THE LEGO® BIG IDEAS BOOK

Written by Daniel Lipkowitz

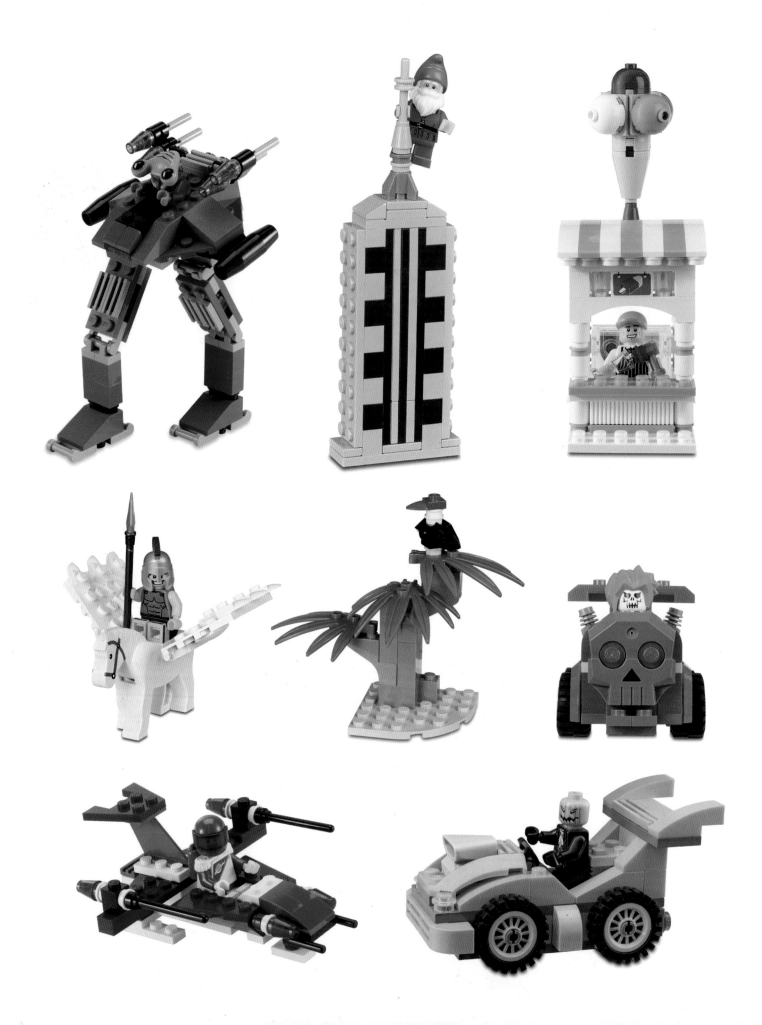

THE LEGO®
BIG IDEAS BOOK

CONTENTS

ON THE MOVE

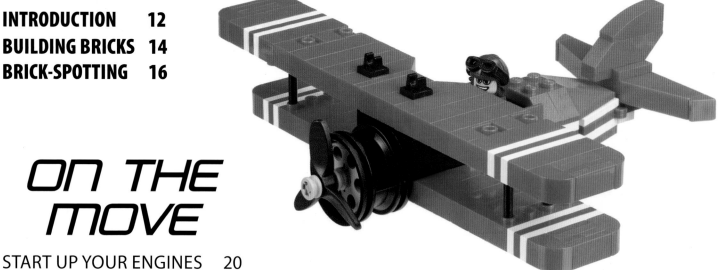

TOWN & COUNTRY

OUT OF THIS WORLD

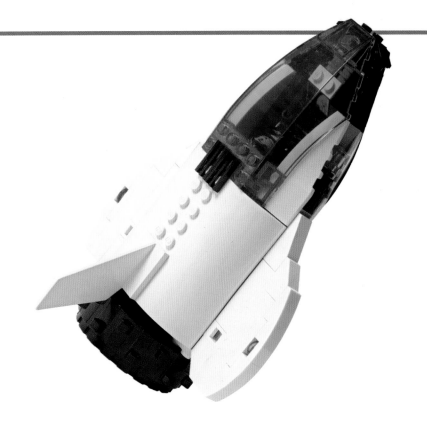

WHEN YOU'RE THIS SMALL, THERE'S EVEN MORE OUTER SPACE TO EXPLORE!

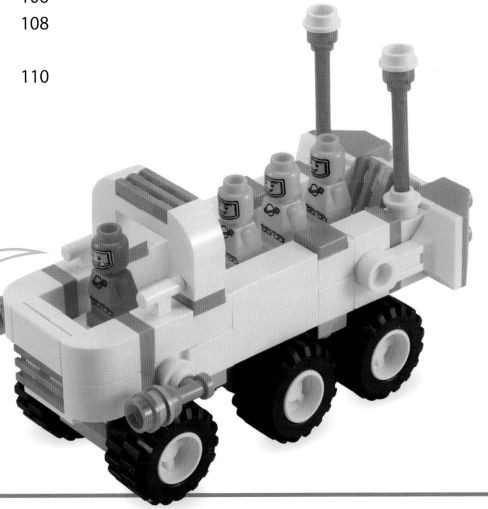

IN DAYS OF OLD

THIS CANNON IS SURE TO GO WITH A BANG!

A WORLD OF ADVENTURE

MAKE & KEEP

Once Upon a Time

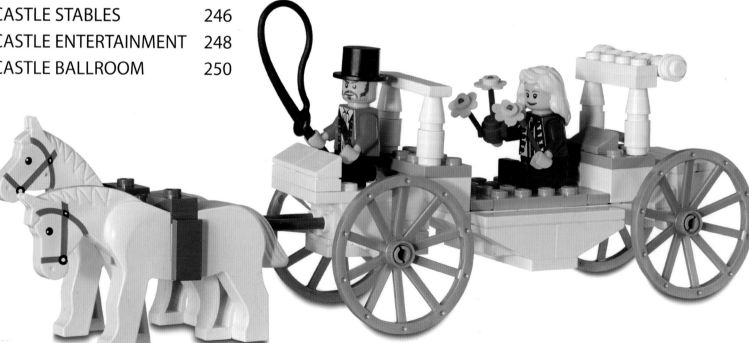

A SMALL WORLD

GO WILD!

THINGS THAT GO BUMP IN THE NIGHT

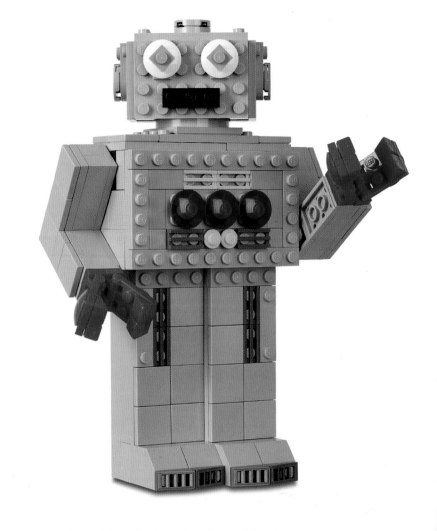

Wish You Were Here

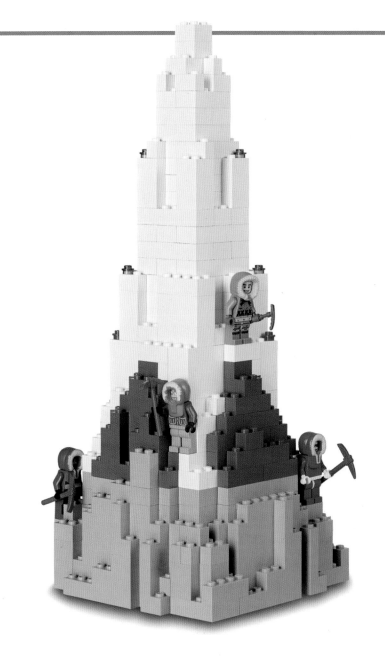

INTRODUCTION

Building with LEGO® bricks is huge fun and endlessly creative. With a bucket of bricks and a bit of practice, you can build just about anything! But even the best builders need some inspiration. That's where this book comes in! In its pages, you will discover a dazzling array of ideas for all ages and abilities.

LOOK OUT FOR THESE SPECIAL FEATURES!

CHALLENGE
Flip to the Challenge panels and pages to find ideas for activities to play with friends and a few LEGO bricks.

BUILDER TALK
The fan builders pop up in their chapters to give insider tips and expert LEGO building advice.

HANDFUL OF BRICKS
On the Handful of Bricks pages, you'll find the fan builders' attempts to prove that you can build just about anything with a handful of bricks and a little imagination! Look up the list of bricks in each "handful" on p.400.

COOL BRICK
The Cool Brick boxes show you versatile pieces and explain why they're so cool.

QUICK BUILD
If time is of the essence or you're looking for ideas for simpler builds, check out the Quick Build features.

BUILDING BRIEF
The building brief is the start point for a model. But remember: if briefed to build a small spaceship, the model you create would be different to anyone else's model. And that's fine!

HOW TO USE THIS BOOK

The ideas in this book will inspire you to create many more models of your own. We don't show building steps or brick lists because it's unlikely you will have all the bricks for each model. Here's how the pages work.

ALTERNATIVE MODEL
The alternative models show different (sometimes simpler) ways of achieving a building effect, using alternative bricks.

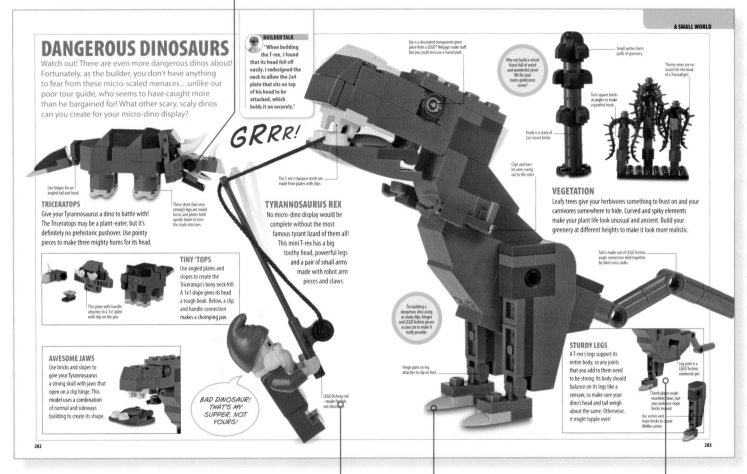

DANGEROUS DINOSAURS

Watch out! There are even more dangerous dinos about! Fortunately, as the builder, you don't have anything to fear from these micro-scaled menaces…unlike our poor tour guide, who seems to have caught more than he bargained for! What other scary, scaly dinos can you create for your micro-dino display?

BUILDER TALK
"When building the T-rex, I found that its head fell off easily. I redesigned the neck to allow the 2x4 plate that sits on top of his head to be attached, which holds it on securely."

GRRR!

Eye is a decorated transparent green piece from a LEGO® Ninjago snake staff, but you could also use a round plate

The T-rex's sharpest teeth are made from plates with clips

Why not build a whole forest full of weird and wonderful plant life for your micro-prehistoric scene?

Small arches form puffs of greenery

Thorny vines are no match for the beak of a Triceratops!

Turn square bricks at angles to make a gnarled trunk

Trunk is a stack of 2x2 round bricks

Clips and bars let arms swing out to the sides

TRICERATOPS
Give your Tyrannosaurus a dino to battle with! The Triceratops may be a plant-eater, but it's definitely no prehistoric pushover. Use pointy pieces to make three mighty horns for its head.

Use hinges for an angled tail and head

These short (but very strong!) legs are round bricks and plates built upside down to turn the studs into toes.

TYRANNOSAURUS REX
No micro-dino display would be complete without the most famous tyrant lizard of them all! This mini T-rex has a big toothy head, powerful legs and a pair of small arms made with robot arm pieces and claws.

VEGETATION
Leafy trees give your herbivores something to feast on and your carnivores somewhere to hide. Curved and spiky elements make your plant life look unusual and ancient. Build your greenery at different heights to make it look more realistic.

TINY 'TOPS
Use angled plates and slopes to create the Triceratops's bony neck frill. A 1x1 slope gives its head a tough beak. Below, a clip and handle connection makes a chomping jaw.

This plate with handle attaches to a 1x1 plate with clip on the jaw

Tail is made out of LEGO Technic angle connectors held together by short cross-axles

Try building a dangerous dino using as many clips, hinges and LEGO Technic pieces as you can to make it really posable.

AWESOME JAWS
Use bricks and slopes to give your Tyrannosaurus a strong skull with jaws that open on a clip hinge. This model uses a combination of normal and sideways building to create its shape.

BAD DINOSAUR! THAT'S MY SUPPER, NOT YOURS!

LEGO fishing rod —made ficklish, not dinoslish

Hinge plate on leg attaches to clip on foot

STURDY LEGS
A T-rex's legs support its entire body, so any joints that you add to them need to be strong. Its body should balance on its legs like a seesaw, so make sure your dino's head and tail weigh about the same. Otherwise, it might topple over!

Leg joint is a LEGO Technic connector pin

Tooth plates make excellent claws, but you could use slope bricks instead

Use arches and slope bricks to create lifelike curves

282

283

LABELS
The labels point out interesting details on a model: important bricks, building techniques and functions. They also suggest changes you could make and different bricks you could use.

MAIN MODEL
The main model is often shown from different angles so you can see just how it's made. But don't just try to copy it. Use it to fire up your imagination – then adapt it to your own collection of bricks.

CONSTRUCTION BOX
The pictures in boxes show some of the construction secrets of the main model – they show it taken apart to explain a useful building technique that you can use in your own models.

BUILDING BRICKS

Are you ready to build? What will you create? Here are a few hints and tips to get you started, but all you really need to know is that you can build just about anything!

WHAT BRICKS DO YOU HAVE?

Organising your bricks into type or colour can really get the creative juices flowing. However many bricks you have, and whatever colour or type they are, you can get building!

LOTS OF THE SAME COLOUR

Build models in all one colour, like this black alphapet. (See p.308.)

NOT MANY BRICKS

Make something small and simple, or try building in micro-scale. Turn to the Small World section on pages 252–293 for inspiration!

WHAT WILL INSPIRE YOU?

Inspiration is all around you – so start looking! Perhaps your ideas will spring from a little research, a single piece or through play with friends.

LOTS OF THE SAME TYPE

Make a model with lots of similar sections, like this slithering snake. (See p.316.)

ONE PIECE

Just one piece can inspire many models. This octagonal plate with bars is part of an octopus (p.274), a flower (p.218) and a spider (p.312). Look for the Cool Brick features in this book for more inspiring bricks.

RESEARCH

Be inspired by images of the kinds of thing you want to build, in books or online.

HOW MUCH TIME DO YOU HAVE?

It doesn't matter! You can build for the whole day, or for the last ten minutes before dinnertime. The important thing is to start.

PLAY

Think about *how* you want to play with your LEGO® bricks and invent models you can use in play with friends. See the Challenge features in this book for inspiration!

NOT LONG

Whiz through the speedy and simple Quick Build models in this book – they can be built in next to no time. On your marks, get set, BUILD!

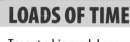

WHAT IF IT GOES WRONG?

If it seems like you have hit a LEGO brick wall, don't panic! Even the most accomplished builders have to try several ways of building something before getting it right.

LOADS OF TIME

Try out a big model or scene, or devise a fun challenge to play with friends.

TAKE IT APART AND TRY AGAIN

Sometimes, you just have to grab your brick separator and start again! See it as a learning experience. You will get it right in the end!

CHANGE IT TO SOMETHING NEW

Maybe your creation could become something else. If your elephant model's head isn't working out, could the model become a rhino instead?

HOW MUCH DETAIL SHOULD I ADD?

It's up to you! The interesting thing about building in a small scale is that you don't need much detail to create the image of something; on the other hand, adding lots of intricate details to your models can be really fun, too.

LOTS

These beautiful beach huts have lots of delicate details that really bring a laidback beach scene to life.

LITTLE

Despite not having buckets (and spades) of detail, this row of tiny beach huts paints a perfect picture.

SHOULD I PLAN MY BUILDS?

Some builders like to plan out their models, while others prefer to just dive into their bricks and see what happens! Either way, the results can be amazing. What kind of builder are you?

PLAN IT OUT

If you want to build a large-scale model or an elaborate scene, it can be helpful to do a rough sketch of your creation and gather your bricks before building.

TRY IT OUT

Sometimes, just starting to build can lead to the most inspiration, especially when creating smaller models or delicate details – though you might reach a few stumbling blocks along the way!

WHAT IF I DONT HAVE THE PERFECT PIECE?

If your collection seems to be missing that one piece that will make your model your showpiece – never fear! It's just another chance to test out your building and creativity skills.

BUILD YOUR OWN

If nothing else will do, try building a piece yourself! No flame pieces to heat up your minifigures' dinner? Make a fire from whatever orange, red or yellow bricks you have.

HOW WILL YOU PLAY WITH THE MODEL?

Remember that LEGO bricks are meant to be played with. Half the fun of building is getting to have fun with your models afterwards! Think about the purpose and function of your model as you build it, so it has ultimate playability.

GET CREATIVE

You might not have *the* brick, but there will be other bricks that achieve the same effect. These bugs have a similar look, but they're made from completely different pieces.

MAKE A MOVE

Making models with moving parts can really bring them to life. This fairy tale dragon wouldn't be quite so scary if it didn't have chomping jaws, flapping wings and fast-moving legs!

TAKE A CHALLENGE

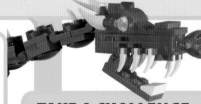

Get competitive with your creativity and build models that can form a game to play with friends. This book's Challenge features should give you some ideas.

TELL A TALE

Build scenes and models with a story in mind. Each chapter in this book tells a tale – use them as inspiration for your own LEGO stories!

BRICK-SPOTTING

Do you know a LEGO® plate from a LEGO tile? If not, don't worry! This book will show you all kinds of pieces, how they function and how they can be used with other parts. To get you started, here are some of the most frequently used or interesting pieces that you will see on the pages of this book. These are good parts to look out for in your own collection. What else can you find?

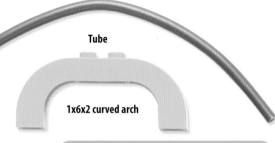

Tube

1x6x2 curved arch

1x1x6 round column

1x1 cone

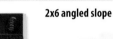

1x2 inverted slope

2x6 angled slope

2x3 slope

2x2 cone

BRICKS

The humble 2x4 brick is the classic LEGO piece, but bricks come in all shapes and sizes. They can all connect to other bricks at the top and bottom. The bumps on the top of a brick, known as "studs," connect to the "tubes" on the bottom of another.

2x2 inverted slope

1x3x2 curved arch

1x2 brick

1x2 curved half-arch

1x5x4 half-arch

2x3 slope

4x4 round brick

2x4 brick

1x3 arch

1x2 slope

1x2x3 slope

1x1x5 brick

2x2 domed brick

1x3x2 half-arch

1x2 log brick

Small wagon wheels and 1x4 axle plate

Ball joint socket

2x2 brick with ball joint

2x2 turntable

1x2 brick with axle hole

1x2 brick-with-hole

1x2 plate with click hinge

MOVING PIECES

Building moving parts into your LEGO models can really bring them to life. LEGO® Technic connecting parts and regular pieces, such as turntables, hinges and winches, can all help you to do this.

LEGO Technic cross-axle 8

1x1 plate with vertical clip

Hinged plates

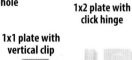

Hinge cylinder

LEGO Technic pin

1x2 plate with handled bar

LEGO Technic half-pin

Ladder with 2 clips

2x4 winch

1x2 plate with click hinge

2x2 brick with side pins and axle hole

16

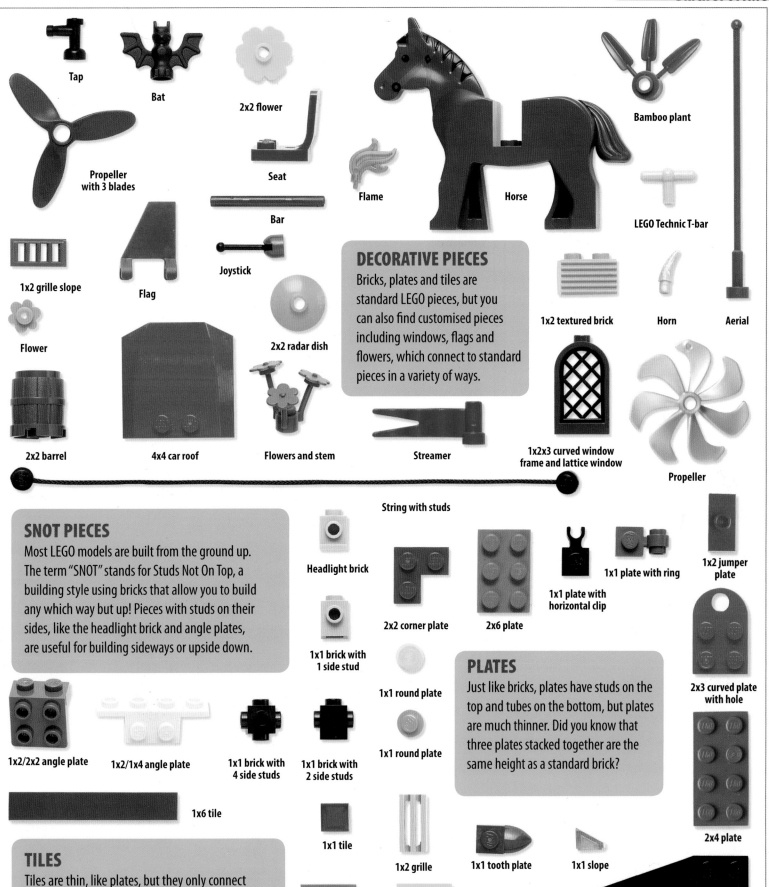

Tap

Bat

2x2 flower

Propeller with 3 blades

Seat

Bamboo plant

Flame

Horse

LEGO Technic T-bar

Bar

1x2 grille slope

Flag

Joystick

Flower

2x2 radar dish

1x2 textured brick

Horn

Aerial

DECORATIVE PIECES

Bricks, plates and tiles are standard LEGO pieces, but you can also find customised pieces including windows, flags and flowers, which connect to standard pieces in a variety of ways.

2x2 barrel

4x4 car roof

Flowers and stem

Streamer

1x2x3 curved window frame and lattice window

Propeller

String with studs

SNOT PIECES

Most LEGO models are built from the ground up. The term "SNOT" stands for Studs Not On Top, a building style using bricks that allow you to build any which way but up! Pieces with studs on their sides, like the headlight brick and angle plates, are useful for building sideways or upside down.

Headlight brick

2x2 corner plate

2x6 plate

1x1 plate with horizontal clip

1x1 plate with ring

1x2 jumper plate

1x1 brick with 1 side stud

1x2/2x2 angle plate

1x2/1x4 angle plate

1x1 brick with 4 side studs

1x1 brick with 2 side studs

1x1 round plate

1x1 round plate

PLATES

Just like bricks, plates have studs on the top and tubes on the bottom, but plates are much thinner. Did you know that three plates stacked together are the same height as a standard brick?

2x3 curved plate with hole

2x4 plate

1x6 tile

1x1 tile

1x2 grille

1x1 tooth plate

1x1 slope

TILES

Tiles are thin, like plates, but they only connect to other bricks at the bottom. The top of a tile has no studs on it, so tiles are great pieces for creating perfectly smooth surfaces.

2x2 tile

2x2 tile-with-pin

3x8 angled plate

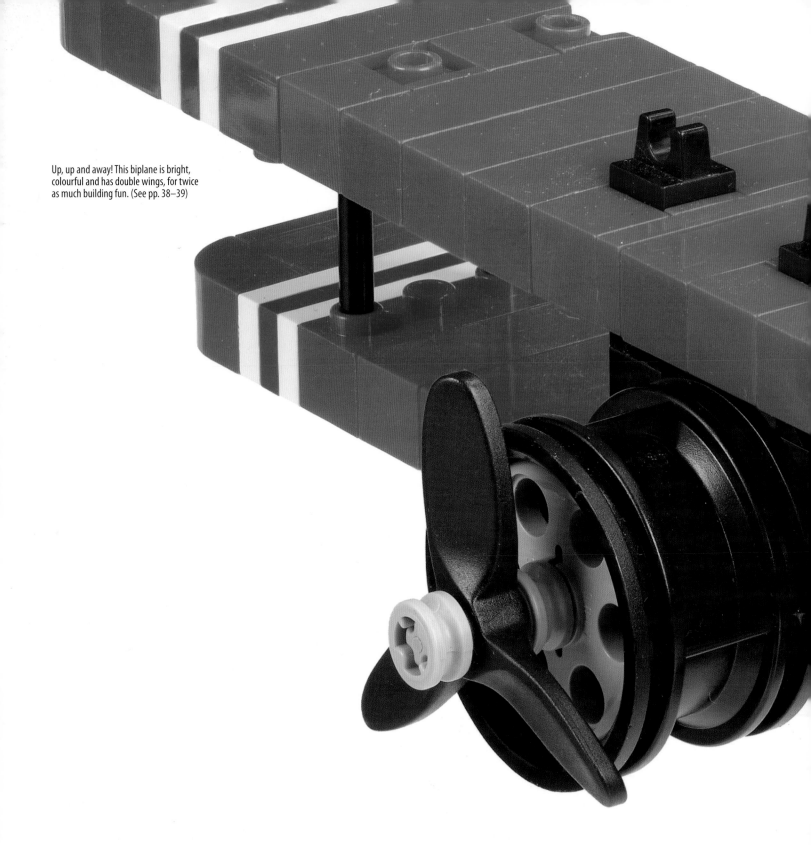

Up, up and away! This biplane is bright, colourful and has double wings, for twice as much building fun. (See pp. 38–39)

ON THE MOVE

It's time to get going! How do you want to travel – by land, sea, air, road or rail? Will your model have two wheels, four wheels, wings, propellers or sails?

TRAIN WHEEL BASE

2x6 ANGLED SLOPE

TUBE

KEEP ROLLING
Wheels and axle plates are useful for planes, trains and automobiles. But if you don't have any, build your own!

2x2 DOMED BRICK

1x6x2 CURVED ARCH

THIN RIM

LEGO® TECHNIC CROSS AXLE

1x2 SLOPE

1x2 INVERTED SLOPE

BAR

2x2 RADAR DISH

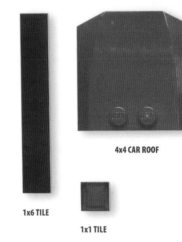

CREATE WITH COLOUR
Bright, bold colours and bricks with studless surfaces are perfect for building eye-catching speedsters.

1x3 CURVED SLOPE

2x3 CURVED PLATE WITH HOLE

WIDE RIMS, WIDE SMOOTH TYRES AND 2x2 AXLE PLATE

4x4 CAR ROOF

SMALL WAGON WHEELS AND 1x4 AXLE PLATE

1x6 TILE

1x1 TILE

1x1 CONE

1x1 SLOPE

LIGHTBULB

1x2 GRILLE

1x1 ROUND PLATE

SMOOTH PIECES
Use tiles and other smooth pieces to give your vehicles a sleek, aerodynamic look.

2x2 PLATE WITH DOUBLE WHEEL

82

1x2 PRINTED TILE

LIGHT 'EM UP
Transparent pieces make great headlights, taillights, navigation lights – even spotlights!

1x1 ROUND PLATE

HC 514

1x2 PRINTED TILE

2x2 PRINTED ROUND TILE

LEGO TECHNIC RIM AND BALLOON TYRE

THIN TREAD TYRE

WHEEL RIM AND TYRE

STEERING WHEEL

SEAT

JOYSTICK

START UP YOUR ENGINES

To build amazing transport vehicles you'll need all the basics – wheels, axles, propellers. But don't just stick to LEGO® car or airplane sets! Look through your entire collection and choose some really exciting pieces to give your models an unusual shape or imaginative detail. Here are some good bricks to look out for.

BARRED WINDOW WITH 4 CONNECTIONS

1x2 GRILLE SLOPE

1x1 BRICK WITH 1 SIDE STUD

1x2 PLATE WITH VERTICAL BAR

1x2/1x4 ANGLE PLATE

ANGLE PLATES
Angle plates are great for attaching grilles and lights to the front or back of your model.

1x2/2x2 ANGLE PLATE

1x1 PLATE WITH SIDE RING

2x2 BRICK WITH SIDE PINS AND AXLE HOLE

1x1 PLATE WITH VERTICAL CLIP

1x1 BRICK WITH VERTICAL BAR

1x2 HINGED BRICK AND 1x2 HINGED PLATE

HINGED PLATES

1x1 HEADLIGHT BRICK

1x2 PLATE WITH HANDLED BAR

SKELETON ARM

1x2 PLATE WITH LEGO TECHNIC BEAM

1x2 JUMPER PLATE

1x2 PLATE WITH HANDLED BAR

1x2 CURVED HALF ARCH

LEGO TECHNIC T-BAR

CHOOSE BRICKS FROM ACROSS ALL YOUR LEGO SETS TO BUILD UNIQUE VEHICLES

2x2 TURNTABLE

1x1 PLATE WITH HORIZONTAL CLIP

LEGO TECHNIC HALF PIN

1x2 TEXTURED BRICK

TRAIN BUFFER

LEGO TECHNIC HALF BUSH

2x2 TILE WITH PIN

2x4 WHEEL GUARD

WHEEL GUARDS
Ready-made wheel guard pieces can help construct the base of your model. Choose printed pieces to add detail! (See Hot Rod, p.25)

PROPELLER WITH 4 BLADES

1x2x2 LADDER

1x2 PLATE WITH SIDE BARS

2x4 WINGED WHEEL GUARD

2x2 BRICK WITH WHEEL ARCH

NEW PURPOSE
Try to think of exciting new uses for your pieces. This webbed radar dish (below) makes a great propeller! (See Swampboat, p.33)

2x4 WHEEL GUARD

1x6 CURVED BAR WITH STUDS

PROPELLER WITH 3 BLADES

2x2 PLATE WITH FRONT GRILLE

A CLEAR PLACE TO START
Windscreens and windows are a good starting point for a vehicle. They can help determine the size of your model.

1x2x2 WALL ELEMENT

LEGO TECHNIC WIDE RIM

6x6 WEBBED RADAR DISH

CURVED WINDSCREEN

1x4x3 WINDOW FRAME WITH WINDOW GLASS

2x4x2 WINDSCREEN

CARS

It's time to hit the road! Before building a car, think about where you're going. For city driving, you could make a compact auto to fit a single minifigure. For off-road vehicles, add some rugged, outdoor features. Whatever you build, make sure the driver fits inside and the wheels can spin freely!

BUILDING BRIEF

Objective: Create small automobiles

Use: Personal travel, transportation

Features: Four wheels, windscreen, headlights, steering wheel

Extras: Roof rack, spare tyre, boot space, additional seats

DOORLESS ENTRY

Doors can be tricky to build, but even if you leave doors out, you can still make a handle using a headlight brick and a 1x1 tile. You could make a petrol cap too!

Roof pops off to let driver in and out

Hood ornament on 1-stud jumper plate

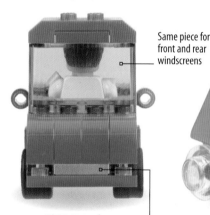

Same piece for front and rear windscreens

REAR VIEW

License plate. You could also use a printed tile

Side mirror, made from plate with side ring. You could attach a 1x1 slope, plate or tile instead

Taillights – transparent tiles built into body of car can be any colour

CITY CAR

To navigate the narrow streets of a bustling city, design a compact car. Build the basic shell first, and then add details like a front grille, headlights and licence plate.

Take off roof and rear windscreen to make a convertible!

WISH I COULD FEEL THE BREEZE THROUGH MY HAIR...BUT IT'S PLASTIC!

1x2/2x2 angle plate

AUTO ANATOMY

This car was built on a base of overlapping rectangular plates with axle plates underneath to attach the wheels. The front details are mounted on an angle plate.

UNDER THE HOOD

The front is held together by an assembly of bricks, clips and sideways building. When you build in multiple directions, the more points of contact you have and the better it holds together.

Roof lights for foggy nights. Use transparent red pieces for hi-tech night vision!

CARGO SPACE

This car has front and back seats and a small boot to store anything your minifigure might need on the road. You could take out the rear seats to make a larger boot.

Pack a spare tyre for emergencies on the back or in the boot

1x1 slopes mirror shape of front of roof

OFF-ROAD CAR

For a more complex car, create something with a special purpose, like driving across rough terrain! This auto was built from the top down, with the roof, hood and windscreen pieces picked out first and then the rest constructed to fit them.

Put transparent slopes on their side for a different effect

Brick-built wheel guards. Make sure the tyres have clearance to turn!

Use different colour bricks in the car's body to add decoration, stripes, dirt or camouflage

MONSTER TRUCKS

Who says that cars and trucks have to be down-to-earth? With a few special pieces and lots of imagination, you can turn your creation into the craziest car around. From towering turbo trucks to super-fast speedsters, these over-amped autos rule the road, the ring and the racetrack!

Elastic band

LEGO Technic half beam

BUILDING BRIEF

Objective: Build souped-up muscle vehicles

Use: Competition, racing, showing off!

Features: Everything a normal vehicle has, but to the extreme!

Extras: Giant wheels, big exhausts, spikes, chains, flames, fins, spoilers

IN SUSPENSE

To make the springy suspension, the wheels are attached to pivoting LEGO Technic half beams. Elastic bands pull the beams toward the centre, so when a wheel is pushed out of position, it springs right back in again.

Boosters made from wheel rims – or use jet engines to go even more over the top!

REAR SIDE VIEW

SKELETON TURBO

Don't let the cheery yellow fool you – this monster means business! It is built around a working suspension system that lets each oversized wheel move independently to conquer or crush any obstacle in its path.

Rollcage built with clips and robot claws

Build a row of bars to clip on mirrors, chains and spikes

Chunky grille made from barred window

Use curved and bumpy pieces as debris to test suspension

Vented engine made from 1x1 round plates

24

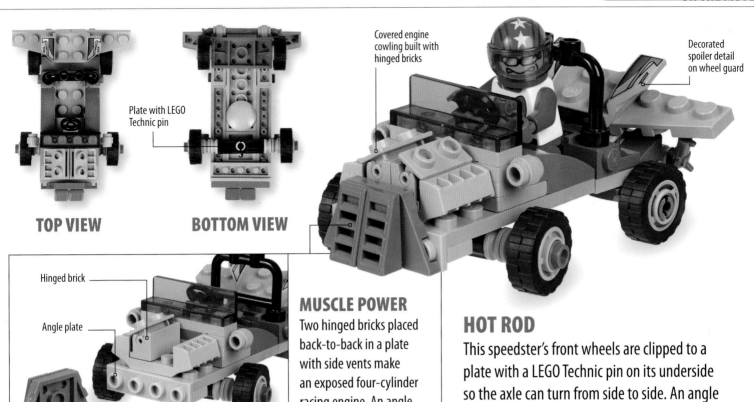

TOP VIEW

BOTTOM VIEW

Plate with LEGO Technic pin

Covered engine cowling built with hinged bricks

Decorated spoiler detail on wheel guard

Hinged brick

Angle plate

Front grille

MUSCLE POWER

Two hinged bricks placed back-to-back in a plate with side vents make an exposed four-cylinder racing engine. An angle plate holds the front section in place.

HOT ROD

This speedster's front wheels are clipped to a plate with a LEGO Technic pin on its underside so the axle can turn from side to side. An angle plate under the front of the car keeps the axle from turning all the way around.

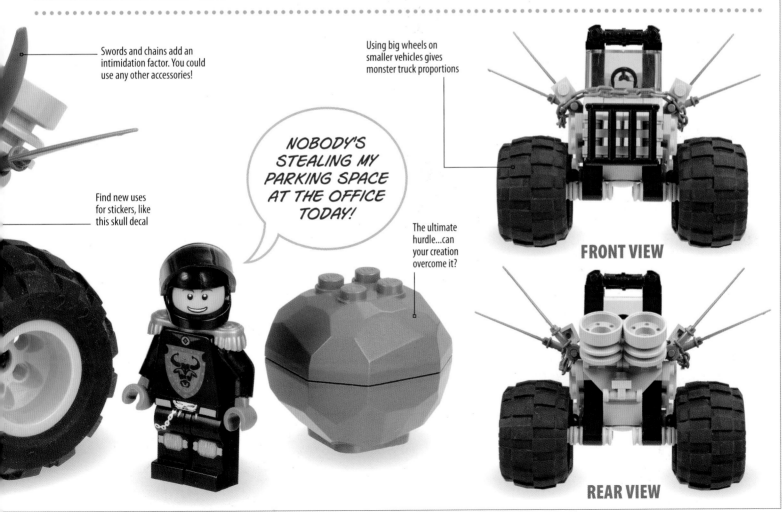

Swords and chains add an intimidation factor. You could use any other accessories!

Using big wheels on smaller vehicles gives monster truck proportions

Find new uses for stickers, like this skull decal

NOBODY'S STEALING MY PARKING SPACE AT THE OFFICE TODAY!

The ultimate hurdle...can your creation overcome it?

FRONT VIEW

REAR VIEW

TRUCKS

Big trucks, little trucks, construction trucks, farm trucks, highway trucks with box trailers, fuel tanker trucks and postal delivery trucks – as long as it has wheels and carries cargo, it's a truck. They might drive cross-country or work at the docks, they might have four wheels or eighteen, but if you have the pieces, you can build them!

TRANSPORT TRUCK

A truck doesn't have to be big to be packed with details. Grey, brown and tan bricks make this classic hauler look well-worn and rustic. It may be carrying cabbages now, but its wooden-slat bed can haul just about anything!

FACING FORWARD

The front grille, headlights and other details are built onto a plate and then connected to the rest of the truck using an angle plate.

Angle plate

Wooden cargo bed made with stacked headlight bricks and long tiles

Slopes create an angled front

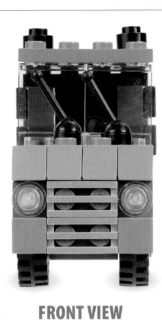

FRONT VIEW

Roof can be removed to make it easier to play inside the driver's cab

A pair of joysticks makes a great set of windscreen wipers. You could also use antennas

DRIVING SEAT

You can secure the driver in place by seating him on a plate or chair – or you can use a tile as his seat to make him easier to remove!

Your truck could be steered using handlebars, joysticks or a steering wheel

If you're clipping a windscreen on, ensure you have enough studs for good clutch power

If you don't have pieces that look like cabbages, choose pieces that resemble different cargo

> LIKE THESE CABBAGES? I GROW 'EM DOWN AT THE OLD ROBOT FACTORY!

Use printed dials, gauges or silver pieces for mechanical details

Leave bed open at back for cargo removal – or build in a simple hinged gate

You could add a trailer or two if there's extra cargo to transport (see p.30)

ICE CREAM VAN

On a hot summer's day, the sight of a friendly ice cream van is always welcome! Make your van fun and colourful with decorative pieces. Don't forget to stock the back with plenty of frozen treats so you can serve all your customers some tasty ice cream!

BUILDING BRIEF

Objective: Make ice cream vans
Use: Transportation, selling treats
Features: Window, removable roof
Extras: Goblets, pieces to personalise your van

CHOOSE YOUR FLAVOUR

The ice cream van has an iconic shape. Use curved half arches at the front of the van to achieve this look. Add tiles to the top of the roof to make it smooth, but don't worry if you don't have enough tiles; exposed studs are okay too.

BOTTOM VIEW

Flower pieces brighten up van

MAIN ATTRACTION

To attract potential customers, make your van eye-catching! You could attach flowers or other accessories to the side of your van with a headlight brick. Coloured round plates could look like scoops of ice cream.

Roof made from plates topped with tiles

Air vent keeps the inside of your van cool

MY ICE CREAMS ARE SPECIAL. WHY? THEY DON'T MELT!

Printed scroll pieces make great menus. What's on offer today?

Built-in window acts as serving hatch

Red wheel arches match the red roof. You could use your favourite colours

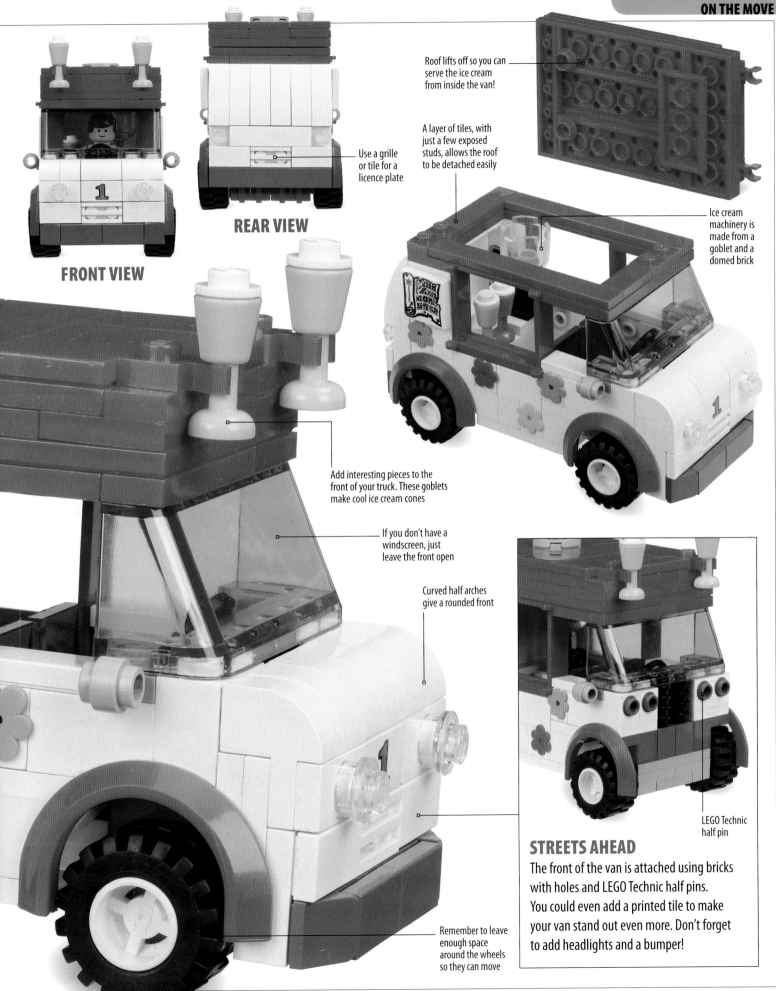

Roof lifts off so you can serve the ice cream from inside the van!

A layer of tiles, with just a few exposed studs, allows the roof to be detached easily

Ice cream machinery is made from a goblet and a domed brick

Use a grille or tile for a licence plate

REAR VIEW

FRONT VIEW

Add interesting pieces to the front of your truck. These goblets make cool ice cream cones

If you don't have a windscreen, just leave the front open

Curved half arches give a rounded front

LEGO Technic half pin

STREETS AHEAD
The front of the van is attached using bricks with holes and LEGO Technic half pins. You could even add a printed tile to make your van stand out even more. Don't forget to add headlights and a bumper!

Remember to leave enough space around the wheels so they can move

SMALL VEHICLES

They're bigger than bicycles but smaller than cars! Small vehicles serve all kinds of purposes for all sorts of drivers, from navigating across bumpy terrain to cruising over a golf course. They can park in small spaces, pass through narrow gaps and fit inside your pocket. Here are some ideas to get you started!

IF YOU'RE GOING TO GO EXPLORING, DON'T FORGET YOUR HAT!

Ears of corn – what else can you transport?

Grille attached with minifigure angle plate

Angle plate holds taillights and licence plate in place

QUAD BIKE

Take your adventures off-road by building an all-terrain vehicle with a compact, tough shape and four big wheels. Add an easy-to-attach trailer for special expeditions!

Standing driver has good control of the vehicle, but you could make it a seated vehicle

Brown bars makes the front grille look chunky and hard-wearing

Make sure wheel guards are raised enough so wheels can turn

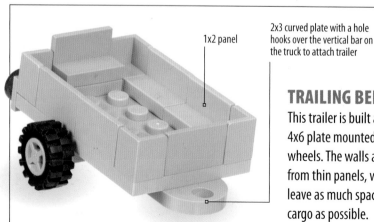

1x2 panel

2x3 curved plate with a hole hooks over the vertical bar on the truck to attach trailer

TRAILING BEHIND

This trailer is built around a 4x6 plate mounted on two wheels. The walls are made from thin panels, which leave as much space for cargo as possible.

1x2 plate with vertical bar attaches trailer

REAR SIDE VIEW

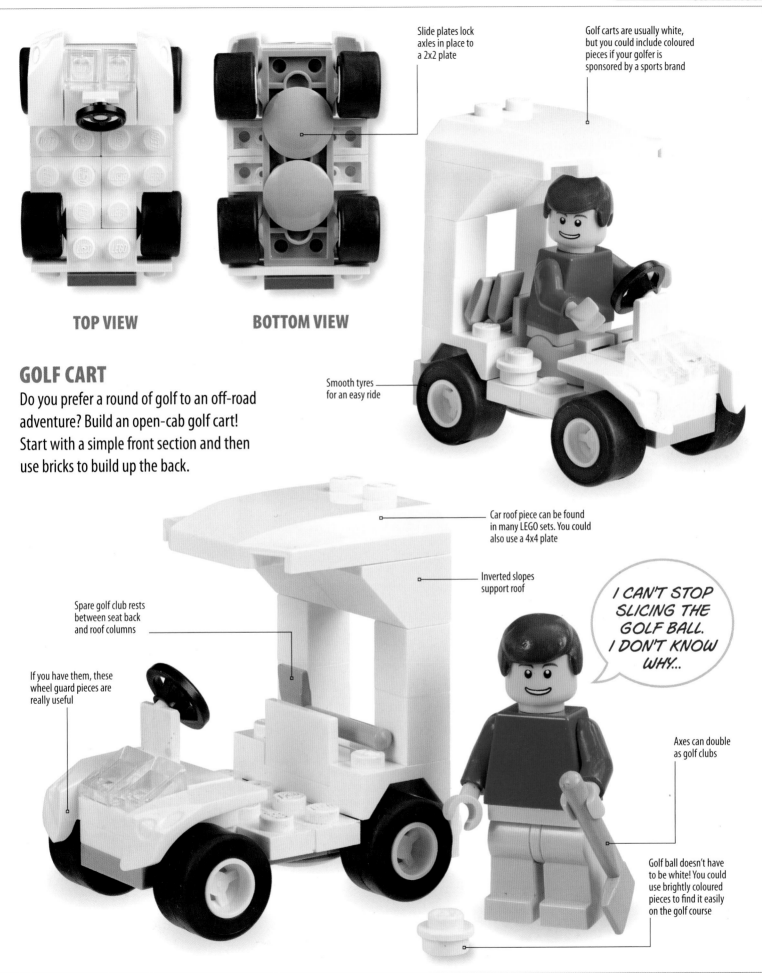

TOP VIEW

BOTTOM VIEW

Slide plates lock axles in place to a 2x2 plate

Golf carts are usually white, but you could include coloured pieces if your golfer is sponsored by a sports brand

Smooth tyres for an easy ride

GOLF CART

Do you prefer a round of golf to an off-road adventure? Build an open-cab golf cart! Start with a simple front section and then use bricks to build up the back.

Car roof piece can be found in many LEGO sets. You could also use a 4x4 plate

Inverted slopes support roof

Spare golf club rests between seat back and roof columns

If you have them, these wheel guard pieces are really useful

I CAN'T STOP SLICING THE GOLF BALL. I DON'T KNOW WHY...

Axes can double as golf clubs

Golf ball doesn't have to be white! You could use brightly coloured pieces to find it easily on the golf course

AROUND THE WORLD

From the rickshaws of Asia and the gondolas of Italy to the swampboats of the Florida Everglades, the world is chock-full of transport vehicles designed to navigate different environments and terrains. What other exotic forms of transport can you think of? Look out for ideas on your next holiday!

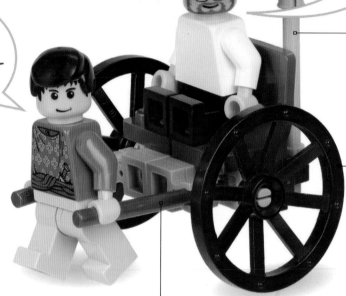

HURRY UP! I'VE GOT A GONDOLA TO CATCH.

THIS JOB MAY NOT PAY MUCH, BUT IT'S GREAT EXERCISE.

Ski pole holds up the roof

RICKSHAW

The base of this foot-powered rickshaw is built on its side, so the bars and wheels can be attached. Make sure the canopy is positioned high enough so that the minifigure passenger can fit in.

Wheels similar to wagon wheels are often used on rickshaws, even today

Make sure the bars are the right width apart that the driver can hold them both at the same time!

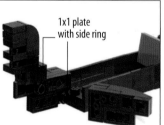

1x1 plate with side ring

Raised prow built with a headlight brick, a stack of plates, a curved half arch and a tile

BOAT BRICKS

Two plates with a side ring hold the curved sides together at the front of the gondola. One of them also attaches the curved sections to the main body of the boat.

GONDOLA

This flat-bottomed Venetian boat combines normal brick stacking with sideways building to create a curved, narrow outline. An angle plate gives the gondolier a set of studs to stand on.

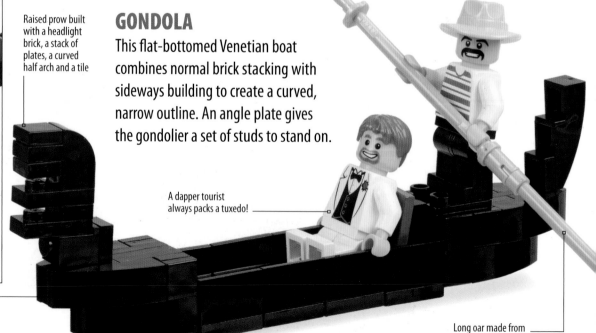

A dapper tourist always packs a tuxedo!

Long oar made from ski pole combined with umbrella pole

SWAMPBOAT

This model started with a great idea for using a big webbed radar dish. Add a propeller, an engine, a platform and some floats, and you've got a good old-fashioned swamp-cruiser!

Webbed radar dish

1x2 plate with handled bar

Don't have bars for a railing? Build a barrier out of bricks and tiles instead!

FLOAT BUILDING

Twin catamaran floats are built upside-down using two pairs of angled slopes. They are attached to the main platform using plates with handled bars.

Streamer adds height and colour to model

Tube railing held in place by skeleton legs

GOOD THING ALLIGATORS CAN'T CLIMB... CAN THEY?

Connect propeller with a LEGO Technic pin so it can really spin!

To build your own wild animals, go to p.167

Big floats raise driver platform above hungry alligators

Engine casings and vent built from curved half arches and a printed tile

CLASSIC TRAINS

To build an old-style train, you don't need a lot of special parts! Find some pictures of steam trains for reference and choose the perfect pieces from your LEGO collection. Then, get building – all you need is a little loco-motivation!

STEAM ENGINE

The key to building a steam locomotive is capturing the shape of the classic train engine: a cylinder with a smokestack in front, a box for the engineer's cabin, and wheels underneath.

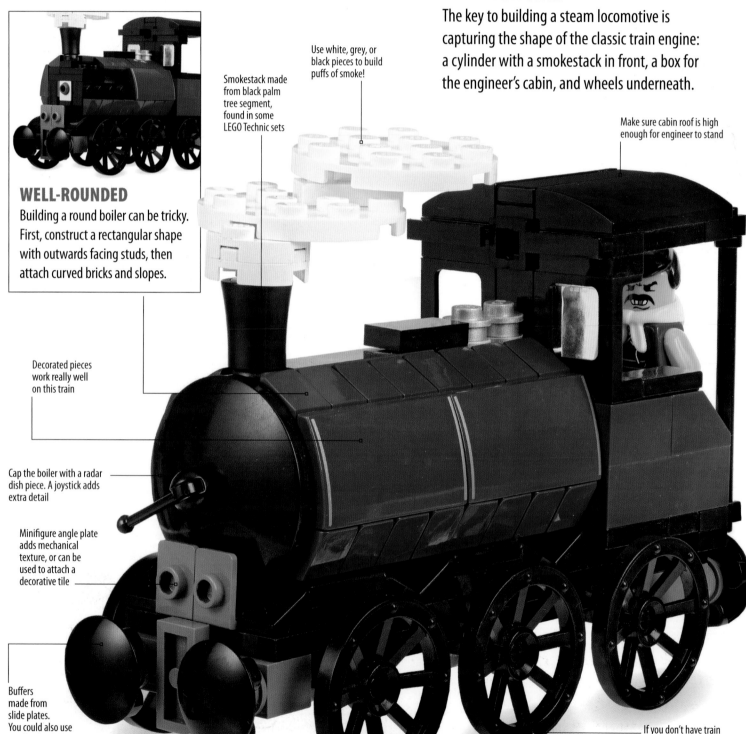

WELL-ROUNDED

Building a round boiler can be tricky. First, construct a rectangular shape with outwards facing studs, then attach curved bricks and slopes.

Smokestack made from black palm tree segment, found in some LEGO Technic sets

Use white, grey, or black pieces to build puffs of smoke!

Make sure cabin roof is high enough for engineer to stand

Decorated pieces work really well on this train

Cap the boiler with a radar dish piece. A joystick adds extra detail

Minifigure angle plate adds mechanical texture, or can be used to attach a decorative tile

Buffers made from slide plates. You could also use small radar dishes

If you don't have train wheels, try using wagon wheels

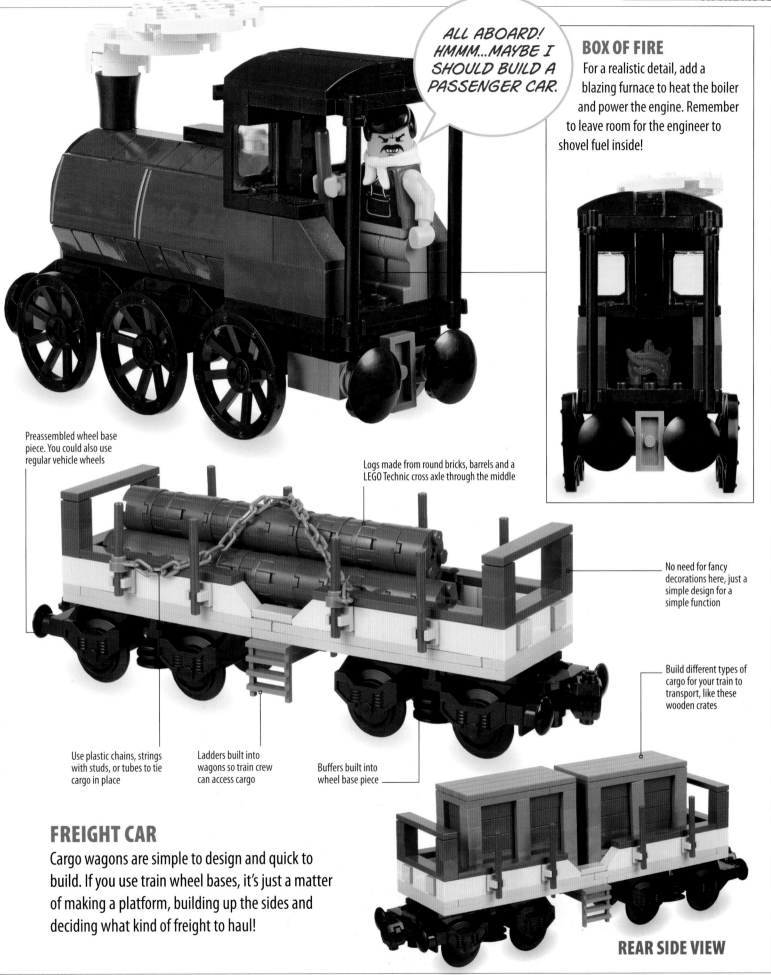

ALL ABOARD! HMMM...MAYBE I SHOULD BUILD A PASSENGER CAR.

BOX OF FIRE

For a realistic detail, add a blazing furnace to heat the boiler and power the engine. Remember to leave room for the engineer to shovel fuel inside!

Preassembled wheel base piece. You could also use regular vehicle wheels

Logs made from round bricks, barrels and a LEGO Technic cross axle through the middle

No need for fancy decorations here, just a simple design for a simple function

Use plastic chains, strings with studs, or tubes to tie cargo in place

Ladders built into wagons so train crew can access cargo

Buffers built into wheel base piece

Build different types of cargo for your train to transport, like these wooden crates

FREIGHT CAR

Cargo wagons are simple to design and quick to build. If you use train wheel bases, it's just a matter of making a platform, building up the sides and deciding what kind of freight to haul!

REAR SIDE VIEW

CITY TRAINS

Trains run through many modern cities, from above-ground commuter lines to trains in tunnels beneath the streets. They are built for speed and efficiency, so they usually have a compact, tube-shaped profile. Match the colours of your favourite city's trains or try building a super-streamlined bullet express!

BUILD-A-BOGIE

The wheeled undercarriage seen on modern trains is known as a bogie. If you don't have train pieces, try making a bogie using LEGO Technic half pins, radar dishes and tiles. You can even link train cars together by adding ball-and-socket joints or plates with vertical bars and holes.

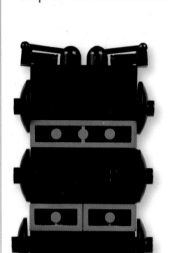

BOTTOM VIEW

Turntable lets the section swivel, but keeps the wheels lined up as it goes around curves

Wheels are made using radar dish pieces held on by LEGO Technic half pins. Can you think of a way to make them rotate?

LEGO Technic half pin

Joysticks, binoculars or antennas can represent braking pins and beams

OPEN-TOP TRAIN

The sections of roof between the doors can be removed easily for quick access to the train's interior.

Curved slopes are perfect to get the shape of this train

Vertical hand rails are a common feature of underground trains

TUNNEL TRAVEL

This train is designed to travel smoothly underground. The distinctive roof is built from curved slopes, with transparent slopes used at the top of the doors.

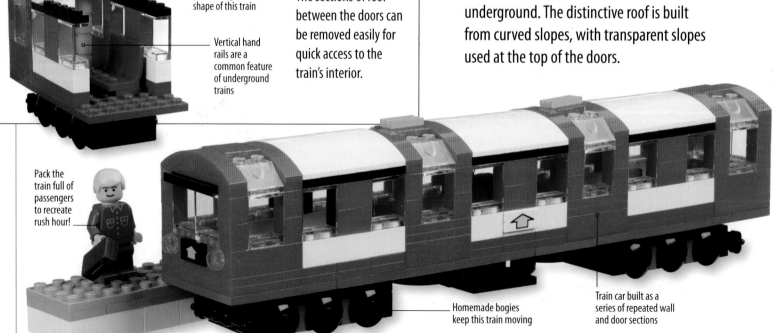

Pack the train full of passengers to recreate rush hour!

Homemade bogies keep this train moving

Train car built as a series of repeated wall and door sections

MIND THE GAP

The windscreen is built onto hinged bricks and plates, which creates a sloping angle at the front of the trolley car. The gaps on either side are hidden by tall slopes.

Tall slope

Hinged brick

Door handles made from plates with side rings

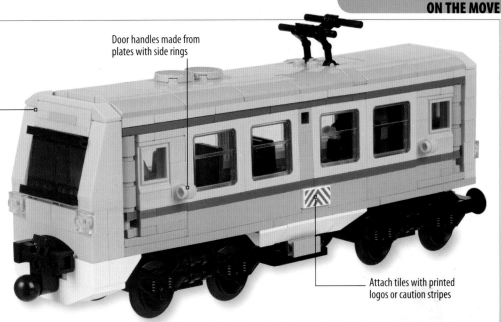

Attach tiles with printed logos or caution stripes

POWER SOURCE

Above-ground trains use roof-mounted devices to collect electricity from overhead power lines. It's easy to build one – you just need some bar pieces and robot or skeleton arms!

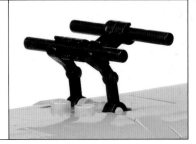

Create doors in a different colour so they stand out from rest of car

Round bricks give door room to swing open

1x1 plate with horizontal clip

Brick with ball joint

ALL ABOARD!

The doors of the train open and close, thanks to two plates with horizontal clips that are built into each door. The clips attach to a vertical bar, which acts as a hinge. You could also use hinged plates or bricks.

ABOVE-GROUND TRAIN

This overground train is built on six-stud-wide plates and rolls on wheel base pieces. Cars can be connected with ball-and-socket joints, so your train can follow curves in the track!

AEROPLANES

There's a whole sky full of aeroplanes for you to build!
You can make a vintage plane with an open cockpit, an
ultra-modern passenger jet or anything in between.
Big planes, little planes, biplanes, triplanes – even cargo
planes with loading ramps and space inside to carry your
auto models. Grab your bricks and prepare for take-off!

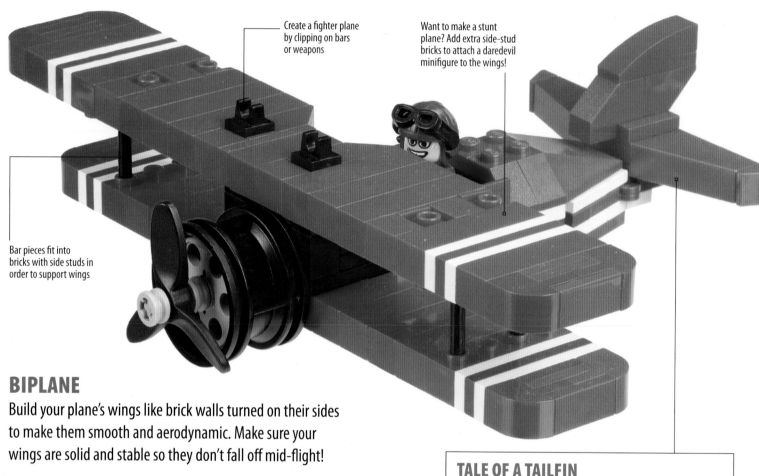

Create a fighter plane by clipping on bars or weapons

Want to make a stunt plane? Add extra side-stud bricks to attach a daredevil minifigure to the wings!

Bar pieces fit into bricks with side studs in order to support wings

BIPLANE

Build your plane's wings like brick walls turned on their sides
to make them smooth and aerodynamic. Make sure your
wings are solid and stable so they don't fall off mid-flight!

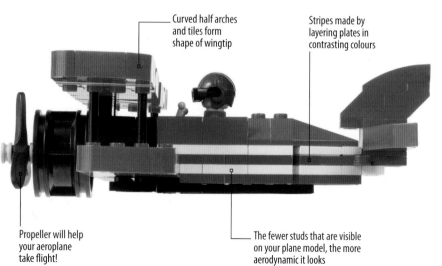

Curved half arches and tiles form shape of wingtip

Stripes made by layering plates in contrasting colours

Propeller will help your aeroplane take flight!

The fewer studs that are visible on your plane model, the more aerodynamic it looks

TALE OF A TAILFIN

Build one tailfin with slopes and curved slopes.
Then create two sideways tailfins and attach them using
back-to-back pairs of headlight bricks and jumper plates.

Jumper plates help centre the vertical tailfin

Headlight brick

MICROPLANE

You don't need to build a big model to make a big plane. Microscale aeroplanes are easy to create and look great. Just make sure you include the key features that make your plane recognisable!

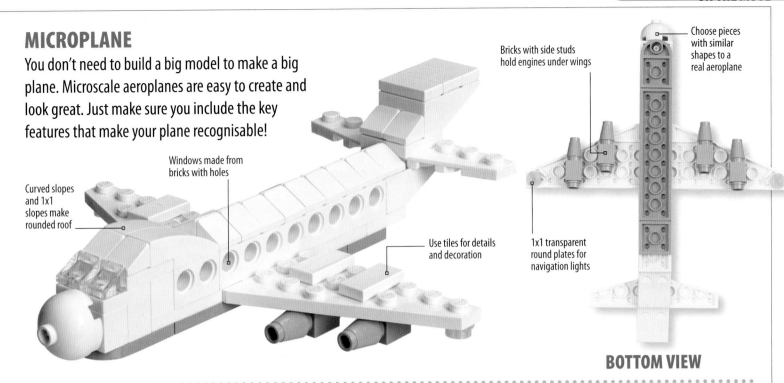

Curved slopes and 1x1 slopes make rounded roof

Windows made from bricks with holes

Use tiles for details and decoration

Bricks with side studs hold engines under wings

Choose pieces with similar shapes to a real aeroplane

1x1 transparent round plates for navigation lights

BOTTOM VIEW

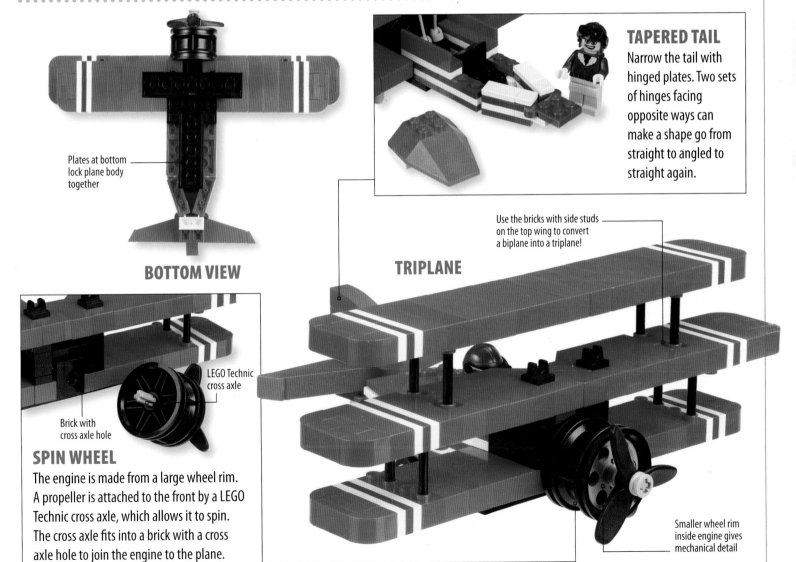

Plates at bottom lock plane body together

BOTTOM VIEW

TAPERED TAIL

Narrow the tail with hinged plates. Two sets of hinges facing opposite ways can make a shape go from straight to angled to straight again.

Use the bricks with side studs on the top wing to convert a biplane into a triplane!

TRIPLANE

LEGO Technic cross axle

Brick with cross axle hole

SPIN WHEEL

The engine is made from a large wheel rim. A propeller is attached to the front by a LEGO Technic cross axle, which allows it to spin. The cross axle fits into a brick with a cross axle hole to join the engine to the plane.

Smaller wheel rim inside engine gives mechanical detail

HOT AIR BALLOON

The most important thing to remember about a hot air balloon is its shape. You may think of a balloon as a sphere, but it's really more like a lightbulb shape. The second most important thing is stability: round shapes need lots of bricks, so make sure they're all locked together securely!

BRICK BALLOON

Build a balloon shape one layer at a time, starting at the bottom and building upward. Overlap the bricks to keep the outline as round as possible. The basket is made from a plate built up with rows of bricks, plates and tiles.

HEAVIER THAN AIR

Build your balloon from the bottom up, gradually stepping outwards and then sharply inwards toward the top. To cut down the weight, make the balloon's centre hollow and strengthen it with crossed bricks inside.

BUILDING BRIEF

Objective: Build hot air balloons
Use: Leisurely trips through the sky
Features: Brightly-coloured balloon top, hanging basket
Extras: Passengers, sandbags, blazing burner

Make a swirl by moving the colours one stud over on each new layer

WAIT...HOW DO I GET BACK DOWN AGAIN?

Add a burner flame to keep the balloon aloft

Long axles attach basket to balloon

Ballast sacks made from plates with vertical clips on blank minifigure heads

1x1 round bricks are good for a wicker texture

HELICOPTER

Helicopters come in all shapes and sizes, and are designed for lots of different jobs. Decide what kind you want to make before you start building: A lightweight news chopper with a camera? A rescue copter with lots of cargo space? Big helicopters can have multiple rotors on top to keep them flying high!

BUILDING BRIEF

Objective: Create helicopters
Use: Controlled hovering flight, transport
Features: Top rotor, tail rotor, cockpit, skids, landing gear
Extras: Cameras, rescue equipment, additional rotors

Boosters or rockets can be held together with a bar or antenna through the middle

Intakes built from harpoons inserted into radar dishes, round bricks and domed bricks

RESCUE COPTER

This emergency chopper's bright colour makes it easy to spot out at sea. Its body is built thinner and thinner toward the tail, tapering from six studs wide to only two.

Add small tools and weapons to equip your chopper for rescue!

Big window shutters make an easy-to-open cargo hatch

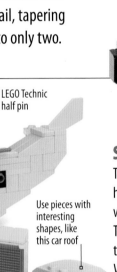

LEGO Technic half pin

Use pieces with interesting shapes, like this car roof

SIDE VIEW

To shape the side of your helicopter, use 1x2 bricks with holes with LEGO Technic half pins in them to secure angled pieces. Windows and slopes add detail too.

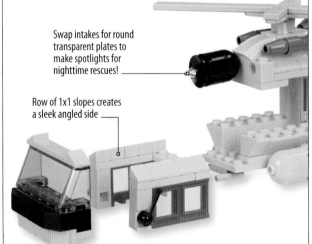

Swap intakes for round transparent plates to make spotlights for nighttime rescues!

Row of 1x1 slopes creates a sleek angled side

Unusual pieces like telescopes and steering wheels used as rescue equipment

COPTER COMPONENTS

Choose your windscreen first and use that as a guide for the helicopter's dimensions. A spacious cockpit with side windows gives your crew a wide view for spotting trouble.

BOATS

What kind of boat do you want to build? Whether you'd prefer a pocket-sized microship or a minifigure-scale vessel with a detailed interior, here are some maritime models to get you started. Build a speedboat for zipping around the bay, or a luxury cruise liner for sailing the seas – just don't forget to give your masterpiece a name!

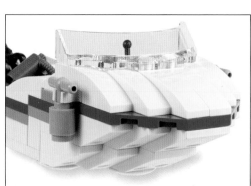

ABOVE THE WAVES

Use two layers of inverted slopes on the bottom of the prow and a layer of curved slopes on top for a streamlined shape!

A LEGO Technic axle connector forms the base of this rooftop radio mast

SPEEDBOAT

This flashy boat's main body is built from white plates, with a tan floor for colour contrast. Blue plates create a wave pattern for a really aquatic look! The cabin roof can be removed, with 1x1 slopes filling the gaps left by the support columns.

Hinged brick and plate allows motor to tilt up and down

Push a T-bar into a round brick for a clip-on float

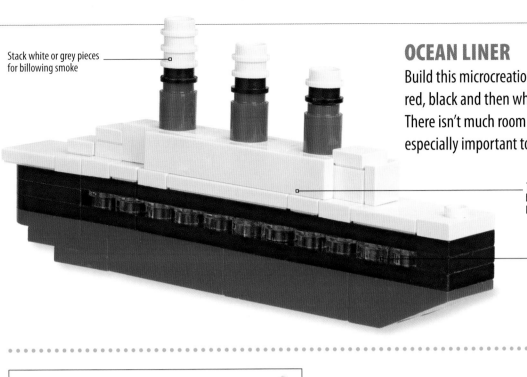

Stack white or grey pieces for billowing smoke

OCEAN LINER

Build this microcreation from the bottom up, layering red, black and then white sections – or any colours you like! There isn't much room for detail on a small vessel, so it's especially important to get the proportions right.

1x6 tile held in place using bricks with holes and LEGO Technic half pins

Windows made with transparent 1x1 round plates, or you could use square plates

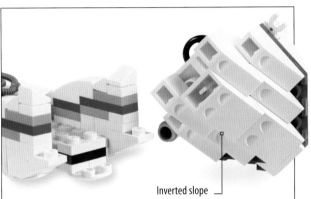

Inverted slope

PROW PARTS

Use inverted slopes to shape the underside of the speedboat. Make sure there are multiple connection points to attach the prow securely to the rest of the boat.

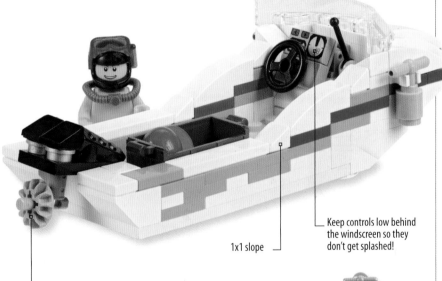

Keep controls low behind the windscreen so they don't get splashed!

1x1 slope

Propeller built using a LEGO Technic gear and firefighter's hose nozzle

2x2 slide plates lock the bottom of the boat together – and let you slide it along a table!

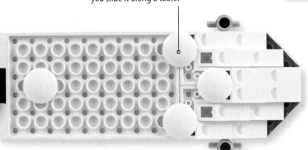

BOTTOM VIEW

TOP VIEW

Include somewhere to store diving gear and supplies

FISHING BOAT

You don't need lots of special pieces to build a fishing boat. You can create the perfect seafaring vessel with some of your own bricks and plenty of imagination. Start with the hull and a cabin, then add nautical details like rigging, anchors and radio equipment. You don't even need to build a whole boat – just build the part that floats above the waves!

GONE FISHING

The toughest part of making a boat without specialised hull pieces is getting the shape right. This model uses hinged pieces to make the shape for the hull, and has lots of improvised building. The front mast was originally the centre of a spiral staircase!

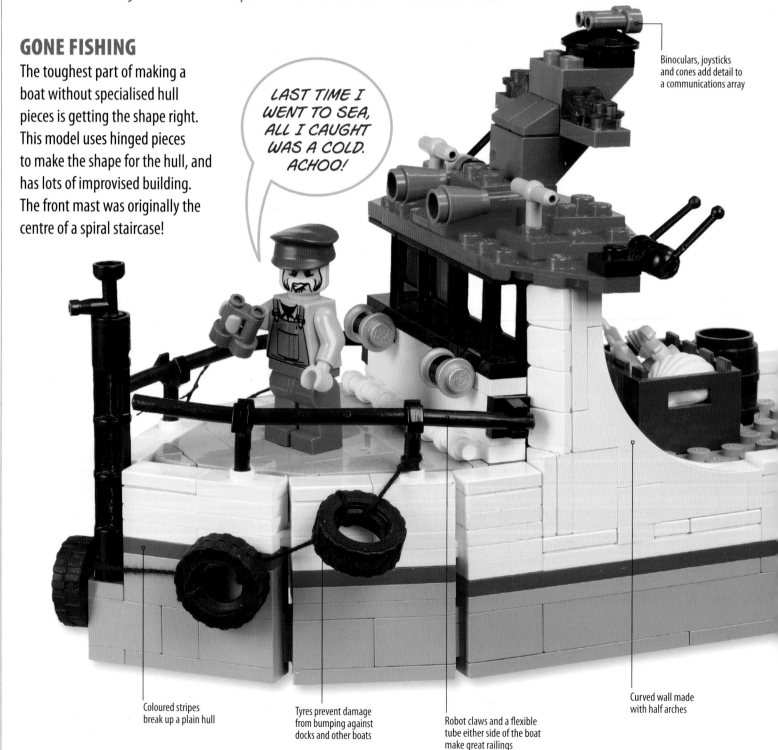

LAST TIME I WENT TO SEA, ALL I CAUGHT WAS A COLD. ACHOO!

Binoculars, joysticks and cones add detail to a communications array

Coloured stripes break up a plain hull

Tyres prevent damage from bumping against docks and other boats

Robot claws and a flexible tube either side of the boat make great railings

Curved wall made with half arches

BOW BUILDING

Connecting sections of bricks with hinged bricks gives the boat its pointed bow. The forward deck is a wall built sideways from the body of the boat. Slopes help shape the deck so it fits into the angled curve of the hull.

Tall slopes give forward deck an angled shape

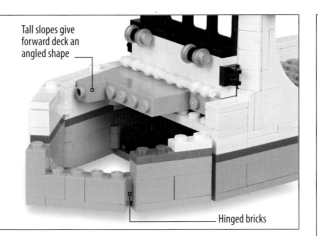

Hinged bricks

BELOW DECK

If you're only building the part of the boat that sticks out of the water, not the whole thing, feel free to leave the bottom open – as long as the hull holds together!

Warning lights made by mounting transparent cones on poles

CRUISE CONTROL

A boat's control cabin is usually loaded with dials, levers, lights, radios and receivers. Fill yours with as many technical-looking pieces as you can!

Working winch built with LEGO Technic pieces and a chain

You can't steer a boat without a rudder!

Fill barrels and crates with fish, crabs, clams... anything you like!

MEET THE BUILDER

BARNEY MAIN

Location: UK
Age: 18
LEGO Speciality: Pirates, transport

How old were you when you started using LEGO bricks?

I was 18 months old when I got my first LEGO®
DUPLO® set, but moved on to LEGO sets shortly
afterwards – and haven't stopped since then!

Which model were you most proud of as a young LEGO builder?

A model of a Viking warrior's head called "Infuriated
Isaac" that I built when I was nine years old. It was
featured in the *LEGO® Magazine*, as "Designer's Choice",
which I was very proud of!

This pirate ship flies through the skies, catching lightning using the nets on the back. It was inspired by the movie *Stardust*, but I added a whole load of my own ideas, such as the lightning-sharks!

Both the blades of the windmill and the wooden boarding on the sides are made by "stepping" plates, and putting tiles on top. It's a very versatile technique, and has a lot of applications.

What are you inspired by?

Anything and everything! The basic idea for a model stems from all sorts
of things – discovering a cool part combination, films and literature or
seeing something in real life. Often I see something that I'd like to
replicate, such as a style of stonework, but only recall it a couple of
months later when I'm building and decide to put it in! Sometimes if I'm
entering a contest with a specific theme, I do my research more
thoroughly: I once had to build a model of my own Dr Seuss story, so I
read through a lot of his books again to get the style right. That said, my
finished models rarely look anything like my initial idea – I just go with
the flow, really, and let the model itself dictate how it's going to look!

What is the biggest or most complex model you've made?

I built a big battle scene from the movie *The
Chronicles of Narnia: Prince Caspian*. The
battlefield was actually raised off the ground so
that I could build the tomb inside the mountain,
and also the sink-hole that opens up in the
ground in the movie. It was really fun making all
the Narnian mythical creatures – griffins,
centaurs, satyrs – as we.. making the famous
cracked Stone Table and

If you had all the LEGO bricks (and time!) in the world, what would you build?

That's a tough one. I enjoy building at real-life scale, so maybe something like a full-size version of myself! I'm also a big fan of the musical *Les Misérables* and would like to do a large, detailed version of the iconic barricade scene.

Models that use only a few colours can look really stylish, but multicoloured models are fun too!

Condensing the various scenes from Charles Dickens' *A Christmas Carol* into one model was a big challenge, as was capturing the characters in minifigure form! Lots of different colours and textures are used to help differentiate the different scenes, and the roof is made out of diving flippers!

The water here is built by turning a wall on its side to get a nice smooth surface. I left holes where I wanted the boats to go. There are loads of different parts supporting the inside of the cliff – pillars, castle towers, LEGO Technic bricks and so on – but you can't see them!

What is your favourite creation?

I really like my life-size version of the Three Blind Mice from the nursery rhyme. I think I captured the mice's expressions, the carving knife and all the gory details really well! The cheese was made from Modulex, which is a miniature LEGO brick from the 196... used for architectural modelling!

What are some of your top LEGO tips?

Brick separators are incredibly useful! I have three lying around in case of an emergency, and it saves having to bite the bricks or ruin your fingernails. As for building, just use what bricks you have, and be creative! Think about what parts you have a lot of – if you've got lots of green bricks, why not make a giant frog? Or if you've got lots of white horns, how about a dragon, using the horns for its spine?

How much time do you spend building?

Normally an hour or two a day.

Although this pirate hideout was designed as a static display scene, it's useful to think about the backstory. Why is the soldier being made to walk the plank? Who hid all the treasure here? Why are the pirates battling each other?

What is your favourite LEGO technique or technique you use the most?

I love coming up with innovative ways to make roofing. For example, diving flippers make a great-looking Gothic tiled roof. I bought 250 black flippers specifically for this!

How many LEGO bricks do you have?

Not enough! At the last count, around 15,000 pieces (although that was a fair few years back).

"Infuriated Isaac"
Barney Main, 9

Building a head is quite similar to building the hot air balloon on p.40, but with added details and facial features. The key to a character is often getting detail around the eyes right – Infuriated Isaac has a very shifty expression!

I JUST GO WITH THE FLOW, REALLY, AND LET THE MODEL ITSELF DICTATE HOW IT'S GOING TO LOOK!

The big challenge for this castle was the steep grassy slopes up to the keep, which were done using hinged bricks and plates. The battlements have some intricate detailing, and the castle even has its own toilet!

What things have gone wrong and how have you dealt with them?

Something I find challenging is being colour-blind. It can be very difficult to distinguish colours, and I have no concept of whether they clash or not. Also, only having a student budget, I don't have nearly the amount of bricks I'd like. I frequently have to make compromises with the size and colour of models, which is why there's normally a lot of grey in them! However, not having enough bricks can be beneficial, as it forces you to innovate and come up with new ways of doing things.

What is your favourite LEGO brick or piece?

That's tricky! There are a lot of parts that I invariably use, but I'll have to go with the headlight brick. It's really useful for turning bricks on their sides or upside down, and you can attach both bricks and bars to it. But be warned — it is actually slightly thicker than a brick, as the stud on the side sticks out a bit, and this can make building with it tricky sometimes.

What do you enjoy building the most?

I don't normally build transport, so this project was venturing into new territory for me. I love pirates and castles – but anything that is green, brown, grey and gritty suits my taste. Urban streets are also fun to do, as there's so much scope for colour and texture. I'd like to get good at making spaceships, but find them really difficult to build, as I always want to add sails or battlements!

Do you plan out your build? If so, how?

Not really! I sometimes do a rough sketch but generally I just start building and hope it goes to plan! I tend to think about the next step in a model when I'm not building, and I've been known to wake up during the night with an idea what to do next! Naturally, I implement it immediately...

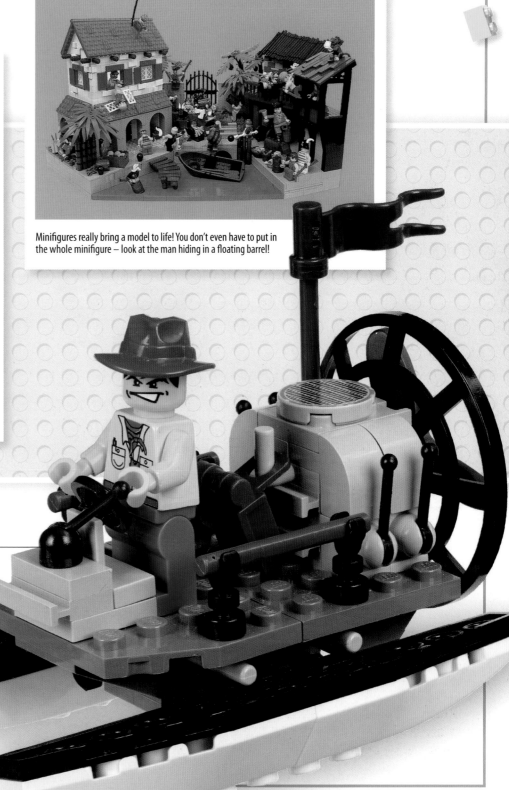

Minifigures really bring a model to life! You don't even have to put in the whole minifigure – look at the man hiding in a floating barrel!

This museum is compatible with LEGO® Modular Buildings, such as Café Corner. It is, however, considerably more dilapidated, with its broken windows and grimy streets.

You can build things that you see around you, things that you may only have seen in books or photographs – like this swampboat – or creations that come entirely from your imagination!

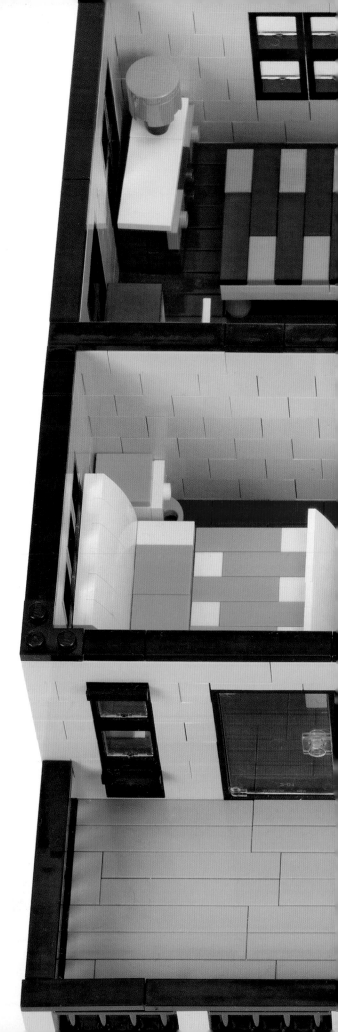

TOWN &
COUNTRY

What kind of structures does your LEGO® world
need? Will you build a place for your minifigures
to live, work or just somewhere for them to hang
out and have fun? You need to get building!

Home sweet home! Your buildings
can be simple or complex, big or small.
This is the top story of a large family
residence. (See pp.58–59)

4x5 DOOR

1x2x3 WALL ELEMENT

1x1x2 HINGE BRICK AND WINDOW SHUTTER

1x6 TILE

2x4 PLATE

2x2 TILE

2x2 TILE

2x3 PLATE

HOME ESSENTIALS

Door and window pieces are useful for building houses. Mix and match colours and styles if you don't have enough of one!

1x6 ARCHED FENCE

1x2x2 WINDOW FRAME

6x6 TILE

BUSH

2x3 CURVED PLATE WITH HOLE

DO IT YOURSELF!

If you haven't got a ready-made piece, try to recreate it yourself.

FLOWER

FLOWER

BALL JOINT

LUGGAGE CART

USE REAL BUILDINGS AS INSPIRATION. THEN ADD SOME IMAGINATION!

1x1 CORNER PANEL

FLOWER WITH OPEN STUD

CARROT

CHERRIES

BAMBOO PLANT

FLOWERS AND STEM

LARGE PLANT LEAVES

SMALL TREE

BARRED WINDOW WITH 2 CONNECTIONS

TAP

USE WHAT YOU HAVE

Be innovative with your bricks. If you don't have a ladder, turn this barred window (above) on its side! (See Children's Bedroom, p.59)

1x2 PLATE WITH SIDE RAIL

1x2 TEXTURED BRICK

CRATE

THE GREAT OUTDOORS

Remember to build both indoor and outdoor spaces to make your scene as realistic as possible.

TELESCOPE

1x4x1 LATTICE FENCE

ORNAMENTAL ARCH

1x4x2 LATTICE GATE

1x4x2 BARRED FENCE

1x8 PLATE WITH SIDE RAIL

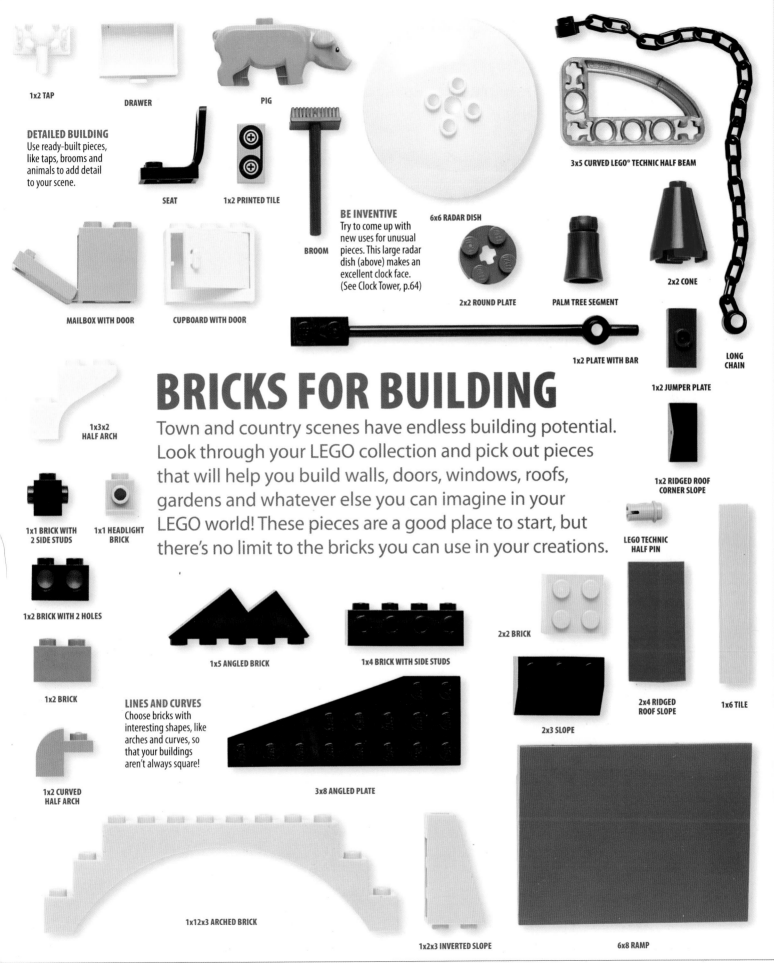

1x2 TAP

DRAWER

PIG

DETAILED BUILDING
Use ready-built pieces, like taps, brooms and animals to add detail to your scene.

SEAT

1x2 PRINTED TILE

BROOM

BE INVENTIVE
Try to come up with new uses for unusual pieces. This large radar dish (above) makes an excellent clock face. (See Clock Tower, p.64)

6x6 RADAR DISH

2x2 ROUND PLATE

PALM TREE SEGMENT

3x5 CURVED LEGO® TECHNIC HALF BEAM

2x2 CONE

LONG CHAIN

MAILBOX WITH DOOR

CUPBOARD WITH DOOR

1x2 PLATE WITH BAR

1x2 JUMPER PLATE

1x3x2 HALF ARCH

1x2 RIDGED ROOF CORNER SLOPE

BRICKS FOR BUILDING

Town and country scenes have endless building potential. Look through your LEGO collection and pick out pieces that will help you build walls, doors, windows, roofs, gardens and whatever else you can imagine in your LEGO world! These pieces are a good place to start, but there's no limit to the bricks you can use in your creations.

1x1 BRICK WITH 2 SIDE STUDS

1x1 HEADLIGHT BRICK

LEGO TECHNIC HALF PIN

1x2 BRICK WITH 2 HOLES

1x2 BRICK

1x5 ANGLED BRICK

1x4 BRICK WITH SIDE STUDS

2x2 BRICK

LINES AND CURVES
Choose bricks with interesting shapes, like arches and curves, so that your buildings aren't always square!

1x2 CURVED HALF ARCH

2x4 RIDGED ROOF SLOPE

1x6 TILE

2x3 SLOPE

3x8 ANGLED PLATE

1x12x3 ARCHED BRICK

1x2x3 INVERTED SLOPE

6x8 RAMP

FAMILY HOUSE

Town construction is all about making detailed models of real buildings – and what could be better than making a home for an entire LEGO family? Plan out your bricks before you start, to see which colours you have the most of. Do you want matching doors and windows? Two floors or three? This is your house – the design is up to you!

If you don't have enough roof pieces and slopes, use plates and hinges to build an opening roof!

You could make each floor a different colour

HOUSE BUILDING

Start your house with a basic brick outline, and decide where you want to put the doors and windows before you make the walls. Plan the layouts of your rooms as you build so everybody has enough space – and remember, you'll want to add furniture, so leave space for that too!

SURE, I'LL REBUILD THE HOUSE THIS WEEKEND!

YOU'LL HAVE TO ASK YOUR FATHER, DEAR.

CAN'T I HAVE A BIGGER ROOM? PLEEEAAASE?

Garden – use flowers, trees and colourful 1x1 plates to design your outdoor space

There are many different types of doors and windows. Will you stick to one style for your family house – or mix and match?

Real lawns aren't totally flat, so use a few plates to add depth

You could build a bigger yard, and add sheds, swings or even a swimming pool!

EASY ACCESS

Make each floor removable by lining the tops of the walls with tiles. Use just a few plates with exposed studs to hold the next level in place.

Inner walls built into outer walls for strength to support upper levels

EXPLODED VIEW

Each row of roof tiles is supported by a layer of bricks underneath

Choose where to place your staircase before finalising the room layout

Each floor is about seven or eight bricks high

Textured bricks add detail and decoration

BRICKS IN THE WALL

If you don't have enough of one colour, build walls with stripes or other patterns. You could try to replicate the look of real bricks – or use crazy colours!

Balcony railing made from barred fence

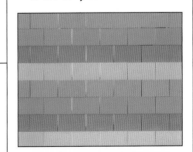

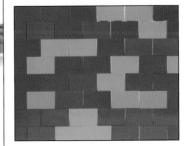

Front walkway, built with tiles. You could add a welcome mat too!

GROUND FLOOR

What does a minifigure family need? Take a look at real houses to decide what rooms and furniture you want. The ground floors of most houses have a front hall, dining room and kitchen, but maybe you want to build a playroom or den as well?

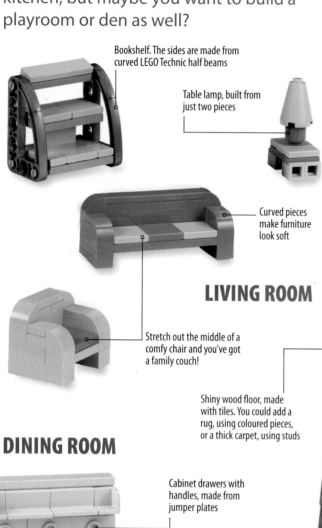

Bookshelf. The sides are made from curved LEGO Technic half beams

Table lamp, built from just two pieces

Curved pieces make furniture look soft

LIVING ROOM

Stretch out the middle of a comfy chair and you've got a family couch!

Shiny wood floor, made with tiles. You could add a rug, using coloured pieces, or a thick carpet, using studs

DINING ROOM

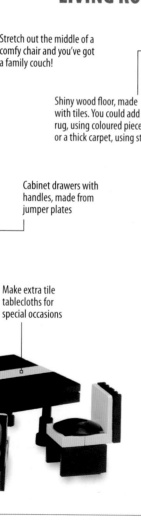

Cabinet drawers with handles, made from jumper plates

Make extra tile tablecloths for special occasions

Table legs made from telescopes

THIS PLACE HAS EVERYTHING PLUS THE KITCHEN SINK!

KITCHEN

Stove, built from a mailbox and two printed videotape tiles

FURNITURE

When building furniture, look at your pieces in new ways. Turn them around or upside-down and see if you can discover part of a chair, lamp or sofa. Remember to build your furniture to minifigure scale!

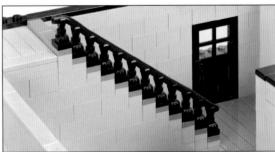

STAIRS

The stairs in this house use a long rubber piece for the handrail, supported by skeleton legs. If you don't have these pieces, you could use 1x1 bricks in alternating colours and 1x1 slopes.

TOP FLOOR

Every member of the family is an individual, so all the bedrooms in the house should be distinct too. Make each one show the interests and personality of whoever sleeps there. You could also put in a guest room, storage room or games room!

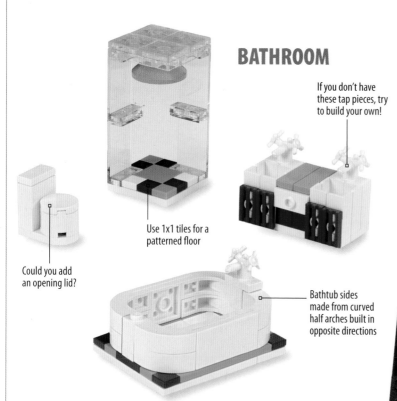

BATHROOM

If you don't have these tap pieces, try to build your own!

Use 1x1 tiles for a patterned floor

Could you add an opening lid?

Bathtub sides made from curved half arches built in opposite directions

TOP FLOOR FURNITURE

When you're building the same piece of furniture a few times, try to make each item unique. Experiment with sizes, colours and styles, and think about how a child's furniture is different from an adult's!

LAMPS

Modern floor lamp made with two radar dishes and an antenna

Master bedroom doors open out onto balcony

Long tiles create wooden plank effect

Crystal lamp base made with transparent plates

For stability, build the balcony directly into the floor of the top story

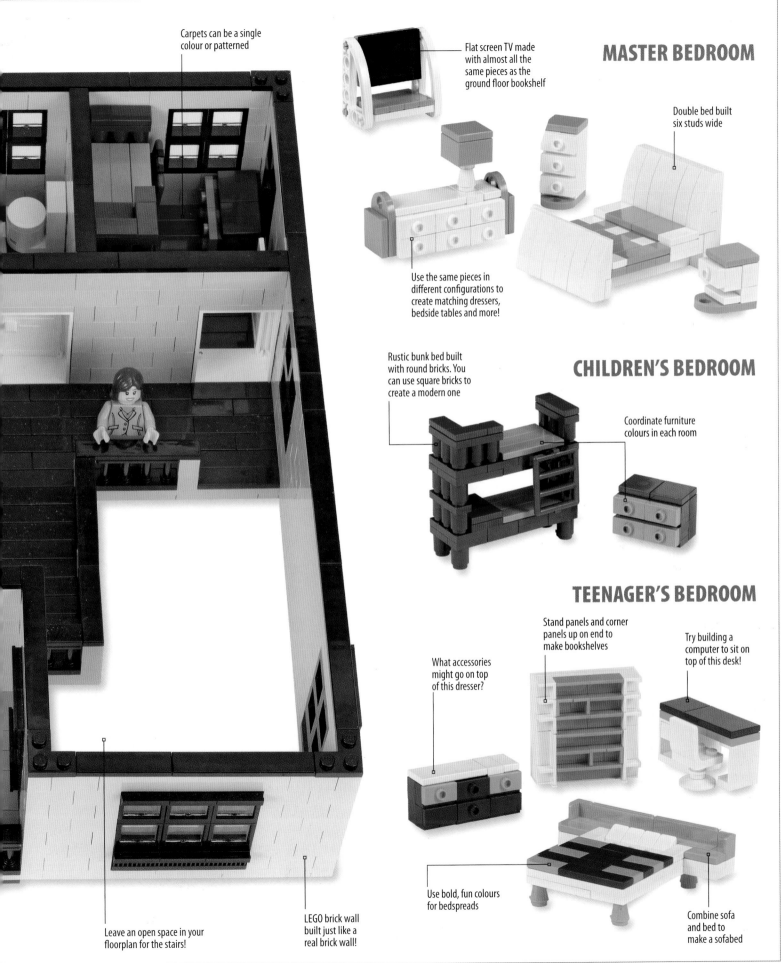

Carpets can be a single colour or patterned

Flat screen TV made with almost all the same pieces as the ground floor bookshelf

MASTER BEDROOM

Double bed built six studs wide

Use the same pieces in different configurations to create matching dressers, bedside tables and more!

Rustic bunk bed built with round bricks. You can use square bricks to create a modern one

CHILDREN'S BEDROOM

Coordinate furniture colours in each room

TEENAGER'S BEDROOM

Stand panels and corner panels up on end to make bookshelves

Try building a computer to sit on top of this desk!

What accessories might go on top of this dresser?

Leave an open space in your floorplan for the stairs!

LEGO brick wall built just like a real brick wall!

Use bold, fun colours for bedspreads

Combine sofa and bed to make a sofabed

MICROBUILDINGS

Want to build a whole town or city, but don't have much space? Try creating microbuildings! With just a handful of standard bricks, a few special pieces here and there and lots of imagination, you can build a landscape that is tiny, but hugely impressive!

BUILDING BRIEF

Objective: Create microbuildings
Use: Part of a microscale town or city
Features: Lots of detail at a tiny scale
Extras: Tiny people, cars, neighbourhoods

LIGHT AND COLOUR

Use transparent plates to create the look of stained-glass windows. You may not be able to capture the intricate detail of the real thing, but the idea will shine through!

Simple colour scheme

Add details to break up plain facades

1x1 slopes look more in-scale than big roof pieces

Small arched frame becomes a giant door

GRAND BUILDING

The scale of your building will sometimes be determined by the best piece for the job. This cathedral-inspired building is built to fit the scale of small arched windows!

1x1 green cones make great hedges and trees

RAISE THE ROOF

The building's roof is built up one row at a time using 1x1 slope pieces, arranged in a simple pattern. Each row is one plate higher than the last one.

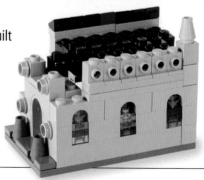

Building fronts don't have to be angular – try using curved slopes

Textured bricks add detail

CANAL HOUSE

Photographs can help you design locations from a particular time or place, like this Dutch canal house. Keep the proportions as close as possible to the real thing.

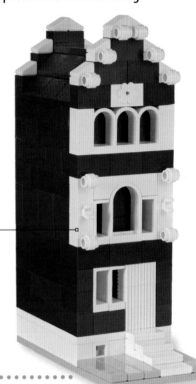

STREET STORES

For a row of buildings, start with a street base, made of plates and tiles. Create each building separately and then attach it to the base. Give each one its own distinct lines, like the green and orange store's curved roof.

Try to choose interesting colour combinations

Add awnings and overhangs to entrances

Building and trim have contrasting colours

Add simple decorative details, but don't overdo it

REAR VIEW

MICROHOUSE

Don't just build a boring box for your microscale house. Experiment with different shapes and pieces! Pick out your windows and doors first so you know how big to make the rest of the building around them.

Windows make great doors at microscale

Same roof pieces as on big houses – just fewer of them!

TRAIN STATION

A train station is a functional building, but that doesn't mean it has to look boring! Try to design your station in an unusual shape, and give it some interesting features, like arched doorways, striking brickwork or a unique roof. You could even build a removable roof so you can access the interior for rebuilding and play.

Roof built in an elongated hexagonal shape

GETTING INTO SHAPE

Building a roof in an unusual shape can be tricky, so focus on this aspect of the model first. When the roof is complete, build the walls to fit.

I'M LATE! DO LEGO TRAINS RUN ON TIME?

ARCHES

Two half arches form the top of a fancy doorway, while a single half arch piece can be used to support part of the roof.

Elevate the main building on a platform to draw attention to it

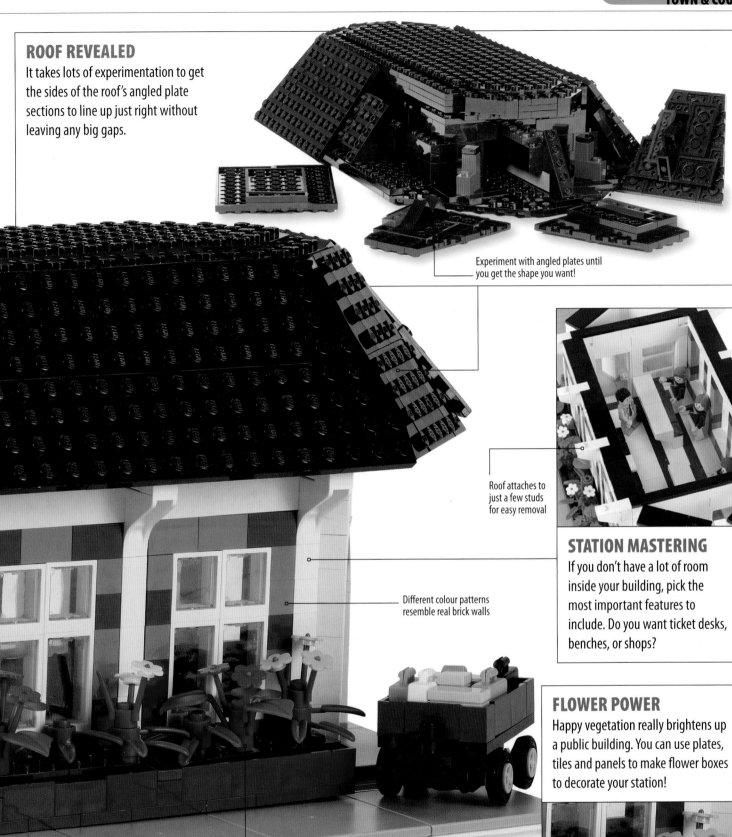

ROOF REVEALED

It takes lots of experimentation to get the sides of the roof's angled plate sections to line up just right without leaving any big gaps.

Experiment with angled plates until you get the shape you want!

Roof attaches to just a few studs for easy removal

Different colour patterns resemble real brick walls

STATION MASTERING

If you don't have a lot of room inside your building, pick the most important features to include. Do you want ticket desks, benches, or shops?

FLOWER POWER

Happy vegetation really brightens up a public building. You can use plates, tiles and panels to make flower boxes to decorate your station!

STATION BUILDINGS

It takes more than one building to make a train station! Look at real stations to get ideas about what else your scene could include. Each building should be different from the others, but perhaps you could incorporate common elements into each of them so they all fit together.

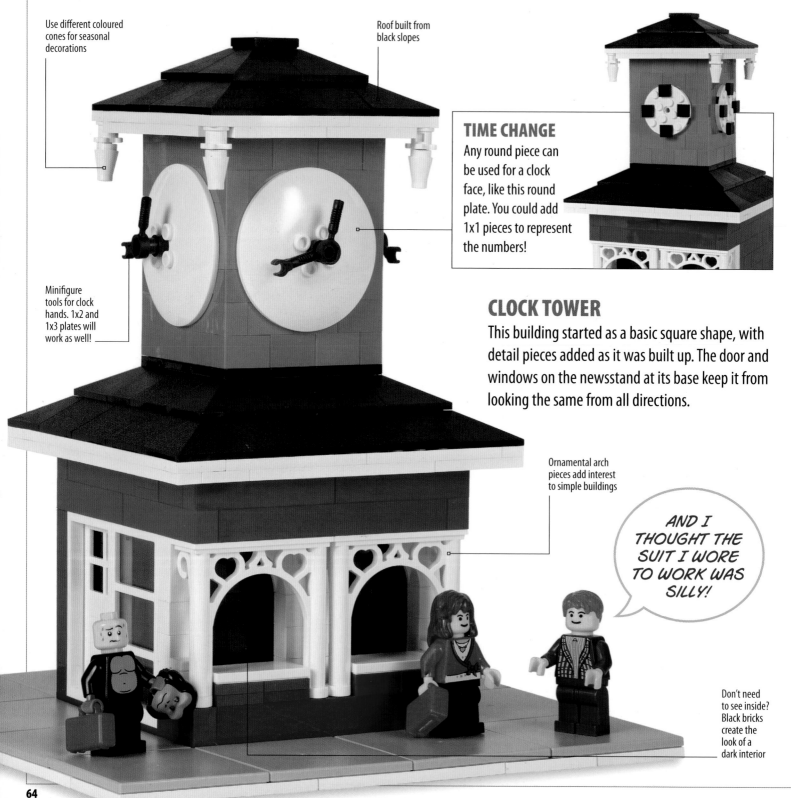

Use different coloured cones for seasonal decorations

Roof built from black slopes

Minifigure tools for clock hands. 1x2 and 1x3 plates will work as well!

TIME CHANGE

Any round piece can be used for a clock face, like this round plate. You could add 1x1 pieces to represent the numbers!

CLOCK TOWER

This building started as a basic square shape, with detail pieces added as it was built up. The door and windows on the newsstand at its base keep it from looking the same from all directions.

Ornamental arch pieces add interest to simple buildings

AND I THOUGHT THE SUIT I WORE TO WORK WAS SILLY!

Don't need to see inside? Black bricks create the look of a dark interior

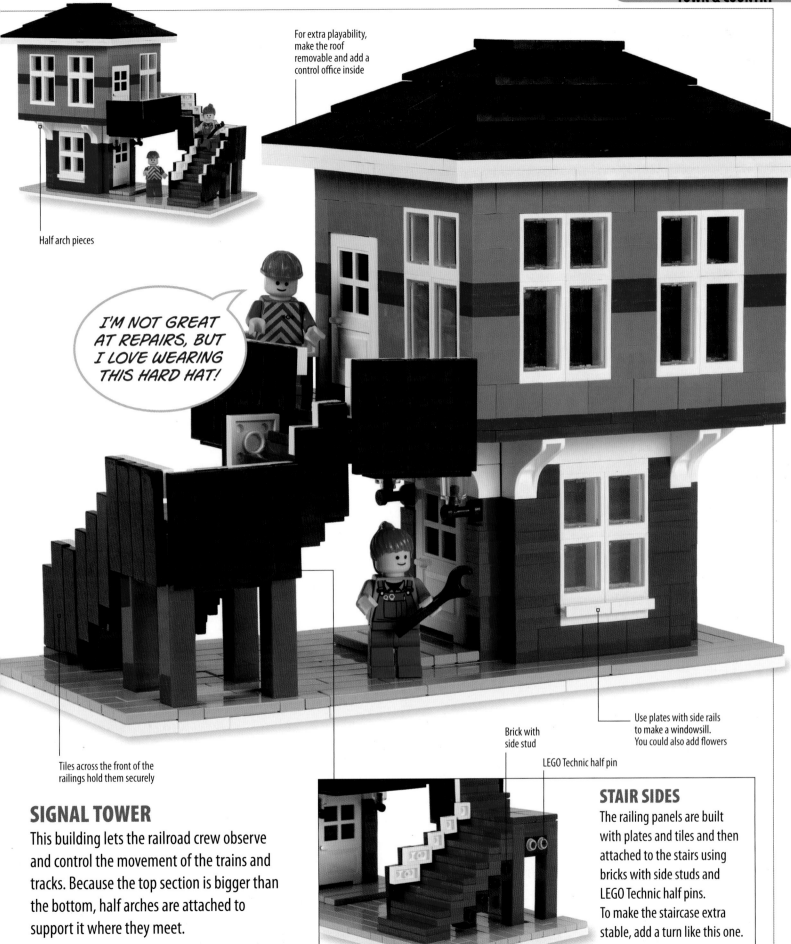

For extra playability, make the roof removable and add a control office inside

Half arch pieces

I'M NOT GREAT AT REPAIRS, BUT I LOVE WEARING THIS HARD HAT!

Tiles across the front of the railings hold them securely

Brick with side stud

Use plates with side rails to make a windowsill. You could also add flowers

LEGO Technic half pin

SIGNAL TOWER

This building lets the railroad crew observe and control the movement of the trains and tracks. Because the top section is bigger than the bottom, half arches are attached to support it where they meet.

STAIR SIDES

The railing panels are built with plates and tiles and then attached to the stairs using bricks with side studs and LEGO Technic half pins. To make the staircase extra stable, add a turn like this one.

INSIDE THE STATION

There are lots of great things you can build inside your train station, from rows of seats and departures desks, to check-in counters and x-ray scanning machines. You could also build waiting rooms, machines and ticket counters for a bus station – or even an airport. Now all you need to do is get your minifigures ready to travel!

DEPARTURES

This is the departure gate, where passengers hand over their tickets before boarding the train. The simple desk is made from red and white pieces, with no sideways building.

You could use transparent pieces to cover the studs and act as desk lights

*BUT I CAN'T SIT NEXT TO **HER** – WE'RE WEARING THE SAME TORSO!*

TICKET COUNTER

White bricks with tiles on top make this ticket counter look sleek and hi-tech. Computer screens are positioned at an angle on jumper plates, and the keyboards are attached with a clip and bar hinge so they can be positioned at an angle.

This ticket counter could also be an airport check-in desk!

You could build the computer desks in the colours of your railway company

Same-colour minifigure torsos look like uniforms

SORRY, BUT MY THREE INVISIBLE FRIENDS ARE SITTING HERE.

SITTING AROUND

Build your waiting area for as many passengers as you like. These red seats clip onto a 2x12 plate. The feet are 1x2 jumper plates with 1x1 round plates on top. Don't forget to add a small side table. Remember: it's all about the details!

2x2 tile used as tabletop

Jumper plates evenly spaced out

Keyboards and computer screens can be found in various LEGO® City sets, but you could use a plain tile or a grille instead

X-ray machine – grey tiles, small panels and cones make it look functional

SECURITY ALERT!

Security is an important feature in airports and some train and bus stations. Make sure your x-ray machine is the right size to scan LEGO luggage, and that the body scanner is tall enough for a minifigure – and his hat – to walk through!

X-ray scanner, made from specialised angled pieces. A stack of 1x2 bricks with slopes on the top corners would work just as well

COUNTRY BARN

Want a break from the hustle and bustle of the big city? Head out to the countryside and build yourself a farm, starting with a good old-fashioned barn. Make it big and sturdy, with plenty of room for animals, crops and equipment inside. Farming life is hard work, but building it can be lots of fun!

BUILDING BRIEF

Objective: Build barns for your farms

Use: Storage of food, tools and livestock

Features: Opening doors, lots of space

Extras: Farming equipment, granary, farm animals

BARN RAISING

The roof is the trickiest part of this model, so build it first, leaving a narrow groove in the underside so it can slot securely onto the barn walls and be removed easily. Match the trim around the doors and windows to the colours of the roof.

Weather vane – try different animals on top too!

With winch parts, you could make the hayloft crane really work

AHHH...DON'T YOU JUST LOVE THAT FRESH COUNTRY AIR?

Vary shape and size of windows

Use 1x3 slopes for the upper roof and 1x2 slopes for the lower roof to get a perfect barn shape!

Don't have enough slopes for roof tiles? Use plates instead!

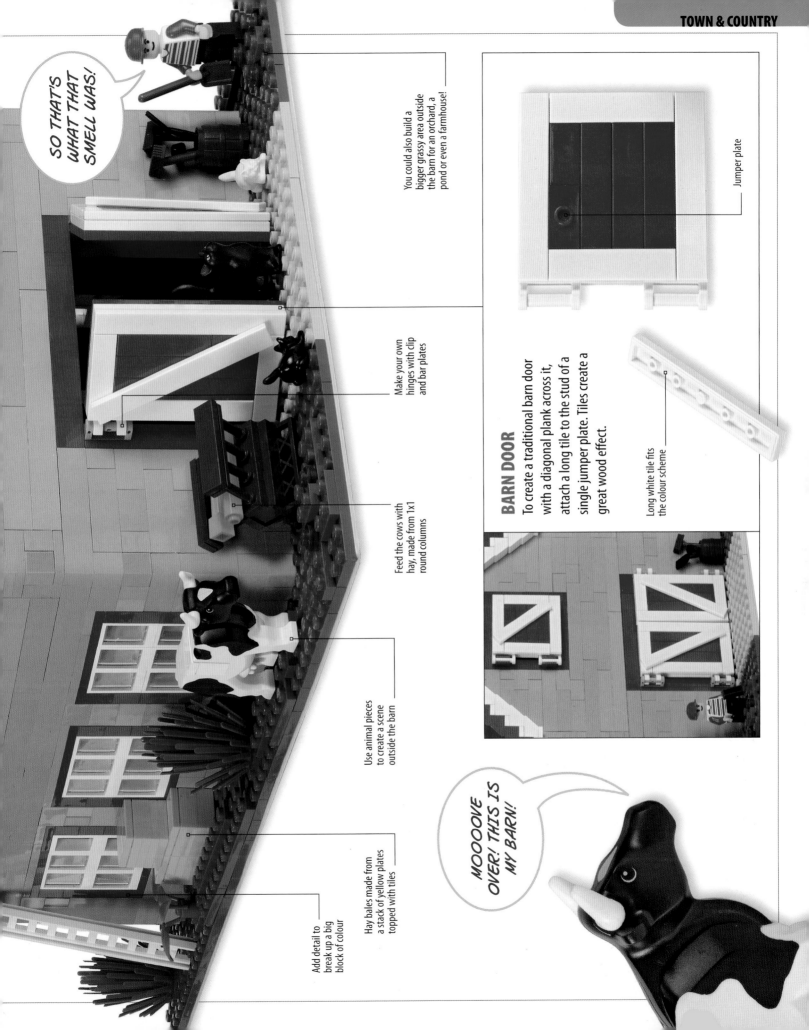

SO THAT'S WHAT THAT SMELL WAS!

You could also build a bigger grassy area outside the barn for an orchard, a pond or even a farmhouse!

Make your own hinges with clip and bar plates

Feed the cows with hay, made from 1x1 round columns

Use animal pieces to create a scene outside the barn

Hay bales made from a stack of yellow plates topped with tiles

Add detail to break up a big block of colour

BARN DOOR

To create a traditional barn door with a diagonal plank across it, attach a long tile to the stud of a single jumper plate. Tiles create a great wood effect.

Jumper plate

Long white tile fits the colour scheme

MOOOOVE OVER! THIS IS MY BARN!

FARMYARD LIFE

With the right bricks and pieces, you can create a whole farm for those hard-working minifigures. Think about what kind of farm you want to run – a dairy farm, an orchard, a ranch – and bring it to life!

BUILDING BRIEF

Objective: Build whole farms
Use: Milking, sowing, feeding, harvesting
Features: Coops, pens, orchards, natural surroundings
Extras: Tractor, field, stable, pen, farmer's house

Some duck houses are built on an island in the middle of a pond. Where will yours go?

COOL COVER

The angled roof of this duck house is made from large ramp pieces, which are built up and locked together with basic plates. You could even attach the roof with a clip and bar hinge so you can play inside!

HOLD ON? THIS IS NICER THAN MY HOUSE!

BRICK FOWL

If you don't have the right LEGO animal, make your own! This duck is made using a few simple colours and pieces, like clip-plate wings and a bill made from a 1x1 cone.

DUCK HOUSE

A duck house doesn't have to be a plain, white hut! Design an unusual roof, add lattice windows or build it on a raised platform so the ducks can wander underneath.

DUCK POND

A pond isn't clean and smooth like a swimming pool, so build yours to look wild and untamed, with plants and mud around the edges.

Water — you could also use transparent blue plates, or white tiles for ice in winter!

Include wildlife like fish, frogs and ducks

Bamboo plant comes in many LEGO sets

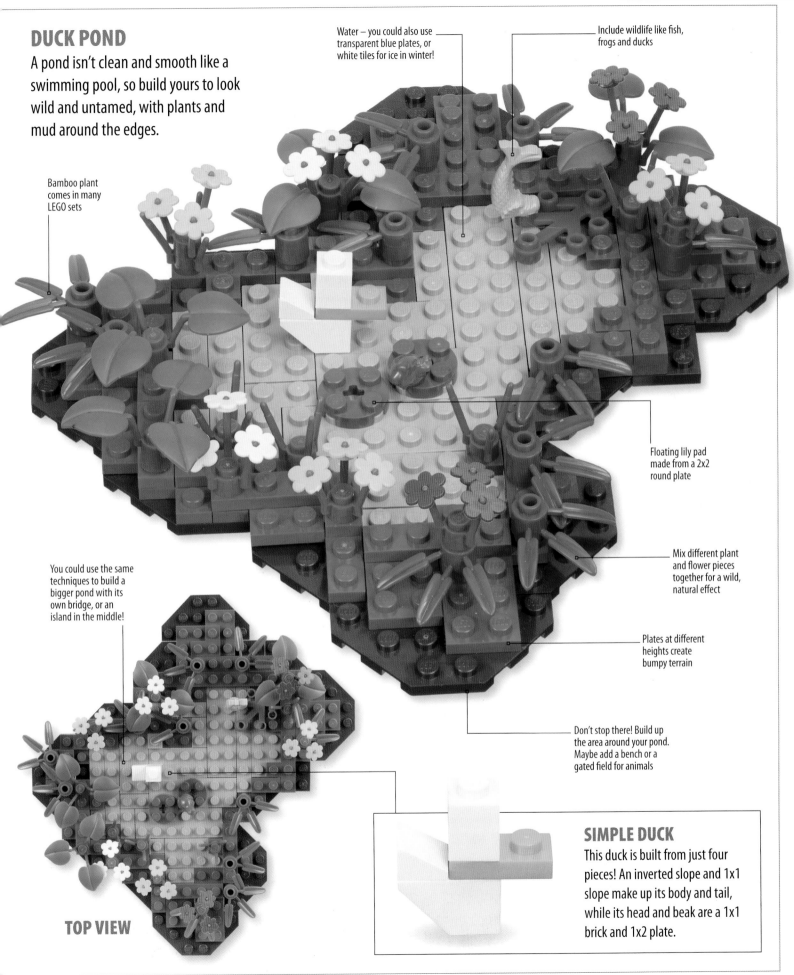

Floating lily pad made from a 2x2 round plate

Mix different plant and flower pieces together for a wild, natural effect

You could use the same techniques to build a bigger pond with its own bridge, or an island in the middle!

Plates at different heights create bumpy terrain

Don't stop there! Build up the area around your pond. Maybe add a bench or a gated field for animals

TOP VIEW

SIMPLE DUCK

This duck is built from just four pieces! An inverted slope and 1x1 slope make up its body and tail, while its head and beak are a 1x1 brick and 1x2 plate.

DOWN ON THE FARM

To bring your farm creations to life, think about the small details: What does a shed's roof really look like? How can you build a realistic gate? What fruit will be growing in your orchard? Don't stop until you're really happy with your model!

TIN ROOF
Long, grey plates with side-rails look like a sheet of corrugated metal when attached side-by-side.

Roof is attached to shed with a 1x6 jumper plate

A plate hung diagonally adds decoration

THAT'S A WHOLE LOTTA FARM TO WATER. I'LL NEED A BIGGER CAN.

TOOL SHED
To make your doors (or windows) look smaller than they are, build a doorway the size you want, then place the door behind it so it opens inwards.

DON'T HOG ALL THE FOOD HAMLET!

A clean, square fence on rough, uneven terrain makes a good visual contrast

PIGPEN
You don't want farm animals to run wild and eat your crops, so build some enclosures! Instead of a single-piece base, this sty has layers of plates to give its surface some depth.

Mud doesn't stay inside boundaries, so let it flow out past the fence

Gate made from lattice gate attached upside-down

BRICK FRUIT

If you don't have pieces of LEGO fruit, make your own! Round or square red bricks make great apples, or use yellow for lemons. Can you think of any other pieces to use?

You could add flowers to your trees too!

Palm tree segments come in many LEGO sets – or you could use round bricks

Build a strong, wide base to support a tall tree

ORCHARD

You could build a well-tended orchard with rows of straight, matching trees – but your farm will look more natural if your tree trunks and branches are different shapes.

If it's autumn, your tree may have fewer leaves on it

Why not build a whole vegetable patch with rows of lettuces, carrots and tomatoes?

Carrot growing out of the ground is really a 1x1 brick topped with a 2x2 plate!

EASY AS ONE, TWO, TREE

Building your own trees is easy! Stack round brown bricks or plates on a sturdy base for the trunk, then add plant leaves or any green pieces as leaves.

2x2 round plate

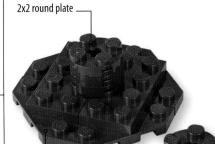

Use green plates if you want your tree to have a base of grass

BRIDGES

It's easy to snap some plates together and call it a bridge, but if you really want to cross a gap with style, try making a bridge that looks like the real thing – and works like it too. Here's a great way to build a gentle humpback bridge for a park or country river crossing.

BUILDING BRIEF

Objective: Build bridges
Use: Crossing streams, rivers and ditches
Features: Strength, stability, walls, railings
Extras: Cars, pedestrians, tollgates, nighttime lightsblazing burner

HUMPBACK BRIDGE

To build this picturesque bridge, start with a central arch. Make a solid base around the arch shape, building steps into it to create height. Then use slopes and tiles to create a smooth finish.

You could add ornamentation to your bridge's walls, like stone sculptures or street lamps

Populate your country scene with minifigures who enjoy outdoor activities like fishing, jogging or family picnics. What else can you think of?

MMM...PLASTIC TROUT – MY FAVOURITE!

THIS BRIDGE IS LOWER THAN I THOUGHT... DUCK!

Build these four-piece ducks in any colours you like!

Make your bridge the right size for your purpose. Should it be wide enough for just pedestrians, or do you want cars to drive over it?

MINI ARCH

The arch is built just like the ones on the big model, but with fewer bricks. Use smaller arch pieces for even tinier bridges.

MICROBRIDGE

You can build a bridge in microscale, too! Try to include all the key features of a bigger model, like arches, support columns, railings and a smooth pathway across.

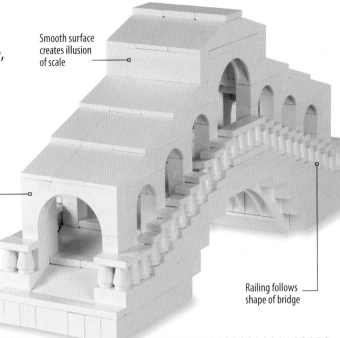

Smooth surface creates illusion of scale

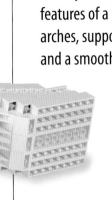

Arched brick

All-white bricks look like polished marble

Railing follows shape of bridge

Use slopes to make the walls follow a gentle curve. You could also use plates to build gradual steps

You could also make a base for your bridge to sit on. Build it up with grass, trees flowers and a river

Attach plant leaves and flowers to jumper plates built into the bridge walls

Your bridge doesn't have to be built out of tan bricks. Use brown pieces for a rustic wooden bridge, or grey for old stone

BULGING BRICKS

To make some of the stones bulge out from your wall, include headlight bricks among your 1x2 bricks and attach 1x2 tiles to them.

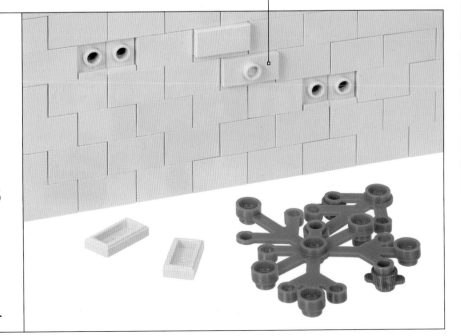

BIGGER BRIDGES

For larger spans of water, you need a bigger bridge! Large bridges usually have more arches to support their length and weight. They're made out of the strongest materials around, so use lots of grey bricks to mimic stone, or LEGO Technic elements for metal girders.

Chains built into sides of pillars

If you don't have chains, use strings with studs, or build railings with bars

Create details to add decoration to your bridge

Build your own cars to drive across the bridge (see p.22)

Archway tall enough for boats to pass below

CITY BRIDGE

The dimensions of the bridge are determined by the size of the key pieces and features, like the length of the chains and how wide the road needs to be to accommodate two lanes of traffic plus pavements. So build the road section first and then construct the arches underneath.

Add more bricks to make supports taller!

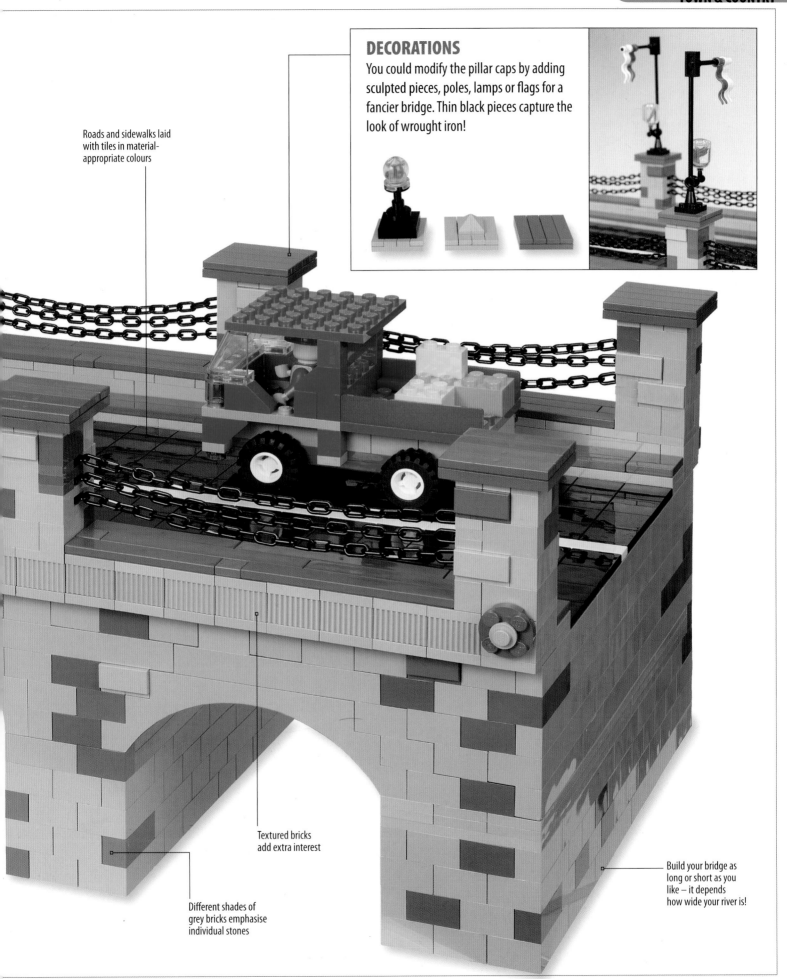

Roads and sidewalks laid with tiles in material-appropriate colours

DECORATIONS

You could modify the pillar caps by adding sculpted pieces, poles, lamps or flags for a fancier bridge. Thin black pieces capture the look of wrought iron!

Textured bricks add extra interest

Different shades of grey bricks emphasise individual stones

Build your bridge as long or short as you like – it depends how wide your river is!

MEET THE BUILDER

DEBORAH HIGDON

Location: Canada
Age: 52
LEGO Speciality: Architecture, furniture

Which model were you most proud of as a young LEGO builder?

I don't remember being particularly proud of one model, but I do remember building houses – I loved the roof pieces and the doors and windows. In a box of things from my childhood, I still have pieces of a large fireplace that I built for my dolls, with candlesticks and a hand-drawn fire. I didn't like playing with dolls as much as I liked building furniture and houses for them!

This is a model of some buildings in the French village of St Paul de Vence. It was my first MOC to win a big competition at a LEGO fan festival.

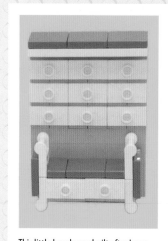

This little bench was built after I saw a picture of a real bench in a Dutch museum. I liked the style and colour and thought I could model it in LEGO bricks.

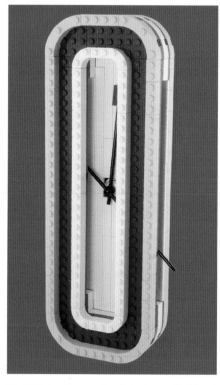

This MOC is based on a modern design I saw on the internet. I changed the colours and some parts of the design to make it work in LEGO bricks. And yes, it really does tell the time!

What is the biggest or most complex model you've made?

Mechanically, a sliding house was the most complex. It appeared to be a huge challenge but it was a simple solution in the end. I hid a motor in the "basement" and had the sliding roof of the house simply sit in a channel and be dragged along. At first, I thought of all kinds of complicated ways to get it to slide, but an AFOL (Adult Fan Of LEGO) friend and I talked about it, and he helped me come up with that simple solution. It doesn't always have to be complicated, sometimes we just think it does!

What is your favourite LEGO brick or piece?

That's really hard to choose but I think my favourite LEGO pieces are tiles. I wish they were all made in every colour, every size! I like them because they really help to make a smooth piece of furniture look almost real. They also help to add small details, which are important when modelling houses and furniture.

If you had all the LEGO bricks (and time!) in the world, what would you build?

I've got a lot of ideas in my head so I don't know where I'd start! On my list of MOCs (My Own Creations) to do, there's a minifigure scale Garden of Versailles in France with all the buildings, fountains and flower beds. I have also thought about a minifigure scale of a Greek fishing village in a mountain like the microscale one I made. But I'd need more than all the LEGO bricks and time in the world – I'd need a new house with an enormous LEGO room and the largest building table in the world!

What things have gone wrong and how have you dealt with them?

Things have fallen apart because I didn't build them strongly enough, especially when I have to travel with my MOCs. Occasionally, things fall on the floor and I have to rebuild them but sometimes I can't remember how I solved a particular problem so I have to rethink. I'm determined to make my ideas work. It takes a lot of patience and determination to rebuild, but it will always be worth it in the end. Often it turns out better than the original!

Another doorway from the series. I thought this could be the entrance to an old castle or manor house.

I tried building just doorways so that I could try different architectural styles without making the whole building. A grey stone doorway like this would be attached to a very big old stone house.

Microscale Rialto Bridge: this famous bridge crosses a canal in Venice, Italy. I wanted to build something like it and I wanted it to look like marble or very white stone, so I used just one colour

I LIKE LOOKING AT VERY ORIGINAL FURNITURE AND THINKING OF HOW I CAN MODEL IT.

What are some of your top LEGO tips?

I think it's important to just play with putting bricks together, not even building anything: two little pieces you put together can suddenly look a bit like something you've seen elsewhere and may give you a brilliant idea for a creation. Look for interesting ways to connect two pieces and find out what fits together. Another good idea is to look at a lot of pictures if you're going to build something in model or replica. Getting tricky bricks apart is much easier with two brick separators – that's an important tip for everyone!

What else do you enjoy making apart from houses/buildings?

I've started to build some small sculptures and useful items like LEGO bookends, a clock and a birdhouse. My first 3-D sculpture was a heart for Valentine's Day and I really enjoyed the challenge of forming the heart to get the curves just right.

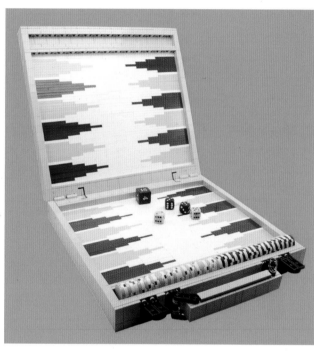

I was starting to build things that weren't houses and furniture so I thought I could start making useful things. I'd never seen a backgammon game made from LEGO pieces so I wanted it to be portable and playable, and it is.

How much time do you spend building?

When I'm in the middle of a project, full of ideas, I spend most evenings and weekends building, which is probably about 10–14 hours a week, sometimes more. At other times I don't build anything for weeks.

This model was built specially for this book. I looked carefully for pieces that could be the "hands" of the clock and I wanted the clock tower to look a little old-fashioned

Do you plan out your build? If so, how?

Only in my head! I think of one central feature of my new MOC (for example, the swimming pool, the main staircase or the roof line) and I'll build the rest of the model around it. I make up my mind as I go along. Sometimes, I'll quickly do a rough sketch of a small part of a building I've seen, then I think of other things I can add to that feature. Sometimes I take pictures to remind me of a nice staircase, porch or window I've seen that I'd like to try to replicate.

My LEGO club often has building challenges. So, for the Valentine's Day challenge I wanted to build something with dark red brick. I also wanted to try some 3-D shaping and a heart seemed a good shape to work with. I also wanted to add frilly lace and a way to curve the square edges so the tooth plates and hinges helped a lot.

What is your favourite LEGO technique or technique you use the most?

I use a lot of hinges, especially the old finger hinges and I like to use LEGO Technic pieces to make interesting furniture. I also love to use a lot of SNOT (a LEGO fan term meaning Studs Not On Top).

What are you inspired by?

Mostly architecture and design – cool building ideas that I see in real life and I want to try to build in LEGO bricks. I like looking at very original furniture and thinking of how I can model it.

This bookend is another useful MOC idea, something that anyone anywhere can enjoy and use. The "books" were fun to build and I printed the titles on clear sticker paper. The building has a little hiding spot for something special.

What is your favourite creation?

This changes all the time, especially after I've just finished a big creation. I think my most favourite will always be St Paul de Vence: I visited that town in France a long time ago. One day I decided to make some of the buildings there in LEGO bricks. There were about seven buildings and I built a walled platform for them, but because they were all separate, I could change the look just by moving the buildings around. Each separate building had a different challenge, which made it more fun to build.

How old were you when you started using LEGO bricks?

I was about seven or eight when I was first introduced to LEGO bricks. I stopped building, like many kids do, but I started again as an adult when I bought LEGO sets for my nieces and nephews. I really started buying and building for myself when I was 40. Then I found the online LEGO community, joined a local club for adults, and started to display publicly and post my work on the internet.

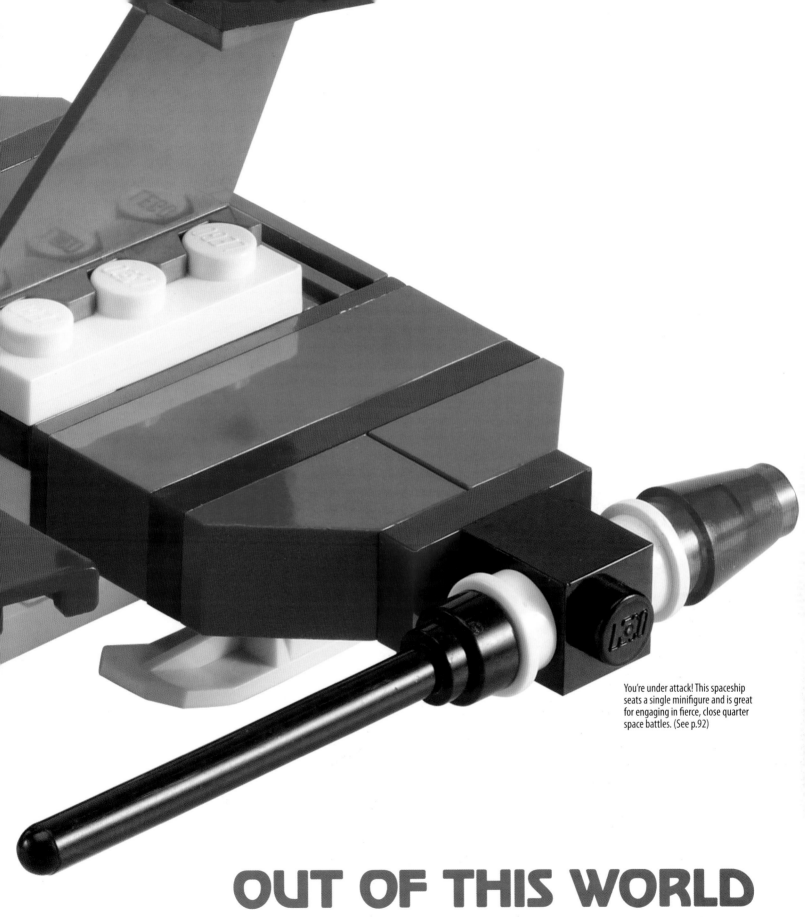

You're under attack! This spaceship seats a single minifigure and is great for engaging in fierce, close quarter space battles. (See p.92)

OUT OF THIS WORLD

Let's go intergalactic! But how will you get there? You need a rocket, plus lots of cool spaceships, moon buggies and other interplanetary vehicles.

STELLAR PIECES

To create spectacular space models, think about what sort of bricks you'll need. Curved pieces, moving parts, metallic details and antennas will give your models a sleek, space-age look. Here are some LEGO® pieces that may come in handy if you have them, but look through your own bricks and you're sure to find many more!

3x4 DOUBLE ANGLED PLATE

2x4 ANGLED PLATE

ALL ANGLES
Angled plates and slopes are great for building wings or giving your model a streamlined shape!

2x2 ROUND TILE

2x2 SLIDE PLATE

2x2 RADAR DISH

2x3 SLOPE

2x3 PLATE WITH WINGED END

1x2/2x2 ANGLE PLATE

STUDWAYS
Pieces with studs facing in more than one direction can help hold different sections of your model together.

1x2 JUMPER PLATE

1x3 CURVED SLOPE

1x2 INVERTED SLOPE

2x2 ROUND BRICK

2x2 ROUND TILE

2x2 DETAILED CURVED SLOPE

1x4 BRICK WITH SIDE STUDS

1x3x2 CURVED HALF ARCH

2x2 PRINTED SLOPE

1x2 PRINTED TILE

LIGHTBULB

LIGHTSABER HILT

LEGO® TECHNIC PIN WITH BAR EXTENSION

2x2 CURVED BRICK WITH TOP STUDS

1x1 PLATE WITH SIDE RING

1x1 CONE

1x1 HEADLIGHT BRICK

1x1 PLATE WITH VERTICAL CLIP

3x3x6 ENGINE

1x1 TOOTH PLATE

JOYSTICK

1x2 BRICK WITH 2 PINS

1x2 BRICK WITH SIDE STUDS AND STAND

LEGO TECHNIC BEAM WITH STICK

BIG BRICKS
A single large piece, such as this engine (above) can become the main body of a microbuild. (See Butterfly Shuttle, p.96)

ANTENNA

SMALL DETAILS
Add detail to your spaceship cockpit control panel with small parts.

2x2 TURNTABLE

HINGED PLATES

1x1 PLATE WITH HORIZONTAL CLIP

1x2 PLATE WITH HANDLED BAR

LOUDHAILER

1x1 SLOPE

BALL JOINT SOCKET

2x2 BRICK WITH BALL JOINT

STEERING WHEEL

ROBOT ARM

HANDLEBARS

1x1 SLOPE

WING-SHAPING
Mix long and short plates until your wings are the exact shape you want.

1x4 TILE

NEW IDEAS
If a piece makes you think of an idea for a specific vehicle, get building! This orange radar dish makes a great flying saucer. (See Flying Saucer, p.97)

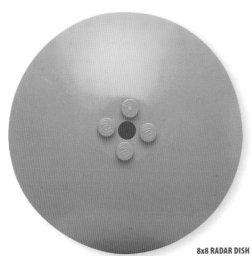
8x8 RADAR DISH

2x4 PLATE WITH SIDE VENTS

1x2x3 WALL ELEMENT

3x12 ANGLED PLATE

6x10x2 WINDSCREEN

CHOOSE AN UNUSUAL WINDSCREEN FOR YOUR COCKPIT AS A STARTING POINT

SPIKED WHEEL

INSPIRING PARTS
Large or unusually shaped pieces, like a spiked wheel (above) or curved arch brick (below), can help you come up with a design for your model. (See Rocket, pp.106–107)

6x4x2 COCKPIT

GOING GREEN
Once you've chosen a windscreen, you could build the rest of the model to match. (See Nova Nemesis, p.95)

FLAG

1x4 HANDLE

AERIAL

1x2 GRILLE SLOPE

1x2 GRILLE

1x2 GRILLE

1x2 GRILLE

1x2 PLATE

1x2x2 LADDER

2x2 RUDDER

INNOVATION
Some pieces are obviously perfect for spaceships, such as turbines, antennas or aerials, but many other pieces can be adapted and work just as well!

8x8x2 CURVED ARCH BRICK

1x2 PLATE WITH JET ENGINE

2x2 PLATE WITH TURBINE

HOVER SCOOTER

When exploring alien worlds, your minifigure might need a small vehicle. But before you get building, ask yourself some simple questions. How will your vehicle travel? Does it roll on wheels, blast around with boosters or zoom along on jet-powered sleds? What do you want your vehicle to do? It could explore space, build a space base...or even deliver pizza to a hungry rocket crew. Anything is possible!

BUILDING BRIEF

Objective: Create space vehicles
Use: Exploration, transportation
Features: Must be able to hover
Extras: Radar, other comm devices

KEEPIN' IT SMOOTH

If you have any curved pieces, try using them to give the front of your vehicle a sleek, aerodynamic profile. Contrasting colours look space-age and striking, especially red and black!

Transparent radar dish could be swapped for a flag or a lightbulb

Thrusters mounted on the underside – you could replace with wheels, or leave the underside flat

FRONT VIEW

I WONDER IF I SHOULD HAVE ADDED SEAT BELTS!

OFF THE GROUND

This single-person hover scooter has an open cockpit at the front and a rear boot for storage. The two sections are made separately, then slotted together. You may not have curved pieces for the front, but think of it like the front of a car and get creative!

Grille piece creates a hi-tech look. Can be swapped for a tile

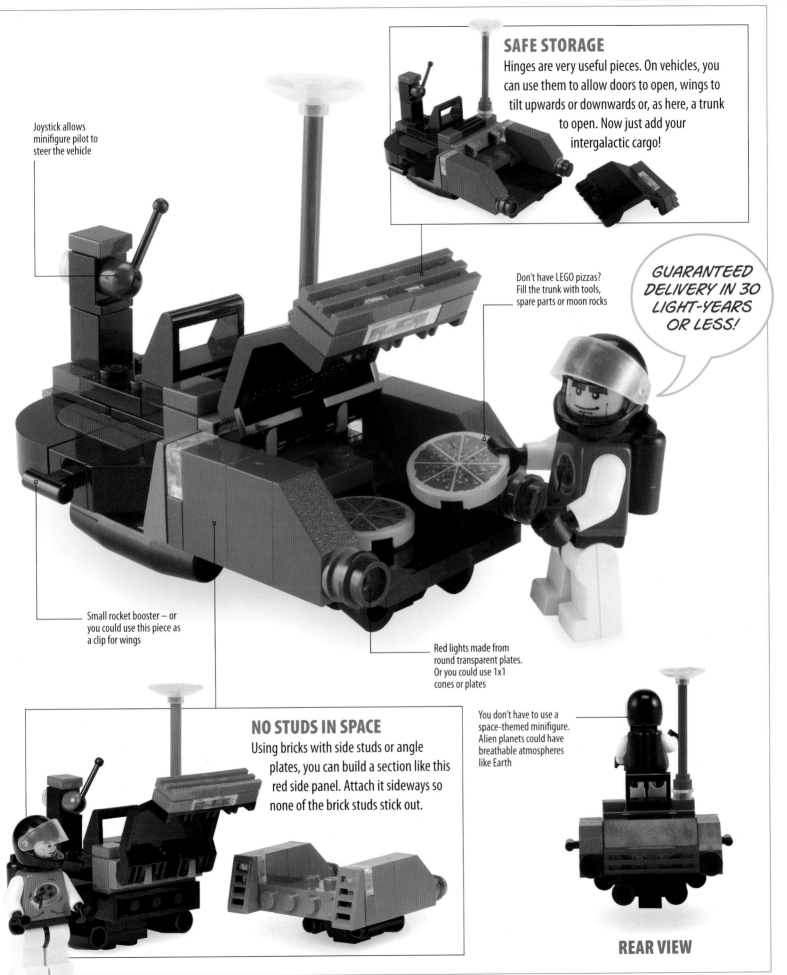

SAFE STORAGE

Hinges are very useful pieces. On vehicles, you can use them to allow doors to open, wings to tilt upwards or downwards or, as here, a trunk to open. Now just add your intergalactic cargo!

Joystick allows minifigure pilot to steer the vehicle

Don't have LEGO pizzas? Fill the trunk with tools, spare parts or moon rocks

GUARANTEED DELIVERY IN 30 LIGHT-YEARS OR LESS!

Small rocket booster – or you could use this piece as a clip for wings

Red lights made from round transparent plates. Or you could use 1x1 cones or plates

NO STUDS IN SPACE

Using bricks with side studs or angle plates, you can build a section like this red side panel. Attach it sideways so none of the brick studs stick out.

You don't have to use a space-themed minifigure. Alien planets could have breathable atmospheres like Earth

REAR VIEW

SPACE WALKERS

Once you've arrived on a distant planet, your minifigures will want to explore! A walker is the perfect vehicle to scale alien terrain. Remember to build a stable, balanced walker: make sure the cockpit is not too big and heavy for the legs to support it.

ZZT QXT LKD FFG KKOJH FJFJ! *

* TRANSLATION: IN THIS WALKER, SPACE CRATERS ARE SMALL FRY!!

BUILDING BRIEF

Objective: Create multi-legged space walkers

Use: Navigating across bumpy planet surfaces

Features: Jointed legs, swivelling cockpit

Extras: Radar, blasters for self-defence

Just flick the robot missiles from the back with your finger to make them fire!

Robot missile launchers made from LEGO® Technic beams with sticks

Using two 1x1 round plates to create an "ankle" is a simple way to add detail to your model

SIDE VIEW

REACHING THE TOP

You can connect the cockpit to the top of the legs using hinges and a flat 2x6 piece. If you have a turntable piece, you can make the cockpit swivel so the pilot can see all around.

SIMPLE WALKER

This simple walker model uses basic hinges to make the legs bend. If you haven't got any hinges, you could build even simpler, straight legs. How about adding a third leg, or even more?

Rocket thrusters attached with angle plate

Blasters could be replaced with wings; then the vehicle could walk...or fly!

Toes made from plates with bars. Think about how to use pieces in different ways!

REAR VIEW

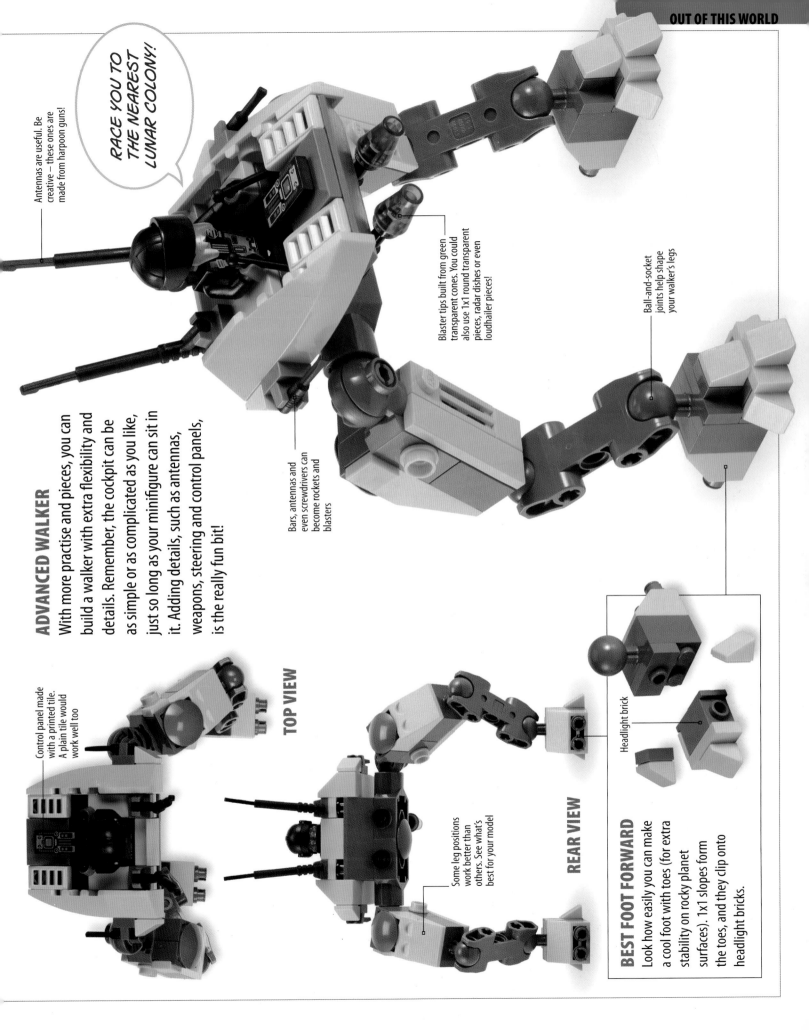

Antennas are useful. Be creative – these ones are made from harpoon guns!

RACE YOU TO THE NEAREST LUNAR COLONY!

ADVANCED WALKER

With more practise and pieces, you can build a walker with extra flexibility and details. Remember, the cockpit can be as simple or as complicated as you like, just so long as your minifigure can sit in it. Adding details, such as antennas, weapons, steering and control panels, is the really fun bit!

Blaster tips built from green transparent cones. You could also use 1x1 round transparent pieces, radar dishes or even loudhailer pieces!

Ball-and-socket joints help shape your walker's legs

Bars, antennas and even screwdrivers can become rockets and blasters

Control panel made with a printed tile. A plain tile would work well too

TOP VIEW

Some leg positions work better than others. See what's best for your model

REAR VIEW

Headlight brick

BEST FOOT FORWARD

Look how easily you can make a cool foot with toes (for extra stability on rocky planet surfaces). 1x1 slopes form the toes, and they clip onto headlight bricks.

SPACEFIGHTER

When building a spacefighter, you could start with a single-minifigure cockpit, big pointed wings, multiple rear engines and big blasters pointing forward for high-speed space duels. Look to your favourite movies or TV shows for inspiration – but don't stop there! Use your imagination to make your model unique and inventive.

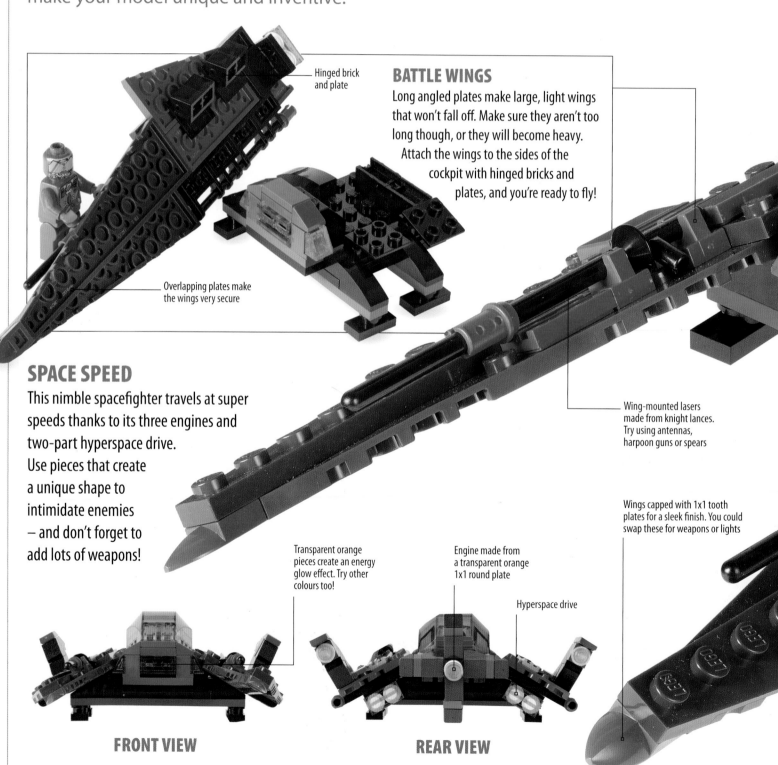

Hinged brick and plate

BATTLE WINGS

Long angled plates make large, light wings that won't fall off. Make sure they aren't too long though, or they will become heavy. Attach the wings to the sides of the cockpit with hinged bricks and plates, and you're ready to fly!

Overlapping plates make the wings very secure

SPACE SPEED

This nimble spacefighter travels at super speeds thanks to its three engines and two-part hyperspace drive. Use pieces that create a unique shape to intimidate enemies – and don't forget to add lots of weapons!

Wing-mounted lasers made from knight lances. Try using antennas, harpoon guns or spears

Wings capped with 1x1 tooth plates for a sleek finish. You could swap these for weapons or lights

Transparent orange pieces create an energy glow effect. Try other colours too!

Engine made from a transparent orange 1x1 round plate

Hyperspace drive

FRONT VIEW

REAR VIEW

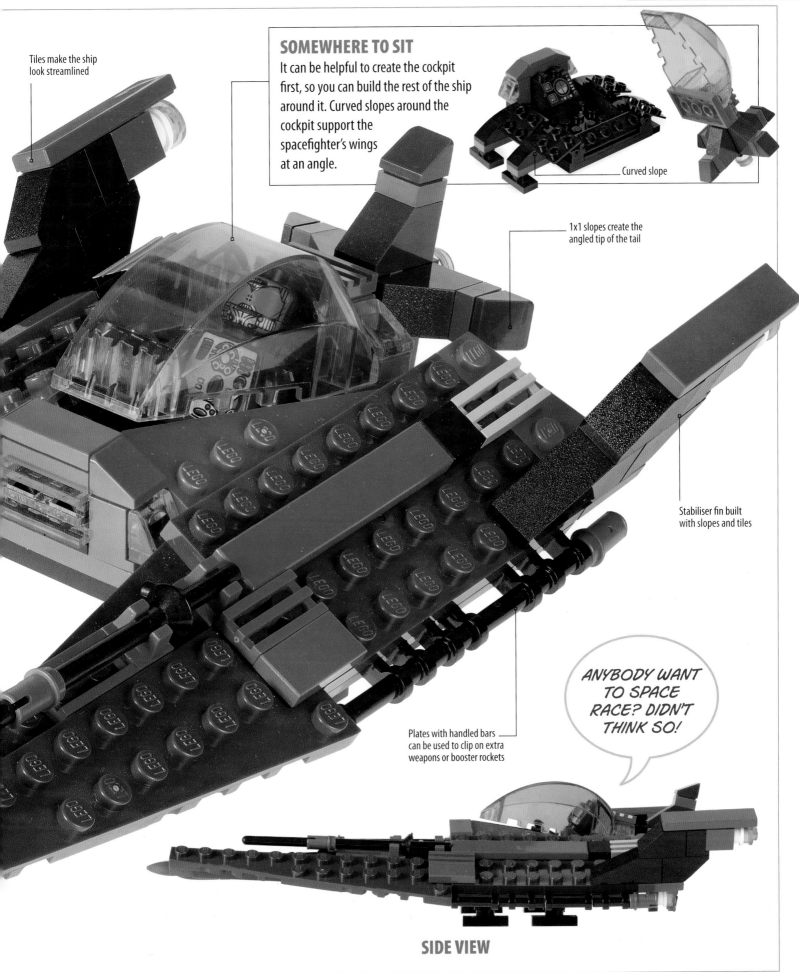

Tiles make the ship look streamlined

SOMEWHERE TO SIT

It can be helpful to create the cockpit first, so you can build the rest of the ship around it. Curved slopes around the cockpit support the spacefighter's wings at an angle.

Curved slope

1x1 slopes create the angled tip of the tail

Stabiliser fin built with slopes and tiles

Plates with handled bars can be used to clip on extra weapons or booster rockets

ANYBODY WANT TO SPACE RACE? DIDN'T THINK SO!

SIDE VIEW

SMALL SPACESHIPS

All you need is a cockpit, some wings and an engine or two, and you can build a small spaceship that's the perfect size for some serious outer-space adventure. Try to find pieces with unusual shapes to complete your build – and remember, there are no rules about what a spaceship should look like! Here are some ideas to get you started.

BUILDING BRIEF

Objective: Create small spaceships
Use: Space travel, adventure
Features: Lasers, tailfins, pilot controls
Extras: Spacefighters, scouts, escape pods, racing ships

ADMIRAL'S INTERCEPTOR

The admiral flies his sleek interceptor into a space battle. The base of the ship is built with the studs facing upward, but the wings are built sideways, with the studs concealed. Landing skids, weapons and a control pad add detail to the ship.

Choose a piece with an unusual shape to make a fancy tailfin

Curved slopes at the front lend a sleek and speedy look

Angled plates make the spaceship's outline look streamlined

You could add extra pieces to the tip to make a more powerful laser

Racing stripes made by placing plates between bricks of a contrasting colour

ALTERNATIVE INTERCEPTOR

This simpler version of the interceptor has wings built with the studs facing up.

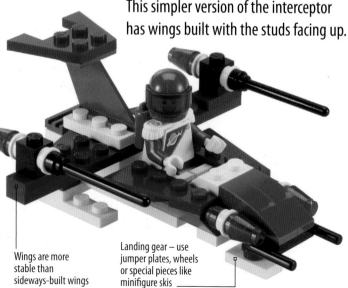

Wings are more stable than sideways-built wings

Landing gear – use jumper plates, wheels or special pieces like minifigure skis

WINGING IT

To create smooth-looking wings, build two small stacks and turn them on their sides. Attach them to the core of the ship with angle plates. Use sloped or curved bricks to give your wings an exciting shape!

1x2/1x4 angle plate

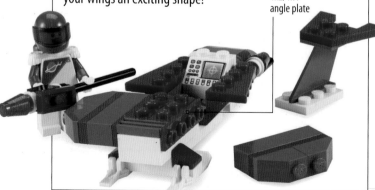

ROCKET SHUTTLE MK I

This nippy little shuttle uses interesting looking pieces for texture, such as grille pieces, plates with bars and a detailed slope as an engine. Using a plate with the studs facing up also adds to the functional look.

HEY BUDDY, RED AND BLUE IS SO 4036!

A steering wheel or handlebars can help your astronaut get around

Angled plates help the rocket zoom through space

TOP VIEW

Detailed curved slope makes a great engine, but curved slopes would work as well

A wall of bricks could act as a back support instead of this tile with handle

Plates with side bars can be lasers or jets

This grille piece could be a cooling fin. Look out for interesting pieces like this

Transparent plates sandwiched between bricks create a strip of lights

Build up the width of the rocket to make it look very different from your original version

Pieces with side studs allow you to add other pieces to your model

LEGO Technic half pin makes the laser longer

TOP VIEW

Want to go for firepower instead of speed? Swap out big rocket boosters for extra lasers!

ROCKET SHUTTLE MK II

Try upgrading your creations by adding extra pieces. The MK II shuttle has the same basic design as the MK I, but it looks more advanced because of its additional bricks and built-up details.

MORE SMALL SPACESHIPS

There are so many ways to build small space vehicles. You could try grabbing a random handful of pieces and seeing what you can make. You might be amazed! Or look around you at the shapes of everyday objects. They could inspire your creations. Now, get building!

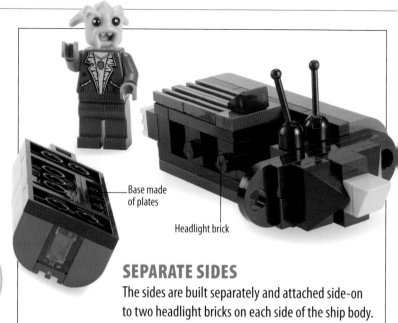

Base made of plates

Headlight brick

SEPARATE SIDES
The sides are built separately and attached side-on to two headlight bricks on each side of the ship body.

> *I LOVE FEELING THE SOLAR WIND BLOWING MY TENTACLES!*

PURPLE PATROLLER

Guess what inspired this small patroller vehicle? A highlighter! The ship is built around a 2x8 plate with purple curved pieces for sides. The highlighter tip could be a sensor device – or maybe it emits a glowing beam!

These purple grilles make great engine cooling vents

1x2 brick with side studs

Front is made from black and green plates and slopes, and attached side-on to a brick with side studs

Side details made from a 1x2 jumper plate and two black 1x1 round plates

Even aliens need to get around!

Blue transparent piece peeps through the grille

Front lights created with a 2x3 curved plate with hole, behind which is a blue transparent piece

Joystick controls, but you could use a steering wheel or handlebars

Exhaust vent made from a transparent 1x2 grille attached side-on to two headlight bricks at the rear

REAR VIEW

SIDE VIEW

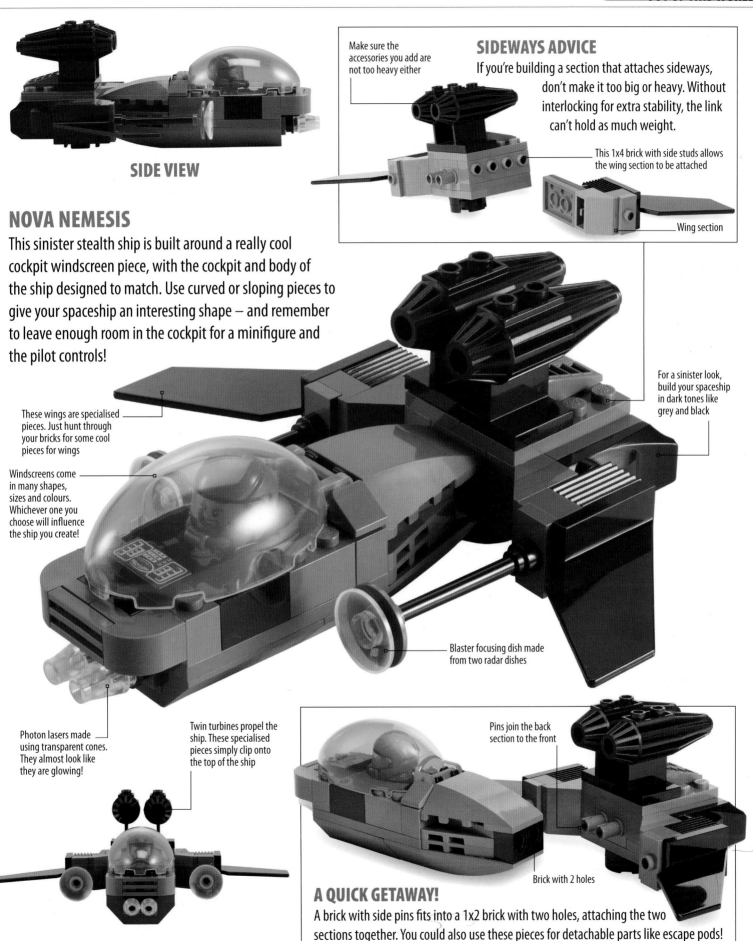

SIDE VIEW

NOVA NEMESIS

This sinister stealth ship is built around a really cool cockpit windscreen piece, with the cockpit and body of the ship designed to match. Use curved or sloping pieces to give your spaceship an interesting shape – and remember to leave enough room in the cockpit for a minifigure and the pilot controls!

Make sure the accessories you add are not too heavy either

SIDEWAYS ADVICE

If you're building a section that attaches sideways, don't make it too big or heavy. Without interlocking for extra stability, the link can't hold as much weight.

This 1x4 brick with side studs allows the wing section to be attached

Wing section

These wings are specialised pieces. Just hunt through your bricks for some cool pieces for wings

Windscreens come in many shapes, sizes and colours. Whichever one you choose will influence the ship you create!

For a sinister look, build your spaceship in dark tones like grey and black

Blaster focusing dish made from two radar dishes

Photon lasers made using transparent cones. They almost look like they are glowing!

Twin turbines propel the ship. These specialised pieces simply clip onto the top of the ship

Pins join the back section to the front

Brick with 2 holes

A QUICK GETAWAY!

A brick with side pins fits into a 1x2 brick with two holes, attaching the two sections together. You could also use these pieces for detachable parts like escape pods!

FRONT VIEW

MICROSHIPS

You may not have a lot of bricks to build with. Or perhaps the space model you want to make would be too complicated at minifigure scale. Or maybe you want a whole fleet of ships for a big space battle. Why not try microbuilding? It is exactly like regular minifigure-scale building but on a smaller scale, and you can assemble some of the coolest – and smallest – spaceships around!

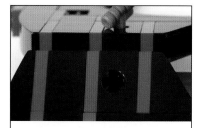

BUILDING WITH HOLES
You'll find that some pieces have holes in them, such as this 1x2 brick with cross axle hole. They are just the right size to grip blasters, antennas and other accessories.

BUILDING BRIEF

Objective: Build microscale spaceships
Use: Everything a big spaceship does...only smaller!
Features: Must have recognisable spaceship features
Extras: Escort fighters, motherships, space bases

Radio antennas built from accessories like harpoon guns or telescopes

Use antennas, lances or blasters as weapons

Hinged plates

Microcockpit – use transparent pieces, solid sloped pieces or even two contrasting 1x1 pieces

Laser weapons – neon transparent pieces look hi-tech

BUTTERFLY SHUTTLE
The wings and body of this microship were built separately, then attached together. The wings are connected to each other with hinged plates, allowing you to fold them at any angle you choose before clipping them onto the main body.

In microscale, a single engine piece can become an entire spaceship body

Lights match the cockpit windscreen here – but they can be any colour!

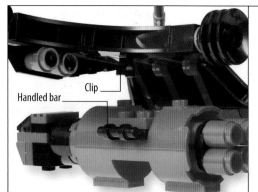

Handled bar

Clip

CLIP-ON WINGS
The wings are built with clips on the underside. These snap onto bars sticking out of the side of the ship's body. It can be tricky to attach the wings, but once they are in place they will look like they are floating!

SIDE VIEW

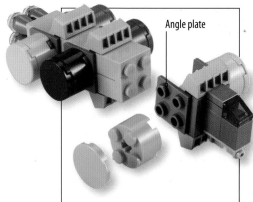

Angle plate

SPACE HAULER

This Space Hauler transports heavy freight across the galaxy. Round barrels full of cargo clip onto the main body of the hauler. The barrels have been unloaded and replaced so many times, it's no wonder they don't match!

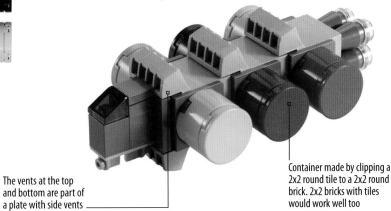

TOP VIEW

The vents at the top and bottom are part of a plate with side vents

Container made by clipping a 2x2 round tile to a 2x2 round brick. 2x2 bricks with tiles would work well too

CARGO COLUMN

The core of the Space Hauler is a simple column of bricks and plates turned on its side. Angle plates form attachment points for the cargo containers.

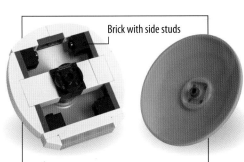

Brick with side studs

INNER WORKINGS

A simple exterior can conceal clever building techniques inside. Here, bricks with side studs support the white curved slopes, and LEGO Technic half pins hold the top and bottom dishes together.

A group of identical flying saucers with different-coloured parts could be a microscale invasion fleet!

FLYING SAUCER

Sometimes you have a piece that you just know would look great as part of a microship. The design of this classic UFO is inspired by a pair of big, orange radar dishes.

Central ring, made of curved slopes attached together to form a circle

Flight wing made from two flag pieces. Rudder pieces would give a similar effect

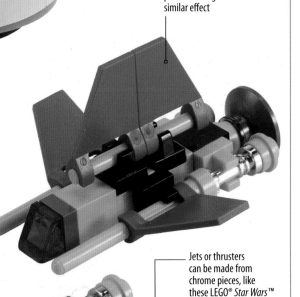

Dish pieces can be engines, cockpits, transmitters or even landing gear!

SHUTTLE AND ESCORTS

For an extra challenge, build a microscale spaceship and then make some even tinier escort vehicles with matching designs to protect it on its interstellar missions!

TOP VIEW

Jets or thrusters can be made from chrome pieces, like these LEGO® *Star Wars*™ lightsaber hilts

MORE MICROSHIPS

The design of your microship should say as much as possible about its purpose and function. Is your mission one of peaceful exploration? Galactic adventure? Combat and conquest? Think carefully about which pieces will best tell the story – because it only takes a few bricks to build a whole ship!

Aerodynamic tailfins made with grille slopes. Regular slopes would work just as well!

Drone escorts protect the stellar explorer!

This piece can be found in LEGO® Games sets. You could also use a 1x1 cone

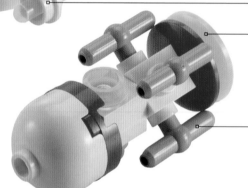

STELLAR EXPLORER

This microship may be small, but its design is actually quite complex. Its bricks face in four different directions: up, down, left and right! Use a central column of bricks with side studs as your starting point. It may take some time to achieve a smooth, sleek look!

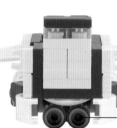

Exhaust nozzles made from two radar dishes in contrasting colours

Thrusters made from LEGO Technic T-bars plugged into a 1x1 brick with 4 side studs

THIS COCKPIT'S A PERFECT FIT! BLAST OFF!

Windscreen attached to the tail by a clip and bar hinge, so it can open and close

Rudder piece is a good size for a microship wing. You could also use flag pieces, or build wings of different shapes!

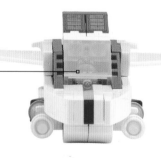

Think these engines are too small? Replace them with one giant engine!

REAR VIEW

Cockpit is a perfect fit for a microfigure from a LEGO Games set

TOP VIEW

FRONT VIEW

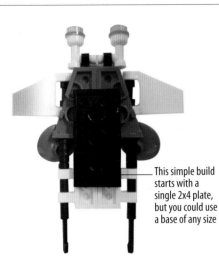

This simple build starts with a single 2x4 plate, but you could use a base of any size

BOTTOM VIEW

APPROACHING TARGET FOR OPERATION MICRO!

STAR CARRIER

The Star Carrier is quite a basic build, but it transports troops and battle vehicles across the galaxy! Plates with horizontal clips hold weapons in place and tiles give a smooth finish.

Harpoon gun is a novel way to attach a radar dish

LEADING THE WAY

A slide plate forms a battering ram at the front — and hides the hollow bottom of the stack. Alternatively, you could use an inverted slope piece to give your cruiser a wedge-nosed shape.

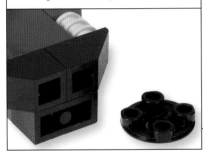

1x1 round plate can be used to dock the microship onto a space station

Engine housings made from LEGO Technic beams with sticks. Swap the transparent pieces for flick-fire space torpedoes!

BATTLE CRUISER

This sturdy, menacing ship is on a mission to smash other microships to smithereens! The battle cruiser is built as a stack of bricks and then turned on its side.

Angled slope

Engine grille

BUILDING SECRETS

Bricks with side studs hold the angled slopes and engine grilles in place. Transparent red pieces under the grille slopes make it look like energy is glowing through the vents.

SPACE AMBASSADOR

Friendly colours and curves, and the absence of weaponry, make this spaceship look like it belongs to a peaceful species. This microship is quite simple to build, but there are lots of areas where detail has been added.

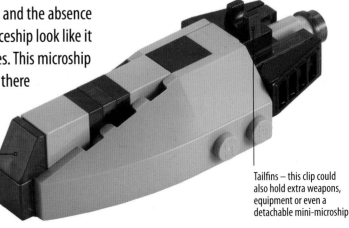

Microcockpit made with 1x1 slope. You could also use a 1x1 plate or a grille piece for an armoured cockpit!

Tailfins — this clip could also hold extra weapons, equipment or even a detachable mini-microship

SMALL TRANSPORTERS

Whether you're carrying supplies or crew, transporters will get your cargo wherever it needs to go. Before you build, think about what you want to transport, how big it is and what might be needed to hold it in place on the journey. There's a whole galaxy of space stuff out there, and someone's got to haul it all!

BUILDING BRIEF

Objective: Create small transporter
Use: Moving people and objects from one location to another
Features: Holds driver and cargo
Extras: Headlights, rocket boosters

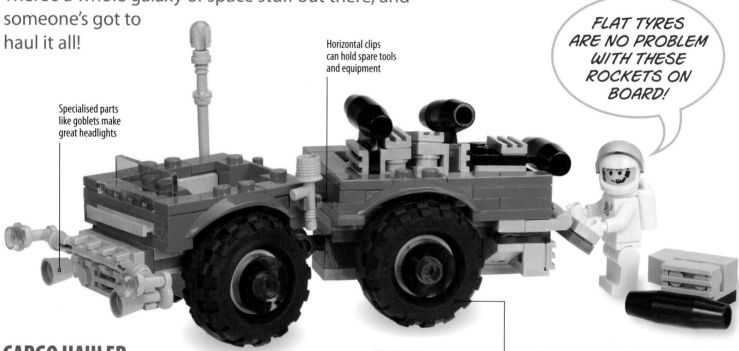

Specialised parts like goblets make great headlights

Horizontal clips can hold spare tools and equipment

FLAT TYRES ARE NO PROBLEM WITH THESE ROCKETS ON BOARD!

CARGO HAULER

The cargo hauler is built in two sections: the driver compartment and cargo trailer. For each section, start with a rectangle of bricks as a base and add wheel guards and other details. A ball-and-socket joint attaches the two sections together.

WHEELY FUN

Choose your wheels before building your wheel arches. There's nothing worse than wheels that don't fit!

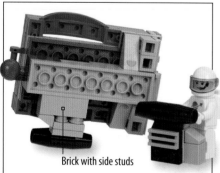

Brick with side studs

NO WHEELS, NO PROBLEM

Attach rockets to the hauler's base using bricks with side studs. Add details like grilles for a hi-tech look.

Navigation beacon built from an antenna, a lightsaber hilt and a lightbulb

ROCKET-POWERED HAULER

Wheels won't get you over every space terrain. That's why this version of the cargo hauler is powered by rockets!

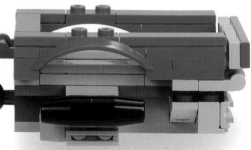

Ball-and-socket joint helps the hauler handle tight turns

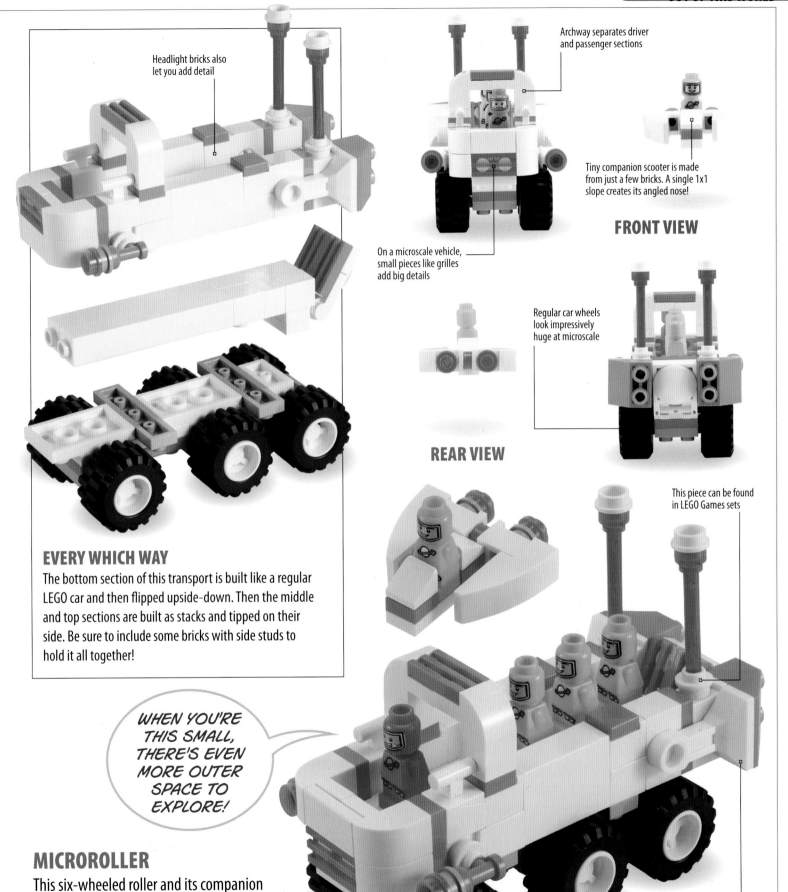

Headlight bricks also let you add detail

Archway separates driver and passenger sections

Tiny companion scooter is made from just a few bricks. A single 1x1 slope creates its angled nose!

FRONT VIEW

On a microscale vehicle, small pieces like grilles add big details

Regular car wheels look impressively huge at microscale

REAR VIEW

This piece can be found in LEGO Games sets

EVERY WHICH WAY

The bottom section of this transport is built like a regular LEGO car and then flipped upside-down. Then the middle and top sections are built as stacks and tipped on their side. Be sure to include some bricks with side studs to hold it all together!

WHEN YOU'RE THIS SMALL, THERE'S EVEN MORE OUTER SPACE TO EXPLORE!

MICROROLLER

This six-wheeled roller and its companion escort flier are built to carry microfigures from LEGO Games sets. You can easily adapt the style of this model for minifigures.

The base of the roller's rear thruster is made from a LEGO *Star Wars* R2-D2 leg!

MOON MINER

When you've got to build a new lunar colony or find valuable space rocks, big mining vehicles are just the thing. Once you've made your rugged mining machine, there are lots of small details to be added. Equip your miner with shovels, claws, saw blades, drills that spin or blast plasma and anything else it takes to get the job done!

BUILDING BRIEF

Objective: Build space mining vehicles
Use: Moving earth and rocks on other worlds
Features: Power, tools to dig through any surface
Extras: Scout vehicle, robot helpers, storage containers

Emergency beacon built from a telescope and transparent plates

HEY! I CAN SEE THE LUNAR OUTPOST FROM UP HERE!

The mining vehicle's base can hold ore containers or a small scout vehicle

TOP VIEW

Elevated control tower lets the driver keep an eye on the drill's work

Don't forget ladders and handles to help the crew climb to the top!

Laser drill

Oversized wheels are great for bumpy alien terrain. Use the biggest ones you can find for a really heavy-duty digger!

MACHINE WITH A VIEW

The Moon Miner is built in two parts: the base and the control tower. Make sure the base is big enough to fit the laser drill, and that the control tower is the right width so it can clip onto the back corners of the base.

Base platform – build it up higher to hold even more ore containers

A 2x2 brick with pin at each corner holds the wheels. They can also attach tank treads or even walker legs

Hinged lids provide easy access for loading and unloading freshly drilled space crystals

ORE CONTAINERS

Hinged lid pieces are great for building ore containers. You could also use a clip and bar hinge to attach a lid to a base, or even build a lid and base from scratch!

Build the base of your container to match the size and shape of the lid

WAIT, THAT'S NOT AN OUTPOST... THAT'S NEPTUNE!

Black slope

ROLL OF THE DICE

Proving that you really can find a use for any and every piece, the head of the laser drill is actually built around a LEGO Games die piece! You could also use two 2x2 bricks or a stack of plates.

MOON MINER WITH TREADS

Treads can be found on some LEGO construction vehicles. Each link is a separate piece, so you can build them as long or short as you want

Mining robots can be attached to the back of the control tower columns for transport

Miniature drills built using palm tree top pieces to match the Moon Miner's drill!

Green light for when crystals are detected underground. Swap it for a red one if your miners find something they don't want to dig up!

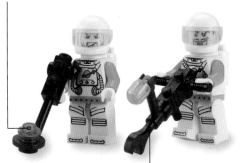

Hi-tech mining device built with a spanner. You could swap a screwdriver or a blaster, for different functions

READY, STEADY, DRILL!

LEGO Technic beam

An arm built from LEGO Technic parts holds the Moon Miner's laser drill. The arm pivots at two points, allowing the drill to be positioned accurately, or folded neatly away! It is supported by a pair of black 1x1 slopes on the support columns of the control tower.

ROBOTIC VEHICLES

Not all space vehicles need drivers! Just like the Mars missions of today, future interplanetary expeditions could make use of robots for exploration. This geological inspection rover is built around a simple stack of bricks, turned on its side and attached to four wheels. Detailed bricks and lots of tools give the rover a functional appearance!

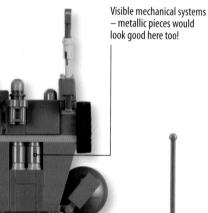

Visible mechanical systems – metallic pieces would look good here too!

No ice pick? Use another minifigure tool, like a magnifying glass, hammer or even a transparent chainsaw

Two antennas – the rover can receive and transmit information at the same time!

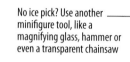

Visible studs add to the industrial look

Mineral sensor built using a clip hinge and small radar dish. Several small antenna pieces would make a bank of sensors

TOP VIEW

Lights sit at different levels. To do this, build one into a socket and push the other forward on a 1x1 round plate

REAR VIEW

ROBOTIC ROVER

Unmanned rovers don't need driver controls or life-support systems, so build a shape that's basic and industrialised. Tools that fold out of the way and a low-to-the-ground profile will help prevent damage from wind and dust.

Cargo crate

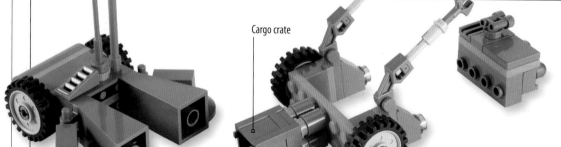

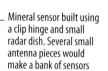

ANATOMY OF A ROVER

The robotic rover is built in three sections, then joined together. Although the shape of the vehicle is quite simple, try using unusual pieces to add detail, like a cargo crate instead of regular bricks.

JETPACKS

What could be more fun than rocketing through space without any need of a spaceship? This is where jetpacks come in, from realistic to wildly inventive. Wings, rockets, jets, blasters – as long as the jetpack can attach to a minifigure, the rest is up to you!

BUILDING BRIEF

Objective: Build single-person jetpacks

Use: Travel and reconnaissance through atmosphere or outer space

Features: Small size, lightweight, high speed, manoeuvrable

Extras: Pilot controls, launch pad, blasters

CAVE RACER

This cavern-exploring vehicle has a core of a few bricks with side studs. A row of slopes on top and blade pieces on the wingtips complete its fierce design.

Handlebars connect minifigure to jetpack

Look for thin pieces like these wall pieces to make a jetpack's lightweight wings

ROCKET GLIDER

The specialised wing pieces on this jetpack can be found in sets like LEGO® Space Police and LEGO® Batman™. You could also use aeroplane wings or flag pieces to achieve the same shape.

Minifigure angle plate fits around minifigure's neck and allows jetpack to be clipped on

SPACEWALK PACK

I JUST NEED TO REMEMBER TO HOLD ON TIGHT!

To perform maintenance and repairs on the outside of a space station, you just need a box shape with some tools built into it. Make sure it is the right size for a minifigure!

These grey bars are just the right distance apart for minifigure hands to clip onto

Flames – LEGO sets with knights and castles are a good place to find these pieces! You can also use any fire-coloured transparent bricks

SIDE VIEW

REAR VIEW

ROCKET

3...2...1...BLAST OFF! This sleek, streamlined rocket launches straight up and then levels out to fly, so it has a big, flat-bottomed main engine, and a tailfin and wings as well. When building your own rocket models, think about where they will travel and what they will encounter on their outer space adventures!

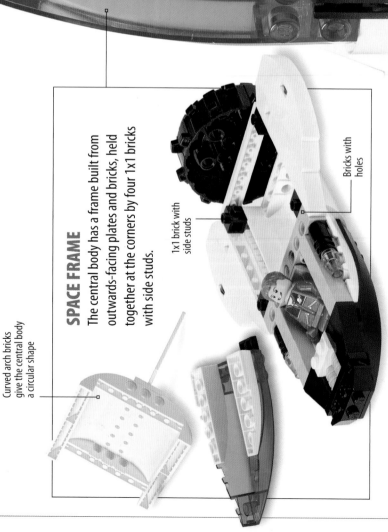

Choose a windscreen to fit your design

Sensor built into sides to keep rocket's profile smooth and sleek

Grille pieces lock windscreen in place in case of bumpy asteroid fields

Curved arch bricks give the central body a circular shape

SPACE FRAME

The central body has a frame built from outwards-facing plates and bricks, held together at the corners by four 1x1 bricks with side studs.

1x1 brick with side studs

Bricks with holes

READY FOR LAUNCH

The front section of the rocket is built with curved wedge pieces and the back section has aeroplane features, giving the model a streamlined, tube-like shape that looks like it could blast right up into space.

Wings built like walls with curved slopes on top, then attached to sides of frame

Fiery engine, made from orange transparent radar dish

WHEEL DEAL

This giant engine was originally a spiked wheel from a LEGO mining vehicle. A pair of jumper plates attached to the rear face of the rocket's central frame holds it in place by two of the many holes in the wheel's back.

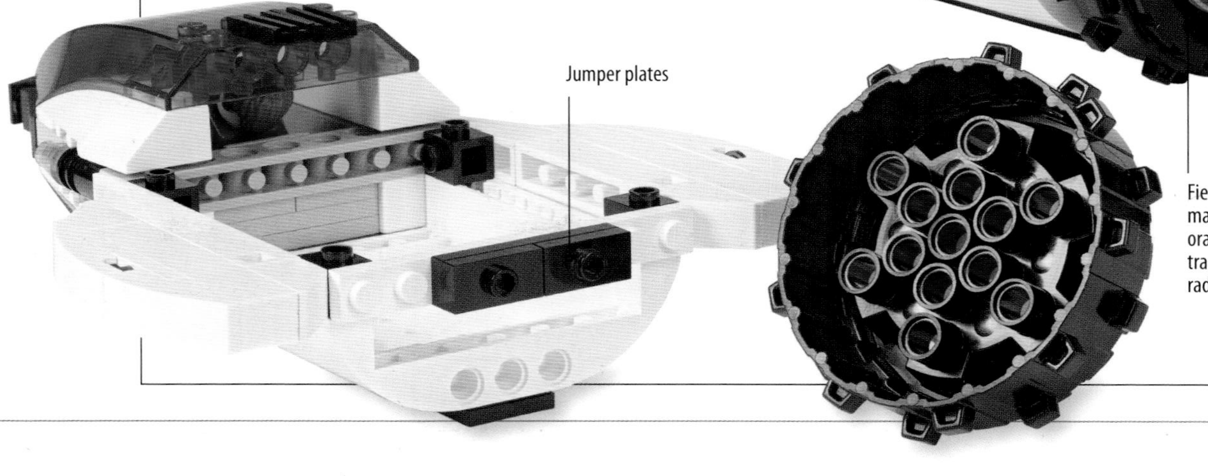

Jumper plates

Navigation lights made from 1x1 round plates built right into wings

You could also build a round rocket body using arched or curved bricks

Aeroplane tailfin. You could also add an extra set of matching wings for the top and bottom!

BOTTOM VIEW

TOP VIEW

ALIENS

When it comes to building alien creatures, if you can imagine it, you can make it. Think about what kind of planet your alien lives on and how it should behave, and then start building your idea of life on the distant world. Try looking at real animals for inspiration and using the most unusual pieces you can find to make your creations look truly out of this world!

BUILDING BRIEF

Objective: Create alien creatures
Use: Friend or foe to space explorers
Features: Limbs for swimming, flying, hopping, climbing...you name it!
Extras: Claws, fangs, suckers, wings, tails, extra limbs

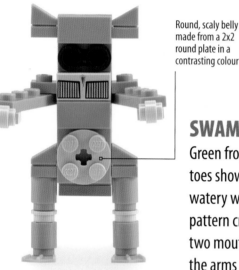

Round, scaly belly made from a 2x2 round plate in a contrasting colour

Creepy glowing eyes are red transparent plates. Glow-in-the-dark pieces would work well too, and some can be found in LEGO® Harry Potter™ sets

SWAMP HOPPER

Green frog-like skin, a long tail and webbed toes show that this alien comes from a watery world. A printed tile with a car grille pattern creates an extraterrestrial face with two mouths. Don't forget to position the arms and tail so it can balance while standing up!

FRONT VIEW

Don't have this flexible tail piece? Try a long, flat plate and add spikes and other details!

Webbed feet are flipper pieces. You could also use a 1x2 plate

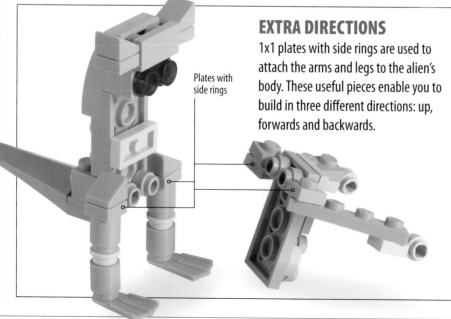

Plates with side rings

EXTRA DIRECTIONS

1x1 plates with side rings are used to attach the arms and legs to the alien's body. These useful pieces enable you to build in three different directions: up, forwards and backwards.

Smooth pieces can be swapped for spiky or textured bricks

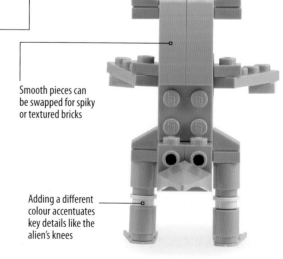

Adding a different colour accentuates key details like the alien's knees

REAR VIEW

ASTEROID INSECTIPEDE

A segmented body and lots of legs make a creature look armoured and insect-like. Each of this alien's six limbs are attached to a jumper plate on its body by a single stud, so they can rotate and be posed to look like it's walking or running.

1x1 round piece can be swapped with a 1x1 slope for a zigzag back or an antenna piece for tall spines

Tail made from antenna. Try using flexible tubes, or tail pieces instead!

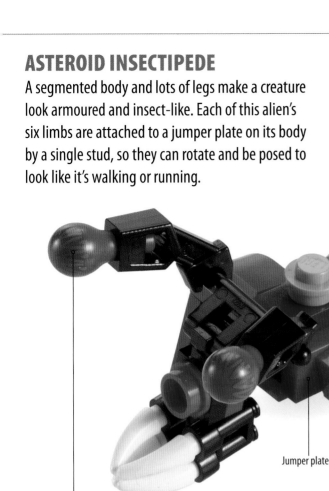

Each leg is made from just three pieces, so it's easy to duplicate for each body segment

Jumper plate

Painted eyes are maracas from the LEGO® Minifigures series

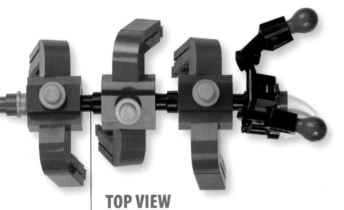

TOP VIEW

Eye stalks made from a robot arm piece that is perfect for angled moving parts

REAR VIEW

STRE-E-E-ETCHING OUT

This alien's body is built out of identical sections joined together using tube studs, so it's easy to add on extra sections to make your creature as long as you want. The longer your alien, however, the less stable it will be. You could even take segments out to make a baby alien!

Tube stud

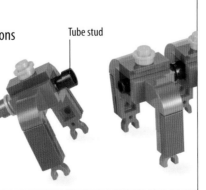

Two pairs of binoculars and four horns make a dangerous-looking set of jaws

FRONT VIEW

MEET THE BUILDER

TIM GODDARD

Location: UK
Age: 34
LEGO Speciality: Microscale space

What are some of your top LEGO tips?

Use SNOT a lot! This is a term that LEGO fans use, it stands for Studs Not On Top and means that you don't just build with the brick studs pointing up. There are loads of interesting bricks that have studs on the side that can be used for this. Another tip is to sort out the bricks in your collection a bit. It may seem like it takes a lot of time, but it can save you time in the long run, as you know just where that brick you need is stored!

This shows the hangar area and part of a road system on a recently settled alien world. This is only part of a large display that was built as a collaboration with another LEGO builder, Peter Reid.

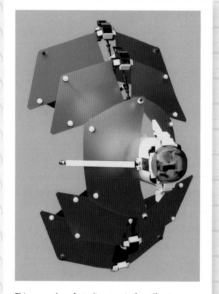

This research craft studies stars in far-off systems. It uses giant solar sails to power its scientific equipment and its engines.

This is the headquarters of the space police. It can communicate over vast distances and is used by commanders to meet up and discuss what the evil aliens have been up to.

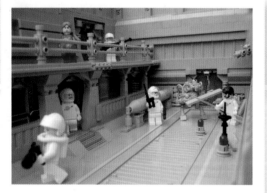

Inside a federation outpost a worker discovers one of the fibre optical cables has been damaged. Did it break or was it sabotage?

THE BEST THING TO DO WITH LARGER MODELS IS PLAN AHEAD.

How much time do you spend building?

It probably averages out at about an hour a day. I don't always have time but I find late in the evening is the best time for inspiration, while playing my favourite music.

What things have gone wrong and how have you dealt with them?

Larger models, such as big spaceships, can be a bit unstable. This is especially a problem when I concentrate more on the detail and shape above the structure of the model. The best thing to do with larger models is plan ahead – build a nice solid frame then add the fancy stuff on top.

What is your favourite creation?

The one I'm working on at the moment! I do like the models that I've made to have a bit of character to them, such as a giraffe I've finished recently. Even robots can have a bit of character – building so you can tilt the head a bit to one side or have the arms in expressive positions is really satisfying.

What is the biggest or most complex model you've made?

The largest things I have built have been a couple of small-scale *Star Wars* dioramas (scenes). I have built a couple about 12ft 11in by 2ft 6in (1.5m by 0.75m) filled with lots of small ships and walkers. The great thing about large scenes is you can gradually build and design the small craft and then make landscape, plants and buildings and gradually add to the whole display. When it is all put together you end up with a great, entirely LEGO environment.

Outside an alien nightclub the space police catch up with a wanted fugitive, but not before he has caused some chaos!

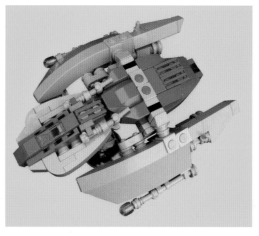

This spaceship is one of the fastest in the galaxy! The yellow and black markings are called bumblebee stripes.

This cargo hauler is specially adapted to travel over bumpy lunar terrain. It has room for one minifigure astronaut

How old were you when you started using LEGO bricks?

I've been building for as long as I can remember! I must have been four or five when I started building.

Do you plan out your build? If so, how?

It depends on what I'm building: I just tend to go for it with smaller models but larger models need a bit more planning. I sometimes sketch out the shape of a spaceship or the layout of a diorama but never in too much detail. I often have an idea of a particular little bit of design – like a wing shape – and just build what I think looks good with it. I carry on designing as I build, seeing what I think looks good as well as using the bricks I have available.

If you had all the LEGO bricks (and time!) in the world, what would you build?

A really big space display that has lots of minifigures and spaceships, with lots of moving parts and brick-built landscaping, and a large moon base with loads of internal detail. I would also like to build what LEGO fans call a SHIP (Seriously Heavy Investment in Parts) of original design, maybe that could land at the moon base above! But these big ideas don't mean I don't enjoy building little models that can fit in your hand.

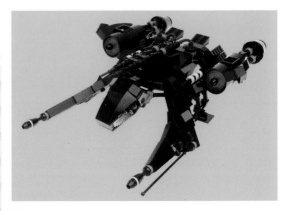

This powerful ship uses a neutralising weapon to catch unsuspecting transport spaceships.

A small submarine discovers some underwater ruins. Could this be the remains of the lost city of Atlantis?

This green space walker, with coordinating green alien minifigure, would be hard to spot on a jungle planet!

How many LEGO bricks do you have?

I have no idea! Lots and lots, but I never seem to have the bit that I'm looking for!

What are you inspired by?

All sorts of things: sci-fi films and TV programmes, buildings and scenery I see when I am driving around, old LEGO® Space sets. But the thing that inspires me to build interesting things more than anything else is seeing other people's LEGO creations.

What is your favourite LEGO technique or the technique you use the most?

SNOT is a real favourite and I use it all the time. I also enjoy combining pieces with clips and bars – it's great for making robots!

What types of models do you enjoy making, apart from space?

I enjoy building everything and anything in LEGO bricks! I like building animals – I've built a giraffe and some hippos. I also like town buildings and anything that involves minifigures. I think the more different things and areas you build in, the better you get as you discover new techniques.

At the robotics development facility the professor of robotics introduces his latest creation to the senior spacemen. The new robot will help around the base, carrying out various maintenance duties.

This trio of aliens are ready to take on the space police. Aliens of all shapes and sizes are welcome here, as long as they are bad!

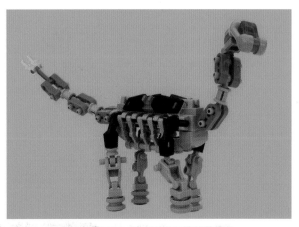

This dinosaur-style mechanical transport is used to traverse treacherous, unexplored planets. It has room for one minifigure pilot to sit in the head section.

What is your favourite LEGO brick or piece?

The standard 2x4 LEGO brick is a real classic, but I think the piece I use the most is a 1x1 plate with side ring. You can do so many things with it!

Which model were you most proud of as a young LEGO builder?

As I was growing up I had a lot of the LEGO Space sets. I made my bedroom into a giant alien planet and had different settlements around the room, one on a shelf and one on a chest of drawers, and had spaceships hanging from the ceiling flying between them. So I suppose the answer is not just one model but a whole series that made up my own world!

I'VE BEEN BUILDING FOR AS LONG AS I CAN REMEMBER!

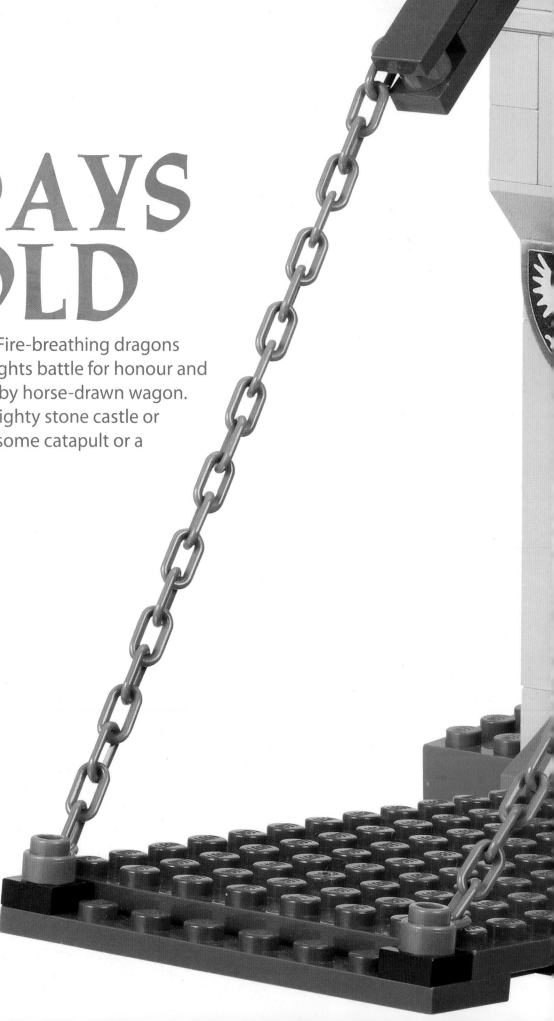

IN DAYS OF OLD

Let's travel back in time! Fire-breathing dragons roam this land, brave knights battle for honour and the way to get around is by horse-drawn wagon. What will you build? A mighty stone castle or a dangerous trap? A fearsome catapult or a gigantic battering ram?

Who goes there? This drawbridge can be pulled up to make the castle safe from invaders. (See p.120)

HARNESS

FLAME

HORN

SHIELD

BAT

ROBOT ARM

2x4 WINCH

READY TO BUILD
Specialised pieces like harnesses, winches and horses are great for building your medieval world. But if you don't have them, you can also make your own. (See Horse of Bricks, p.129)

FLAG WITH 2 CLIPS

MEDIUM WAGON WHEEL

BIONICLE® SHIELD

TUBE

MIX AND MATCH
Use pieces from all your LEGO sets to build your medieval scenes – don't just stick to LEGO® Castle sets!

PLANT

LADDER WITH 2 CLIPS

HORSE

LONG CHAIN

STREAMER

SEAT

PIECES OF HISTORY

Who needs a time machine when you can build your own medieval models? Search your LEGO® collection for wheels, weapons and chains. Brown and grey pieces make good wooden or stone structures, while LEGO® Technic parts can help create working mechanisms. Here are some pieces that might come in useful – what else can you find?

4x6x3 ROLLCAGE

TAIL

TORCH

SWORD

SPEAR

LANCE

4x8 DOOR

MEDIEVAL WEAPONRY
Your minifigures can wield weapons – or you could incorporate them into your models as traps or defensive features. (See Siege Tower, p.137)

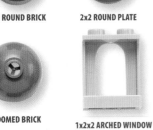

2x2 ROUND BRICK

2x2 ROUND PLATE

SMALL NARROW RIMS AND 2x2 AXLE PLATE WITH 2 PINS

1x1 ROUND PLATE

CRANK

LEGO TECHNIC RIGHT ANGLE AXLE CONNECTOR

LEGO TECHNIC LIFT ARM

2x2 DOMED BRICK

1x2x2 ARCHED WINDOW

1x2 TILE WITH TOP BAR

1x1 ROUND BRICK

LEGO TECHNIC
LEGO Technic pieces can make wheels turn, cannons tilt and drawbridges drop. (See Crank Drawbridge, p.120)

LEGO TECHNIC AXLE CONNECTOR

1x2 TEXTURED BRICK

1x4 PANEL

2x4 RIDGED ROOF SLOPE

1x1 SLOPE

1x1 CONE

COMPLETE CASTLES
Roof pieces, cones and slopes can add the perfect finishing touch to your castles.

LEGO TECHNIC CROSS AXLE 8

2x2 PLATE WITH 2 RINGS UNDERNEATH

1x2 JUMPER PLATE

1x1 BRICK WITH 4 SIDE STUDS

LEGO TECHNIC 12 TOOTH GEAR

1x1 BRICK WITH HOLE

LEGO TECHNIC HALF PIN

1x2 BRICK WITH HOLE

1x2 BRICK WITH CROSS AXLE HOLE

2x2 TILE

1x6 TILE

1x2x3 SLOPE

4x4 ROUND BRICK

1x1 PLATE WITH SIDE RING

1x1x6 ROUND COLUMN

2x16 ANGLED SLOPE

2x4 ANGLED PLATE

2x2 INVERTED SLOPE

1x2 PLATE WITH HANDLED BAR

1x2 PLATE WITH CLICK HINGE

1x1 HEADLIGHT BRICK

2x2 CORNER PLATE

2x2 TURNTABLE

1x2/2x2 ANGLE PLATE

EVEN SIMPLE MODELS CAN HAVE MOVING PARTS AND LOTS OF DETAIL!

4x4 PLATE

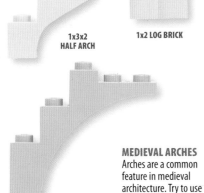

1x3x2 HALF ARCH

1x2 LOG BRICK

1x1x5 BRICK

1x3 ARCH BRICK

MEDIEVAL ARCHES
Arches are a common feature in medieval architecture. Try to use them in your buildings.

1x6 ARCH BRICK

1x4 BRICK WITH SIDE STUDS

1x5x4 HALF ARCH

1x12 PLATE

1x4 HINGE PLATE AND 4x4 HINGE PLATE

CASTLE

Medieval castles are huge, sturdy structures. Other than that, you can build your model however you want: grand, ornate, plain, strong, majestic, or crumbling. You could even build it as a combination of all these things! Look at pictures of ancient castles, or find inspiration in your favourite books and movies. Think about including details like flags, wall-mounted torches and knight minifigures to bring your creation to life.

BUILDING BRIEF

Objective: Build medieval castles

Use: Home for royalty and knights, defending the village, location of jewels and treasure

Features: Must be big and strong, able to withstand attack, majestic architecture

Extras: Interior rooms, inner courtyards, drawbridge, moat, gardens, a whole town within the castle walls

CURVED BATTLEMENTS

Rounded battlements can help your knights keep a lookout in all directions. Use hinged plates to connect several sections of wall together. Then angle the walls into a circle, semicircle or whatever shape you want.

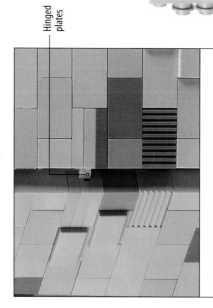

Hinged plates

ARCHITECTURE

An interesting architectural feature can really give your model a boost. Here, a smaller arch has been built in behind a larger arch, which adds depth and detail to the chapel walls. Cones, round bricks and round plates are stacked to make decorative columns. Be inventive!

CASTLE FORTRESS

Castles are built up over time as each king or queen adds what he or she needs. Start with an impressive doorway and a grand central building. Then add on sections to house sleeping quarters, viewing platforms, dining rooms, chapels, stores and anything else you can think of. They don't even have to match!

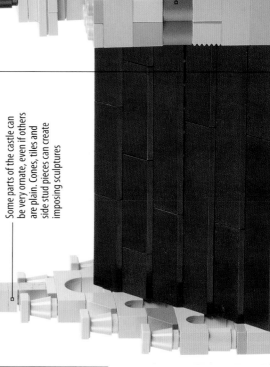

Different sections can be built from different materials. Use brown bricks for wooden walls and grey for stone

Log bricks are great for medieval building

Some parts of the castle can be very ornate, even if others are plain. Cones, tiles and side stud pieces can create imposing sculptures

Fly flags in your army's colours. You could also display shields or printed tiles to identify your king or queen

This castle even has a chapel attached

Arched windows. If you haven't got arched bricks, use half arches or inverted slopes

Arrow slits made from bricks with cross axle holes

A green brick here and there looks like a moss-covered stone!

Bricks in different shades of grey, textured bricks and log bricks help break up large stone walls

Green baseplate is a good starting point, but why don't you try building your castle on a hill, or on an island in the middle of a lake?

Scattered plates and tiles look like fallen ruins

Overgrown foliage suggests an old castle. You could build a well-tended garden instead

Imposing entrance. You could also add a gatehouse with a way to keep invaders out! (See pp.120–123)

Wooden structures with lattice windows look really medieval!

DRAWBRIDGES

Every castle needs protection from invading armies. First build a simple gatehouse as an imposing front to your fortification. Then, think about how best you want to defend your castle and design a mechanism to suit. You could create a portcullis, a heavy stone door or a drawbridge. Here are two clever ways to build a drawbridge!

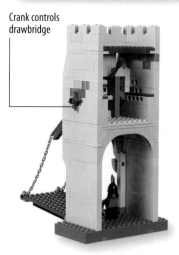
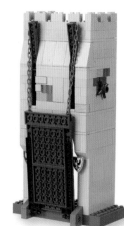

Crank controls drawbridge

OPEN   **CLOSED**

GATEHOUSE

A simple gatehouse can be the first point of protection for your castle. Grey bricks and LEGO Technic half pins on either side of the door attach the drawbridge.

Make sure the doorway is high enough for a knight to ride through on horseback!

LEGO Technic half pin allows drawbridge to pivot

Push lever to release gears and send drawbridge crashing down!

MEDIEVAL MECHANISM

LEGO Technic gears turn to raise the lift-arms. These pull the chains, raising the drawbridge. A lever secures the drawbridge in place by locking an axle connector against the gears.

CRANK DRAWBRIDGE

A crank system is a simple way to raise and lower a drawbridge. This mechanism is housed in a stone battlement that connects to the top of the gatehouse. It uses LEGO Technic bricks, axles and gears that allow you to operate the drawbridge using a crank on the side of the building.

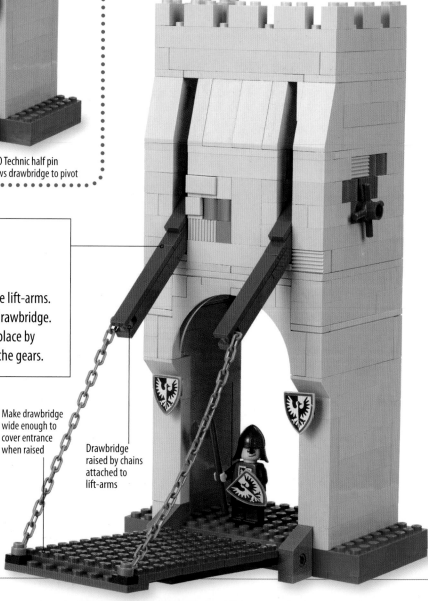

Make drawbridge wide enough to cover entrance when raised

Drawbridge raised by chains attached to lift-arms

CABLE DRAWBRIDGE

There's more than one way to raise a bridge! This version of the gatehouse uses a spool and string cable system instead of chains and lift-arms. The mechanism is housed in a rustic-style gatehouse room.

CLIPPING THE CABLES

Use plates with handled bars to secure your drawbridge's cables. Thread the cable through both handles before clipping them to the underside of the drawbridge.

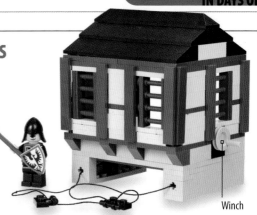

Winch

Not enough grey bricks? Build the top of your gatehouse using wood colours instead!

Hand-cranked winch is not as fast as a gear system, but it gets the job done!

SPOOL SYSTEM

The cables are attached to a winch inside the gatehouse, which is turned by a handle on the outside. This system takes up little space, which leaves room in the gatehouse for guards and ammunition.

Use a brick with cross axle hole in it to feed the cables through

Don't have LEGO Technic parts? Use hinged bricks or plates to build a movable drawbridge

Plate with handled bar

CLOSED

Winch

OPEN

PORTCULLIS

A portcullis is a heavy gate that can be raised and lowered on a pulley system. It is another great way to let friends into your castle – and keep enemies out! Start with a simple gatehouse like the one on the previous page, and adjust it to house your portcullis.

AW. THANKS TO THAT PORTCULLIS, WE NEVER GET TO BATTLE ANYBODY ANYMORE!

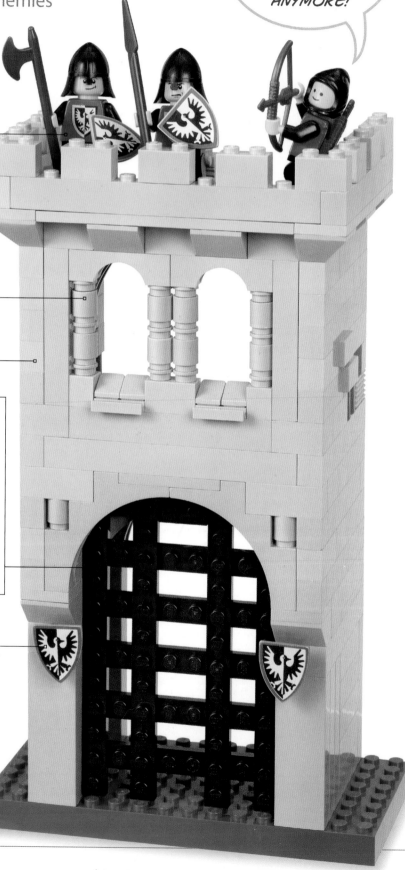

Put knights and soldiers on top to defend gatehouse

One-brick-wide channel between two layers of the front wall

Tall gatehouse tower leaves room for portcullis to slide all the way up

Decorative windows built with 1x1 round bricks, plates and small arches

GATE GAP

Build two layers into the front wall of the gatehouse, leaving a narrow channel between them. Drop the portcullis into this gap before building the roof, so it is trapped inside the gatehouse, but able to slide up and down freely.

PORTCULLIS

This portcullis is built from crisscrossed long, thin plates, with no special pieces needed. A string attached to a plate with handled bar at the top raises it through a channel created by the space between the two layers of the front walls.

Display your castle's coat of arms on the gatehouse walls. You could also fly flags or hang weapons!

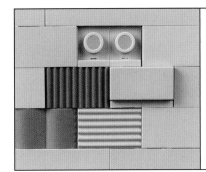

BRICKS IN THE WALL

To add realistic textures to a stone wall, include textured bricks and log bricks among regular bricks, or attach 1x2 tiles to pairs of headlight bricks so they protrude from the wall.

NO ONE GETS IN UNLESS THEY KNOW THE PASSWORD!

When portcullis is closed, brick at end of drawstring sits on top of the tower

Plate with handled bar attaches string to door

To raise gate, pull brick down and attach it to top of archway, holding portcullis in place

REALLY? OK... THE PASSWORD IS "LET ME IN OR ELSE"!

PORTCULLIS LOWERED

You could also put a portcullis behind your castle's front door!

Portcullis moves smoothly because nothing blocks its way

PORTCULLIS RAISED

123

CASTLE DOORS

When building a door for your castle, think about what it's for. Royal processions and grand entrances? Then make it really big and fancy! To keep out unwanted guests, make it sturdy and strong with a way to lock it from inside. Or perhaps you'd like a secret door to protect a room full of treasure? It's all up to you!

DOOR OF DANGER

The door to a villain's castle should say "keep out!" to any heroes who approach. This simple door is made from standard bricks and tiles and attaches to the frame with clips and handled bars.

A bat or a flaming torch would look just as scary here!

Rattling chain hints at the spooky danger waiting inside

Use pieces with unusual or dramatic shapes to make creepy decorations

UNHINGED

Build the doors of this creepy entrance first. Next, construct the doorframe around them so you can position the clip pieces correctly.

Horn pieces warn intruders to keep out. You could also use tooth plates or tools

OPEN   **CLOSED**

Locking mechanism – a LEGO Technic cross axle slides through a brick with a hole through it to lock the door

No welcome mat here!

You could add a clip to the front of your doorway to hold a sword, shield or torch that could double up as a secret lever

Old stone walls, built with grey bricks of different shapes and shades

Textured bricks look old and crumbling. Great for a haunted castle!

SECRET DOOR

The trick to building a secret door is to make it blend in with the castle's wall. First build an arched doorway with two clip plates at the back. Then design your door to match!

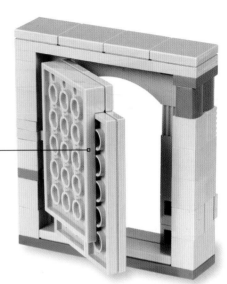

With just a push, the secret passage is revealed

REAR – OPEN

FRONT – CLOSED   **FRONT – OPEN**

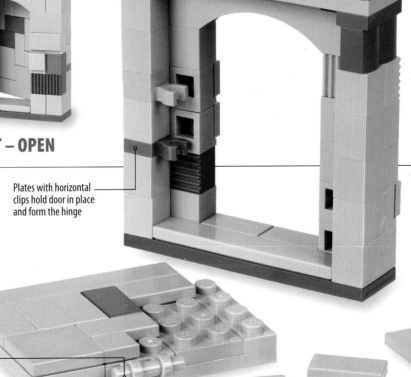

Plates with horizontal clips hold door in place and form the hinge

DOOR DESIGN

Just a few basic plates form the foundation of the door. Cover them with tiles that match the colour and design of the tiles around the doorframe. Now your door will be camouflaged! Make sure there's enough space around the door for it to swing open smoothly.

Plate with handled bar secured with overlapping pieces

TRAPS

To build up your medieval scene, why not add some extra detail to your castle? Perhaps your castle has hidden treasure, which needs protecting from thieves. Or maybe you'd rather design a clever way to trap your enemies. Design some sneaky traps to keep your secrets safe! Adding moving parts to your models really brings them to life!

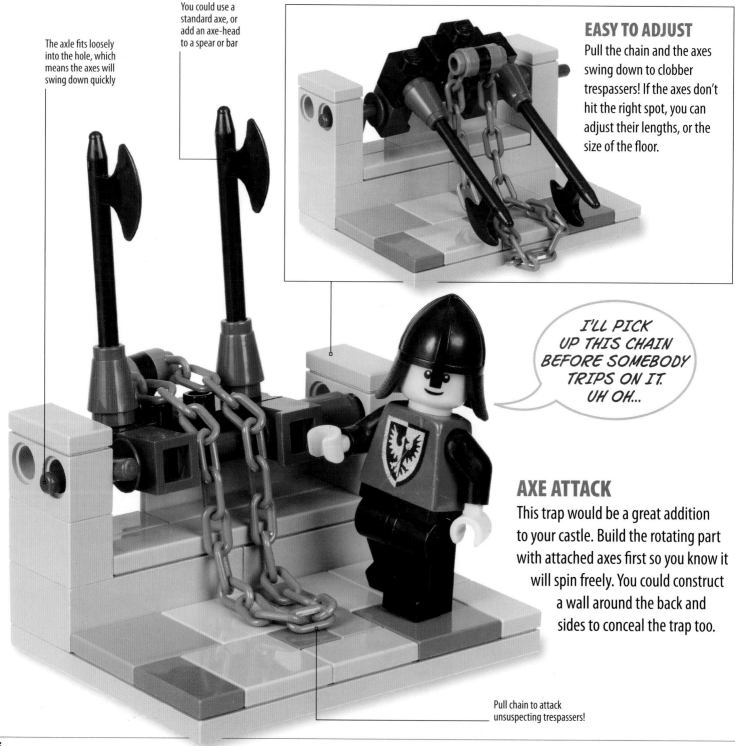

The axle fits loosely into the hole, which means the axes will swing down quickly

You could use a standard axe, or add an axe-head to a spear or bar

EASY TO ADJUST

Pull the chain and the axes swing down to clobber trespassers! If the axes don't hit the right spot, you can adjust their lengths, or the size of the floor.

I'LL PICK UP THIS CHAIN BEFORE SOMEBODY TRIPS ON IT. UH OH...

AXE ATTACK

This trap would be a great addition to your castle. Build the rotating part with attached axes first so you know it will spin freely. You could construct a wall around the back and sides to conceal the trap too.

Pull chain to attack unsuspecting trespassers!

TRAPDOOR

A trapdoor needs to swing down to drop people out of sight, so build it up high. The door should match the rest of the floor (whether wooden or stone) so it's a huge surprise for unsuspecting minifigures!

POLES APART

Two lance pieces support the door. One acts as a hinge, while the other can be pulled out to send the door swinging down.

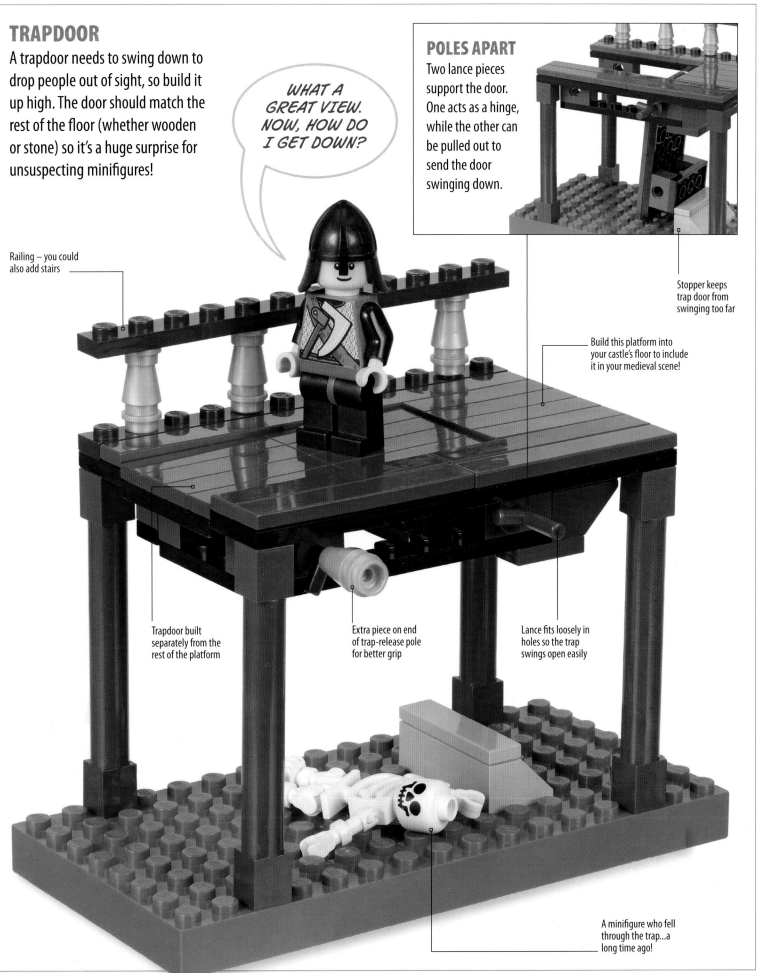

WHAT A GREAT VIEW. NOW, HOW DO I GET DOWN?

Railing – you could also add stairs

Stopper keeps trap door from swinging too far

Build this platform into your castle's floor to include it in your medieval scene!

Trapdoor built separately from the rest of the platform

Extra piece on end of trap-release pole for better grip

Lance fits loosely in holes so the trap swings open easily

A minifigure who fell through the trap...a long time ago!

KNIGHTLY STEEDS

What's a knight without his faithful horse? On foot, that's what! Many LEGO Castle sets include horses, but you can also build your own. It's simple to give each horse its own individual character! Build and customise special saddles and barding (the name for horse armour). You can even build your knight's armour to match!

Don't have plume pieces? You could use flames, feathers or Viking horns!

NOW THIS IS WHAT I CALL RIDING IN STYLE!

BUILDING BRIEF

Objective: Make horses worthy of a knight!

Use: Riding forth for deeds of derring-do

Features: Must be interesting and colourful

Extras: Coat of arms, plumes, pennants, weapon and shield clips

Helmet has holes for plumes and other decorations

Swap the sword for a lance when it's time for a jousting tournament!

LEGO armour comes in many colours and styles. Choose something that matches your army's colours

You could also add a horse battle helmet to protect your steed

Chain makes horse look tough and armoured

Barding built from angled plates and tiles. Use different plate shapes to create unique saddle designs

MOUNTED KNIGHT

The only buildable surface on a LEGO horse is where the rider's feet attach. So to make your own barding, you'll need to build out from there. Clip and bar plates can help you build in two directions.

Flag pieces make good barding too!

Use different colours to build up your army's identity

You can use a LEGO saddle or build your own!

MY HORSE IS TOTALLY OFF THE CHAIN!

1x1 plate with horizontal clip

This clips to 1x1 plate with horizontal clip on saddle

A tile locks the plates together without adding too much bulk

Two-toned coat, created by mixing classic and modern brown bricks. Create your own patterns!

Ears made from cone pieces

HORSE OF BRICKS

If you don't have a horse for your knight, try building one! This brick-built horse has a gap to fit a minifigure. Its body is built from simple bricks and plates, with a few slopes and inverted slopes.

You could make the bricks around the gap a different colour to resemble a saddle

Hooves made from round black bricks

WAGONS & CARTS

Every medieval villager needs a trusty horse-drawn wagon to get them to the market. Before building your cart or wagon, think about what you want it to carry: food, equipment, passengers? You could even make an armoured battle-wagon with lots of spears and spikes!

BUILDING BRIEF

Objective: Create carts and wagons
Use: Travel, transportation
Features: Pulled by horse, carry supplies
Extras: Lanterns, repair tools, horse food

WOODEN WAGON

This wagon has plenty of room for carrying supplies from town to town. Build the part that attaches to the horse first to ensure everything is the right height and all four wheels touch the ground to roll evenly.

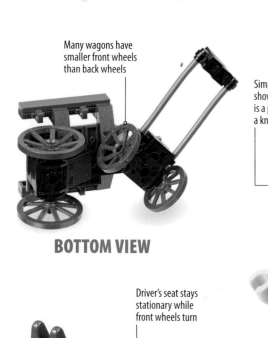

Many wagons have smaller front wheels than back wheels

BOTTOM VIEW

Simple hood shows that driver is a peasant, not a knight or king

OFF TO THE MARKET WITH A LOAD OF FRESHLY PICKED BRICKS!

Driver's seat stays stationary while front wheels turn

Wooden boarding, built from brown tiles. You could use bright colours for a festive painted wagon

Make sure wheels aren't blocked by back of wagon when it turns

If you don't have a LEGO horse, try building your own! (See p.129 and p.153)

TURNING THE WAGON

As the horse changes direction, it turns the front axle, which pulls the rest of the wagon along behind. You can use different pieces to make a turning wagon, from a turntable to a LEGO Technic pin.

Round brown plate is attached to a turntable, allowing front axle to turn

HORSE-DRAWN CART

Unlike a wagon, a cart has only two wheels so it doesn't need a steering mechanism. There are lots of ways to connect a horse to a cart! This one uses long bars and plates with side rings.

Back of cart swings down to unload cargo

Robot arms attach grille to back of cart's frame

A CART APART

The rollcage is attached to the base with LEGO Technic half beams. A plate with two rings underneath holds the cross axle in place.

LEGO Technic half beam

Rollcage from LEGO construction vehicle sets

Plate with two rings underneath

Big round brick used instead of wagon wheel

Plate with side ring

Seat is high enough for driver to see over horse

Half-barrel-shaped wagon body built from curved bricks. You could also use curved half arches

Harness piece designed to attach horses to vehicles

Wheels connected to axle plate with pins

GREEN WAGON

This wagon uses a single harness piece to connect the horse to the steerable front axle. Design your wagon around any specialist pieces you have, and then customise it to look however you want!

BODY BUILDING

Your wagon's body can be any shape and size you choose! This model's body is built around a black rectangular plate. Bricks with side studs hold the side panels in place.

Brick with side studs

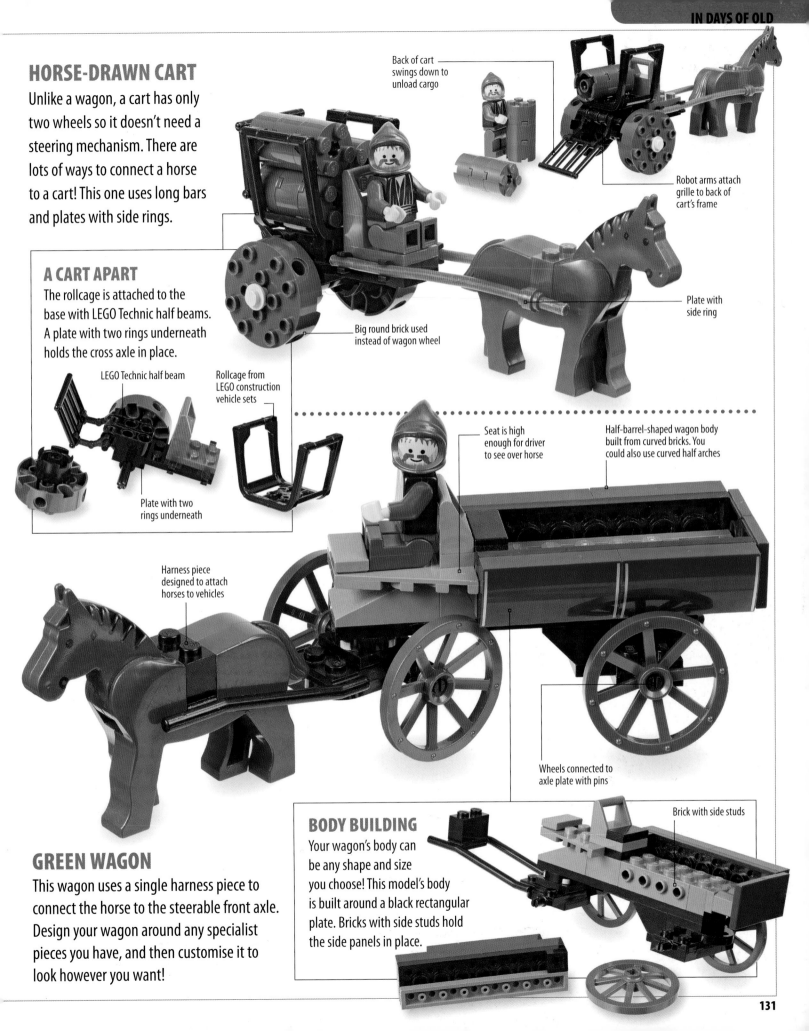

DRAGONS

No medieval world is complete without a fierce, fire-breathing dragon. Dragons are mythical creatures, so there are no rules about what they should look like. Give yours spikes, fangs, horns, tails, chains, curves and as many wings as you like! What else can you think of?

BUILDING BRIEF
Objective: Build hot air balloons
Use: Leisurely trips through the sky
Features: Brightly-coloured balloon top, hanging basket
Extras: Passengers, sandbags, blazing burner

FLYING SERPENT

This lean, agile dragon has a twisted body built from lots of LEGO Technic parts. Its back is shaped and held together with ball-and-socket joints, while axles and LEGO Technic half beams make up the front arms.

Horns face backwards so dragon is streamlined when flying

Don't have these horn pieces? Use screwdrivers, daggers or bars – anything long or pointy will do!

Neck joint is not fixed in place so the head can be posed as you like

ALL IN HIS HEAD

The dragon's head is built in four different directions. The bottom part has studs facing up, the sloped sides are built outwards to the left and right, and the inside of the mouth has a jumper plate facing forwards, which holds the flame piece in place.

Angle plates allow sideways building

Printed angled slopes add detail

Jumper plate faces forwards

I MIGHT BE MADE OF HEAT-RESISTANT PLASTIC, BUT I'M STILL SCARED!

Use joints to create posable ankles and knees

Build the shape of your dragon using ball-and-socket joints

Can your minifigure tame the dragon?

Dragons don't have to have feet! Why not build some claws instead?

Make hip platform wide and sturdy

BOTTOM VIEW

Small transparent pieces make scary, glowing eyes

If you don't have these pieces, use hinged plates or clip and bar pieces to create a movable joint

SIDE VIEW

KEEPING IN SHAPE
Although the dragon's spine is made from LEGO Technic joints, its position has been secured so the model doesn't fall forwards due to its weight. Angled plates are clipped in place along the dragon's back to hold it in a fixed shape.

Bony spine made from blue minifigure heads

Double angled plates attached with clip and bar plates

If you don't have specialist dragon wing pieces, build your own!

Flexible tail built with slopes and joints

You could also use spikes, tentacles or antennas to build the tip of the dragon's tail!

Add width by building sideways, using angle plates

BALANCING ACT
When building a tall model like this one, extra attention must be paid to stability. Large, wide feet are a good way to help the dragon balance when it stands.

BATTERING RAMS

A battering ram is like a medieval tank: heavy, tough and almost unstoppable. It needs a sturdy frame and a strong, swinging ram that can smash through your enemy castle's best defences. It needs a set of wheels too, so your LEGO knights can move the huge contraption around!

BUILDING BRIEF

Objective: Build battering rams
Use: Breaking through the fortifications of enemy castles
Features: Strength, stability, swinging mechanism
Extras: Wheels, shields, armour plates, flags

SWING AND SMASH

A swinging mechanism is built into this ram's support frame. The castle's attackers stand behind the ram, pull it back as far as they can, and then let go. Gravity and momentum take care of the rest!

Axles at the top and bottom of the lift arms let the battering ram swing back and forth freely

Battering ram hangs from two pairs of LEGO Technic lift arms

You could also use wagon wheels for a lighter, faster battering ram

Swinging hinge made from LEGO Technic cross axle and bricks with holes

REAR SIDE VIEW

Make the frame as sturdy as you can with overlapping bricks

Angle plates attach sides to the base

Silver plates look like bolted metal to hold heavy loads

I LOVE THE SOUND OF CASTLE GATES CRASHING DOWN IN THE MORNING!

134

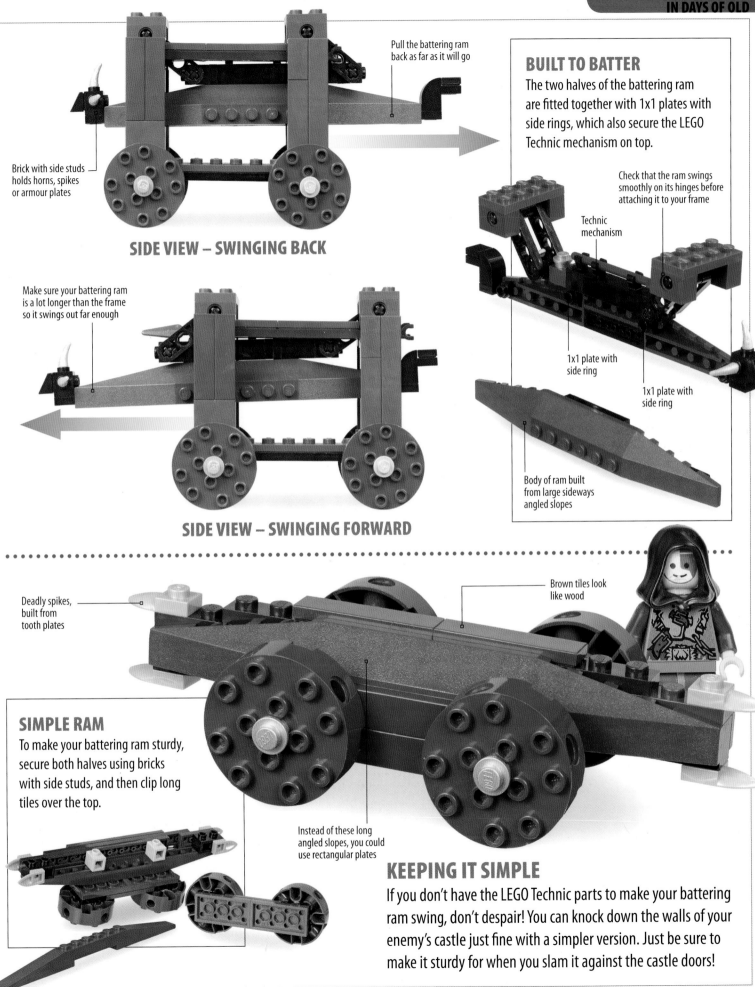

Pull the battering ram back as far as it will go

Brick with side studs holds horns, spikes or armour plates

SIDE VIEW – SWINGING BACK

Make sure your battering ram is a lot longer than the frame so it swings out far enough

SIDE VIEW – SWINGING FORWARD

BUILT TO BATTER
The two halves of the battering ram are fitted together with 1x1 plates with side rings, which also secure the LEGO Technic mechanism on top.

Check that the ram swings smoothly on its hinges before attaching it to your frame

Technic mechanism

1x1 plate with side ring

1x1 plate with side ring

Body of ram built from large sideways angled slopes

Deadly spikes, built from tooth plates

Brown tiles look like wood

Instead of these long angled slopes, you could use rectangular plates

SIMPLE RAM
To make your battering ram sturdy, secure both halves using bricks with side studs, and then clip long tiles over the top.

KEEPING IT SIMPLE
If you don't have the LEGO Technic parts to make your battering ram swing, don't despair! You can knock down the walls of your enemy's castle just fine with a simpler version. Just be sure to make it sturdy for when you slam it against the castle doors!

LAYING SIEGE

Laying siege to an enemy castle is no easy task! You can build all kinds of equipment for your army of knights. A portable shield will protect them from spears and arrows as they advance across the battlefield, while a tall siege tower will help them climb over the castle walls.

PORTABLE SHIELD

Offering protection for knights on the move, this shield wall is made by alternating 1x2 log bricks with 1x1 round bricks. This structure makes the wall flexible enough to bend into a curve.

IT'S LIKE A GAME OF HIDE AND SEEK...READY OR NOT, HERE WE COME!

Use grey bricks to create a stone wall – but remember, a stone wall wouldn't be portable!

Cones at top create the look of wooden poles bound together

Siege army is safe and sound behind the wall!

Plate with click hinge

Rolling wheel rims allow knights to push wall toward castle

REAR VIEW

ROLLING WALL

The portable shield rolls on small wheel rims without tyres. You can attach a horse to the click hinge at the front to tow the wall to the battlefield!

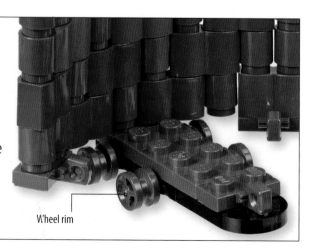

Wheel rim

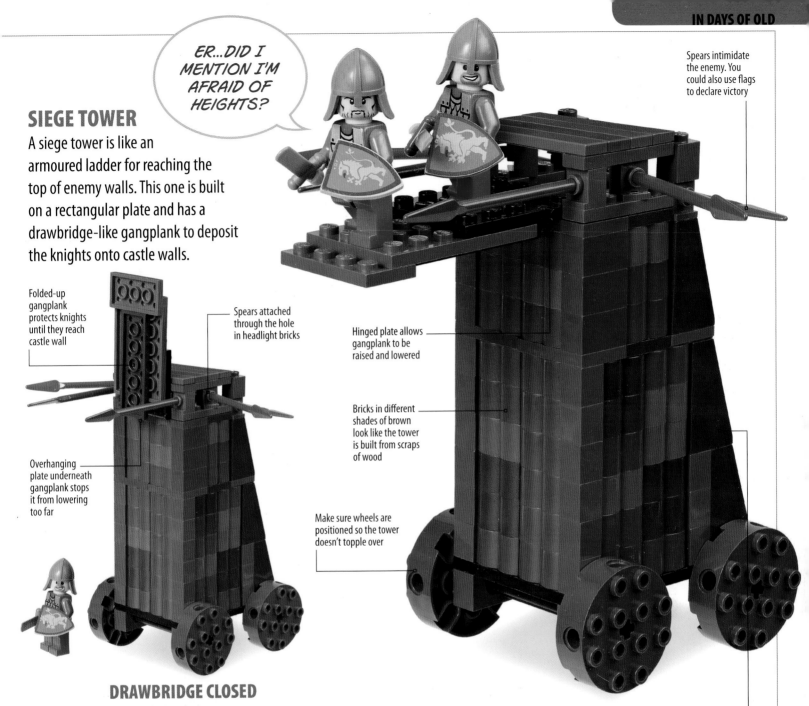

ER...DID I MENTION I'M AFRAID OF HEIGHTS?

SIEGE TOWER

A siege tower is like an armoured ladder for reaching the top of enemy walls. This one is built on a rectangular plate and has a drawbridge-like gangplank to deposit the knights onto castle walls.

Spears intimidate the enemy. You could also use flags to declare victory

Folded-up gangplank protects knights until they reach castle wall

Spears attached through the hole in headlight bricks

Hinged plate allows gangplank to be raised and lowered

Bricks in different shades of brown look like the tower is built from scraps of wood

Overhanging plate underneath gangplank stops it from lowering too far

Make sure wheels are positioned so the tower doesn't topple over

DRAWBRIDGE CLOSED

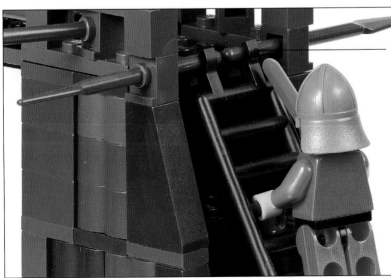

Knights climb up ladder or take shelter inside open back of tower

HOLLOW INSIDE

The back of the siege tower is left open so that the knights can hide inside. A ladder is clipped on to two of the side spears. It can be folded out to allow the knights to climb up it.

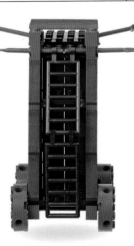

REAR VIEW

CANNONS & CATAPULTS

Siege weapons are designed to throw objects at or over a castle's walls. Beyond that, the only limit is your imagination! So be creative and keep an eye out for parts that would work as catapult buckets or cannon barrels. And remember – don't aim anything at your eyes!

BUILDING BRIEF

Objective: Build siege weapons

Use: Attacking castle walls and towers

Features: Ability to throw, fling or launch projectiles

Extras: Wheels, guards, spare ammo wagons

TILT TO AIM

This cannon can be tilted up and down thanks to a few LEGO Technic pieces. The barrel is built around two bricks with holes, through which is fitted a cross axle.

Axle allows cannon to tilt

Brick with a hole

Barrel made from 2x2 round bricks with a domed brick at the back

Frame uses LEGO Technic parts so the barrel can move up and down

BOTTOM VIEW

Wagon wheels make a heavy cannon more portable

MICROCATAPULT

The basic components of a catapult are a bucket attached to an arm and a sturdy base to support them. With a rotation point in the middle of the throwing arm, this catapult works like a see-saw.

Rotation point

Radar dish for bucket

Push this end down, and the other goes up!

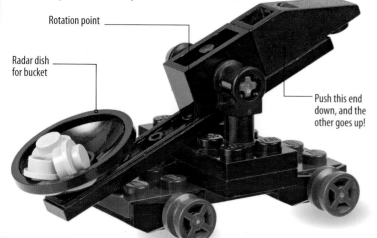

MICROCANNON

For a siege on a smaller scale, you can make a microcannon. This model is built out of two LEGO Technic tubes, supported by headlight bricks.

ASSEMBLE YOUR WEAPONS!

The LEGO Technic tubes are connected by a plate with horizontal clip, which attaches to the headlight bricks with 1x1 round plates.

1x1 round plate

Plate with horizontal clip

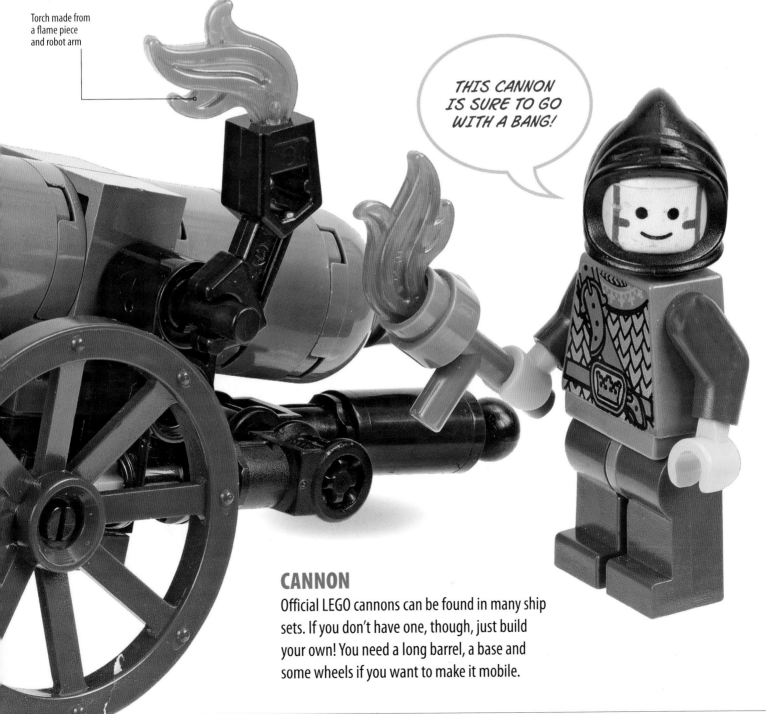

Torch made from a flame piece and robot arm

THIS CANNON IS SURE TO GO WITH A BANG!

CANNON

Official LEGO cannons can be found in many ship sets. If you don't have one, though, just build your own! You need a long barrel, a base and some wheels if you want to make it mobile.

MICROMEDIEVAL

Have you ever wanted to build a really big castle, but didn't have enough bricks? Try shrinking it down! Build it at a smaller-than-minifigure scale to make huge structures from just a few bricks. Your LEGO knights might not fit inside, but with the right pieces and some imagination, you can create churches, houses, animals – even a whole micromedieval world!

FANTASY CASTLE

This magical castle may be small, but it has plenty of interest. A small arch is used to top the front gate, a tile can be a drawbridge and round 1x1 bricks make the towers. The roofs are covered in 1x1 dark grey slopes, cones and tiles to complement the sand-coloured walls.

TOP VIEW

Make your castle as elaborate as you want!

Columns built with 1x1 round bricks and plates

Drawbridge is a single tile supported by plates

A 1x1 cone makes a great tree at microscale!

Square windows are actually the backs of headlight bricks

Castle roof made from ridged roof slopes

Arched window

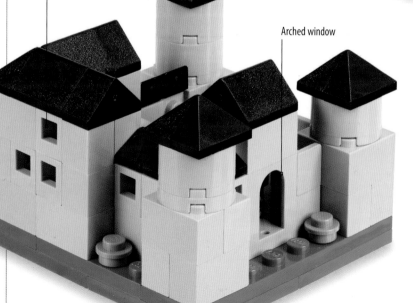

STONE CASTLE

For a traditional-looking castle, start with a few plates to make a base. Next, add the corner towers and then build the rest of the castle between them. Pointy roofs, arched doors and thin walls complete the look!

Tree made from 1x1 round brick

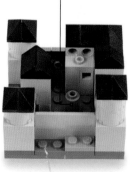

TOP SIDE VIEW

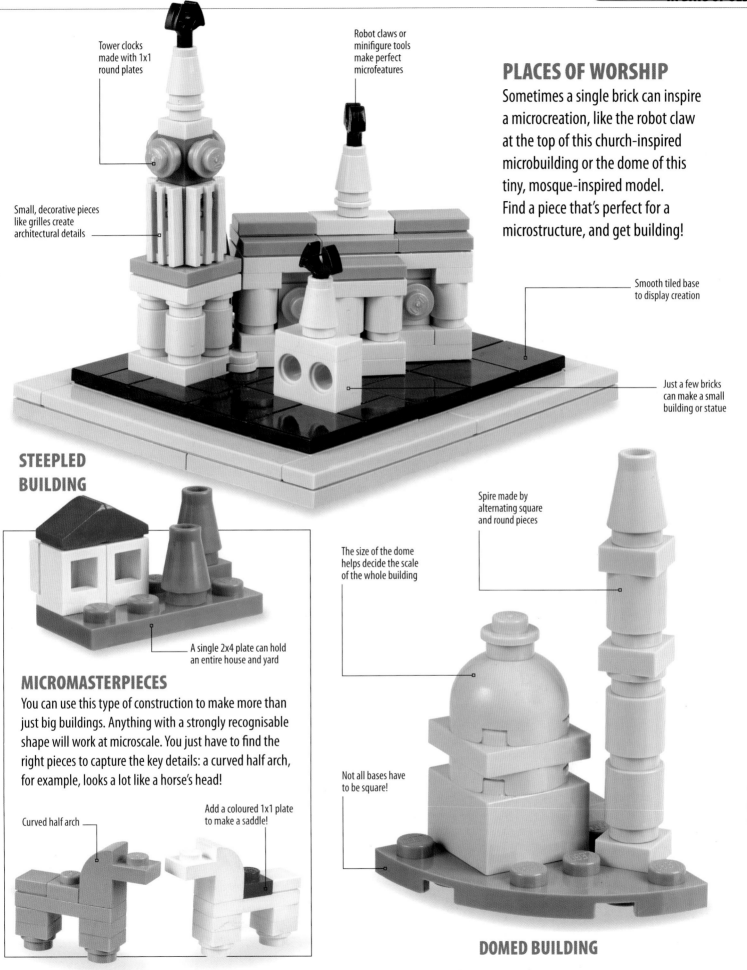

Tower clocks made with 1x1 round plates

Robot claws or minifigure tools make perfect microfeatures

PLACES OF WORSHIP

Sometimes a single brick can inspire a microcreation, like the robot claw at the top of this church-inspired microbuilding or the dome of this tiny, mosque-inspired model. Find a piece that's perfect for a microstructure, and get building!

Small, decorative pieces like grilles create architectural details

Smooth tiled base to display creation

Just a few bricks can make a small building or statue

STEEPLED BUILDING

A single 2x4 plate can hold an entire house and yard

Spire made by alternating square and round pieces

The size of the dome helps decide the scale of the whole building

MICROMASTERPIECES

You can use this type of construction to make more than just big buildings. Anything with a strongly recognisable shape will work at microscale. You just have to find the right pieces to capture the key details: a curved half arch, for example, looks a lot like a horse's head!

Not all bases have to be square!

Curved half arch

Add a coloured 1x1 plate to make a saddle!

DOMED BUILDING

MEET THE BUILDER

SEBASTIAAN ARTS

Location: The Netherlands
Age: 27
LEGO Speciality: Castles and other medieval buildings

What are you inspired by?

I mostly make buildings, so I often get inspiration just walking around town. Whenever I watch documentaries or read articles about castles and medieval buildings, my fingers really itch to build! I also get a lot of inspiration from movies – I pay particular attention to the background buildings and scenery. Seeing LEGO creations by other builders is also a great source of inspiration: sometimes I'll see a clever building technique or part of a creation that makes me think, so I can't stop myself from sitting down and building.

Placing part of your building at an unusual angle can really make your castle a lot more interesting looking.

It's not all about castles! You can also build churches, houses and farms in a medieval setting. This model is based on the church of Scherpenheuvel in Belgium.

To the walls! Siege towers like this were used very widely in the Middle Ages. Invaders could approach their enemy's castle walls protected in their siege tower and then use the height of the tower to climb up and over the castle walls.

If you had all the LEGO bricks (and time!) in the world, what would you build?

This is a subject that has come up in conversations with other fans many times before, and for me that's an easy answer. There's a castle on a rocky island in the north of France named Mont Saint-Michel. I would love to build that whole castle in full minifigure scale. That would be my dream creation.

NOTHING IS IMPOSSIBLE WITH LEGO BRICKS!

What is your favourite creation?

The "Abbey of Saint Rumare", a fictional fortified church built on a rock. It's big, complex and full of different techniques and building styles – the landscape alone combines water with landscaping, rocky surfaces and vegetation. The main structure has a huge church in tan, grey fortifications and lots of different buildings inside in different colours and styles, to create that messy, thrown-together look that you would often find in medieval castles.

What things have gone wrong and how have you dealt with them?

My first response to any question like this would be that nothing is impossible with LEGO bricks! If you're building something that doesn't quite fit, there's always a different combination of parts that will fit. If you can't figure it out, step back for a bit, do something else and go back to your "problem" later – you'll often suddenly see a solution.

What is the biggest or most complex model you've made?

The biggest model I've made is the "Abbey of Saint Rumare". This model was also quite complex, because everything is built at different angles. My most complex model by far was a star-shaped fort, which I named "Herenbosch". The star shape created a series of odd angles linked together, which then had to fit snugly with the buildings inside the castle. This took a lot of work – mostly trial and error – to find exactly the right angles for every part of the castle.

Height can add another dimension to your creation. A tall castle can look a lot more impressive than a bigger, more spread out one. This is my favourite creation, the Abbey of Saint Rumare.

How old were you when you started using LEGO bricks?

On my fourth birthday I received my first LEGO sets, and it all started there: I got hooked straightaway. For every birthday that followed, all I wanted was more LEGO sets. From an early age, I always enjoyed building my own creations.

A drawbridge can also be used as an effective door. However, you need to make it big enough to cover the gate when raised

What are some of your top LEGO tips?

When building a castle, don't limit yourself to just one or two colours. Real castles often took a long time to build, and sometimes bits were added later with a different material. You should also be open to building in different directions: Don't have enough bricks to build a wall? A plate with tiles on its side makes a perfect wall. Don't have enough tiles to make a smooth floor? Try building a wall and placing it on its side to make the floor.

Do you plan out your build? If so, how?

Yes, definitely. Whenever I have a building in mind, I draw a plan of it first, to determine how big each part of the castle should be compared to the other parts around it. I really love building at odd angles, so this requires quite a bit of measuring before I can even start building. I always get the plan on paper before I start building, that way when I do start building, I know exactly where to begin. Of course, I leave enough room for improvisation – if something doesn't quite fit as planned, or if I suddenly come up with a better idea when I actually have the bricks in my hands. So, even if I have drawn a plan to begin from, I usually change it and improvise while building.

Adding detailed and uneven terrain around your castle looks more realistic and also more dynamic.

Star-shaped forts such as my "Herenbosch" model were very common in the late Middle Ages, after the invention of gunpowder and cannons. The angle of the walls makes it more difficult for cannonballs to punch straight through them.

> I OFTEN GET INSPIRATION JUST WALKING AROUND TOWN.

What else do you enjoy making, apart from castles?

I really love everything that I can make with LEGO bricks! I'm mostly into buildings – not just medieval buildings but also more modern town buildings or even science-fiction laboratories or spaceship hangars. Apart from that I also enjoy building cars, spaceships, pirate ships and heavy machinery such as bulldozers or excavators. It really depends what I'm in the mood to build.

Which model were you most proud of as a young LEGO builder?

I was always into castles as a kid too, so my most fond memories are of the biggest castles I could build. I would use as many of my LEGO pieces as I could to build the biggest possible castle. One castle I can particularly remember being proud of was one that had a big dragon's head as a gate – that was very tricky to make and I thought it looked very real and menacing.

What is your favourite LEGO technique or technique you use the most?

I always love finding new ways to make the same thing, and I love using as many different techniques in the same creation as I can, while still keeping it coherent. What I use the most is the technique of using different-coloured and different-shaped bricks to break up an otherwise boring grey wall. Other than that, I love building at all sorts of odd angles to make any building look more interesting. There are many ways to place things at an angle, and there's really no right or wrong way to do it, as long as your chosen technique achieves the correct angle.

What is your favourite LEGO brick or piece?

That's an easy choice for me: the headlight brick.

How much time do you spend building?

This really depends on how inspired I am. Sometimes, I don't build at all for a few weeks. But sometimes, when I have an idea in my head I just can't stop building, and I build from the moment I get home from work until the moment I get so tired that I just have to go to bed.

Don't have enough bricks of the same colour? You can always combine different colours. In this case I used grey for stone and red for clay bricks.

How many LEGO bricks do you have?

I don't know the exact number, because I buy bricks in bulk and trade bricks with other LEGO fans. However, based on other people's collections and logical guesswork, I estimate my collection at about 700,000–750,000 pieces.

If you build a trapdoor, make sure it looks just like the rest of the floor, so it's not easy to spot

A WORLD OF ADVENTURE

Where will your imagination take you? Will you become a treasure-seeking pirate? Will you sail the seven seas in a Viking longship? Will you explore dangerous jungles? Or will you invent a super cool robot? Go ahead, it's your LEGO® fantasy!

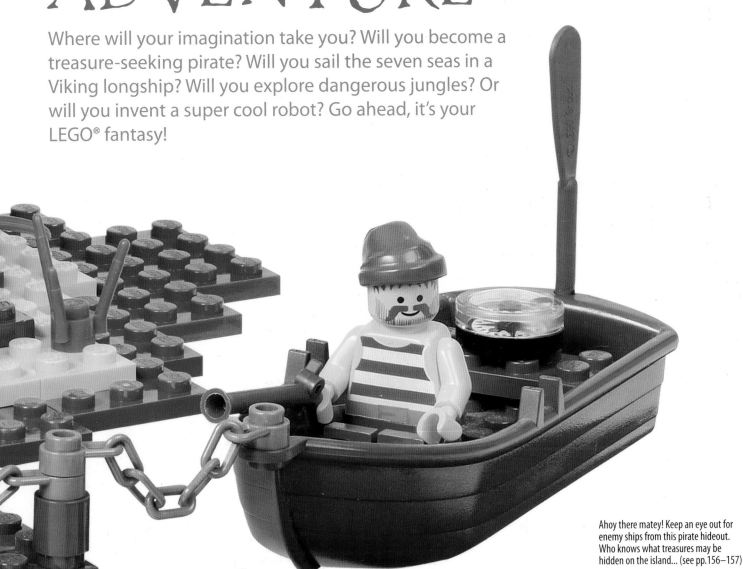

Ahoy there matey! Keep an eye out for enemy ships from this pirate hideout. Who knows what treasures may be hidden on the island... (see pp.156–157)

BRICKS FOR ADVENTURE

In your world of adventure, anything is possible. Swinging vines, towering ships and hi-tech robots all have a place in your LEGO world. Here are some bricks that might be useful when building your fantastic adventures, but search your own collection for cool pieces, and use them! What else can you build?

PLANT

VINE/WHIP

CARROT TOP

TELESCOPE

FLAME

LEGO® TECHNIC DISK

SKELETON HEAD

PALM TREE LEAF

TURKEY

LIGHTBULB

1x1 TOOTH PLATE

ANTENNA

HORN

1x1 ROUND PLATE

THAT FINAL TOUCH
Keep an eye out for small pieces that will add detail to your adventure scene. A flaming candlestick can bring a Viking celebration to life! (See Feasting Table, pp.160–161)

2x2 PALM TREE BASE

TAIL

1x1 ROUND PLATE

LONG BONE

2x2 PALM TREE BASE

1x2x3 CURVED WINDOW FRAME AND LATTICE WINDOW

FLOWER WITH OPEN STUD

1x1 CONE

2x2 PRINTED SLOPE

SMALL WAGON WHEELS AND 1x4 AXLE PLATE

1x2 GRILLE

2x2 BARREL

PALM TREE TOP

MUSKET

1x1 ROUND BRICK

1x1 ROUND BRICK

1x2 PRINTED TILE

1x4x2 BARRED FENCE

AERIAL

VERSATILE PIECES
Long pieces like aerials and antennas are very versatile. They can be used for anything, from a flagpole to a bowsprit. (See Pirate Ship, pp.150–151)

OAR

1x4 PRINTED TILE

STRING WITH STUDS

HINGED PLATES

SHORT CHAIN

1x1 PLATE WITH HORIZONTAL CLIP

1x1 PLATE WITH VERTICAL CLIP

LEGO TECHNIC PIN

1x2 INVERTED SLOPE

1x2 PLATE WITH CLICK HINGE

1x2 JUMPER PLATE

1x1 BRICK WITH VERTICAL BAR

LEGO TECHNIC HALF BEAM

1x2 PLATE WITH HANDLED BAR

HINGE CYLINDER

HINGE CYLINDER WITH PIN

1x2 PLATE WITH VERTICAL BAR

HOOKS AND HOLES
Pieces with clips, bars, hooks and holes can help turn a good model into a great model!

6x6 ANGLED PLATE

RIGGING

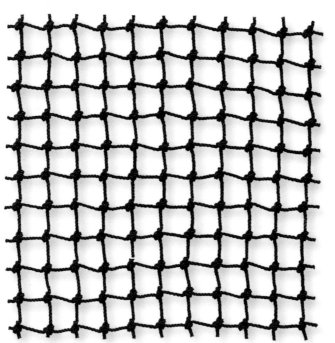

NET

LEGO TECHNIC CROSS AXLE 8

SPIRAL TUBE

LEGO TECHNIC RIM

2x2 ROUND PLATE

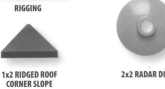

1x2 RIDGED ROOF CORNER SLOPE

2x2 RADAR DISH

BE ADVENTUROUS!
BUILD WITH DIFFERENT
TEXTURES, SHAPES
AND COLOURS

2x2 ROUND BRICK

2x2 ROUND BRICK

CREATE WITH COLOUR
Choose colours to help you tell your story. Use grey bricks for stone and rock, brown for wooden structures, green for grass and blue for oceans and waterfalls!

1x1x6 ROUND COLUMN

3x3 CURVED PLATE

4x4 ROUND BRICK

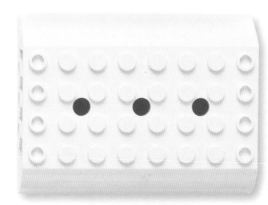

6x8x2 CURVED BRICK WITH HOLES

STRANGE SHAPES
Unusually shaped bricks and plates will make your models interesting. Try to use both big and small pieces.

1x6 TILE

2x6 ANGLED SLOPE

2x12 PLATE

MAST

149

PIRATE SHIP

Ready to set sail for plunder and adventure, me hearties? Build yourself a mighty pirate ship! You'll need a tall mast with a sail and a fearsome skull and crossbones, a treasure hold for all your loot, a plank to make the landlubbers walk, a cannon or three and, of course, a scurvy gang of buccaneers as crew!

BUILDING BRIEF

Objective: Make pirate ships
Use: Sailing the seven seas in search of treasure
Features: Masts, sails, pirate flags, cannons, planks, steering wheel
Extras: Figureheads, treasure chests, crew quarters, rigging

A BOATLOAD OF BRICKS

There are all kinds of specialist pieces that you can use to build a pirate ship, from hulls to cannons to bowsprits, but here's a way to make one using mostly standard bricks and pieces.

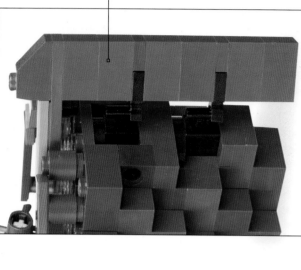

Rudder is important for steering the ship

STEER CLEAR

The movable rudder is built from 1x2 bricks and 1x1 plates. Two clip plates attach it to bricks with vertical bars on the ship's squared-off back end.

Railings built from tiles and supported by 1x1 round bricks

Skull and crossbones pirate flag made from a skeleton minifigure head and bone accessories

REAR SIDE VIEW

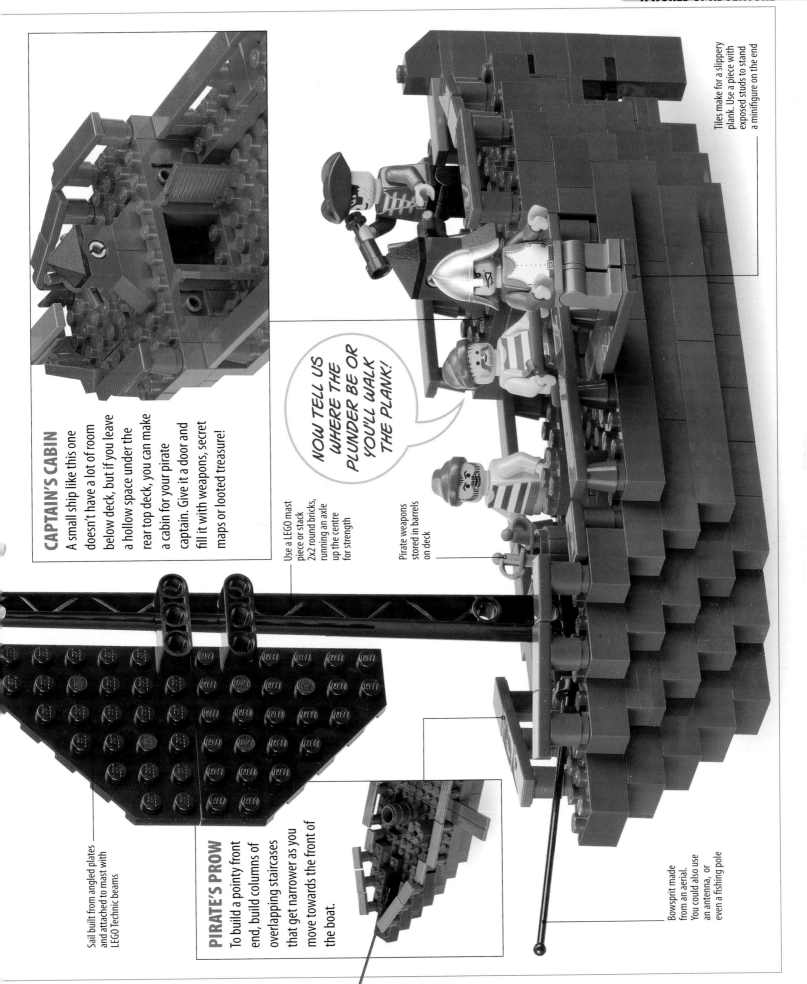

CAPTAIN'S CABIN

A small ship like this one doesn't have a lot of room below deck, but if you leave a hollow space under the rear top deck, you can make a cabin for your pirate captain. Give it a door and fill it with weapons, secret maps or looted treasure!

Use a LEGO mast piece or stack 2x2 round bricks, running an axle up the centre for strength

Pirate weapons stored in barrels on deck

PIRATE'S PROW

To build a pointy front end, build columns of overlapping staircases that get narrower as you move towards the front of the boat.

Sail built from angled plates and attached to mast with LEGO Technic beams

Tiles make for a slippery plank. Use a piece with exposed studs to stand a minifigure on the end

NOW TELL US WHERE THE PLUNDER BE OR YOU'LL WALK THE PLANK!

Bowsprit made from an aerial. You could also use an antenna, or even a fishing pole

A PIRATE'S WORLD

There is more to being a pirate than just sailing around in a ship! You can create an entire world for your bold buccaneers full of buried treasure, rival bands of pirates, cannon battles and daring captures and rescues. There's plenty of swashbuckling action to be had!

Wing made from tooth plate

Feet made from plate with horizontal clip

Beak made from horn

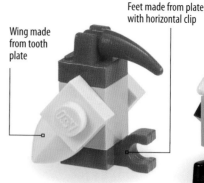

PARROTS

Every bad pirate should have a parrot! Start with a body of a 1x1 brick with side studs and clip on feet, wings and a beak to create a colourful bird. You could use a 1x1 tile and feather pieces to add plumage.

Build a giant box to store your own valuables (see pp.190–191)

Lock made from plate with handled bar

ALL THAT GLITTERS

Create treasure using transparent and metallic pieces for gems, coins and gold. Make sure your treasure chest is big enough to hold it all!

ARR, I'VE GOT THE TREASURE... NOW I JUST NEED A BIG HOLE TO BURY IT IN!

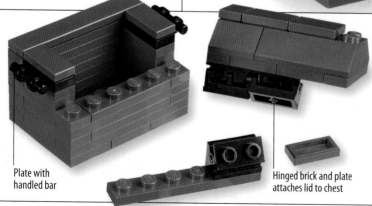

Plate with handled bar

Hinged brick and plate attaches lid to chest

PIRATE TREASURE

You could make a removable lid, but why not use hinged bricks and plates to allow your chest to open and close? You could even add a keyhole by using a brick with a hole.

TREASURE CHEST

Once you've found your treasure, you'll need somewhere to hide it away! You can build treasure chests in all shapes and sizes using plates and tiles that resemble wooden boards. Handles can be made using any piece a minifigure hand can clip onto.

PIRATE CANNON

Here's a cannon of a piratey variety. The flat platform and small wheel rims are ideal for rolling across the deck of a ship during a pitched sea battle.

READY... AIM... BUILD!

Rounded end-cap, made from domed brick

Cannon barrel built from 2x2 round bricks with LEGO Technic axle through the centre

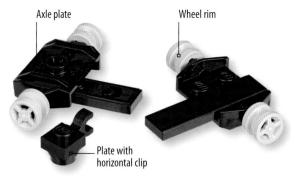

Axle plate

Wheel rim

Plate with horizontal clip

CANNON AID

For the cannon platform, attach wheel rims to upside-down axle plates held together by tiles. Then attach a clip to a handle on the cannon so it can tilt for aiming!

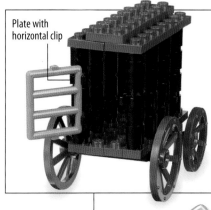

Plate with horizontal clip

LOCK-UP

A door hinge is created by building plates with horizontal clips into one of the bars of the cage. A single clip plate on the opposite bar makes a latch to close the door.

PRISON WAGON

Make a horse and wagon to whisk a captured pirate prisoner off to jail. For extra adventure, you could also build a secret hatch into the roof or floor for last-minute escapes!

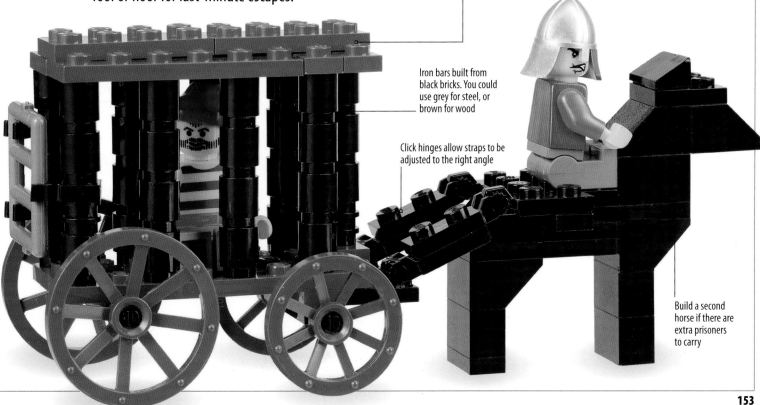

Iron bars built from black bricks. You could use grey for steel, or brown for wood

Click hinges allow straps to be adjusted to the right angle

Build a second horse if there are extra prisoners to carry

SHIPWRECK

Why not give your minifigures a pirate shipwreck scene to play in? You'll need a stormy sea, some ruinous rocks and a pirate ship smashed to smithereens! Think of what else you could add to the scene – perhaps some floating treasure or escaping prisoners? You could even build a rowboat to rescue any survivors!

BUILDING BRIEF

Objective: Build shipwreck scenes
Use: A scene to pose or play with your pirate crew
Features: Wrecked ship, rocks, water
Extras: Seagulls, waves, floating debris

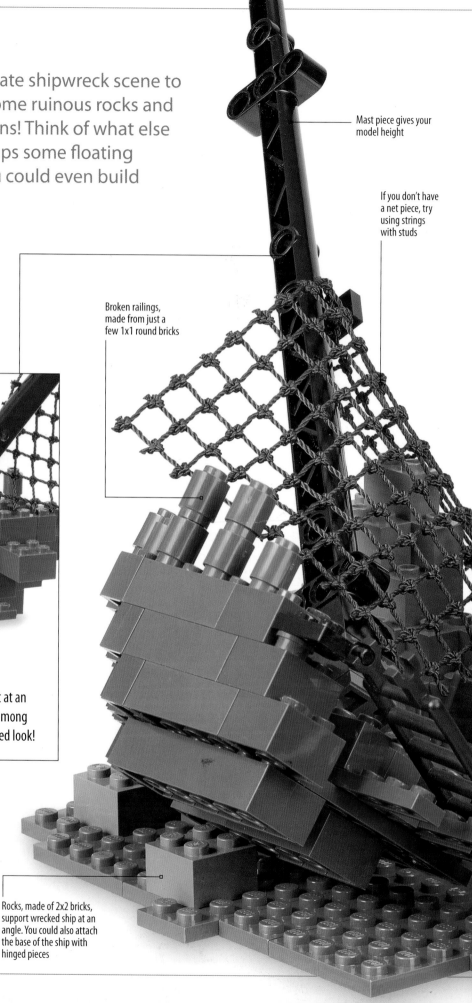

Mast piece gives your model height

If you don't have a net piece, try using strings with studs

Broken railings, made from just a few 1x1 round bricks

Rocks, made of 2x2 bricks, support wrecked ship at an angle. You could also attach the base of the ship with hinged pieces

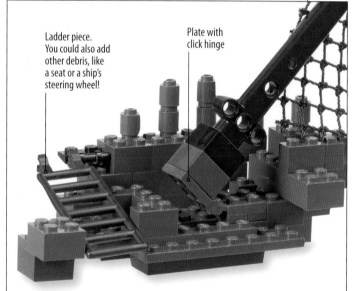

Ladder piece. You could also add other debris, like a seat or a ship's steering wheel!

Plate with click hinge

DECK DETAILS

Attach the mast with hinged plates so you can position it at an angle as if it's been snapped at the base. A black ladder among the brown bricks adds interest and creates a really wrecked look!

HALF A SHIP

Once you know how to construct a ship, a wrecked one is easy – just build part of it! Make the edges of the hull uneven and add deck plates of different lengths so they look like boards smashed up by rocks in a storm.

ROWBOAT

Build a rowboat just like you would make a pirate ship, but on a smaller scale. Use a rectangular brick or plate across two 1x2 bricks to make the pirate's seat.

NOW THE TREASURE'S ALL...OOPS, I FORGOT TO TAKE THE TREASURE!

Oars attached to clips that move back and forth

You could perch a parrot on the prow!

Flagpole, made from antenna. You could attach a small sail or pirate flag

TOP VIEW

You could use bricks in different colours for a patchwork boat made from salvaged materials!

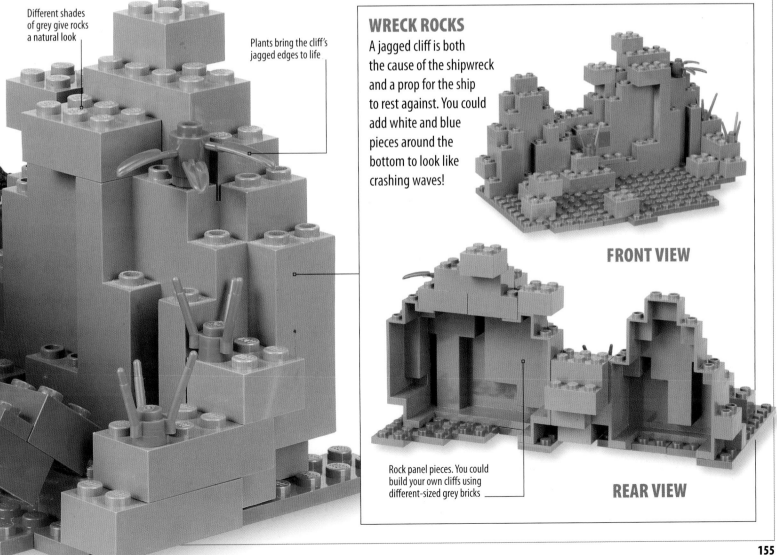

Different shades of grey give rocks a natural look

Plants bring the cliff's jagged edges to life

WRECK ROCKS

A jagged cliff is both the cause of the shipwreck and a prop for the ship to rest against. You could add white and blue pieces around the bottom to look like crashing waves!

FRONT VIEW

Rock panel pieces. You could build your own cliffs using different-sized grey bricks

REAR VIEW

PIRATE ISLAND

Even the most hardy sea dogs need somewhere to call home! Expand your pirate play with a pirate island. Imagine you're a pirate and think about what you might need in a hideout: how about a lookout for spotting enemy soldiers on the horizon? Or somewhere to moor your ship, or hide your treasure?

PIRATE PATCH

You could build a fancy fort or a humble home for your pirates. This hideout has a simple but interesting design, with two main levels and a lookout level, all built on a small patch of land anchored in the middle of the sea.

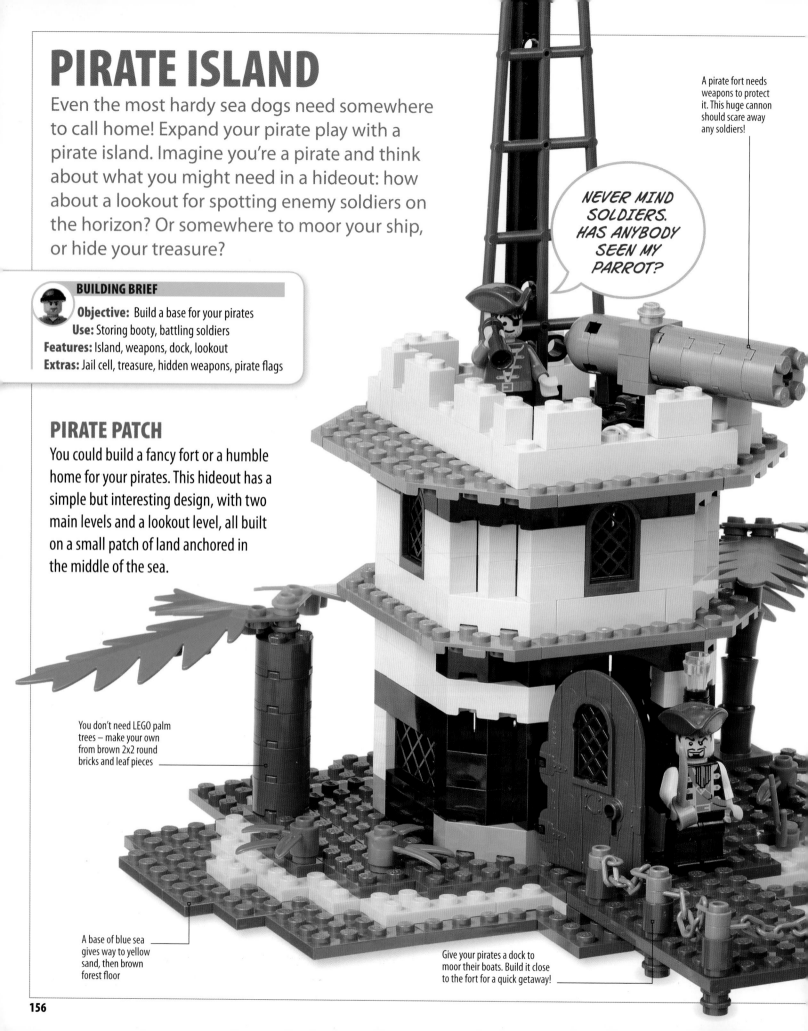

A pirate fort needs weapons to protect it. This huge cannon should scare away any soldiers!

NEVER MIND SOLDIERS. HAS ANYBODY SEEN MY PARROT?

You don't need LEGO palm trees – make your own from brown 2x2 round bricks and leaf pieces

A base of blue sea gives way to yellow sand, then brown forest floor

Give your pirates a dock to moor their boats. Build it close to the fort for a quick getaway!

Angled bricks connect the four walls together

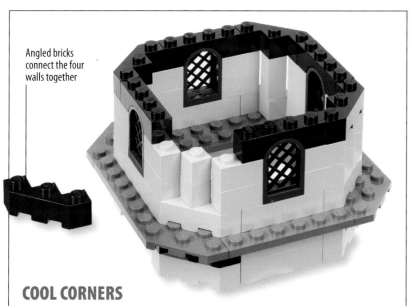

Add mast or hull pieces to your pirate base to make it look like it was built with salvaged parts from a shipwreck!

It's easy to build your own cannon! (See p.153)

Rigging attached to the lookout for the pirates to climb up

COOL CORNERS

A tower made mostly from square bricks doesn't have to be square! On this second level of the fort, angled bricks frame stacked 1x1 bricks to make the corners of the tower an interesting shape.

Plenty of plants bring your pirate island to life!

REAR VIEW

I'VE GOT A BOAT AND A COMPASS...NOW I'M OFF TO FIND TREASURE!

If you don't have a LEGO boat, turn back to p.155 to see how to make one

This lantern not only helps the pirates see at night – it can be moved sideways to lock the door!

GROUND UP

The ground level features a large doorway and windows made from lattice fences. Dark tan bricks show where the tower has become dirty from the brown forest floor. Pirates aren't known for their cleanliness!

VIKING LONGSHIP

Are your minifigures ready to set sail and conquer the world? They'll need a longship for their Viking adventures. Viking longships have a distinctive look, with low walls and a tall bow and stern, but the rest of the details are up to you. How many oarsmen do you need? What figurehead will you build at the front of your model? You could even add a second level to your ship, or billowing sails!

BUILDING BRIEF

Objective: Create Viking ships
Use: Transportation, exploration, plunder
Features: Must hold a lot of oarsmen, stability, distinctive Viking appearance
Extras: Sails, additional levels, escort ships, enemy fleets

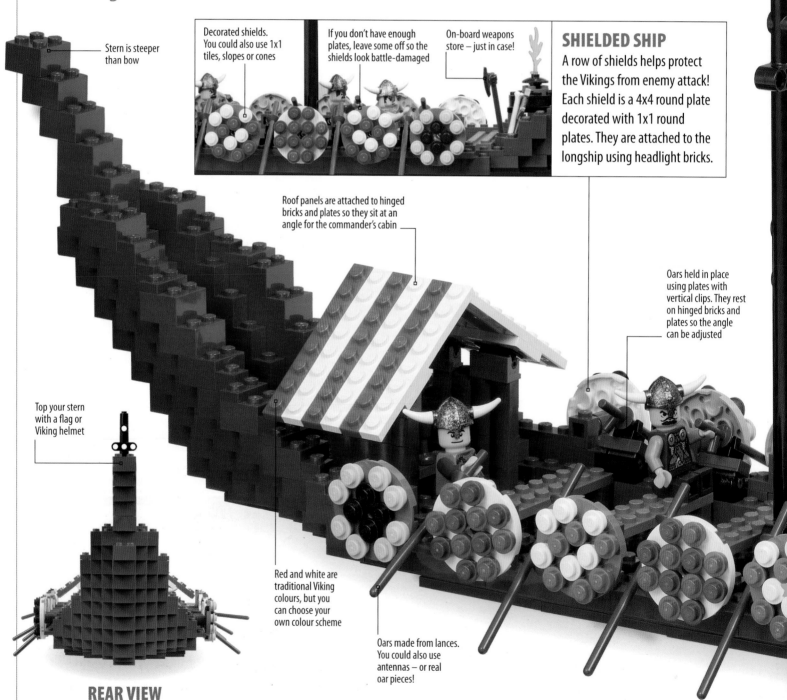

Stern is steeper than bow

Decorated shields. You could also use 1x1 tiles, slopes or cones

If you don't have enough plates, leave some off so the shields look battle-damaged

On-board weapons store – just in case!

If you don't have a LEGO mast, you could build a stack of round 1x1 or 2x2 bricks

SHIELDED SHIP

A row of shields helps protect the Vikings from enemy attack! Each shield is a 4x4 round plate decorated with 1x1 round plates. They are attached to the longship using headlight bricks.

Roof panels are attached to hinged bricks and plates so they sit at an angle for the commander's cabin

Oars held in place using plates with vertical clips. They rest on hinged bricks and plates so the angle can be adjusted

Top your stern with a flag or Viking helmet

Red and white are traditional Viking colours, but you can choose your own colour scheme

Oars made from lances. You could also use antennas – or real oar pieces!

REAR VIEW

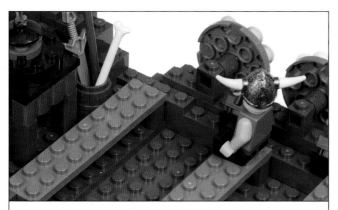

This model is 16 studs wide. Decide how wide your longship will be. How many crew will it hold?

BOTTOM VIEW

Overlap plates to create a flat, sturdy base

MANPOWER

Viking ships are powered by a crew of strong oarsmen. Build a row of benches to seat the crew next to their oars. You could also add a furnace to provide light during the night.

Dragon head has white round plates for eyes and teeth

A REALLY LONG SHIP

To get the shape of your longship right, start with a wide base of overlapping plates. Build the front and back sections separately using columns of stepped bricks that get narrower toward the bow and stern. Connect it all together at the base and secure with more plates if necessary.

Flame held in place by a plate with vertical clip on top of a jumper plate

IF US DANES WANT TO CONQUER THE WORLD, WE SHOULD CONCENTRATE ON THE TOY MARKET.

Furnace built with log bricks, round bricks and a radar dish on top

Curved neck built from stepped 2x3 bricks

This style of building is also used for the Pirate Ship (see pp.150–151)

Don't have enough brown bricks? Use different colours for Viking war paint!

VIKING VILLAGE

Even the toughest Viking needs somewhere to come home to after a long sea voyage. Build him a village and fill it with everything you think a Viking clan would need, including hearty food, fresh water, a welcoming fire and a place to sleep. You could even build a wooden fence to protect the village from marauding enemies!

THE FACT THAT WE FOUGHT THE BAD VIKINGS AND WON, REMEMBER?

FEASTING TABLE

For a village feast, build long wooden tables and matching benches, then add as much food as you can find or build. Make it big enough for the whole clan to celebrate their Viking victories together!

SO WHAT ARE WE FEASTING ON THIS WEEK, GUYS?

Candlestick made from a telescope and a flame piece

If you don't have any Viking minifigures, combine armoured bodies with bearded faces

160

The longer your table, the more 1x1 round bricks you'll need to support it

UNDER THE TABLE

Long, narrow plates make good table planks, and 1x1 round bricks can be stacked to make legs. Small plates underneath hold the long plates together.

MESSY MEAL

Who needs table manners? If you have a piece that resembles food, stick it on the table. Bones and empty plates suggest the feasting has been going on for a while!

Don't forget goblets for toasts and quaffing!

I'M JUST PROUD THAT I BUILT THIS TABLE ALL BY MYSELF!

Bench made in the same way as table, just with shorter legs

Knives, axes and swords come in handy at the dinner table, too!

JUNGLE ROPE BRIDGE

You may never have been to a jungle, but everyone knows what they look like. Lots of green leaves, plants and vines. Ancient, twisted trees. Rivers and waterfalls. There are so many possibilities! And when you create the natural world in bricks, you can be as free form as you like – if you haven't got enough pieces to finish a tree, leave it as a stump!

BUILDING BRIEF

Objective: Create jungle scenes
Use: Exploration, adventure, discovery
Features: River, hanging bridge
Extras: Foliage, ladders, flowers

Vegetation placed on irregular tree surfaces for a natural effect

Only middle slat is doubled up to hold the string; string hangs loose elsewhere

This is a great piece to make a jungle vine, which only needs one stud. You could also build in clips into your tree to attach extra plants

ROPE BRIDGE

The coolest way to cross a jungle river is by rope bridge! This one is made from four lengths of string with studs on the ends. The slats are brown 1x4 plates. The trees are made from bricks, inverted slopes and plant leaves, arranged to look random and natural, with lumps and bumps all over.

Bumpy forest floor, created using brown and green plates arranged in an irregular pattern

Access to the bridge is via a ladder, attached to the tree with a plate with handled bar

FALLEN LOGS

Logs fall on the forest floor and plants grow around them. Side branches may also have leaves growing from them. These leaves grow in different directions, which is what this model is replicating.

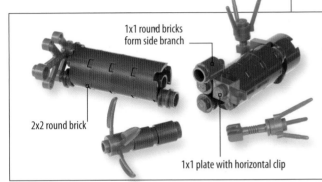

Logs can be strewn around your jungle scene for extra realism

1x1 round bricks form side branch

2x2 round brick

1x1 plate with horizontal clip

CLIP-ON LEAVES

The central trunk of the log is made from brown 2x2 round bricks. Then, a 1x1 plate with horizontal clip is fitted in so the plants can grow upwards from the trunk.

CAMP FIRE

Here's a camp fire for cooking or warmth – even the jungle can get cold at night. Brown 1x1 round bricks form the logs and robot arms and tube studs hold the flames.

If you don't have flames, you could create smouldering embers with any small red and orange pieces

Palm tree leaves come in many LEGO sets

PALM TREES

The trunks of palm trees often have a natural bend, which can be recreated in bricks using various pieces. Any round brown bricks or cones would work, topped with leaves.

Specialised palm tree segment

INTO THE JUNGLE

Time to expand your jungle landscape! You can add mystery and adventure by building ancient ruins and long-lost forbidden temples. Not everything has to be man-made, either – how about a raging river full of snapping crocodiles or a rushing waterfall? Go wild with your creations!

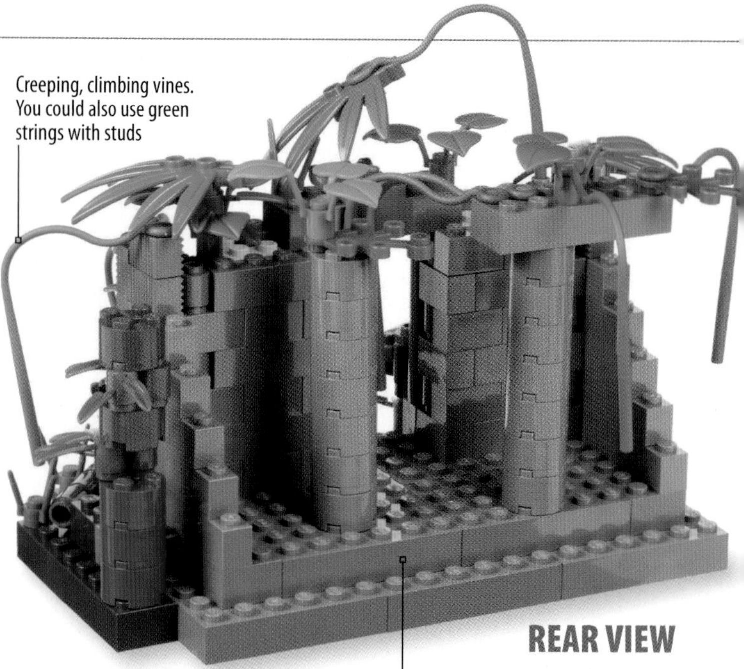

BUILDING BRIEF

Objective: Expand your jungle
Use: New places to play and explore
Features: Crumbling ruins, waterfalls
Extras: Jungle animals, trees, mountains

Creeping, climbing vines. You could also use green strings with studs

REAR VIEW

You could build trapdoors or tile mosaics into the floor

Mix different types of leaves and plants for an overgrown look

JUNGLE RUIN

To create an old, crumbling building, leave some of the walls incomplete so they look like they've fallen apart over the centuries. Creeping vines and other greenery show the jungle growing back over the ruins!

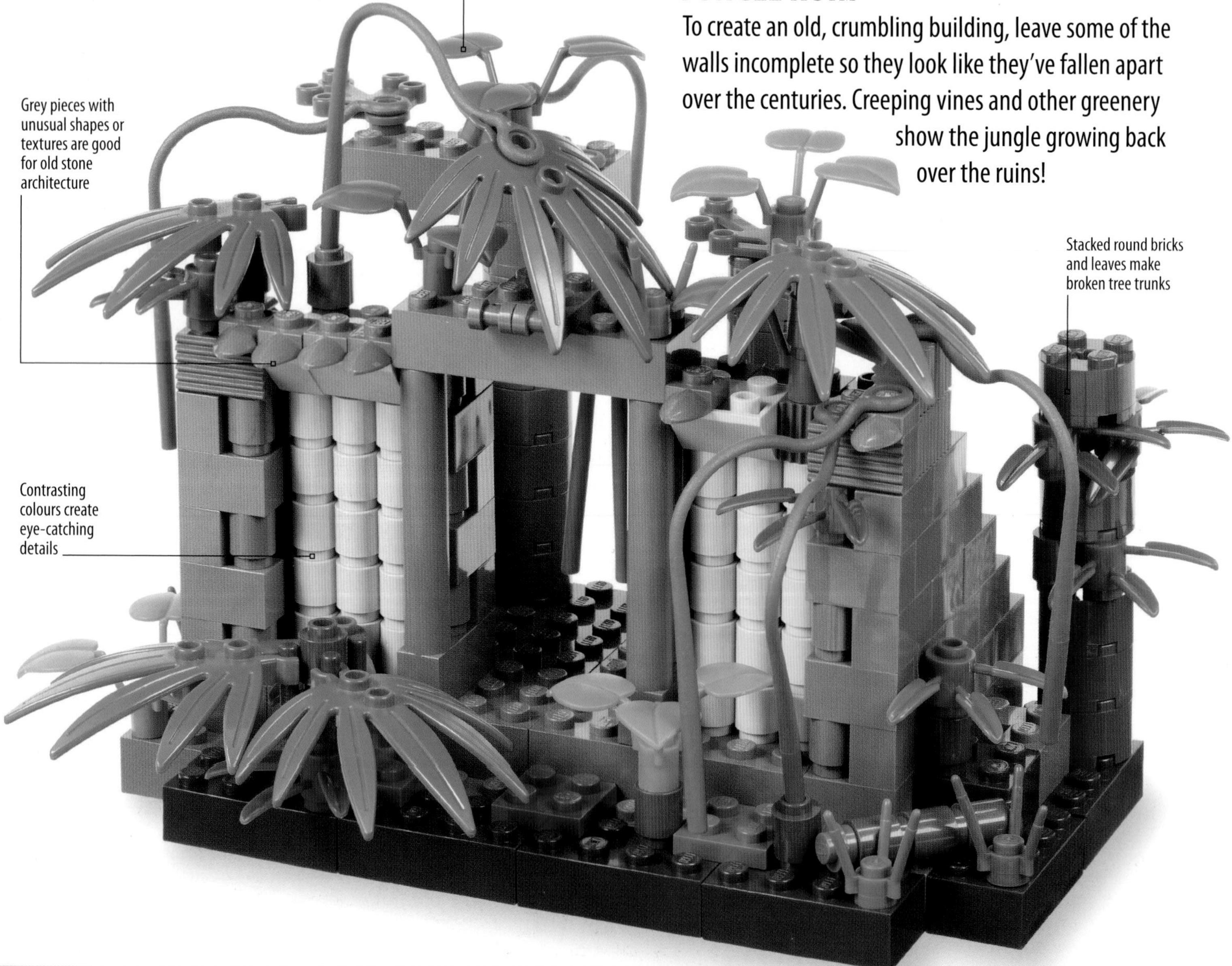

Grey pieces with unusual shapes or textures are good for old stone architecture

Stacked round bricks and leaves make broken tree trunks

Contrasting colours create eye-catching details

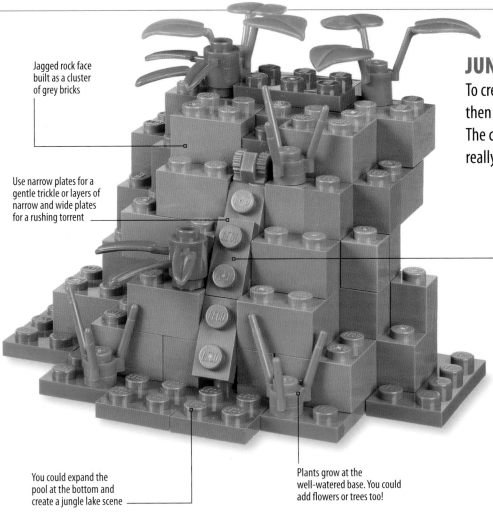

Jagged rock face built as a cluster of grey bricks

Use narrow plates for a gentle trickle or layers of narrow and wide plates for a rushing torrent

You could expand the pool at the bottom and create a jungle lake scene

Plants grow at the well-watered base. You could add flowers or trees too!

JUNGLE WATERFALL

To create a waterfall, first build a rocky base, then add blue bricks for running water. The coolest part is making it look like it's really flowing downhill.

FALLING WATER

The stream of this waterfall is made with one-stud-wide blue plates built onto plates with click hinges. Hinges allow the waterfall to be angled so it flows down the rocks. If you don't have hinges, try building the blue pieces directly onto the rock face.

GRAND ENTRANCE

The temple gate is built from a barred fence turned sideways. It is clipped to an antenna that is secured in the doorway. Use a plate with handled bar for the door handle.

Plate with handled bar

You can build the temple as large as you want!

You could completely cover your temple with vegetation and vines so it looks lost and forgotten

LOST TEMPLE

Even a small jungle building can make a big impact. This secret temple may look like an ordinary pile of rocks, but the barred gate hints that something important is hidden inside. What that is...is up to you!

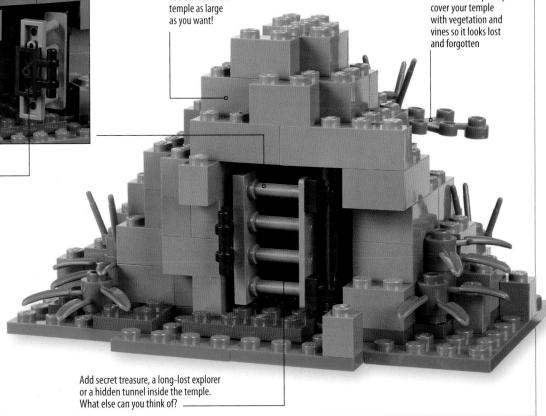

Add secret treasure, a long-lost explorer or a hidden tunnel inside the temple. What else can you think of?

WILD ANIMALS

Fill your jungles, plains and savannas with wild animals of all species! Identify the shapes, proportions and patterns of your chosen animal and try to stick as close to the real thing as you can! The more you can show what makes the animal unique, the better your model will be!

BUILDING BRIEF

Objective: Make animal models
Use: Living in a jungle, zoo or desert
Features: Stability, distinct features
Extras: Opening jaws, moving limbs

GIRAFFE

A giraffe's most recognisable feature is its long neck. Use a variety of bricks and slopes to get the body shape and markings just right. You could build a bigger head so you have more room for facial features.

Eyes, ears and horns attach to bricks with side studs

You could build a longer neck, but remember, the longer it is, the less stable it will be!

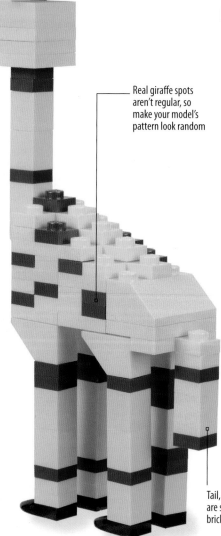

Real giraffe spots aren't regular, so make your model's pattern look random

Inverted slope creates natural shapes at base of neck and top of legs

Tail, legs and neck are stacks of 1x1 bricks and plates

Pointy hooves, made from tooth plates. You could use round plates for small hooves

Studs on back resemble tough elephant skin

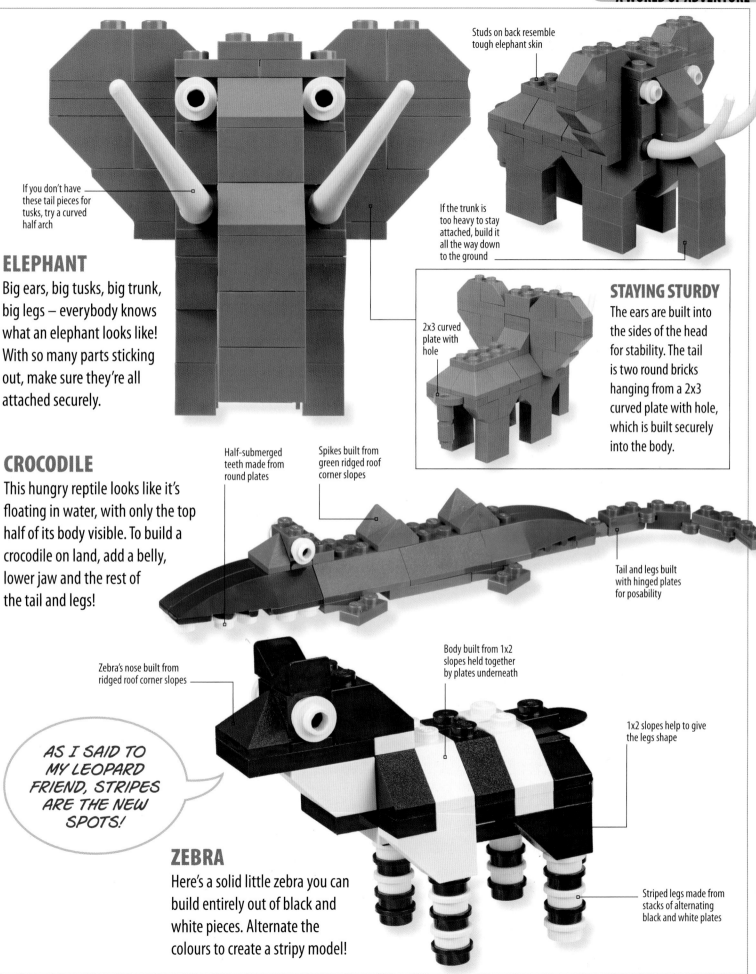

If you don't have these tail pieces for tusks, try a curved half arch

ELEPHANT

Big ears, big tusks, big trunk, big legs – everybody knows what an elephant looks like! With so many parts sticking out, make sure they're all attached securely.

If the trunk is too heavy to stay attached, build it all the way down to the ground

2x3 curved plate with hole

STAYING STURDY

The ears are built into the sides of the head for stability. The tail is two round bricks hanging from a 2x3 curved plate with hole, which is built securely into the body.

CROCODILE

This hungry reptile looks like it's floating in water, with only the top half of its body visible. To build a crocodile on land, add a belly, lower jaw and the rest of the tail and legs!

Half-submerged teeth made from round plates

Spikes built from green ridged roof corner slopes

Tail and legs built with hinged plates for posability

Zebra's nose built from ridged roof corner slopes

Body built from 1x2 slopes held together by plates underneath

1x2 slopes help to give the legs shape

AS I SAID TO MY LEOPARD FRIEND, STRIPES ARE THE NEW SPOTS!

ZEBRA

Here's a solid little zebra you can build entirely out of black and white pieces. Alternate the colours to create a stripy model!

Striped legs made from stacks of alternating black and white plates

ROBOTS

When building robots, anything goes! They can be simple or complicated, silly or cool. Who needs normal feet when you can roll around on wheels or clank across the floor with big stompers? Use hinges, joints and turntables to add posability, and try adding printed tiles, radar dishes and LEGO Technic pieces for mechanical details!

YOU CAN'T MISS ME, EVEN IN A CROWD OF ROBOTS!

BUILDING BRIEF

Objective: Build robots of all shapes and sizes
Use: Heavy lifting, major computation, battle
Features: Movable sections, tools
Extras: Swappable parts, lights, motorised functions

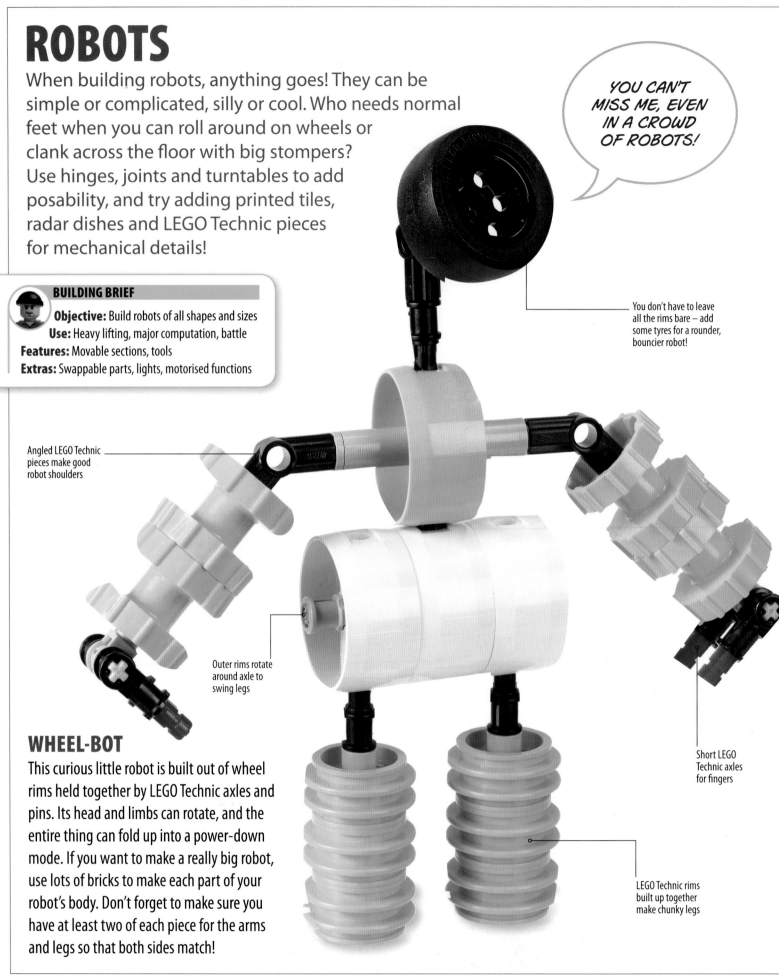

You don't have to leave all the rims bare – add some tyres for a rounder, bouncier robot!

Angled LEGO Technic pieces make good robot shoulders

Outer rims rotate around axle to swing legs

Short LEGO Technic axles for fingers

WHEEL-BOT

This curious little robot is built out of wheel rims held together by LEGO Technic axles and pins. Its head and limbs can rotate, and the entire thing can fold up into a power-down mode. If you want to make a really big robot, use lots of bricks to make each part of your robot's body. Don't forget to make sure you have at least two of each piece for the arms and legs so that both sides match!

LEGO Technic rims built up together make chunky legs

ROBO-MOTION

Axle holds big wheel rims together back-to-back

The digger-bot's arms rotate on a LEGO Technic cross axle running through its body, so it can swivel each tool into place as and when needed!

DIGGER-BOT

It may not be the most mobile of robots, but put the digger-bot near a mine cave wall and watch it go! Minifigure tools, LEGO Technic gears and a construction vehicle shovel give each arm its own special function.

Long-distance antenna for communication with surface

Use any printed tiles you want for a control screen

Use different tools for different jobs

Radar dish for a base, but you could add wheels or treads so it can move around

If you don't have these hemisphere-dome eyes, try building crazy eyes of your own!

Hand made from palm tree top plugged into hinge cylinder with a LEGO Technic pin end

BUG-EYED BOT

Here's a big-eyed bug-eyed robot! It uses the same base as the digger-bot, but you could try adding legs if you wanted. Its round body complements its domed eyes, while the hinged arms make it really posable.

Spherical body built from overlapping plates. Or build a body in any shape you like!

Claw lets robot grab and hold on to other robots!

169

CREATURE 'BOTS

Robots don't need to have arms, legs or even heads. They can be wide, skinny, tall, short, huge or tiny. They can resemble real-life creatures or look like nothing you've ever seen before! Use unusual pieces to create your creature 'bots – the crazier the better!

You could add functional accessories to the tip of the tail, like a computer screen or spy camera!

Plug in an antenna for a long tail

Use clips to attach weapons or equipment to bars all over body

Posable legs can fold under the body while in flight

Want to go faster? Substitute rocket boosters for wings!

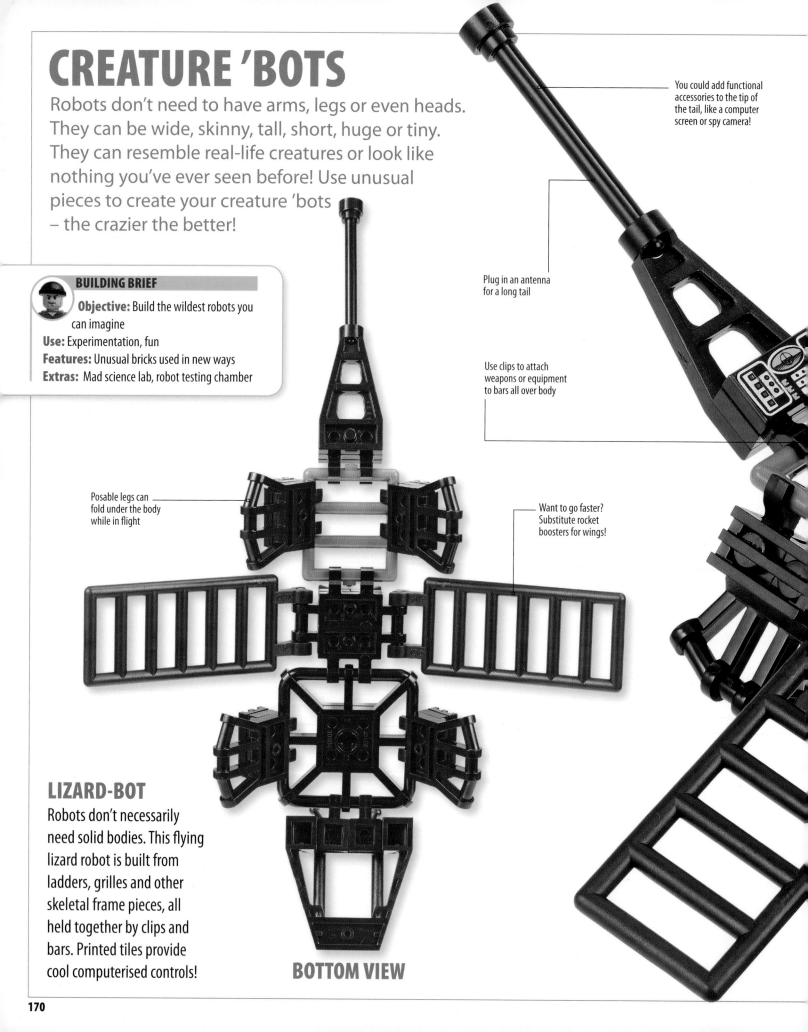

LIZARD-BOT

Robots don't necessarily need solid bodies. This flying lizard robot is built from ladders, grilles and other skeletal frame pieces, all held together by clips and bars. Printed tiles provide cool computerised controls!

BOTTOM VIEW

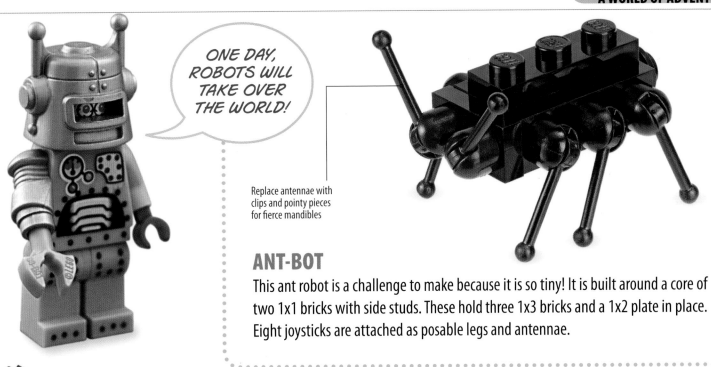

ONE DAY, ROBOTS WILL TAKE OVER THE WORLD!

Replace antennae with clips and pointy pieces for fierce mandibles

ANT-BOT

This ant robot is a challenge to make because it is so tiny! It is built around a core of two 1x1 bricks with side studs. These hold three 1x3 bricks and a 1x2 plate in place. Eight joysticks are attached as posable legs and antennae.

You could add a seat so a minifigure can fly on the lizard-bot

Head made from cockpit roll cage

REAL-WORLD ROBOTS

Robots aren't only from science fiction. They're all around us in the world today – assembling cars, working with dangerous objects, exploring the depths of the ocean and outer space and performing all kinds of other tasks that human beings can't safely do. When building a real-world robot, think about its function and what kind of design and tools it needs to do its work!

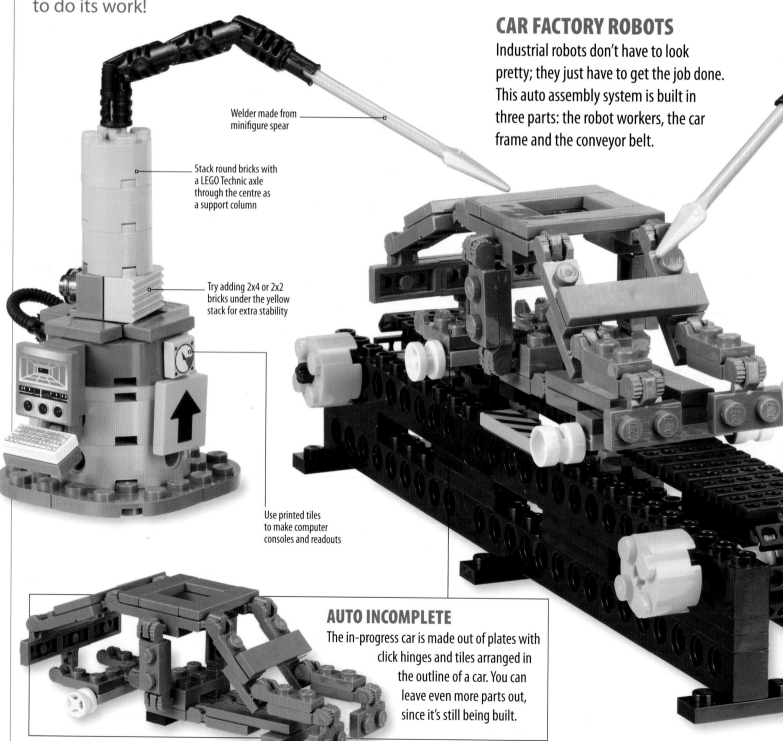

Welder made from minifigure spear

Stack round bricks with a LEGO Technic axle through the centre as a support column

Try adding 2x4 or 2x2 bricks under the yellow stack for extra stability

Use printed tiles to make computer consoles and readouts

CAR FACTORY ROBOTS

Industrial robots don't have to look pretty; they just have to get the job done. This auto assembly system is built in three parts: the robot workers, the car frame and the conveyor belt.

AUTO INCOMPLETE

The in-progress car is made out of plates with click hinges and tiles arranged in the outline of a car. You can leave even more parts out, since it's still being built.

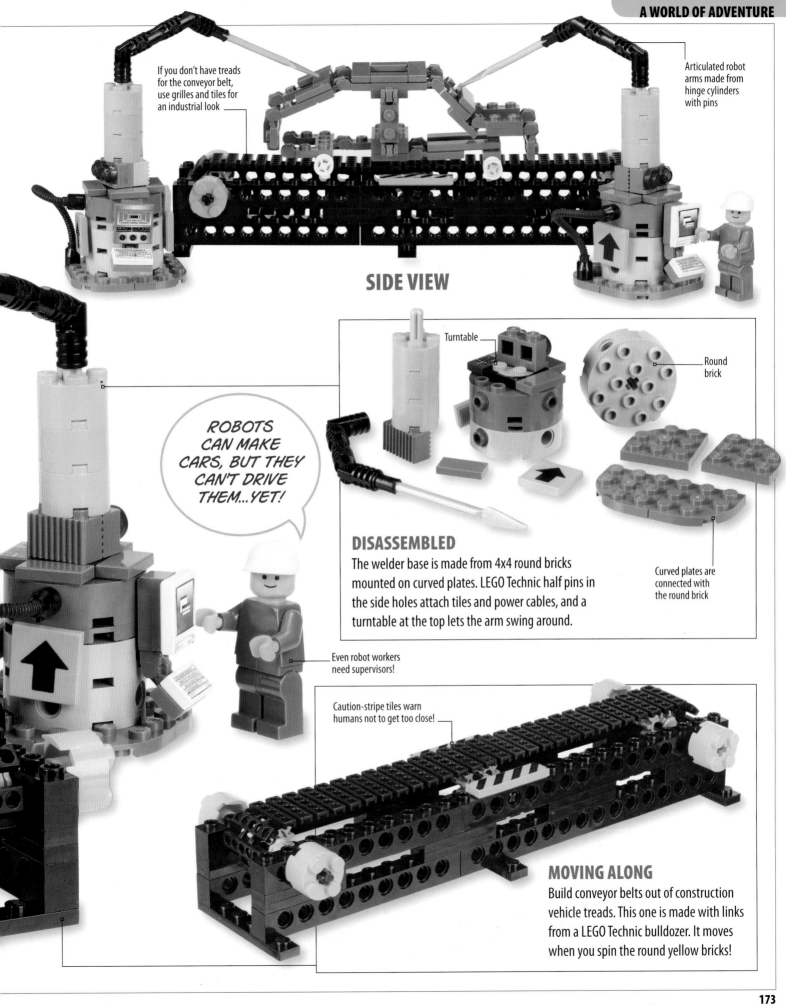

If you don't have treads for the conveyor belt, use grilles and tiles for an industrial look

Articulated robot arms made from hinge cylinders with pins

SIDE VIEW

Turntable

Round brick

ROBOTS CAN MAKE CARS, BUT THEY CAN'T DRIVE THEM...YET!

DISASSEMBLED

The welder base is made from 4x4 round bricks mounted on curved plates. LEGO Technic half pins in the side holes attach tiles and power cables, and a turntable at the top lets the arm swing around.

Curved plates are connected with the round brick

Even robot workers need supervisors!

Caution-stripe tiles warn humans not to get too close!

MOVING ALONG

Build conveyor belts out of construction vehicle treads. This one is made with links from a LEGO Technic bulldozer. It moves when you spin the round yellow bricks!

MEET THE BUILDER

DUNCAN TITMARSH

Location: UK
Age: 40
LEGO Speciality: Mosaics

What is the biggest or most complex model you've made?

I made a large version of LEGO set #375. It was the first castle the LEGO Group ever made and was in yellow. To make it bigger I built all the bricks six times bigger – some were easy but there were a few more difficult bricks to make, such as the hinges. I was then able to assemble the set from the original instructions and make a very large castle.

My wife likes the artist Banksy's pictures, so I built this LEGO mosaic version of it for her. It hangs in our hallway at home.

This is another of my mosaics. I wanted to see what a flower would look like so I picked a daisy and built it using 9,216 1x1 plates.

How much time do you spend building?

Every day. I have turned my hobby into a job and I am one of only 13 LEGO® Certified Professionals in the world. I build larger-than-life creations for companies who want to promote their products. I also build family pictures from 1x1 plates to form LEGO mosaics.

I THINK I HAVE IN THE REGION OF 1,000,000 BRICKS!

What is your favourite LEGO brick or piece?

The 1x2 brick is my favourite brick because you can use it to build big walls. You don't even need any 1x1 bricks as you can turn the 1x2 on its side to fill the gap. When building with these it gives a great looking brick wall effect. If you want to make a curved wall, add some round 1x1 bricks between the 1x2 bricks.

What is your favourite creation?

I made a mosaic of one of the pieces of wall art by the artist Banksy. It took a couple of days to do but I think it looks great.

What are some of your top LEGO tips?

I always use a brick separator as it's made for the job and you don't break your fingernails or damage the bricks. If I have a LEGO Technic pin stuck in a beam, I use an axle to push from the other side.

What things have gone wrong and how have you dealt with them?

You can be working close up on a model and it seems alright, but when you stand back it's not quite right or you have missed some detail that could look better. The only thing to do is to take some of the model apart and rebuild it. You always feel better in the end, even though it takes longer.

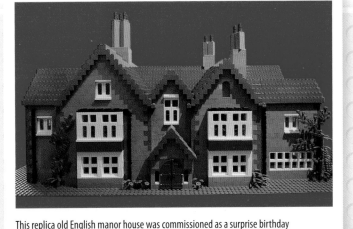

This replica old English manor house was commissioned as a surprise birthday present. Using only photographs for reference, it took me less than a day to build. The actual house is in Surrey, England.

The LEGO Group make specific boat hull pieces, but not everyone has them in their collection. I wanted to show you can make a boat just from regular bricks and this is my small pirate ship. I have added a gang plank and a pirate with a telescope. I made the skull and crossbones from new LEGO bone pieces

What are you inspired by?

I really enjoy building items that people see and use. The London underground map is a good example. I was on the Tube and the idea came to me, then I worked out what LEGO colours to use and it grew from there.

Do you plan out your build? If so, how?

I plan some builds using graph paper. I draw the outline of the model first then draw a square around it. This helps as a starting point for the shape of the model.

Which model were you most proud of as a young LEGO builder?

I built a town and the aim was to use all the LEGO bricks I had. I had lots of wheels so rather than build lots of cars I built a shop that sold wheels. This build helped me be creative with the bricks I had at the time.

How many LEGO bricks do you have?

I have not counted them all, but I think I have in the region of 1,000,000 bricks!

I was commissioned to make a model of the famous Bullring shopping centre in Birmingham, UK. This was the first section I built.

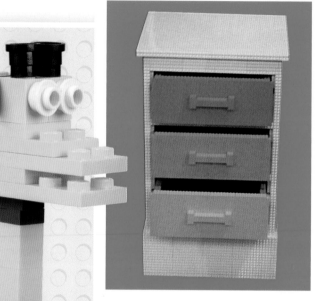

I wanted to build some furniture that actually worked. I built this chest of drawers for my daughter and it now stands proudly in her bedroom.

When building from real life you need to think of the key features to make your model recognisable. In this case, it's the giraffe's markings and long neck!

If you had all the LEGO bricks (and time!) in the world, what would you build?

If I had that much time I would really like to build a full-size town with all the shops and cars in it. I don't think it would be very practical, but it would be good fun to build!

What is your favourite LEGO technique or technique you use the most?

Using the bricks with side studs, which come as 1x4 and 1x1 bricks. The side-on build allows you to give a lot more detail to a model. For example, you can add lettering to the side of a building without having to build it in the wall by building the detail on a plate and then attaching it to the side studs.

How old were you when you started using LEGO bricks?

I was about four years old when I had my first LEGO set, but I was about 34 when I started building really big creations. Later, I met with some other fans of LEGO and the models got bigger and better!

What else do you enjoy making apart from adventure themes?

I really enjoy making pictures: it's like drawing but with bricks. Also, if you go wrong it is easy to change. My daughter likes to do them as well so it allows us to spend time together.

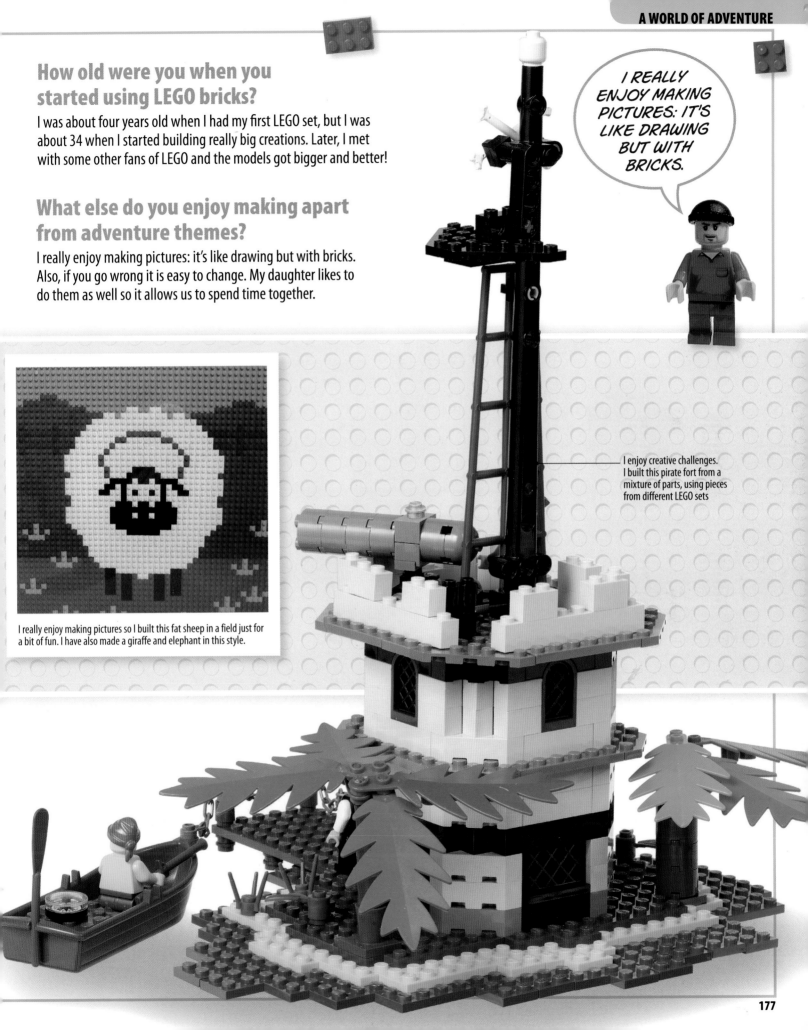

I REALLY ENJOY MAKING PICTURES: IT'S LIKE DRAWING BUT WITH BRICKS.

I really enjoy making pictures so I built this fat sheep in a field just for a bit of fun. I have also made a giraffe and elephant in this style.

I enjoy creative challenges. I built this pirate fort from a mixture of parts, using pieces from different LEGO sets

MAKE & KEEP

Here's an idea! Why don't you create some models that are so useful you won't ever want to break them up? LEGO® board games, pictures and small household items not only look great, they can have practical functions too.

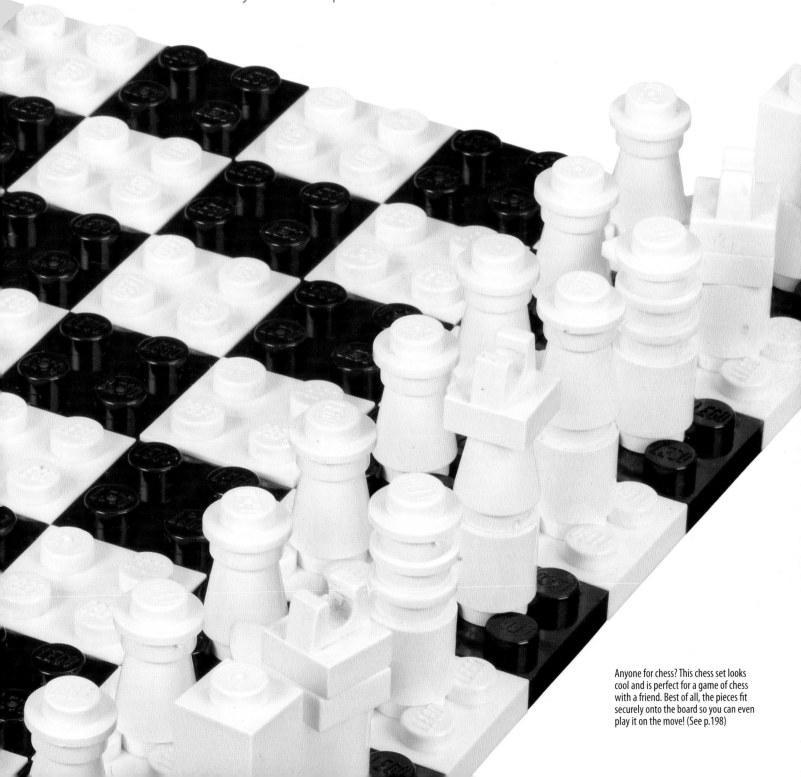

Anyone for chess? This chess set looks cool and is perfect for a game of chess with a friend. Best of all, the pieces fit securely onto the board so you can even play it on the move! (See p.198)

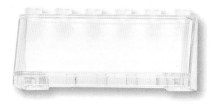

2x6x2 WINDSCREEN

1x2 BRICK

1x2x2 BRICK

2x2x3 BRICK

2x2x3 SLOPE

USEFUL PIECES

When building practical models, stability is key. Use lots of square or rectangular bricks to build a solid base before adding fancy and decorative pieces. To make your models exciting, build them up with different types of pieces, including bricks, plates, slopes, dishes, arches and cones. Here are some useful pieces to keep in your tool kit!

1x2 SLOPE

1x2x3 SLOPE

1x6 TILE

1x2 BRICK

1x2 PLATE WITH HANDLED BAR

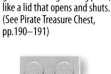

1x2 PLATE WITH BAR

1x6 PLATE

2x8 PLATE

1x6 BRICK

1x4 BRICK

1x1 BRICK

1x1 BRICK

HINGES
Clip and bar plates are an easy way to build a hinge. Hinges are great for adding moving parts, like a lid that opens and shuts. (See Pirate Treasure Chest, pp.190–191)

2x2 PLATE

1x2 TILE

1x2 TEXTURED BRICK

COOL COLOURS
Choose your colours carefully. Do you want your model to match something in your house or room?

2x3 BRICK

2x2 CURVED BRICK

2x2 BRICK

2x2 INVERTED SLOPE

2x4 ANGLED PLATE

2x4 DOUBLE ANGLED PLATE

4x4 CURVED PLATE

2x2 FLOWER

2x2 FLOWER

1x1 ROUND BRICK

1x1 PLATE WITH VERTICAL CLIP

1x1 TOOTH PLATE

1x1 HEADLIGHT BRICK

2x2 CURVED BRICK

BAMBOO PLANT

1x1 ROUND PLATE

1x1 SLOPE

1x1 CONE

1x1 TOOTH PLATE

CLEAN CURVES
Curved pieces will help build models with rounded edges.

1x3x2 HALF ARCH

1x2 CURVED HALF ARCH

VEGETATION DECORATION
Small pieces, such as flowers, plants or transparent plates, can decorate simple builds like a picture frame. (See Flower Power, p.193)

LEGO® TECHNIC T-BAR

THINK ABOUT WHAT YOU WANT TO MAKE, SELECT YOUR BRICKS AND GET BUILDING!

1x3x2 CURVED HALF ARCH

2x2 ANGLED CORNER BRICK

SMALL PLANT LEAVES

2x2 ROUND BRICK

1x3 CAR DOOR

2x2 BRICK WITH WHEEL ARCH

2x2 ROUND PLATE

2x2 RADAR DISH

WIDE RIM, WIDE TYRE AND 2x2 AXLE PLATE WITH 1 PIN

2x2 ROUND BRICK

LEGO TECHNIC CROSS AXLE 4

1x2 HINGED BRICK AND 2x2 HINGED PLATE

SPECIAL PIECES
If you have an unusual piece in your collection, invent a model to include it in! This white girder (below) works well in a space-age display stand. (See Space Station Display, p.187)

2x2 DOMED BRICK

CONNECTING PIECES
Pieces that have holes and extra studs are a great way to connect different sections of your model together – and provide places to attach decorative pieces.

4x4 ROUND PLATE

1x6 CURVED BAR WITH STUDS

4x4x2 CONE

1x6x5 GIRDER

DESK TIDIES

Sort out your stationery with a LEGO desk tidy! Before you start, think about what you want to keep in your desk tidy: Pens, rulers, erasers? Do you need drawers? How big should it be? A desk tidy should be practical and sturdy, but it can also brighten up a workspace, so add decoration in your favourite theme or colour scheme!

CASTLE DESK TIDY

This cool desk tidy has boxes for your pens and pencils, a drawer for smaller stationery – and it looks like a miniature castle! Start with the drawer and make sure it is big enough to fit whatever you want to store inside.

STEP-BY-STEP
After you've built the drawer, make a box that fits neatly around it. Once the box is high enough to cover the drawer, top it off with some plates, adding decoration and open boxes.

Layer plates, bricks and tiles to build the drawer and the box it fits into

Need even more room for your stationery collection? Build boxes in various widths and heights

Simple, square open-topped boxes hold pencils and pens

Decorate your desk tidy with plates in contrasting colours

FRONT VIEW

Grey, white and black bricks are good for a castle theme, but you can use any colours you want!

You could use a large plate to build the base of the drawer, but several small plates work if you reinforce them

Build a plate with handled bar into the drawer front so you can open it

SEA MONSTER

Scare away stationery stealers with a sea monster desk tidy! Begin with a basic box shape, build in dividers, then add the features that make a monster of the deep. Can you think of other creatures that could keep your stationery safe? Have a go at making those too!

To make your sea monster even more frightening, add horns or fangs!

FRONT VIEW

A high, pointed tail can support bigger pens

Exposed studs on bricks create a scaly effect

Eyes made from 1x1 round plates inserted into headlight bricks

A red mouth adds detail and looks pretty scary!

BRING ME A NET TO CATCH THAT SEA MONSTER! THOSE PENS WILL BE MINE!

Dividers can keep different kinds of stationery separate

Sea monsters are mythical creatures, so no one really knows what they look like. What colour and shape will yours be?

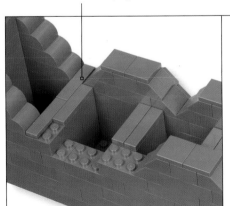

SEA SLOPES

The sea monster's humped body and pointed tail get their smooth shape from slopes topped with tiles. You could also create humps by stacking bricks in stepped layers.

4x4 slope

Curved bricks make a long, sloping neck

REAR SIDE VIEW

TRUCK TIDY

Your desk tidy can look like anything you like. Why not take inspiration from everyday objects as with this colourful truck? It can deliver a truckload of stationery straight to your desk! What are your favourite things? What kind of shapes would make a good desk tidy? Try building one based on a car, an animal or a spaceship. Go ahead – it's your workspace!

Add lots of contrasting colours to brighten up your workspace!

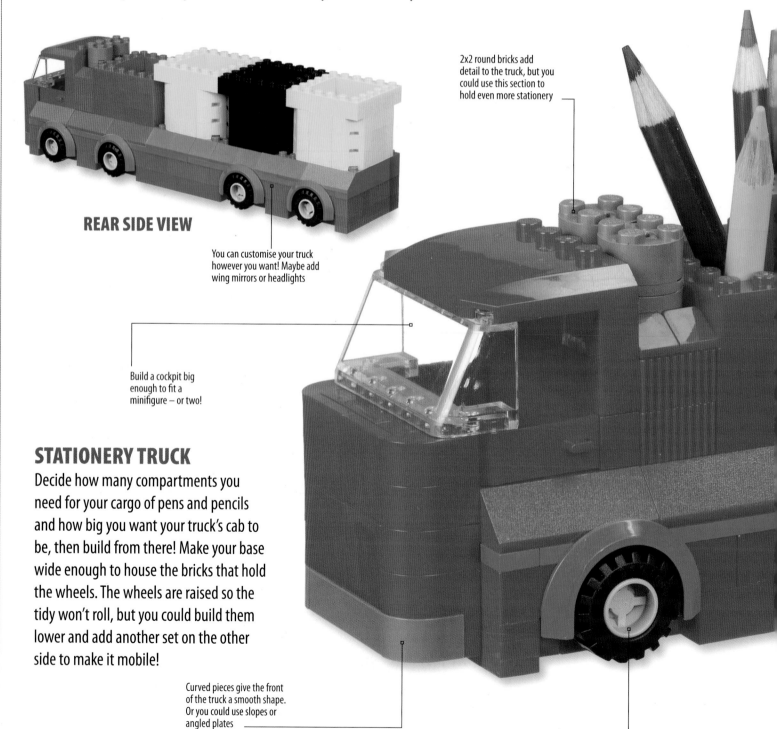

REAR SIDE VIEW

2x2 round bricks add detail to the truck, but you could use this section to hold even more stationery

You can customise your truck however you want! Maybe add wing mirrors or headlights

Build a cockpit big enough to fit a minifigure – or two!

STATIONERY TRUCK

Decide how many compartments you need for your cargo of pens and pencils and how big you want your truck's cab to be, then build from there! Make your base wide enough to house the bricks that hold the wheels. The wheels are raised so the tidy won't roll, but you could build them lower and add another set on the other side to make it mobile!

Curved pieces give the front of the truck a smooth shape. Or you could use slopes or angled plates

2x2 wheels fit into 2x2 bricks with wheel arches

SIDE VIEW

A brick separator could come in handy when you're building your desk tidy!

Compartments can be varying sizes, depending on what you want to store in them

HANG ON... IF I'M IN HERE, WHO'S DRIVING THIS THING?!

Large buckets look like a real truck's cargo!

Try using curved bricks instead of angular bricks to give your compartments a different look

This side sticks out from the cab so it can accommodate the wheels

TOP VIEW

MINIFIGURE DISPLAY

Be proud of your minifigures! Show off your building skills by making a display stand to house your growing collection. You can add to your stand every time you get a new minifigure. You can even build stands in different styles to display minifigures from different LEGO themes!

BUILDING BRIEF

Objective: Build display stands
Use: Storage, decoration
Features: Sturdy enough to hold minifigures
Extras: Doors, moving parts

DISPLAY STAND

You can make a display stand with simple bricks and plates. Build a basic structure that is stable and balanced. Then use special or interesting bricks to add detail. Choose exciting colours, or maybe use a colour that matches your bedroom. It's up to you!

REAR VIEW

NEW HEIGHTS

A height of five bricks is tall enough to fit most minifigures nicely, but if yours has a large hat or helmet you may need to make the level higher.

You will know straight away if one of your figures is missing!

A mix of minifigures makes your display stand interesting to look at

Use pieces like curved half arches if you have them

Unusual shapes built with half arches. Inverted slopes would work too

Use plates, not tiles, so your figures can't fall off

Headlight bricks could hold tiles that correspond to minifigures

NOW'S MY CHANCE TO MAKE A RUN FOR IT!

Accessorise to match the theme of your stand. Add antennas, or some droids!

SPACE STATION DISPLAY

This space station stand is out of this world! White girders make this display stand look like something from outer space. If you decide to use fun and unusual bricks for your walls, make sure they're tall enough to house your minifigures!

Build the stand as wide as you need to contain all your minifigures

If you don't have a big enough plate, overlap smaller plates to whatever size you want

You could give your minifigures a control panel or an escape pod!

5...4...3...2...1... BLAST OFF! WHOA, WAIT FOR ME!

Girders come in a few LEGO® Town sets. Use any specialised bricks you have that fit your theme

REAR VIEW

WORK IT OUT

How many minifigures do you want to display in your stand? Once you know, build each layer accordingly using pieces that fit your theme. These white girders look really space-age.

Choose colours to match your theme. For an underwater theme, use blue and green. What else can you think of?

If you don't have these pieces, try building with transparent bricks like windows – they look great as part of a space theme!

BOXES

Are your LEGO pieces all over the place? Pencils scattered over your desk? These boxes are the answer. Think about what you will put in your box and how big it should be. It will need to be strong and stable to hold all your treasures. Choose a simple colour scheme and design – or just go crazy with your imagination. Don't feel boxed in!

BUILDING BRIEF

Objective: Make boxes to store your belongings
Use: Workspace organisation
Features: Hinges, drawers
Extras: Handles, dividers, secret drawers

FRONT SIDE VIEW

SHINY BOX

This box will brighten up any desk – and make it tidy too! The bottom is made of large plates, and the sides are built up with interlocking bricks and topped with tiles for a smooth finish. The lid is built as a wall that is slightly larger than the top of the box.

A row of shiny tiles finishes off the box lid

Choose your favourite colours for your box

You could increase the height of your box so you have more room inside

NOT SURE THESE COLOURS ARE THE BEST FOR A GOOD NIGHT'S SLEEP!

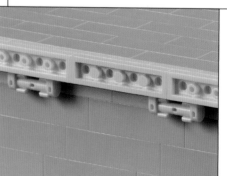

JOINTS THAT JOIN

The hinges are made from pairs of plates with bars and plates with horizontal clips. They are held in place by a row of tiles on top. To increase stability so you can use the box for longer, add more hinges.

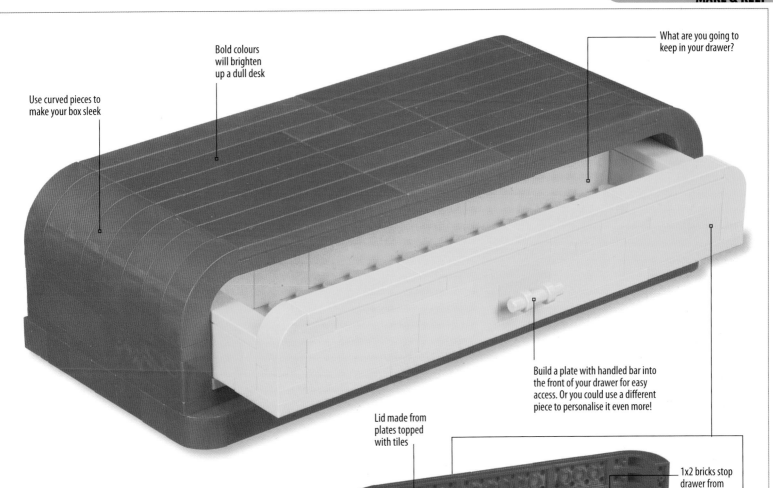

Use curved pieces to make your box sleek

Bold colours will brighten up a dull desk

What are you going to keep in your drawer?

Build a plate with handled bar into the front of your drawer for easy access. Or you could use a different piece to personalise it even more!

Lid made from plates topped with tiles

1x2 bricks stop drawer from sliding in too far

Layer of tiles

COOL CURVES

Boxes don't need to be boxy – they can be curvy too! Use curved pieces to create your desired shape. Make the drawer first, then build the box around it. Finally, create a base as a wall turned on its side. Use bricks with side studs to attach the base to the box.

Curved half arch

FRONT VIEW

SLIDING DRAWERS

To help the drawer slide easily, fix some tiles to the base of the box. These will create a smooth layer so the drawer won't catch on the studs as it slides in and out.

TREASURE CHEST

You can make boxes in all shapes and sizes – and to match any theme you like! Maybe you want a medieval wooden trunk with big metal locks to store your knight minifigures. Or a hi-tech, zero-gravity space capsule for your astronauts and aliens. Use different colours to style your box, and remember, the lid doesn't have to be flat!

BUILDING BRIEF

Objective: Create fantasy boxes
Use: Storage, play
Features: Hinged lid, drawers
Extras: Secret compartments, decorations

PIRATE TREASURE CHEST

This treasure chest has a secret drawer at the bottom for hiding your most precious LEGO pieces (or any other treasures)! First, the lower half is built around the sliding drawer. Then the top half is constructed on top of that, with a hinged lid, built sideways. The more hinges you use, the more stable the lid will be!

A layer of plates divides the secret drawer from the chest above it

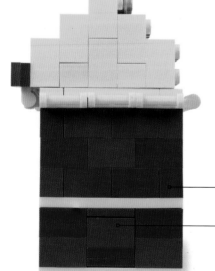

Overlap bricks for stability

Press on this secret brick and the drawer will slide out the other side!

Use different colours to theme your box – brown and yellow look like a pirate's treasure chest

SIDE VIEW

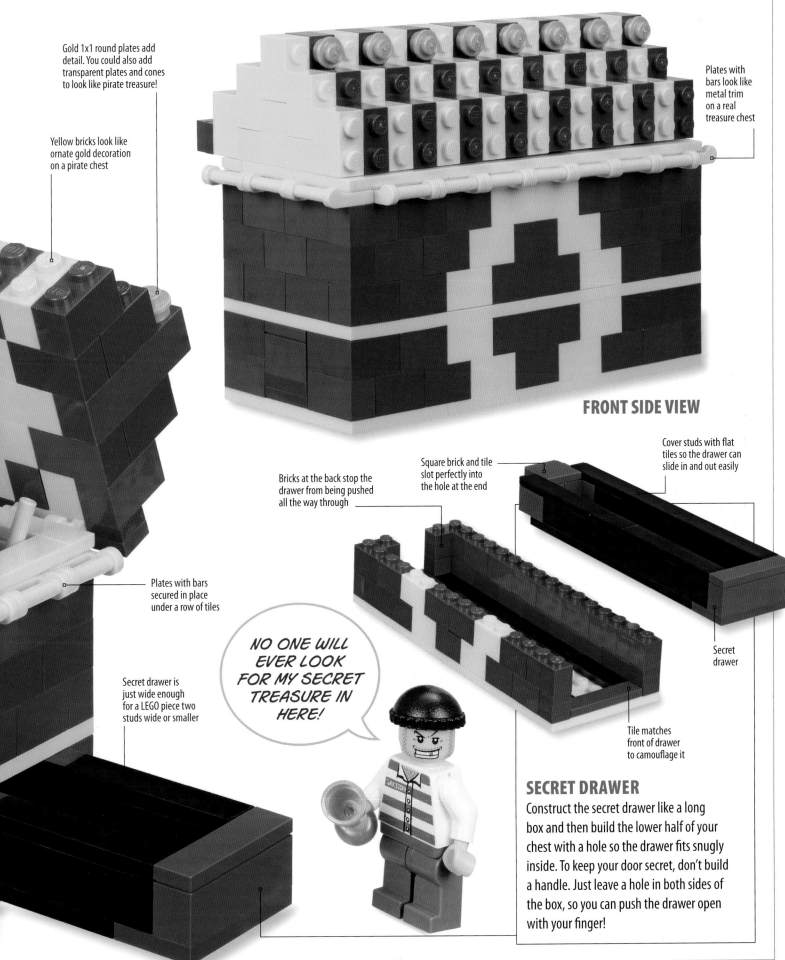

Gold 1x1 round plates add detail. You could also add transparent plates and cones to look like pirate treasure!

Plates with bars look like metal trim on a real treasure chest

Yellow bricks look like ornate gold decoration on a pirate chest

FRONT SIDE VIEW

Plates with bars secured in place under a row of tiles

Bricks at the back stop the drawer from being pushed all the way through

Square brick and tile slot perfectly into the hole at the end

Cover studs with flat tiles so the drawer can slide in and out easily

Secret drawer

NO ONE WILL EVER LOOK FOR MY SECRET TREASURE IN HERE!

Secret drawer is just wide enough for a LEGO piece two studs wide or smaller

Tile matches front of drawer to camouflage it

SECRET DRAWER
Construct the secret drawer like a long box and then build the lower half of your chest with a hole so the drawer fits snugly inside. To keep your door secret, don't build a handle. Just leave a hole in both sides of the box, so you can push the drawer open with your finger!

PICTURE FRAMES

Say "cheese"! How about building something to display your special pictures? You can use photos of your favourite LEGO models or treasured pictures of family and friends. Once you have a basic frame you can decorate it any way you want. You can even change the theme of your frame whenever you change the photo!

BUILDING BRIEF
Objective: Make frames for pictures
Use: Display your favourite pictures
Features: Sturdy frame, ability to stand
Extras: Multi-frames, themed frames, different shaped frames

BASIC FRAME

If you want your photo to be the main attraction, keep the frame simple. Use interlocking rows of plates to make two identical rectangles. A middle layer of one-stud-wide plates holds the two rectangles together and creates a gap to slide the photo in.

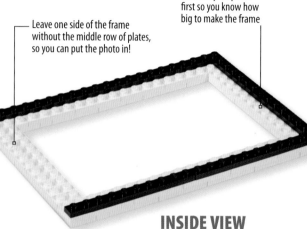

Measure your photo first so you know how big to make the frame

Leave one side of the frame without the middle row of plates, so you can put the photo in!

INSIDE VIEW

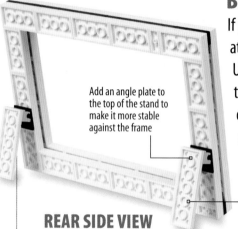

Add an angle plate to the top of the stand to make it more stable against the frame

Use a plate and a clip and bar hinge to build a stand

REAR SIDE VIEW

You could alternate the colours of the plates for a cool effect

SIDE VIEWS

I SURE MISS THE GANG FROM THE OLD NEIGHBOURHOOD!

FLOWER POWER

Now that you have the basic frame, you can get creative! Do you like flowers? Make them into a pattern to frame your pretty picture. You could also add some foliage or even a microbutterfly. Putting pieces at different angles creates an interesting pattern and helps fit more pieces on.

Use pieces that match your chosen theme

These radar dishes and transparent plates look really space-age

Use pretty flowers in your favourite colours

SPACE AGE

Why not decorate your frame to match your picture? This space frame has lots of translucent pieces and even a spaceman minifigure! To make the frame fit a portrait photo, simply move the position of the stands at the back of the frame.

Clip minifigures to bricks with side studs to add them to your frame!

Make extra pieces stick out to change the frame shape

Think of other pieces that would add to the jungle theme. Maybe a rope bridge or a mini waterfall?

JUNGLE FEVER

Add different coloured bricks to your frame to match your theme. Use brown pieces for a jungle theme and add lots of green foliage. You could even add animal figures. Go wild!

MOSAICS

Mosaics are the art of making pictures or patterns from small pieces of material, such as glass, stone...or LEGO bricks! First, plan how you want your mosaic to look. Will it lie flat or stand upright? Will it let through light? Will it be 3-D? You will have your own LEGO art gallery in no time!

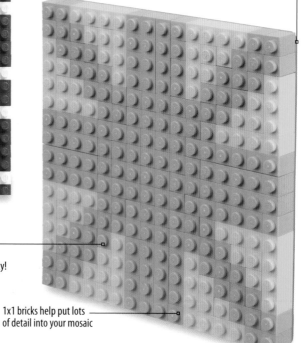

BASEPLATE

A 16x16 baseplate supports these flag mosaics, but you can build your mosaic on any size base you like! You could also attach several plates together if you don't have the right size.

BUILDING BRIEF

Objective: Make mosaics

Use: Decoration, gifts

Features: Must be stable, especially if it stands upright

Extras: 3-D effect, recreate famous artworks, stands, frames

FUN FLAGS

Get patriotic and make your country's flag into a LEGO mosaic! These Union Jack designs are made from 1x1 bricks, with a few wider bricks where larger blocks of colour appear.

Use wider bricks for less detailed flags – it will save you some time!

Your flag doesn't have to be in the traditional colours – go colour crazy!

1x1 bricks help put lots of detail into your mosaic

1x1 and 1x2 bricks are stacked like a wall to make this simple design

FLOWER ART

Say it with LEGO flowers! This flower mosaic stands upright to look like two flowers growing against a clear blue sky. Tall slopes form a stable base to hold the mosaic up.

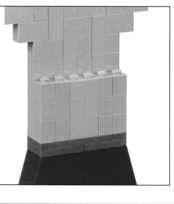

WIDER BASE

Toward the bottom of the mosaic, an extra layer of bricks is built into the design to provide extra support for the base. The ledge is only visible on the back.

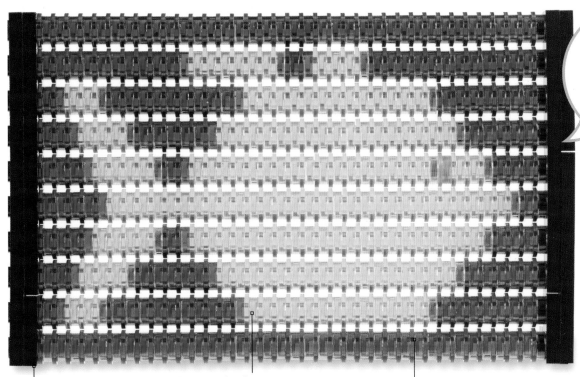

> *I KEEP SWIMMING, BUT I JUST CAN'T SEEM TO GET PAST THESE END PLATES!*

MARINE MOSAIC

This mosaic is entirely made from transparent 1x1 round plates. Ten rows have been carefully planned and assembled to make a floating yellow fish! Long black plates frame the rows.

Transparent plates let light through, so the mosaic seems to glow!

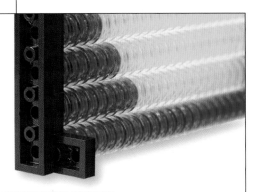

SUPPORT STAND

Add small plates at right angles to the end plate at both bottom corners. These allow the mosaic to stand up vertically, like a picture frame. If your mosaic is smaller, it will be even more stable.

CONSTRUCTION

The design of this mosaic takes careful planning. Transparent plates are stacked according to the pattern, then the stacks are attached on their sides to the end plates.

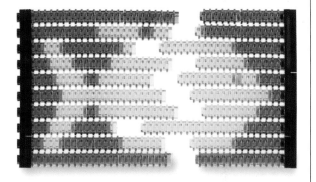

ORANGE FISH

If you don't have enough transparent round plates to make an entire mosaic, it doesn't matter. You can mix and match! This orange aquatic artwork includes white round plates too. You can include 1x1 square plates as well!

3-D MOSAICS

Mosaics don't always have to be flat. If you have bricks in different shapes and sizes, you could try adding 3-D elements to your LEGO mosaics to make them really stand out! First choose what picture you want to create, then decide which features will work best in 3-D. What do you want to draw the most attention to?

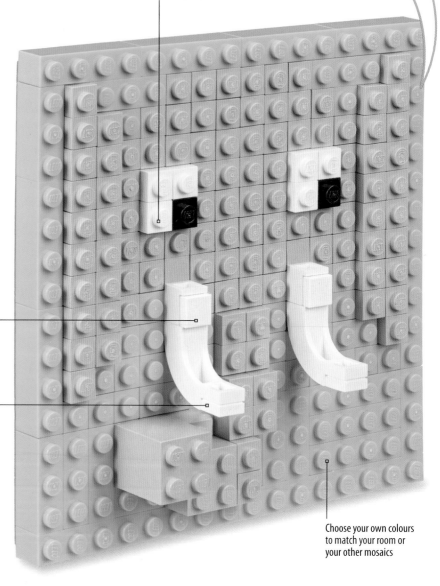

DID YOU REALLY HAVE TO DRAW EVEN MORE ATTENTION TO MY EARS?

Layer bricks at different heights to add perspective

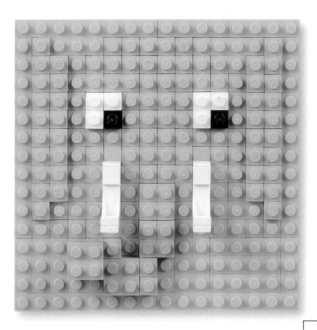

FRONT VIEW

White 1x1 tile covers the exposed stud on headlight brick

Choose your own colours to match your room or your other mosaics

TUSK TASK

The elephant's protruding tusks really bring the mosaic to life! They are made from curved half arches, which attach to the green background with white headlight bricks.

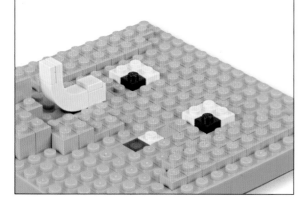

ELEPHANT

What is your favourite animal? Try making its likeness in 3-D! A 16x16 plate forms the base of this mosaic. The baseplate is completely covered in bricks, which form a green background and a basic grey elephant head shape. More bricks and plates are added to make the 3-D features.

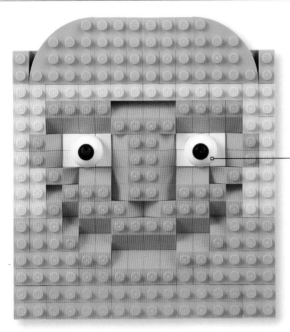

FRONT VIEW

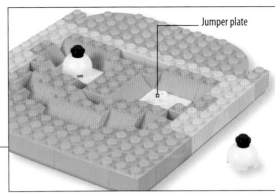

Jumper plate

EYE-POPPING

You don't have to stick to square bricks for your mosaics! Here, the eyes are made from domed bricks and black round plates. The domed bricks attach to white jumper plates.

FUNNY FACE

Don't restrict yourself to square bricks! Think about how you can form 3-D details with all different kinds of pieces. This girl's facial features are almost entirely formed from pink slopes! Used this way, the pieces create a cool, crazy-looking mosaic style.

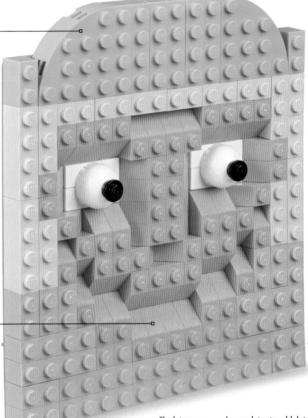

Curved plates form the rounded sides of the girl's green hat

Arrange opposite-facing slopes to make smiling lips

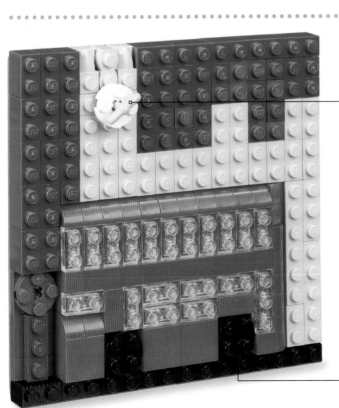

Big Ben's hands are a T-bar

CITYSCAPE

Lots of unusual bricks are used in this London cityscape. The clock tower, tree and red bus are all built using a variety of bricks. How inventive can you be?

Wheels are round plates

Clock tower built with tooth plates

Layer plates to add detail, like the transparent windows on this red bus

FRONT VIEW

197

CLASSIC BOARD GAMES

Classic board games can provide hours of fun. LEGO board games are no different – and they are ideal for long journeys because the pieces stay in place! All you need is a simple base and some game pieces. Don't know the rules? Ask your family or look online. You can even adapt the game to suit your favourite theme.

FINALLY, IT'S MY CHANCE TO CAPTURE THE KING!

CHESS

A 16x16 base is a good size for lots of board games, including chess. If you don't have a baseplate, build one with overlapping plates to create a square. Then add eight rows of eight 2x2 plates in alternate colours to create a chessboard.

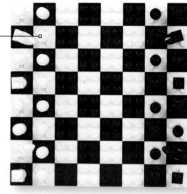

Each side has eight pawns, two knights, two rooks, two bishops, one king and one queen

TOP VIEW

A standard chessboard has black and white squares, but you can use any colours you want!

1x1 plate with vertical clip

Tooth plate for a horse's nose

CHECKMATE!

The chess pieces – pawns, knights, rooks, bishops, queens and kings – should be easy to distinguish. Will your queen have a big crown? Maybe your knight will have shining armour? Make sure the pieces are sturdy because they will be moved around a lot.

Pawn

Bishop

Knight

King

Queen

Rook

Pawn

Bishop

Knight

King

Queen

Rook

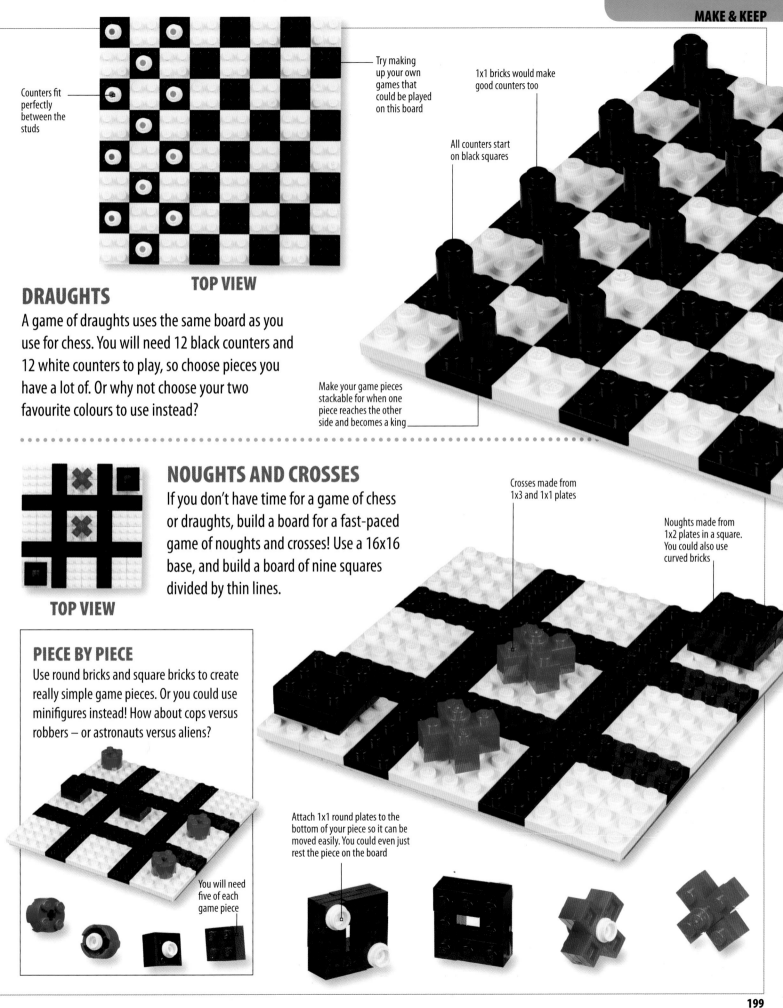

Counters fit perfectly between the studs

Try making up your own games that could be played on this board

1x1 bricks would make good counters too

All counters start on black squares

DRAUGHTS

A game of draughts uses the same board as you use for chess. You will need 12 black counters and 12 white counters to play, so choose pieces you have a lot of. Or why not choose your two favourite colours to use instead?

Make your game pieces stackable for when one piece reaches the other side and becomes a king

TOP VIEW

NOUGHTS AND CROSSES

If you don't have time for a game of chess or draughts, build a board for a fast-paced game of noughts and crosses! Use a 16x16 base, and build a board of nine squares divided by thin lines.

TOP VIEW

Crosses made from 1x3 and 1x1 plates

Noughts made from 1x2 plates in a square. You could also use curved bricks

PIECE BY PIECE

Use round bricks and square bricks to create really simple game pieces. Or you could use minifigures instead! How about cops versus robbers – or astronauts versus aliens?

You will need five of each game piece

Attach 1x1 round plates to the bottom of your piece so it can be moved easily. You could even just rest the piece on the board

MORE BOARD GAMES

Now that you can build board games out of bricks, you and your friends will never be bored again! You can make all your favourite games, and even make up your own. Before you start building, try to organise the pieces you need. Think about how many people are going to play and what colours you want to use. You could even use your favourite minifigures as pieces.

Any small pieces can be used as game pieces. You could also use cones or minifigure heads

DID SOMEONE SAY JUDO?

TOP VIEW

LUDO

Start your Ludo board with a square base. You'll need four different colours – one for each player. Make each corner a different colour, and design a path from the corner to the middle for your pieces to follow.

You don't have to use red, yellow, blue and green. Any colours will work if you have enough bricks

Each piece follows the black and white path until they return to their coloured staircase

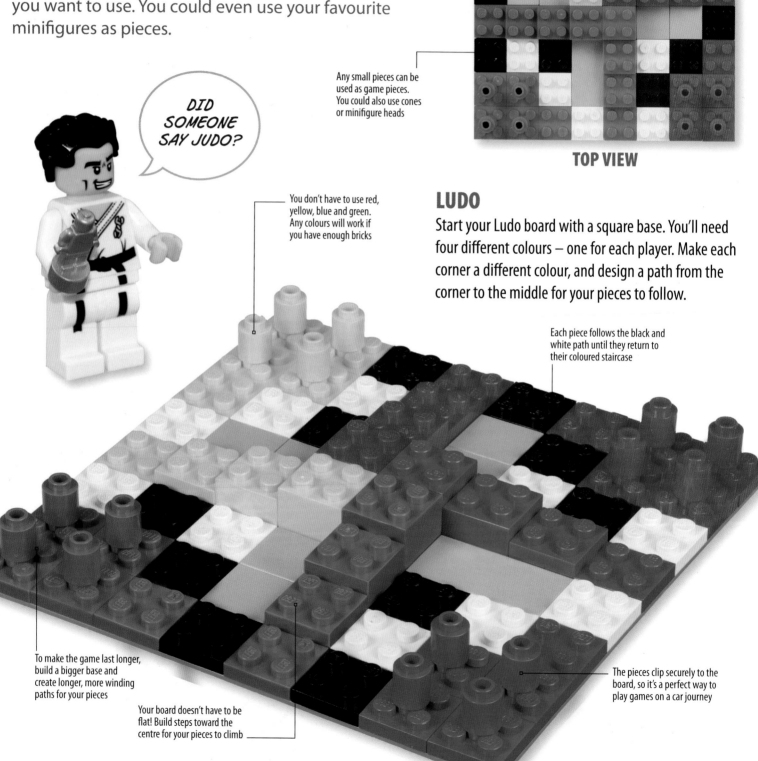

To make the game last longer, build a bigger base and create longer, more winding paths for your pieces

Your board doesn't have to be flat! Build steps toward the centre for your pieces to climb

The pieces clip securely to the board, so it's a perfect way to play games on a car journey

SUMMIT

Try making up your own game. This one's called Summit because the aim of the game is to reach the top of the mountain. Build your board like a spiralling pyramid, with a path that gets a step higher each time it goes round a corner.

COLOUR CRAZY

Choose one or two colours to use as the default board. This model uses red and white. Every so often, substitute a different colour for a square on the board to add rewards and pitfalls to the game.

The winner is the first to reach the square at the top

TOP VIEW

You could place a flag or a treasure piece at the summit

You don't have to stick to a mountain shape. How about a castle shape where the first to reach the top is crowned king or queen?

Make up your own rules. For example, if you land on a black square you miss a go and if you land on a blue square, you move forward three spaces

BUILDING REALITY

You may have built lots of fantasy models to play with, from flying saucers to pirate ships. But now it's time to face reality! Recreating everyday household items is a different challenge, since you can pick up the real thing and take a good look before planning the best way to make it. Create life-sized models or minifigure-scale objects – it's up to you!

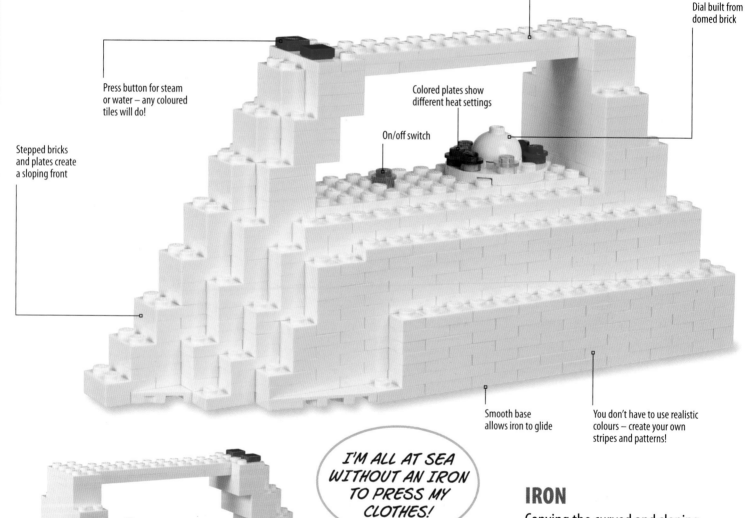

Handle must be strong enough to support the iron. The more bricks and plates you add, the more stable it will be!

Dial built from domed brick

Press button for steam or water – any coloured tiles will do!

Colored plates show different heat settings

On/off switch

Stepped bricks and plates create a sloping front

Smooth base allows iron to glide

You don't have to use realistic colours – create your own stripes and patterns!

I'M ALL AT SEA WITHOUT AN IRON TO PRESS MY CLOTHES!

REAR SIDE VIEW

IRON

Copying the curved and sloping shape of an iron with LEGO pieces is a challenge, but it can be done! Add dials, lights and buttons to bring your model to life – without the fear of burning your clothes! Just make sure any real iron is turned off and unplugged before you touch it!

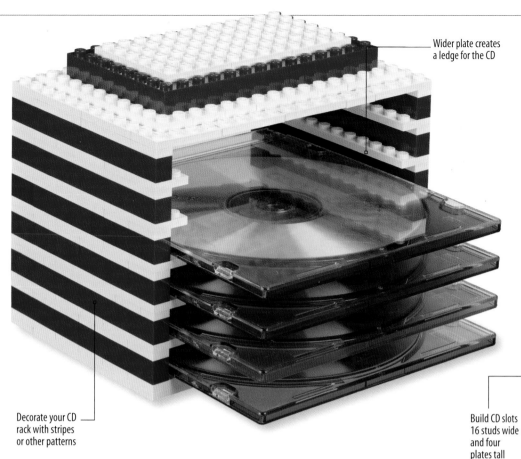

Wider plate creates
a ledge for the CD

Decorate your CD
rack with stripes
or other patterns

CD RACK

Sometimes LEGO builds are so realistic, they can function like the real thing! This CD rack is big and sturdy enough to hold your CD collection. Build two walls on opposite sides of a base, adding wider plates at regular intervals for your CDs to rest on.

Build CD slots
16 studs wide
and four
plates tall

REAR SIDE VIEW

SALT AND PEPPER

These shakers can be the beginning of your LEGO dining experience. Try and recreate what might be on a dining table, from crockery to silverware, or even a candelabra!

Holes in the bricks mean that these models
don't hold real-life salt and pepper!

Corner bricks surround
a central column of two
stacks of 1x1 bricks

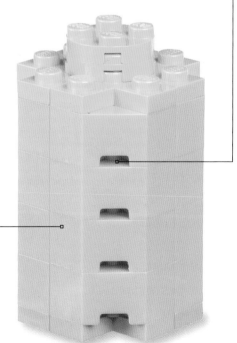

SHAKE IT UP

These salt and pepper shakers are made from angled corner bricks, but you could use curved bricks, square bricks or curved half arches to create your own!

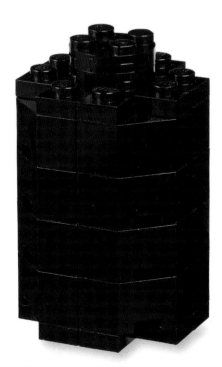

YOUR OWN DESIGNS

Now it's time to create some beautiful household objects using your own imagination! Instead of copying something directly, build a LEGO masterpiece of your own design. Use your favourite colours to build a decorative sculpture, or think up original designs for a set of coasters that you can use – for cold drinks only!

Mixing round and rectangular bricks helps create a curve

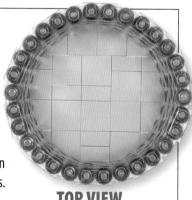

This sculpture is delicate. Can you think of a way to make it more stable?

Secure the round plates and cones with 1x2 bricks and plates

COLOURFUL SCULPTURE

Stack rows of round plates, rectangular plates, cones and bricks to make your sculpture as tall or short as you like. Choose your own colours and patterns to match the colour of the room you will display the sculpture in. You could even try building different shaped sculptures.

BACK TO BASICS

Build a circular base using plates covered with tiles. At four points around the edge, position 1x2 plates and jumper plates, to which you can attach the circular sides.

TOP VIEW

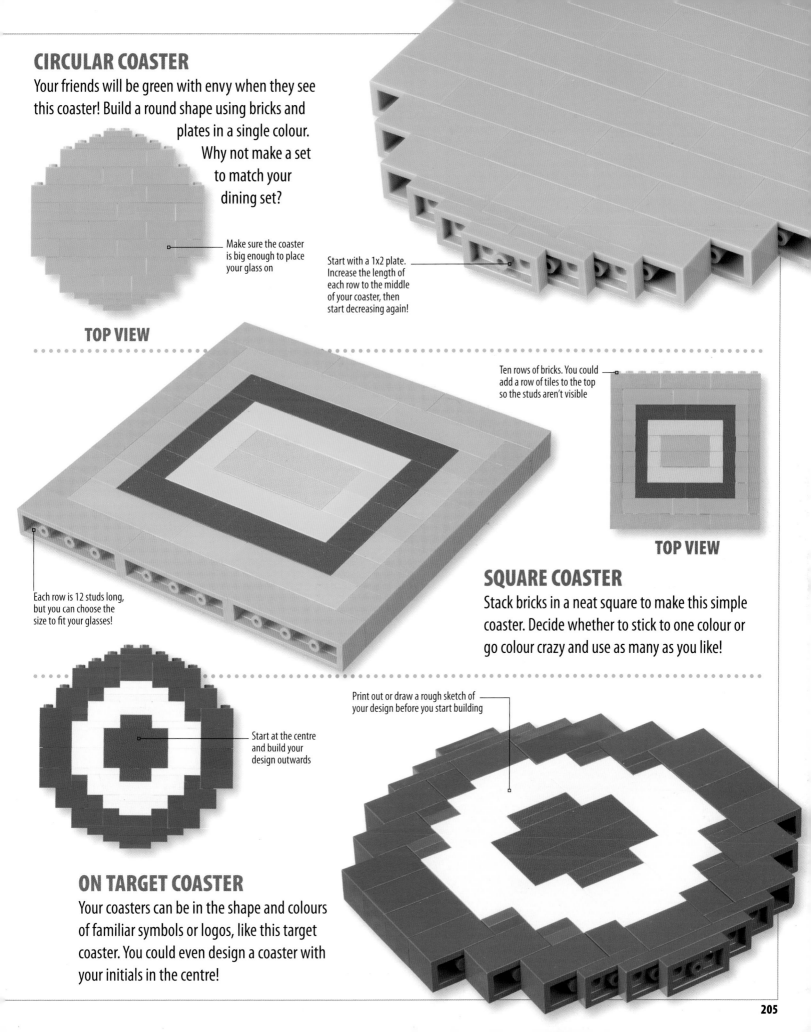

CIRCULAR COASTER

Your friends will be green with envy when they see this coaster! Build a round shape using bricks and plates in a single colour. Why not make a set to match your dining set?

Make sure the coaster is big enough to place your glass on

TOP VIEW

Start with a 1x2 plate. Increase the length of each row to the middle of your coaster, then start decreasing again!

Ten rows of bricks. You could add a row of tiles to the top so the studs aren't visible

TOP VIEW

Each row is 12 studs long, but you can choose the size to fit your glasses!

SQUARE COASTER

Stack bricks in a neat square to make this simple coaster. Decide whether to stick to one colour or go colour crazy and use as many as you like!

Start at the centre and build your design outwards

Print out or draw a rough sketch of your design before you start building

ON TARGET COASTER

Your coasters can be in the shape and colours of familiar symbols or logos, like this target coaster. You could even design a coaster with your initials in the centre!

MEET THE BUILDER

ANDREW WALKER

Location: UK
Age: 45
LEGO Speciality: City, trains and still life

How old were you when you started using LEGO bricks?

I'm pretty sure I always had LEGO bricks to play with. I think they must have belonged to my older sisters and brothers. We kept them in an old baby bath, and I remember always rummaging around in it looking for the parts I needed to build. However, when I was 13 my brother sold all the family LEGO pieces so I was without it for many years. I have only started building again in the last five years.

This market stall sells LEGO pets. The little boy seems happy with his new pet snake!

This is a model of Stephenson's Rocket, one of the first steam trains. The most difficult part of the building process was mounting the barrel and getting the piston to work.

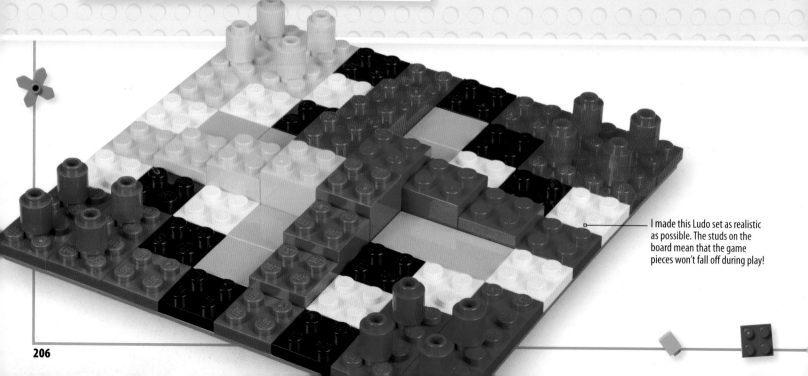

I made this Ludo set as realistic as possible. The studs on the board mean that the game pieces won't fall off during play!

What are you inspired by?

I'm inspired most often by recreating memories, whether it's a train I've ridden on or a cinema I used to visit when I was young. I also enjoy recreating scenes and models from films.

What is the biggest or most complex model you've made?

One of the great things about LEGO bricks is that you can build together: I recently worked with five other LEGO enthusiasts at a model railway exhibition to build a train layout 19ft 8in (6m) wide and 6ft 6in (2m) deep. We all brought our small individual models to build a lively and exciting town and railway. It looked great and all the visitors enjoyed our collaboration.

What things have gone wrong and how have you dealt with them?

I have often built the body of a train only to find out that when I put the wheels on it won't go round the track or connect to any of the carriages or wagons! If you build your train too long it will overhang and hit everything else as it goes round the corner, so you need to be aware of the size and shape of your track. The wheels on trains are also important – if attached in the wrong place the train will not be able to travel around the track. To avoid this, always start with the wheels and base of your model. Check how it goes around the track and connects to the rest of your rolling stock, and then build the body of your model.

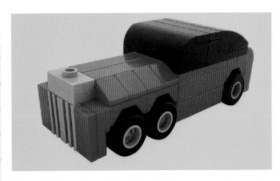

This model of a classic car takes us into the future of personal transport. It has a distinctive classic long nose and front grille, and I've added six wheels, a bulbous cabin, smooth sides and curved boot.

This space display, called Asteroid 478, was designed around many space vehicles. The command centre has solar panels, radar, communication dishes, sliding doors and its own repair robots.

If you had all the LEGO bricks (and time!) in the world, what would you build?

One of my favourite landmarks is the Eiffel Tower. I know the LEGO Group has built an official model, but I would like to make one at minifigure scale with working lifts.

What is your favourite creation?

I have made a model of the "Mole" tunnelling machine from *Thunderbirds*. I love how the body fits together and the LEGO bricks come together to make a round shape.

I really enjoyed building somewhere for my collectible minifigures to stay. It's great to display your favourites!

What are some of your top LEGO building tips?

Try to keep up to date with new developments. The LEGO Group are continually bringing out new bricks, which really helps you when trying to build something from real life. Some of my favourite recent bricks include: the headlight brick, which enables other bricks to be connected in different ways and can help you build in close quarters; bricks with side studs, which revolutionise how we can build details into our models; and the 1x1 plate with side ring which enables the bottom of two bricks to be joined together.

Which model were you most proud of as a young LEGO builder?

When I was about seven years old, I won a town themed building competition in a local department store. I built a jail in a town scene and enjoyed spending the prize money on more LEGO bricks!

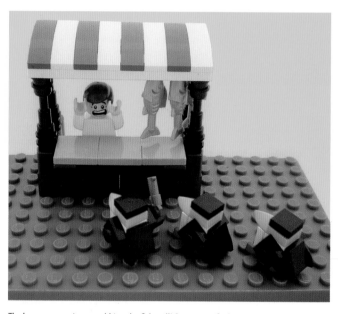

Building this underground rescue vehicle with drill presented some interesting challenges: using curved pieces to create a round body and using LEGO Technic beams to attach it to the base.

The hungry penguins are robbing the fish stall! Sometimes finding just the right minifigure head for your scene can be difficult, but this minifigure has the perfect expression!

The little figures on this clock tower are supposed to be like those that come out when the clock strikes the hour. When the LEGO Group released the trophies I knew what I had to make!

ONE OF THE GREAT THINGS ABOUT LEGO BRICKS IS THAT YOU CAN BUILD TOGETHER.

What else do you enjoy making, apart from practical makes?

Practical items are really amazing to make. I also enjoy building town scenes, with all the cars, trains, buildings and people needed to make an accurate mini model of real life.

What is your favourite LEGO building technique or technique you use the most?

In the AFOL (Adult Fans Of LEGO) forums we refer to SNOT (Studs Not On Top) – the ability to build shapes that are smooth, round and flat, without any studs showing. This is how I like to build.

How much time do you spend building?

I usually build for one or two hours a day, depending on what project I have on the go. Sometimes I might also have to do some sorting or tidying up.

How many LEGO bricks do you have?

I must have over 50,000 by now.

Do you plan out your build? If so, how?

Planning is often very helpful. I use the LEGO Group's Digital Designer virtual building software, which helps me go over designs and particular techniques until I am happy. I also use spreadsheets to help me plan out the number of bricks I need to buy. However, if I have to make something using only the bricks I have already then I just start building and use trial and error to work it out.

My creation of this iconic British train is one of my most recent builds. Getting the doors at the rear right were the final piece of the build.

Using parts from some of the LEGO Group's most recent sets I tried to recreate my own car with a minifigure inside. With models like this, you may have to compromise or adapt to get your model to fit together.

What is your favourite LEGO brick or piece?

I think my favourite at the moment is the 1x1 slope that has been introduced over the last couple of years.

This treasure chest is the perfect place to hide all your favourite LEGO pieces! Building using specific colour design requires a little extra planning to make sure that the pieces colour coordinate but also fit together securely

Once Upon a Time

How do you create a fairy tale adventure? You'll need a place where the tale begins, and scenes that take place along the way. Make up some fantastic creatures to be ferocious monsters or brand-new friends. Don't forget some tricky traps and puzzles, too. Get out your bricks and start building your own story!

MEET THE BUILDER:
BARNEY MAIN

Age: 20
Day Job: Engineering design student
LEGO® Specialities: Castles, pirate ships
Brick Collection: 25,000 parts
Favourite Brick: Round LEGO® Technic connector
Did You Know? Barney once built some weighing scales using a LEGO plane model when he was baking a cake and needed to weigh out the ingredients.

> FAREWELL, MOTHER! I'M OFF TO FACE DIRE PERILS IN THE WILDERNESS.

> HAVE FUN, DEAR.

COUNTRY COTTAGE

Goodbye, home-sweet-home! Jack lives with his mother in a country cottage deep in the woods. Jack doesn't know what lies beyond the woods – but he can't wait to find out! (See p.216.)

TELLING A FAIRY TALE
BARNEY MAIN

"I really enjoyed working on my chapter, as I got to read loads of children's books as my research! I also used cartoons and history books for inspiration. I had a good idea of how I wanted each fairy tale model to look, but I made lots of changes as I went along. I especially like how the larger fairy tale characters (pp.220–221) came out, as I'd never built anything like them before."

> WE CENTAURS HAVE NO NEED OF GOLD.

JACK'S JOURNEY

"Hear ye, hear ye, the Royal Nugget is missing. Whoever finds it will be granted stuff."
– Signed, The King

Little Jack has spent all his young life in one place and longs to have an adventure. When a cry goes up across the land that the King's Royal Nugget has been stolen, Jack knows that at last this is his chance to see the big, wide world. The King requests that all heroes in the kingdom go in search of the Royal Nugget. The one to return it to him will be granted a rich reward. Jack decides to pack his backpack and set out to find the Royal Nugget – and his fortune!

ALAS! WHERE COULD IT BE?

WOODLAND WONDERS

Jack discovers mythical woodland realms on his travels. Will the strange plants and creatures he finds there be his friends or his foes? (See p.218.)

FEE-FI-FO-FUM, I'VE GOT SOME ROAST CHICKEN. YUM!

GIANT TROUBLE

Nowhere is out of reach for little Jack – even the kingdom of the giants, way up in the clouds. Will Jack become the giant's next dinner? (See p.228.)

NO NUGGET HERE, KID. SCRAM!

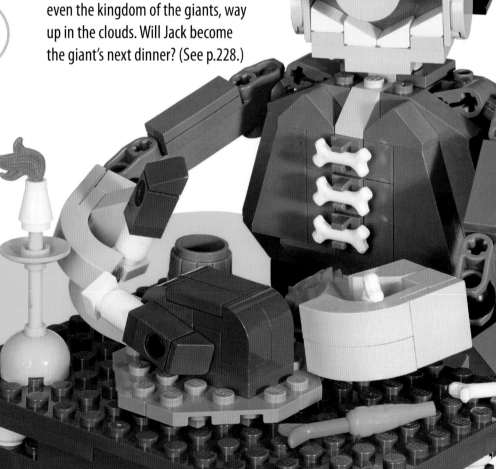

TROLL TERROR

Jack's quest to find the Royal Nugget takes him over a troll-guarded bridge. Better run, Jack – that troll doesn't look too happy! (See p.224.)

SQUEAK!

FAIRY TALE COTTAGE

Jack is setting out on his adventure, and where better to start his story than the quaint country cottage where he grew up? A cottage is a nice place to stop and rest after a long day of walking. Will your cottage be on farmland, or deep in the woods? You could even make extra cottages and change their colours around to create an entire village!

This door was built first, then the frame was constructed around it

Fancy window is the bottom of a small turntable piece

FRONT VIEW

Latticed windows lend a rustic feel

KITCHEN

Give your minifigures everything they could need, including the kitchen sink! In the cottage kitchen there are jars of food on the shelves, a powerful oven and a nice mug of LEGO broth waiting on the table.

The oven door is made from a tile with clips

Pose and accessorise your characters so they're doing something, like gardening or repairing the house

IT'S SO HARD TO KEEP A COTTAGE WARM WHEN IT SPLITS OPEN IN THE MIDDLE!

A roof of stepped yellow bricks looks like it's made out of straw. Make sure it's built to support its own weight so it doesn't collapse!

Try building a secret hiding place inside your cottage's roof.

Flowers are a sign of a well-cared-for home

Use small tiles to make a tiled floor, or long brown ones for wooden floorboards

Cone bricks can be used for the legs of a chair, table, or stool

Tabletop is the base from a LEGO® Minifigures collectible character

COSY HOME

Building from reference can really inspire your choice of colours and shapes for your fairy tale cottage, so take a look at your favourite fairy tale books for ideas! Brown timber frames around white plaster walls give this building a half-timbered style.

LIVING SPACE

Fill your cottage with furniture and decorations that fit a pastoral setting, like a rug, a picture and a fireplace. Use transparent orange elements to make a roaring fire, and have some firewood at the ready for when it starts to go out!

What will your occupants need in their home? Build in details to suit your minifigures.

Stack white plates like a staircase to make a plume of puffy smoke

Attach a 1x4 tile to a 1x1 brick with side stud for a diagonal brown beam

REAR VIEW

Use more than one hinge plate for strength and stability

Decorated and stickered tiles make great paintings. Attach them to bricks with side studs

Windows and curtains help make a house into a home

An auto mudguard can also be a shady window overhang

SIDE VIEWS

Stone chimney built from grey bricks in different shapes and colours

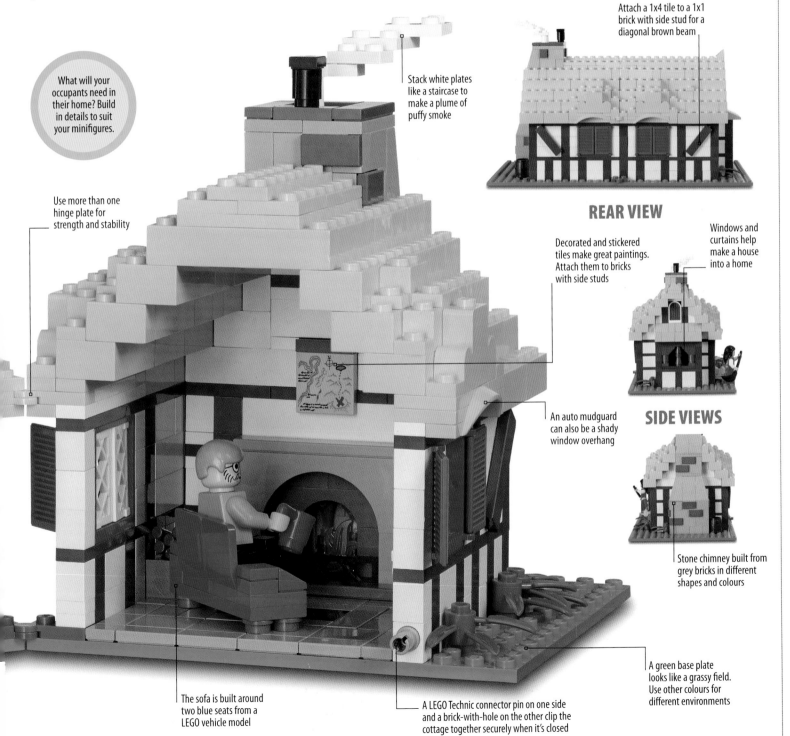

The sofa is built around two blue seats from a LEGO vehicle model

A LEGO Technic connector pin on one side and a brick-with-hole on the other clip the cottage together securely when it's closed

A green base plate looks like a grassy field. Use other colours for different environments

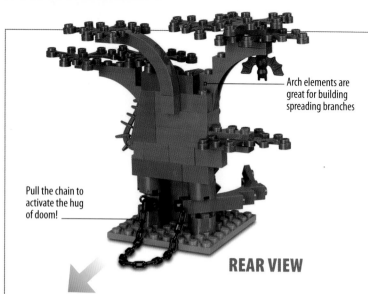

Arch elements are great for building spreading branches

Pull the chain to activate the hug of doom!

REAR VIEW

BUILDER TALK

"Getting the monster tree's arms to grab a minifigure was tricky. I came up with a technique that I'd never used before: the arms swing together when you pull on a chain that connects them."

ENCHANTED FOREST

A walk in the woods sounded like fun, but Jack has gotten lost. Yikes, did that tree just move? Storybook forests are always full of mystery and adventure. They can be home to ferocious monsters and beasts, or helpful fairies and magical creatures. Build a forest with caves, rocks, rivers and lots of trees in different shapes and sizes!

If you don't have LEGO leaf pieces, use any green bricks and plates – or just leave the branches bare!

What is this tree protecting? Or does it just not like minifigures?

Pieces with unusual curves and shapes make a forest creation look organic and growing

Two barrels attached with LEGO Technic cross-axles make a pair of creepy, hollow eyes

Use slopes and bricks to build up the shape of a big, sturdy tree trunk

Build in roots for a natural look

HUG OF DOOM

The tree's grabbing arms are half-arch pieces built on their sides, with L-shaped plates for the branch-hands on the ends. They move on pivot points made with LEGO Technic bricks and axles.

MONSTER TREE

This tree's arm-like branches can close to capture a LEGO minifigure. To make your own living tree, just build a regular one and then add creature features like eyes, hands or even big pointy teeth!

It doesn't matter what colour pieces you use on the inside – they'll be hidden from view!

INSIDE THE PINE

This pine tree is built around a central core of bricks with studs on their sides, and plates attached to them sideways. Stacking more plates on the bottom creates a tapered shape.

Studs pointing outwards make the tree look bristly

PINE TREE

Some LEGO sets include single-piece pine trees, but you can build your own versions to plant in your forest! This pine tree is built to fit into the same base as the chopping tree below, so the two are interchangeable.

Try blue trees for a magical forest, or white for a snowy one.

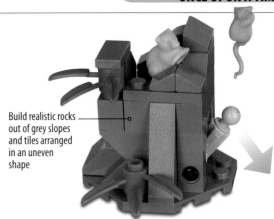

Build realistic rocks out of grey slopes and tiles arranged in an uneven shape

SECRET SURPRISES

What would a fairy tale forest be without a few surprises? This "ratapult" launches a rat out of a hollow rock to scare unwary adventurers! You can build all kinds of fun tricks and traps into your forest creations.

CHOPPING TREE

Some people work in forests – even enchanted ones! A woodcutter makes his living by cutting down trees. This chopping tree is perfect for lumber as it's straight, tall and thin enough to be cut up and hauled away. Its trunk is made from stacked 2x2 round bricks, with plant leaves built in.

Light green leaves look healthy and vibrant

OH BOY! I HOPE I GET MADE INTO SOMETHING REALLY COOL...LIKE A BATTERING RAM!

A LEGO Technic towball inside the hollow base pushes up on the trunk to dislodge it

Push down here to topple the tree

Build the trees for your forest with different heights and leaf patterns to make them look unique

TIMBER!

TOPPLING TREE

This tree is built with a special action feature: when you push down on the LEGO Technic towball at its base, it topples over as if the woodcutter has just chopped it down.

Stacked 2x2 round bricks

FOREST FLORA

Strolling through the woods, Jack spots all sorts of strange and wondrous things. Maybe getting lost isn't so bad after all! When building flowers and mushrooms for an enchanted forest, look at real plants for inspiration – but don't stop there. Let your imagination take root and grow by giving your creations new shapes, wild colours and magical features.

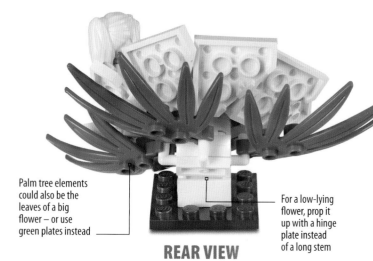

Palm tree elements could also be the leaves of a big flower – or use green plates instead

For a low-lying flower, prop it up with a hinge plate instead of a long stem

REAR VIEW

BUILDING ROUND

A plate with an octagonal bar around it forms the centre of this flower, with one petal clipped to each bar segment to create a circular flower shape. The three leaves clip onto 1x2 plates with bars that are attached underneath.

GIANT FLOWER

This big flower may have a lovely aroma, but don't get too close or it might fold its petals shut to catch you tight! The most important step in building a giant flower is finding the right piece to go in the middle. Look for parts that can connect to a ring of petals.

Sticking out of the centre is a classic LEGO plant piece

Legend says this flower is allergic to frogs. Will one help your hero escape?

IT SMELLS SO NICE HERE. MAYBE I COULD TAKE A QUICK NAP...

Clip-and-bar connections let petals close in to catch a minifigure – or to form a fairy's bed!

Each petal is made from two pieces: an angled plate and a 1x1 plate with a clip on top

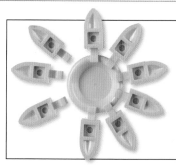

PETAL POWER

To build this flower, you only need a few types of LEGO pieces: a dinner plate element for the circular centre, and a set of petals made from tooth plates attached to 1x1 plates with clips.

TALL FLOWERS

Flowers can be even more realistic if you build them on top of stems. It may be tricky to make a stem that is tall and thin, but also sturdy and well-balanced. Here are some different ways to create them.

Angled-plate leaves attach to a brick with side studs

Stacked 1x1 round bricks, with slope bricks for leaves

Petals are double angled plates connected to plates with clips, which clip on to handled bars around the centre

FOREST FUNGI

Decorate your fairy tale forest with mushrooms and toadstools in many sizes and colours. You could make tiny ones with small radar dishes and round bricks, or build your own giant mushrooms like this one out of bigger bricks and plates.

Build from the top down, creating descending steps in all directions

Jumper plates help to line up the pieces at the bottom

Use textured bricks for a stalk

★ CHALLENGE

SPINNING FLOWER TOPS

In a magic forest, flowers don't have to be attached to the ground! Why not build a flower that can spin around like a spinning top? Build some with your friends and see whose spinning tops can spin the longest, travel the furthest or knock the other forest flowers down.

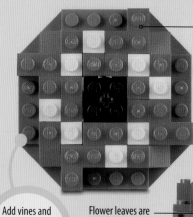

Keep your flower's pieces balanced. A lopsided top doesn't spin as well as one with the same weight on all sides

Add vines and spikes to make a scary-looking battle flower top!

Flower leaves are green plate pieces

SIDE VIEW

SECURE SPIN

Push a LEGO Technic cross-axle through the centre of your spinning top for a point on the bottom and a spinning-handle on top. Use bricks with axle holes through them to hold the cross-axle in place.

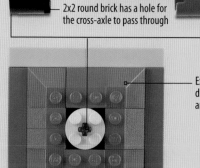

2x2 round brick has a hole for the cross-axle to pass through

Experiment with different colours and patterns of bricks

What will your colours look like when your top is spinning around?

SIDE VIEW

FAIRY TALE CREATURES

The world is an incredible place when you're on an adventure. Jack bumps into all kinds of amazing creatures on his quest! Animals and fantasy creatures bring lots of new storytelling possibilities to fairy tale models. You can add extra parts to your minifigures to make some, or build them entirely out of your bricks.

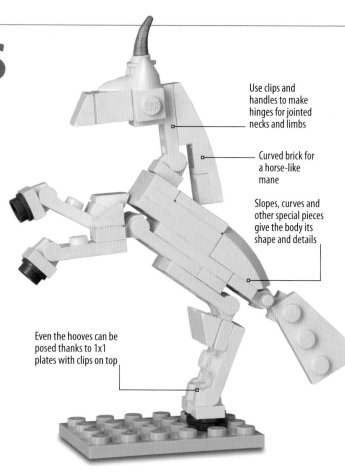

Use clips and handles to make hinges for jointed necks and limbs

Curved brick for a horse-like mane

Slopes, curves and other special pieces give the body its shape and details

Even the hooves can be posed thanks to 1x1 plates with clips on top

UNICORNS

Unicorns are usually portrayed as white horses with horns growing from their foreheads. Beyond that, the details are up to you. This posable unicorn looks like it's ready for battle!

HONK!

FEATHERED FORM

The adult swan's wings are built separately to the body. They are made up of curved bricks on top, slope bricks below, and a stacked pair of tooth plates for feathers in the back.

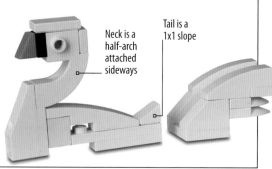

Neck is a half-arch attached sideways

Tail is a 1x1 slope

ELVES

Your stories can involve different kinds of elves, from tiny cobblers to tall and graceful warriors. These Fair Folk of the woods wear green and brown so they blend in with the trees. Will they help your hero or play mischievous tricks?

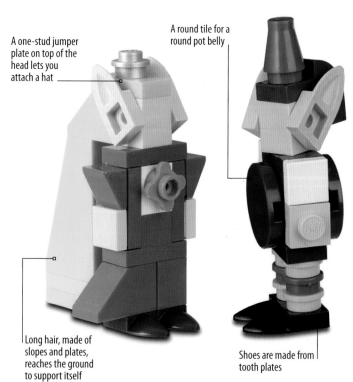

A one-stud jumper plate on top of the head lets you attach a hat

A round tile for a round pot belly

Both swans use the same bricks for their eyes and beaks, but extra pieces make the adult's head longer

A hinge base for a stubby tail

Feet are minifigure flippers

Long hair, made of slopes and plates, reaches the ground to support itself

Shoes are made from tooth plates

SWANS

Remember the ugly duckling that turned out to be a swan? You can build both! Baby animals often look cute and clumsy, with big heads, eyes and feet. A grown-up swan should have graceful curves and smooth features.

ADVENTURE ACCESSORIES

Use your bricks to create unique items for your story's minifigures. For a staff, all you need is a long handle, antenna or bar. Attach other elements to the end or clip them to the sides to make different styles.

WANT TO TRADE?

WELL, I DO HAPPEN TO HAVE THIS MYSTIC, TREASURE-FINDING STAFF...

A skull and axe blades make this look like a villain's weapon

You can include magical special effects, too!

A wise wizard might carry this ancient stone walking stick

This could be a sorcerer's staff...or add a flame in the middle for a tall torch

Try to match the colours of the hair piece and the horse body

DON'T BELIEVE HIM. THAT STAFF ONLY FINDS TURNIPS!

Is your centaur a scholar or a fighter? It's all in the choice of minifigure parts and accessories!

CENTAURS

Half-horse and half-human, these galloping creatures of myth can be created by building new four-legged lower bodies with two-stud attachments on top for minifigure torsos.

Two pairs of minifigure legs make great horse legs!

Round plates for hooves

Stacks of plates and bricks for legs — or make them posable like the unicorn's

QUESTS

As your heroes travel on their fairy tale adventure, they're sure to discover challenges that test their courage and skills. They might have to cross a rickety bridge high above a lava-filled chasm, face a monster in its den or track down a king's missing treasure. Whatever quests you can imagine, you can make them come to life with your LEGO bricks.

MAGIC WELL

This could be an enchanted well that grants your wish if you drop in a brick. Or maybe it has a curse on it that turns anybody who drinks from it into a frog. Better ask the witch, to be on the safe side!

Roof shingles built from brown plates

Plates with clips make nice decorations

DOUBLE, DOUBLE, TOIL AND TROUBLE... I'VE FORGOTTEN WHAT I PUT IN THIS ONE!

OKAY, I'VE GONE UP THE HILL AND FETCHED A PAIL OF WATER. NOW WHAT?

Make a deeper well by building your structure on a raised platform

For a bucket, you could also use a barrel or a 2x2 brick

Tiles on top hold the walls together

Bricks with side studs hold the roof at an angle on both sides

1x1 brick-with-hole

The round shape of the well is built with curved bricks

If you don't have a chain, try using a string

THE MAGIC REVEALED

Just turn the lance to wind up the chain and discover the magic potion inside the well. The lance goes through bricks with holes at the tops of the support posts, and has a cone over its end at the far side so it won't slide out.

Tan side-by-side 1x4 plates blend in with the rest of the surface

Strange plants and dangerous animals make a scene appear weird and foreboding

Skull and crossbones tile from a LEGO pirate game

I WONDER WHAT THAT SIGN SAYS. OH WELL, IT CAN'T BE TOO IMPORTANT.

Use brown pieces to make a dirt trap, or white for a pit full of snow.

QUICKSAND

In a fairy tale world, you never know where you'll encounter a trick or a trap. What looks like a stretch of solid ground might really be a treacherous pit full of quicksand!

It's a good thing this adventurer checked the sand with his walking stick first!

Pull this slider to release the trap

To reset the trap, just take the 1x4 plates out and push the slider back in again

ACTION VIEW

Smooth tiles keep trap pieces from snagging on studs when you slide it out

A T-shaped end keeps the slider from being pulled out too far

SAND, QUICK!

When you pull the plate with handle on the slider, the loose 1x4 plates that are resting on top fall into the deep pit beneath – taking anyone standing there along with them!

ARGHH!

TROLL BRIDGE

"Hold it right there! If you want to cross this bridge, you'll have to pay the troll." Jack has come upon a classic fairy tale peril: an evil troll that lives under a bridge. To get past it, he might have to solve a riddle, battle his way across or distract the troll with a tasty snack. But step carefully, because this bridge has a built-in surprise!

THE BRIDGE

A bridge should be built like an arch – good and strong. This one is made out of dark grey bricks with lighter grey bricks for accent stonework. Tan bricks form steps to let a minifigure (or goat) walk up and across the span.

I CAN SEE MY HOUSE FROM HERE!

Top plate rests on a thin lip at one end and smooth tiles at the other. Nudge it out of place and gravity takes care of the rest!

You could also make a hinged trap door, or one that works like the quicksand trap on p.223.

TRAP DOOR

Step in the wrong spot on top of the bridge and the secret hatch falls down, sending you tumbling into the clutches of the troll below! Some LEGO sets include trap door elements, but you can also build your own in whatever style you like.

A 2x4 double angled plate for a keystone

1x1 slopes turn jagged bumps into smooth curves

Use an antenna or spear with a round brick on the end to make bulrushes

Include wetlands details such as muddy banks, plants and frogs

Does your bridge go over water? Then build a base of transparent and solid blue plates!

224

TROLL

This mean-tempered troll is big enough to bully a minifigure, but small enough to hide under the bridge. Add a plate with clip to his hand so he can hold a spiked club – and shake it angrily at any trespassers!

WHO'S WALKING ON MY BRIDGE? I'LL GOBBLE THEM UP, BRICKS AND ALL!

TROLLISH FEATURES

Four headlight bricks with hollow side studs make up most of the troll's square head. His little round nose is a folded-up hinge plate.

Horn pieces from a LEGO cow plug into the headlight bricks' hollow studs

Eyes are round plates from a LEGO® Games set

Hinge plate

Spiked club comes from the LEGO Minifigures line

Arms are built out of hinges, clips and plates with handles

Clawed fingers and toes are made from tooth plates

Legs are made from 2x2 round bricks and plates

FRONT SIDE VIEW

Set one foot in front of the other for a sense of movement and action

Big feet make a two-legged model more stable

QUICK BUILD

BILLY GOATS GRUFF

Each of these three billy goat brothers is bigger and tougher than the last. You can build them in two shakes of a goat's tail if you have similar pieces! First design your goat's head, then use slopes or arches lined with plates for the body, and cones and round plates for legs and feet.

Tail piece used as a horn

Include features in common, like headlight brick eyes and little clippity-clop hooves

You can use these same techniques to make little versions of big animals or big versions of little ones!

Attach cow horns to 1x1 round plates with open studs

Don't forget a beard for the biggest billy goat

Horn piece for a stubby tail

Hooves are flowers with open studs

CASTLE SIEGE

Jack hears a rumour about a kingdom that is under siege. Some people say the attackers are bandits. Some say it's a gold-hungry dragon! Here's a challenge to test both your building skill and your aim. Build a castle and use catapults to launch LEGO pieces inside. Who amongst you and your friends can get the most bricks over the wall?

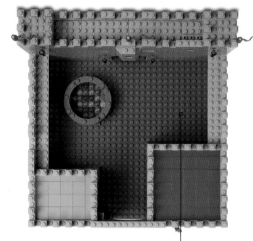

TOP VIEW

Get 1 point for landing your brick in the courtyard

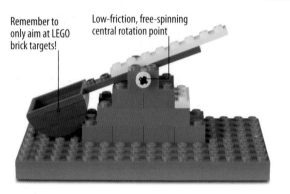

Remember to only aim at LEGO brick targets!

Low-friction, free-spinning central rotation point

SIEGE PLANS

Your castle should have a high wall and a central courtyard where you want the launched pieces to land. For an extra challenge, build coloured tower platforms and award extra points for hitting more difficult targets!

See p.240 for more tips on building castles!

CATAPULTS

Assemble a catapult and use it to toss 1x1 round bricks over the castle walls. Here are some ideas to get you started – what will yours look like?

Experiment with different heights and arm lengths to get your catapult just right

Wheels let you move a catapult around quickly

Use 1x1 round bricks for your catapult ammunition

Include a basket or bucket to hold the ammunition

A sturdy base keeps a catapult steady when it's fired

A long throwing arm acts like a lever to fling the bricks

If you don't have the pieces to build a castle, you could make anything you like – even just a simple ring.

Get 4 points for getting your brick through the castle door

What happens if you hit these torches? That's up to you!

Get 5 points for landing your brick in the little well – the toughest shot of all!

Get 3 points for landing your brick on the green tower

Get 2 points for landing your brick on the red tower

INCOMING BRICK... EVERYBODY DUCK!

IT'S YOUR JOB TO SNEAK INTO THE CASTLE AND BRING BACK THE MISSILES.

BAH!

Get a bonus point if your brick goes through the gateway instead of over the wall

Building on a big base plate will help keep your castle walls stable

Use coloured plates or tiles to mark special target zones

Try attaching ammunition-blocking defences to the castle battlements, such as knights with shields.

227

GIANTS

When Jack climbed up a beanstalk, he never expected that he'd discover a land in the clouds, much less one filled with hungry giants! If you're tired of tussling with trolls, then try a giant on for size. These fee-fi-fo-fearsome creatures are really tough because they can be as smart as a human (or a minifigure), but they're a whole lot bigger and stronger.

BIG HEAD

There are lots of ways to build your giant's head. Experiment with your pieces to find the features and expression you like the most. This giant's grinning face uses bracket pieces for the sides of the mouth, and round tiles for the nose and cheeks.

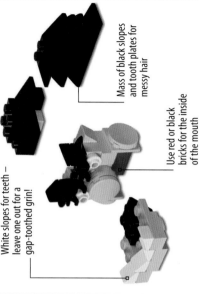

Mass of black slopes and tooth plates for messy hair

Use red or black bricks for the inside of the mouth

White slopes for teeth – leave one out for a gap-toothed grin!

A row of forward-facing clips makes a shaggy mono-brow

Eyes are hollow-stud 1x1 round plates from LEGO Games sets

EVIL GIANT

Better run, Jack – this giant's legs are a lot longer than yours! They are attached to LEGO Technic bricks with ball joints to make them posable. All giants are tall, but they are also individuals, so give your giants all kinds of different faces, clothes and body shapes.

Tunic is shaped by slope bricks

Bones for shirt toggles

Use ball-and-socket pieces from LEGO buildable action figures to create articulated arms

A giant-sized belt to hold up giant-sized pants!

SIDE VIEW

JUST THE RIGHT SIZE FOR A LIGHT SNACK!

EEK!

You can also use basic bricks and hinges for bendable arms

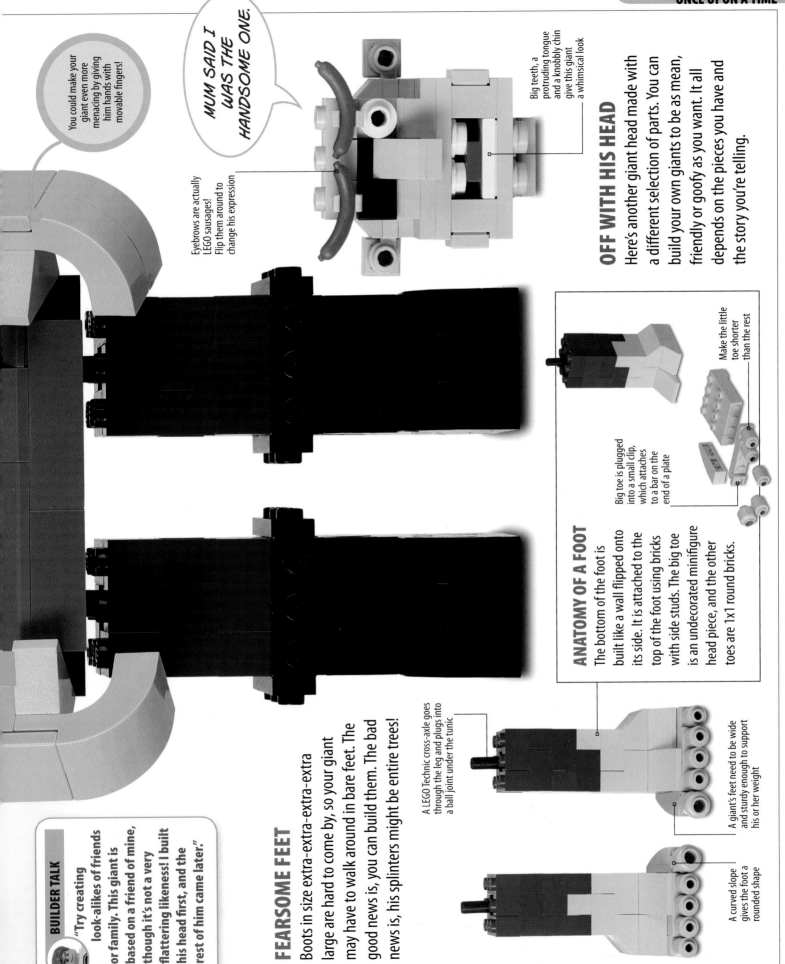

You could make your giant even more menacing by giving him hands with movable fingers!

MUM SAID I WAS THE HANDSOME ONE.

Eyebrows are actually LEGO sausages! Flip them around to change his expression

Big teeth, a protruding tongue and a knobbly chin give this giant a whimsical look

OFF WITH HIS HEAD

Here's another giant head made with a different selection of parts. You can build your own giants to be as mean, friendly or goofy as you want. It all depends on the pieces you have and the story you're telling.

Make the little toe shorter than the rest

Big toe is plugged into a small clip, which attaches to a bar on the end of a plate

ANATOMY OF A FOOT

The bottom of the foot is built like a wall flipped onto its side. It is attached to the top of the foot using bricks with side studs. The big toe is an undecorated minifigure head piece, and the other toes are 1x1 round bricks.

BUILDER TALK

"Try creating look-alikes of friends or family. This giant is based on a friend of mine, though it's not a very flattering likeness! I built his head first, and the rest of him came later."

FEARSOME FEET

Boots in size extra-extra-extra-extra large are hard to come by, so your giant may have to walk around in bare feet. The good news is, you can build them. The bad news is, his splinters might be entire trees!

A LEGO Technic cross-axle goes through the leg and plugs into a ball joint under the tunic

A curved slope gives the foot a rounded shape

A giant's feet need to be wide and sturdy enough to support his or her weight

GIANT'S KITCHEN

As Jack explores the land of the giants, he starts to feel a bit like a mouse. Everything here is so huge! Don't just build a giant for your adventure – construct a whole world for it. What kind of furniture and tools would exist in a giant's home? Does your giant use regular-sized objects in new ways, like a sword for a butter knife or a lion for a house pet?

NOW WHERE HAS THAT LITTLE MORSEL GONE?

ROAST CHICKEN

For an appetising dinner, use curved bricks and tiles to hide the studs. LEGO Technic pins let the drumsticks attach at an angle, and pop right off if your giant is feeling hungry!

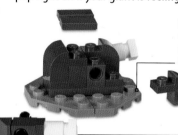

LEGO dinner plates will work for small dishes, but for big ones, make your own!

CHAIR

Can you match the look of your table and chairs? This chair has a wooden frame of brown bricks and plates, with tan grilles in the seat to make a wicker pattern. Just like the table, the legs are topped with minifigure skulls.

A radar dish, an antenna and a dome make a fine candlestick

A green LEGO® EXO-FORCE™ hair piece resembles a leafy head of cabbage

Bones are the remains of previous meals

A whole barrel can be a giant's drinking cup

GULP

Tabletop made from overlapping plates

DINNER TABLE

Building a giant table is just like building a small one: it needs four sturdy legs and a big flat top. Look for the biggest pieces in your collection, or assemble it in sections from lots of small bricks.

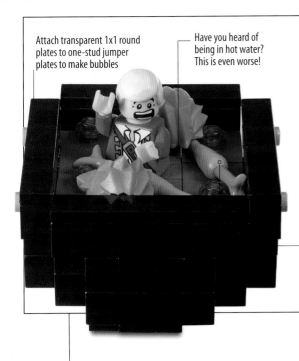

Attach transparent 1x1 round plates to one-stud jumper plates to make bubbles

Have you heard of being in hot water? This is even worse!

SOUP'S ON!

What's in the pot? An upper surface of green tiles, some vegetables made from more LEGO EXO-FORCE hair (this giant likes his greens!), and a secret ingredient or two. You can use any pieces and colours you like for your giant's stew.

LEGO carrots can be found in many farm and house LEGO sets

COOKING POT

No hero wants to land in a giant's pot, but imagine the adventure you can have getting back out! This pot could be found in the forest or the kitchen of the giant's castle. It could work for a witch's cauldron, too.

FIRE PIT

Build wood for a giant's bonfire just like you would make sections of a tree trunk (see p.216) – after all, that's exactly what they are! The logs and flames in this model are attached with brackets and clips.

You could build a roasting spit instead, or even some sticks with giant-sized marshmallows!

HEY! WHEN I ASKED IF I COULD HELP MAKE THE STEW, I WASN'T VOLUNTEERING TO BE PART OF IT!

Use plenty of flame pieces to make a roaring fire

A rough, uneven shape makes the fire pit look simple and crude

Use long LEGO Technic cross-axles to make poles, and hang the pot from them with chains

Iron pot built by stepping bricks up and out to make a cup shape

Include a pile of small black pieces in the centre for ash and charcoal

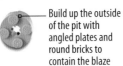

Build up the outside of the pit with angled plates and round bricks to contain the blaze

PLAY OPTIONS

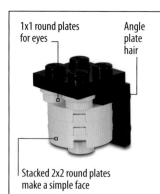

1x1 round plates for eyes

Angle plate hair

Stacked 2x2 round plates make a simple face

Think about how you want to play with your brick character. Build some extra body parts to swap in and give your characters different looks and poses. This knight also has an unhelmeted head for when he doesn't have to stand guard at the castle!

There are lots of ways to build a helmet. Create some different designs of your own!

FAIRY TALE CHARACTERS

Your fairy tale doesn't have to just star minifigures. You can use your bricks to build bigger and more detailed characters, too. They can be as colourful and as fantastical as you like! You can even mix them in scenes with minifigures so they become super-sized heroes.

Armour built out of curved and angled pieces

Side stud bricks for hands allow the knight to hold his sword and shield

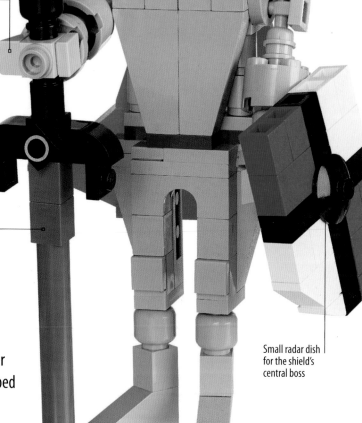

Sword blade is a long, round column, but you could build a stack of 1x1 round bricks

Small radar dish for the shield's central boss

KNIGHT

Cape attaches to the body at three points

Start out a brick character with the basics – a head, two arms, two legs, and a body – and then add any other parts you want. This knight is equipped with a sword, a shield, a cape, and a helmet with a fancy feather plume.

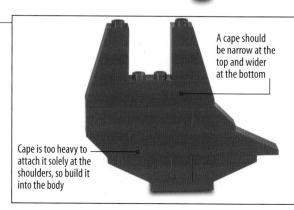

Calves are gray minifigure heads

REAR VIEW

A cape should be narrow at the top and wider at the bottom

Cape is too heavy to attach it solely at the shoulders, so build it into the body

BRICKS IN MOTION

Solid bricks can be used to create dynamic motion. The knight's cape is built just like a LEGO brick wall, with slopes and inverted slopes to give it a swooshing shape, as if it is being blown by the wind.

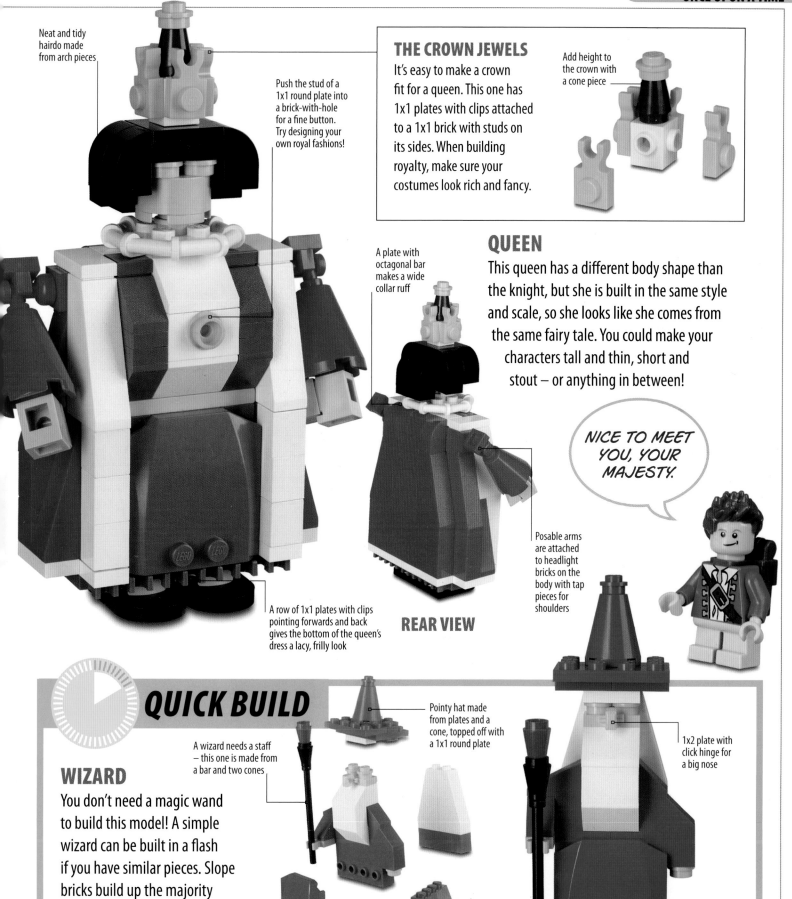

Neat and tidy hairdo made from arch pieces

Push the stud of a 1x1 round plate into a brick-with-hole for a fine button. Try designing your own royal fashions!

THE CROWN JEWELS

It's easy to make a crown fit for a queen. This one has 1x1 plates with clips attached to a 1x1 brick with studs on its sides. When building royalty, make sure your costumes look rich and fancy.

Add height to the crown with a cone piece

A plate with octagonal bar makes a wide collar ruff

QUEEN

This queen has a different body shape than the knight, but she is built in the same style and scale, so she looks like she comes from the same fairy tale. You could make your characters tall and thin, short and stout – or anything in between!

NICE TO MEET YOU, YOUR MAJESTY.

Posable arms are attached to headlight bricks on the body with tap pieces for shoulders

REAR VIEW

A row of 1x1 plates with clips pointing forwards and back gives the bottom of the queen's dress a lacy, frilly look

QUICK BUILD

A wizard needs a staff – this one is made from a bar and two cones

Pointy hat made from plates and a cone, topped off with a 1x1 round plate

1x2 plate with click hinge for a big nose

WIZARD

You don't need a magic wand to build this model! A simple wizard can be built in a flash if you have similar pieces. Slope bricks build up the majority of the body and the hair.

Create a cloak with a car roof

UNDERSEA CHARACTERS

While taking a swim, Jack is so surprised that he almost forgets to hold his breath…there are people living under the sea! The seas of a fairy tale world are brimming with mythical, magical creatures, from krakens and sea serpents to mermaids and mermen. If you don't have any mer-minifigures, don't flounder about – use your bricks to build some!

MY HAIRSTYLE? I LIKE TO GO FOR THE WET LOOK.

Curved and clip pieces make her hair look wild and wave-tossed

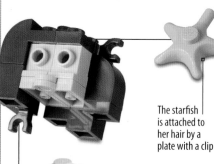

The starfish is attached to her hair by a plate with a clip

MER-CONSTRUCTION

The mermaid's mouth is three stacked jumper plates in front of two headlight bricks, her rounded nose is a folded hinge plate, and her eyes are two more headlight bricks.

1x2 curved half-arch piece for a curving forearm

A plate with side ring can hold a hairbrush

Seashells are a traditional underwater fashion

Build in a 1x1 round plate for a bellybutton!

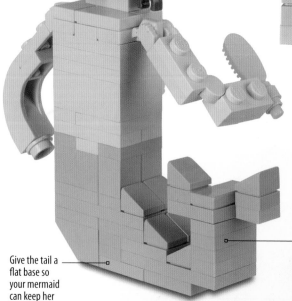

Give the tail a flat base so your mermaid can keep her balance!

REAR VIEW

Use bricks and plates for the main structure of the tail, and shape the curves with slope elements

MERMAID

Building a mermaid is like building any other fairy tale character, except that she has a tail instead of legs. Search through your collection for sea-themed accessories that you can use to give your mermaid her own unique, aquatic style.

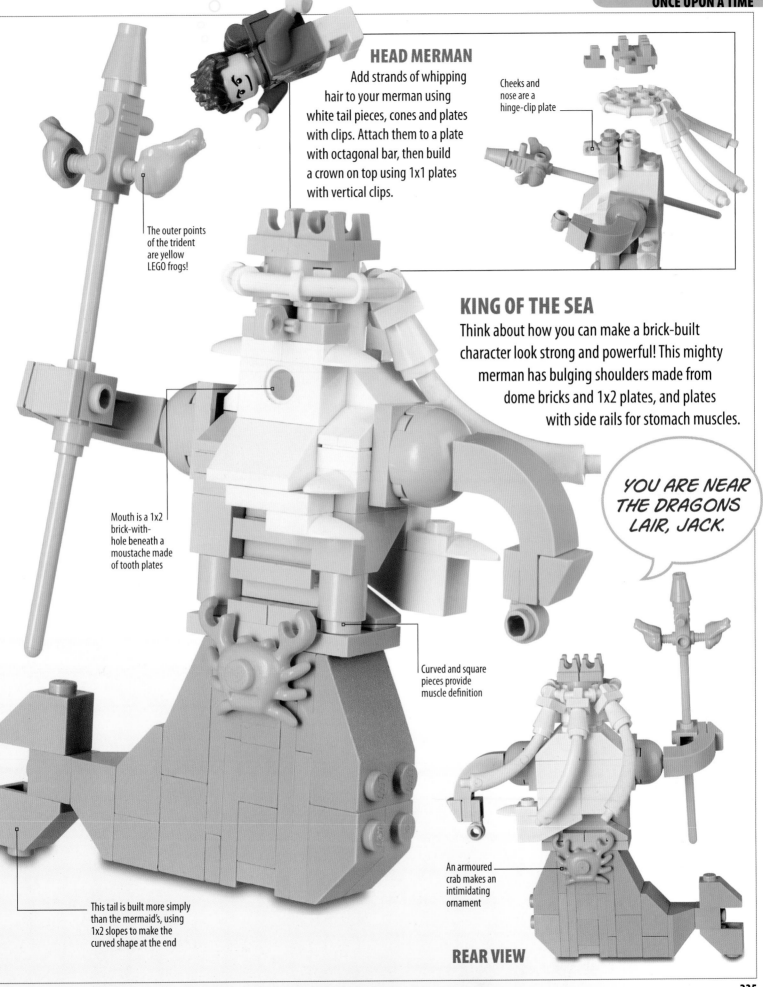

The outer points of the trident are yellow LEGO frogs!

HEAD MERMAN

Add strands of whipping hair to your merman using white tail pieces, cones and plates with clips. Attach them to a plate with octagonal bar, then build a crown on top using 1x1 plates with vertical clips.

Cheeks and nose are a hinge-clip plate

KING OF THE SEA

Think about how you can make a brick-built character look strong and powerful! This mighty merman has bulging shoulders made from dome bricks and 1x2 plates, and plates with side rails for stomach muscles.

Mouth is a 1x2 brick-with-hole beneath a moustache made of tooth plates

YOU ARE NEAR THE DRAGONS LAIR, JACK.

Curved and square pieces provide muscle definition

An armoured crab makes an intimidating ornament

This tail is built more simply than the mermaid's, using 1x2 slopes to make the curved shape at the end

REAR VIEW

DRAGON

Jack never dreamed that his search for the Royal Nugget would lead him to the cave of a fire-breathing dragon! He will have to rely on all of his luck and courage (and some help from a fearless dragon catcher) to get out of this in one piece. Defeating a dragon can be the ultimate quest for a hero. Build yours with lots of teeth, scales and spikes – and don't forget a big pair of wings.

Gems aren't just for treasure – these ones make the dragon's big, glowing eyes!

Horn elements can attach to clips and bricks with hollow studs to make spikes and frills

Neck joints are made with clips and handles

FIRE BREATH

Smaller LEGO flame pieces plug into small brick holes, and bigger ones can attach to LEGO Technic cross-axle holes. Build pieces with attachment points into your dragon's head for a fiery-breath attack!

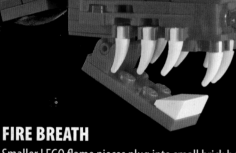

HEY, BIG AND SCALY! LOOK OVER HERE!

Surely the dragon won't be able to resist this dragon catcher's delicious bait?

BUILDING A DRAGON

You can build a dragon in any size, shape or colour – it's your fairy tale! Design your dragon's head first, and then the neck and body. Add a tail, wings and legs next, making sure it isn't too heavy or off-balance to stand up. Then give it lots of spikes and other ferocious details!

What reason will your hero have to brave the dragon's lair?

Add taloned toes to your dragon's feet

Look through your collection for gold and silver elements, jewels, swords, crowns and other precious items

"At first the dragon's knee joints kept folding forwards, making it fall over. To solve it, I locked them so they couldn't bend the wrong way, and built a longer tail for balance."

Neck spikes plug into 2x2 round plates

Use plenty of hinges to make your dragon super-posable!

Wings are built out of overlapping angled plates to give them their shape

TOP VIEW

HEAD DESIGNS

The dragon's head can inspire the rest of the body, so it's a good place to start building. Here are some head ideas for a long-horned blue dragon, an Asian-style green dragon and a majestic golden dragon.

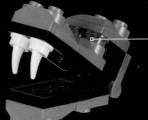

Transparent round plates for eyes

Use pointy white pieces for horns or fangs

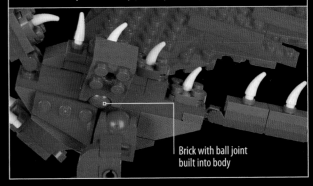

SHHHHHH!

LEGO Technic pin helps to rotate the knee joint

Tail spikes plug into jumper plates

Jack has found the Royal Nugget under the dragon's foot!

The tail is built out of segments held together by clip hinges to let each one swing up and down

WINGS

All the scariest dragons have the power of flight! This dragon's vast wings are braced by LEGO Technic cross-axles inside the body, which hold the ball joints in place and allow them to pose and flap. The ball and socket pieces need to be locked in place solidly so they don't pop loose.

Brick with ball joint built into body

HANDFUL OF BRICKS

Each of the fan builders was given a handful of common LEGO elements and asked to make as many different models as they could using only those pieces. Here's what Barney came up with.

Pieces with printed eyes are great for making expressive animals and people

Posing the tail at an angle gives it a sense of life and movement

WHO? WHO?

MINI DRAGON
You have already met Barney's evil dragon — now here's a much friendlier-looking one, made mostly out of red bricks. Perhaps it could keep Jack company on his adventures!

ME, THAT'S WHO!

OWL
With its big eyes and upraised wings, this owl looks pretty surprised! Barney used a printed radar dish element for its round, feathery tummy.

Placing the brick at an angle gives baby bird's shell a nice dimension

BABY BIRD
This baby bird has just popped out of its shell! A foot at the bottom will let it hop around until it's ready to hatch all the way.

A smaller 2x2 radar dish looks like a budding flower

Sandwich a plate between two bricks to make a stripe

BEE AND FLOWER
With a tap for a nose and an antenna for a stinger, Barney's bee is all abuzz about this flower. The same radar dish that gave the owl colourful feathers gives this flower delicate petals!

Angled plates are perfect for creating wings on small models

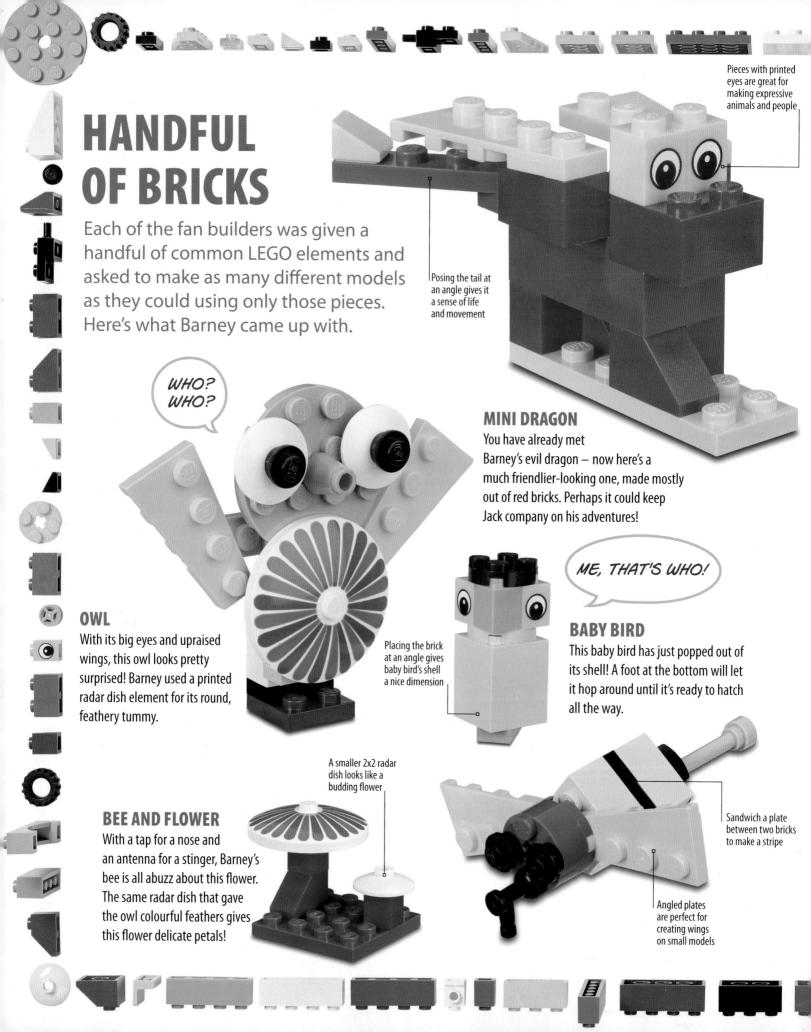

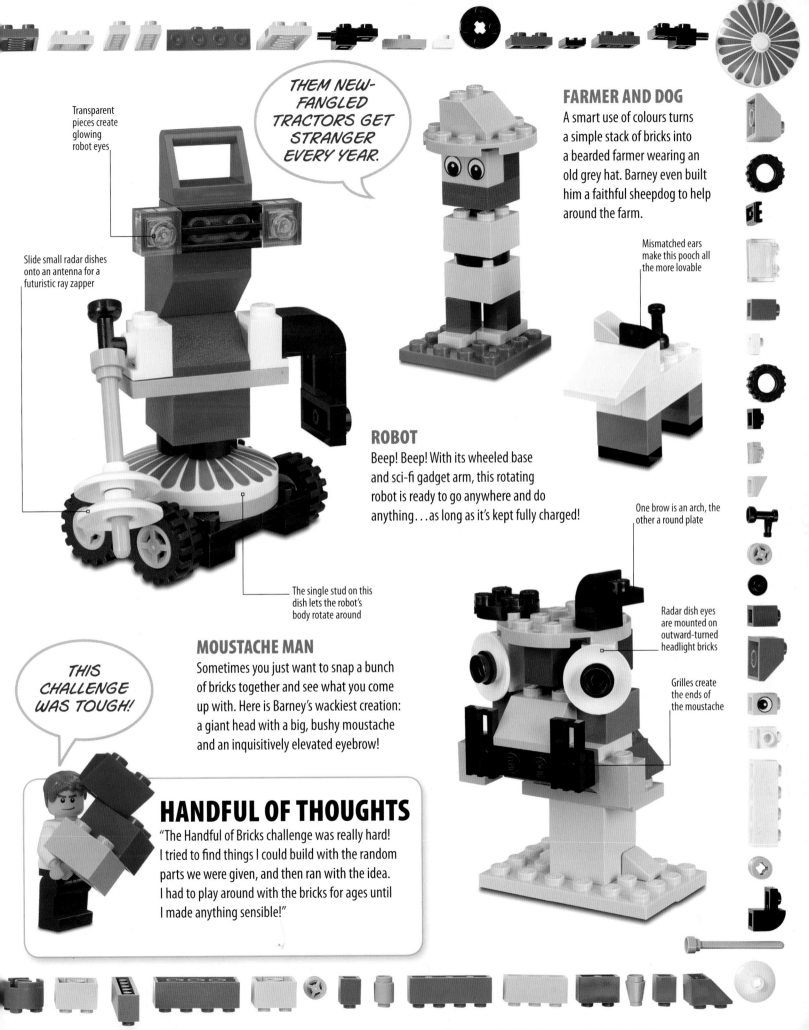

THEM NEW-FANGLED TRACTORS GET STRANGER EVERY YEAR.

Transparent pieces create glowing robot eyes

Slide small radar dishes onto an antenna for a futuristic ray zapper

FARMER AND DOG

A smart use of colours turns a simple stack of bricks into a bearded farmer wearing an old grey hat. Barney even built him a faithful sheepdog to help around the farm.

Mismatched ears make this pooch all the more lovable

ROBOT

Beep! Beep! With its wheeled base and sci-fi gadget arm, this rotating robot is ready to go anywhere and do anything...as long as it's kept fully charged!

The single stud on this dish lets the robot's body rotate around

One brow is an arch, the other a round plate

Radar dish eyes are mounted on outward-turned headlight bricks

Grilles create the ends of the moustache

MOUSTACHE MAN

Sometimes you just want to snap a bunch of bricks together and see what you come up with. Here is Barney's wackiest creation: a giant head with a big, bushy moustache and an inquisitively elevated eyebrow!

THIS CHALLENGE WAS TOUGH!

HANDFUL OF THOUGHTS

"The Handful of Bricks challenge was really hard! I tried to find things I could build with the random parts we were given, and then ran with the idea. I had to play around with the bricks for ages until I made anything sensible!"

FAIRY TALE CASTLE

Recovering the Royal Nugget has earned Jack an invitation to the king's castle. While real medieval castles were usually built to keep enemy armies out, and were more practical than beautiful, the castle of a fairy tale kingdom can be colourful and ornate. Give it elegant peaked turrets, festive flags and banners and decorative designs that show off the magic and majesty of your fantasy kingdom.

TURRET

Make your castle's turrets hollow with strong walls and an opening door so you can easily place minifigures inside. Will you put a palace guard or a captured prisoner in there?

Arches support the weight of the turrets from underneath

Studs on the floor stop the door from swinging too far in

Turret cones are built from the top down, stepping out each lower layer

Battlement crenellations are 1x2 bricks topped with 1x1 slopes

Pennant flags can be found in castle-themed LEGO sets – or build your own out of plates and clips!

Bricks in the middle of the turret cone keep it strong

Alternate round and square pieces to make columns around windows

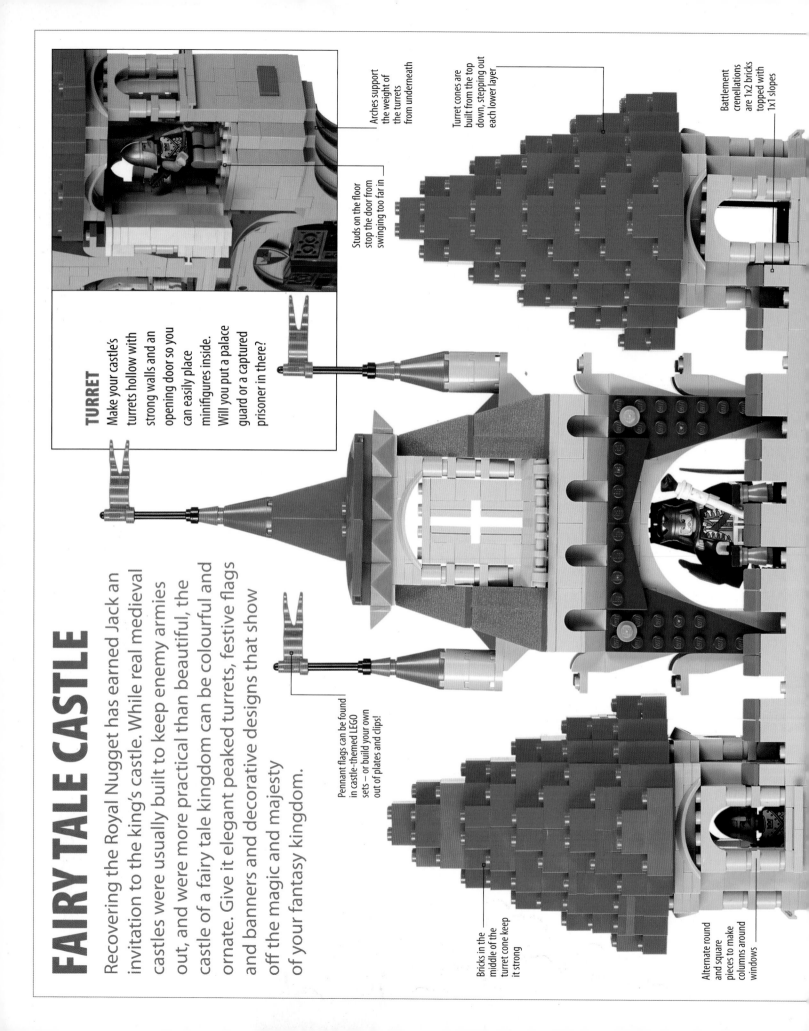

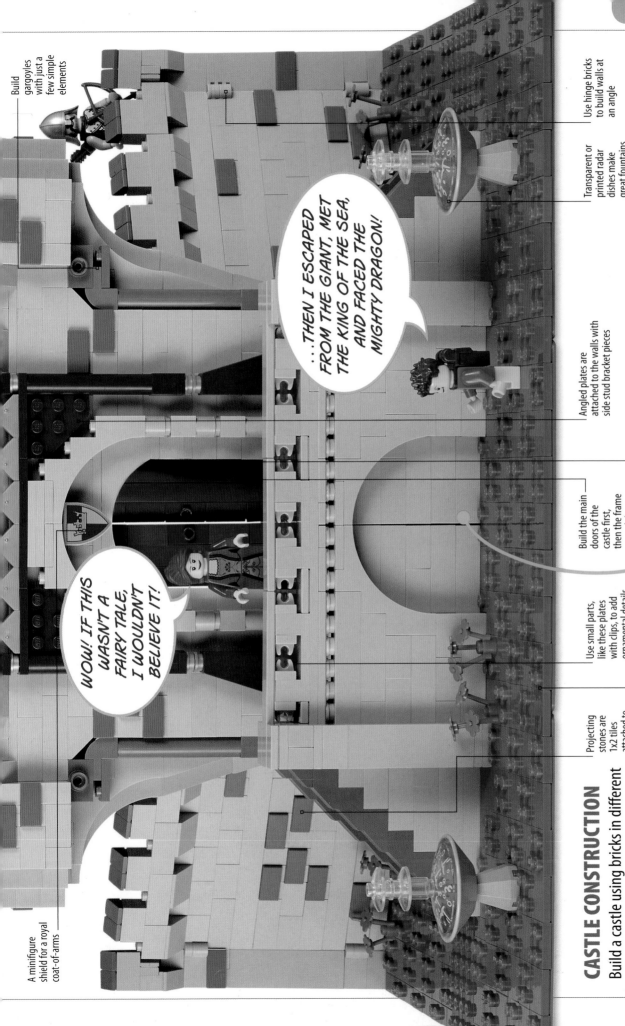

Build gargoyles with just a few simple elements

Use hinge bricks to build walls at an angle

Transparent or printed radar dishes make great fountains

…THEN I ESCAPED FROM THE GIANT, MET THE KING OF THE SEA, AND FACED THE MIGHTY DRAGON!

Angled plates are attached to the walls with side stud bracket pieces

Doors open on clip-and-bar hinges

Build the main doors of the castle first, then the frame around them

What secret does this balcony hide? Turn the page to find out!

WOW! IF THIS WASN'T A FAIRY TALE, I WOULDN'T BELIEVE IT!

Use small parts, like these plates with clips, to add ornamental details

For a fancy groomed lawn, make a checkerboard pattern of green 2x2 plates and tiles

Projecting stones are 1x2 tiles attached to headlight bricks in the walls

CASTLE CONSTRUCTION

Build a castle using bricks in different shades of grey to resemble stone. Here, contrasting dark orange brickwork adds texture and realism. More light grey pieces will make it look friendly, while dark grey will create a foreboding appearance.

A minifigure shield for a royal coat-of-arms

BUILDER TALK

"Take inspiration from a mixture of your favourite books. This castle design was inspired by the castle in the fairy tale *Cinderella*, with a lawn based on the Queen of Hearts's castle in Lewis Carroll's *Alice in Wonderland*."

MEET THE KING

Jack finds that even an old stone castle can be full of excitement. Not only does he meet a king, he is also given his very own fairy godmother! Building special features into your fairy tale castle will help you to tell even better stories with your bricks and minifigures. How about giving your castle a damsel in a tower, an ogre in the basement or a secret treasure chamber?

Steep pointed roof is made with slopes and cones on top of 4x4 car roof pieces

HIS MAJESTY'S TOWER

Some kings have huge throne rooms, but this one prefers a spot high in his castle where he can see the entire kingdom. The royal blue and gold around the archway tells all who behold it that their king is watching over them.

Gold, triangular slopes make a crown-like ring

ARROW SLIT

Many fairy tale castles have narrow windows to let archers inside fire at enemies outside. Combine 1x1 bricks and tiles, then add decorative columns built from 1x1 round bricks. Hold them in place with 2x3 curved plates with holes.

2x3 curved plate with holes

Use 2x2 round bricks and cones to make small turrets and towers

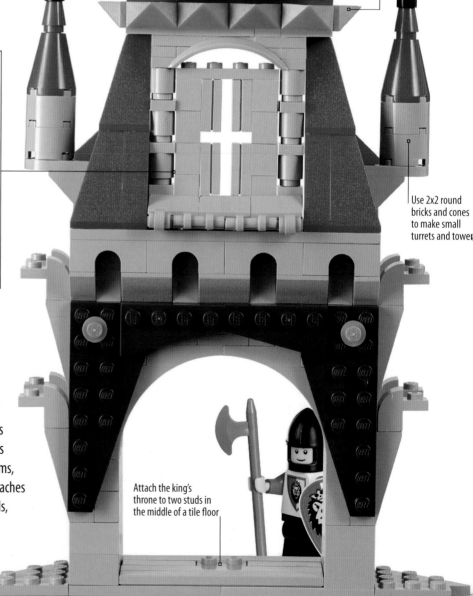

Jewels add the finishing touch to the royal throne

ROYAL THRONE

The royal throne is no mere chair! Flanked by gold swords and topped by a trio of jewels mounted on golden robot arms, this one is fit for a king. It attaches to the tower on just two studs, so it's easy to get in and out.

Attach the king's throne to two studs in the middle of a tile floor

HUZZAH FOR JACK THE HERO!

PEGASUS

A messenger on a winged horse travels the length of the kingdom to spread the news that the nugget has been found by a boy named Jack! Build your own flying steed by adding wings made of angled plates and clip hinges to a LEGO horse.

Angled plates held together with sliding plates

Minifigure attaches to studs on the horse's back

I GRANT YOU THREE WISHES!

A glowing magic wand, a crown and a kindly expression show that this fairy is a friend

Wings are overlapping angled plates attached to a minifigure neck bracket piece

If you don't have a decorated dress piece, you can use a plain slope brick instead

FAIRY GODMOTHER

This friendly fairy godmother will bestow Jack's reward for finding the nugget. She has three wishes for Jack to do with as he pleases! Your fairy could be good or evil. Use colours, faces and wing shapes to decide which yours is.

Instead of treasure, this chamber could house a powerful beast or knightly guardian to protect the castle!

TREASURE CHAMBER

Sliding doors beneath the entrance conceal the castle's secret treasure chamber. Perhaps Jack's brave deeds will have earned him an item of his choice. Flickering candles and hanging spiderwebs can create a creepy atmosphere.

Treasure chests are found in many LEGO® Castle and LEGO® Pirates sets – or build your own!

MOVING WALL

These secret panels are built to match the castle walls, but they're not locked into position. A base of smooth tiles beneath lets them slide back and forth, while pillars hold the sliding walls in place so they don't fall forwards.

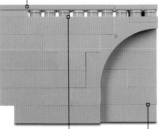

A row of tiles conceals the top of the door but leaves it free to move

Pillars made from a 1x2x5 brick and two 1x2 bricks

Add detail to the door with 1x1 round plates

Archway detail hints at the secret chamber beyond

THANKS FOR GETTING OUR TREASURE BACK FROM THAT BIG LIZARD, JACK!

CASTLE COMFORTS

Jack has never seen so much wealth in one place before. Palace life is definitely the life for him! Your castle's royal residents are used to luxury, so build them some of the finer things in life. A good use of colour goes a long way in making brick-built objects look expensive, and don't forget the fancy ornamentation.

A plate with handle holds the plates together and looks like artistic scroll work

For a rounded top, use car roof elements or substitute with arch and bow pieces

Tan angled plates are held on by 1x4 bricks with studs along one side

To make elegant carved columns, stack round bricks and cones with square bricks at the top and bottom

FOUR-POSTER BED

For inspiration in building old-fashioned furniture, look in a storybook…or a history book! With its resplendently thick mattress, softly curving sheets and sparkling gems, this covered bed is truly fit for a princess.

Design a different colour combination for every member of the royal household!

DON'T TELL ME I'M SUPPOSED TO MAKE THE BED MYSELF!

Double-hinge at the foot of the bed

You could attach feather plumes or other accessories to these jumper plates.

Build a stud-free surface for silken sheets and bedclothes

Raised platform made with plates

Use taller arches for the downturned top of the sheets

ALL TUCKED IN

This bed has a cosy hinged duvet on top. Swing it up and you can fit the lower half of a sleepy minifigure inside. When the minifigure is removed, the hinged part of the duvet blends in with the rest of the bed.

Harnesses connect to minifigure lances plugged into 1x1 bricks with one side stud

COOL BRICK

"This versatile brick adds fancy decoration to the royal carriage. It has also been used on the cottage (p.214) and castle (p.240) – can you spot where?"

REMOVABLE ROOF

Make the roof removable by clicking it onto just a few studs, so that you can move your characters around inside the carriage. This one rests its weight on the front supports, but only attaches at the back.

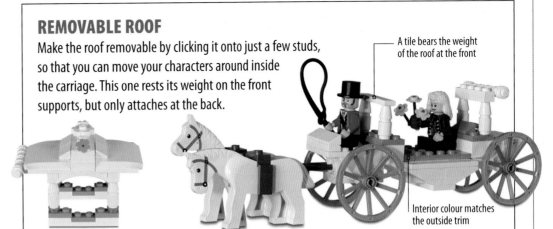

A tile bears the weight of the roof at the front

Interior colour matches the outside trim

White bricks make a model look like it's made of polished marble, ivory or painted wood

Decorative flowers on top

Roof provides shade and privacy

ROYAL CARRIAGE

A basic carriage has big round wheels, horses to pull it and spots for the driver and passengers to sit. For a royal carriage, add lots of curves, slopes and decorations. You could make other modifications to create prison carriages, mail coaches and racing buggies.

Roof supports built like shorter versions of the four-poster bed columns

Make sure your carriage's wheels have enough clearance to turn without bumping the sides

STEERING WHEELS

This carriage is built in two sections. The front part where the coachman sits is connected to the passenger portion with a 2x2 turntable plate, allowing the front wheels to steer and navigate winding roads.

These large wagon wheels can be found in many castle-themed LEGO sets

A turntable plate lets the back half of the carriage move separately

1x1 bricks with side studs are under these tiles

The wheel is attached with a free-spinning LEGO Technic pin

CASTLE STABLES

Feed the horses…sweep the stables… there's so much work for Jack to do around the palace! Every good castle has horses to pull its carriages and carry its knights, and those horses need somewhere to rest when they're not on duty. Build a strong wooden stable to house your kingdom's loyal steeds in the safety and comfort they deserve.

WATER TROUGH

This whole trough is built around a core of two 1x1 bricks with four side studs. For the trough's long sides, use one 2x4 tile or two 2x2 tiles, and 1x2 tiles for the short sides. Add water for thirsty horses by using a blue 1x4 tile.

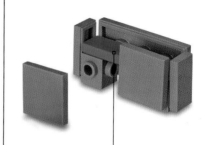

Switch out the blue tile for a different colour to make a food trough instead!

Yellow 2x2 bricks serve as bales of hay for the horses' mealtime

Rear wall mixes dark grey bricks with dark tan 1x2 log bricks for a stone-and-wood appearance

LEFT SIDE VIEW

REAR VIEW

RAISE THE ROOF

Enhance the play potential of your stable by building it with a removable roof. This stable's roof is only attached at two points on the back wall, so it can be removed completely. The roof can also be flipped back for play thanks to LEGO Technic bricks and pins.

RIGHT SIDE VIEW

CAN THESE HORSES TALK?

You can use curved barred fences to build secondary enclosures

The king's knights can mount up at this hitching post, built from 1x1 round bricks and headlight bricks

BUILDER TALK

"The biggest challenge with this build was getting the horses to actually fit inside. The solution: make the stables larger!"

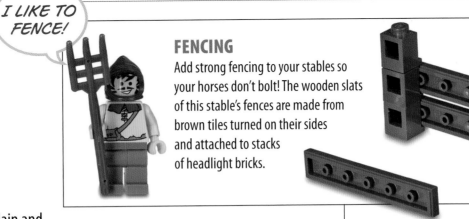

I LIKE TO FENCE!

FENCING

Add strong fencing to your stables so your horses don't bolt! The wooden slats of this stable's fences are made from brown tiles turned on their sides and attached to stacks of headlight bricks.

THE ROYAL STABLE

Stables are usually built to be plain and serviceable. Since the structure has so many open areas, take care to make the roof well-supported by the back wall and pillars. Include wide gates so the king's royal horses can get in and out with ease.

Roof is textured with a repeating pattern of tiles and 1x1 slopes

A farmer's stable might only have space for one or two horses, but a castle's stables need plenty of room for all the king's horses!

An overlapping framework of plates supports the roof and holds the pillars in place

NEIGH!

Single-piece round columns in the corners are stronger than stacks of individual bricks

A tan base looks like mud – or use yellow for scattered straw

Gates are attached to clips to let them swing open

CASTLE ENTERTAINMENT

Walking through the castle grounds, Jack stumbles upon the preparations for the grand ball that will be held in his honour. When he hears the musicians practising their songs, he can't help but join in! Kings and queens have a lot of responsibilities, and one of them is keeping all of their guests entertained. Make sure your fairy tale castle is well-stocked with food, entertainment and party supplies.

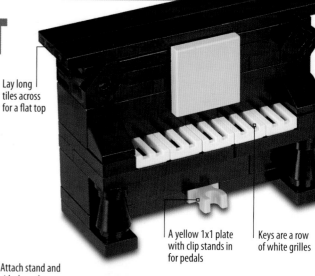

Lay long tiles across for a flat top

A yellow 1x1 plate with clip stands in for pedals

Keys are a row of white grilles

UPRIGHT PIANO

An upright piano is built like a series of walls assembled together, so use bricks and shape elements such as slopes and cones to recreate its design.

HIC!

Flame is a stack of two transparent orange 1x1 round plates

Candle stand is a small barrel

Attaching this plate upside-down lets you reverse the white cone for a unique candle shape

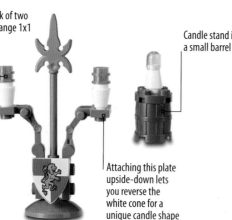

Attach stand and side-branches to bricks with side studs

Almost any piece can become part of a candlestick. These arms are handles from a pair of ninja nunchuks

CANDLESTICKS

To make candlesticks, look through your smallest pieces and see what you have in the same colour, then combine them in interesting ways. Use white 1x1 round bricks or cones as candles, and transparent orange, red or yellow pieces for flames.

A LEGO Technic half-beam holds the stand and barrel together

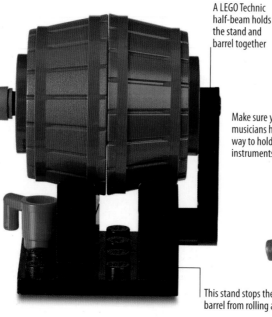

BEVERAGE BARREL

On its own, a half-barrel piece makes a handy washing basin or medieval bathtub. When you connect two together with a LEGO Technic axle-with-stud, then add a tap and stand, you've got a beverage barrel large enough for the biggest castle party!

This stand stops the barrel from rolling away

EVERYBODY READY? A-ONE, A-TWO AND...

Make sure your musicians have a way to hold their instruments!

GRAND PIANO

A grand piano takes a little more work. If this design is too complex, you can simplify things by using regular bricks. Give the pianist somewhere to sit, and provide a few refreshments for long performances!

> IF YOU CAN HUM IT, I WILL PLAY IT!

A pianist's stool can be made with tiles, a plate beneath and a radar dish for a stand

A small radar dish does double-duty as the teapot's lid and base

Teapot has a cow's horn for a handle and a horn for a spout

Keys are black grilles and a white tile

Use white elements for fine china

CASTLE BAND

Build your own musical instruments for the band. Look at real instruments and see how you can copy their shapes with your LEGO elements. You can stick to authentic medieval instruments, but since this is a fairy tale, you don't have to!

MAKE SOME MUSIC

The front and middle of the grand piano are fairly basic builds. The back is constructed sideways, using bricks and plates for the core. The curves are made from small and medium arches.

A tile with a printed scroll works well for sheet music

Each leg is built with a 1x1 round brick, round plate and a square plate

Use screwdrivers or bars as drumsticks

Centre drums are made from sliding plates and upside-down domes

> ♫ JACK! JACK! I'M A LEGO MANIAC! ♫

Saxophone is made from two taps, a goblet, a 1x1 plate with clip, and a round plate on the bottom

CASTLE BALLROOM

Here in the castle's grand ballroom, Jack almost feels like a prince himself. A ballroom makes a great story setting for medieval minifigures who want to party. It can include places for characters to sing and dance, eat and drink, and give speeches or play music. It's also a good location for daring swordfights and rescuing damsels in distress.

Attach tiles to bricks with side studs for trim around columns and wall edges

STAIRCASE

Your ballroom's staircase can be as tall, wide, long or short as you want it to be. Build the sides a little higher than the steps, and add detail bricks on top for a decorative railing.

This railing design is made of 1x1 slopes on top of pairs of 1x1 round plates, with a 1x1 square plate underneath

Each level of the staircase is two plates higher than the last one

Create mood with colour. A bold black-and-red ballroom could belong to an evil tyrant!

THEY CALL ME TWINKLE TOES ON THE DANCE FLOOR.

HELP! CAN ANYONE READ SHEET MUSIC?

BUILDER TALK

"I got the idea for this ballroom model from an animated fairy tale movie. I had to stop myself from putting in even more detail!"

HAVE A BALL!

A castle ballroom should be vast and well-lit. Create a wide-open look by building your ballroom's floor and walls in light colours. Add lavish decorations such as carpets, statues and wall hangings – plus a big central staircase so your guests can make a royal entrance.

Make a pattern with studded plates for a thickly carpeted dance floor, or use smooth tiles for something a little shinier

Use a different colour and some inverted-slope elements to turn a projecting layer of wall into a big curtain around the window

Telescopes make great hanging tassels!

GREAT WINDOW

Build a big window to let light flood in! Try stacking small windows together to make a large one, or build a wall out of coloured transparent bricks for a beautiful stained glass window.

If you don't have enough small window pieces, build a hollow frame instead

STATUES

Combine minifigure parts in solid colours to make gargoyles and other statues for your castle interior. Grey, for stone, looks most realistic, but you can use any colour you like.

Lampstand is built out of an upside-down spear, two LEGO® Space laser guns, and a brick with studs on its side to hold them together – plus matching flames!

Gargoyle's face is an alien mask from the LEGO® Space Police theme

A TOAST TO OUR NEW FRIEND JACK!

Roll out the red carpet for your minifigures by building a strip of red plates down the centre of the stairs

A double-layered base gives your model strength and stability, and lets you make the carpet on the same level as the ballroom floor

Have you ever wanted to build something big, but didn't have enough bricks? Try making it in micro-scale! By shrinking down the scale of your models, you can create vehicles, buildings and entire landscapes, all in a smaller size. In this section, you'll find ideas for making the most of even your tiniest LEGO® elements.

PLEASED TO MEET YOU!

MEET THE BUILDER:
TIM GODDARD
Age: 36
Day Job: Analytical chemist
LEGO Speciality: Microscale
Brick Collection: No idea, but it's pretty big!
Favourite Brick: 1x1 round plate (at least it is today!)
Did You Know? Tim took part in a workshop at LEGO headquarters to help with the initial planning of the LEGO® Legends of Chima™ theme.

TINY TRAVEL

When you are as small as the Gnome, it's easy for people to overlook you. That's why he likes micro-scale building so much. It makes him feel like he is enormous! The Gnome might usually be a tiny creature in a big world, but when he switches to micro-scale, he can be the biggest thing around. Join him on his travels through LEGO® models that recreate the past, present, and future…all in miniature form!

GNOME TO MARS BASE: I'M ABOUT TO LAND.

FROM SMALL BEGINNINGS COME GREAT THINGS!

MAKING A MICRO-WORLD
TIM GODDARD

"For this chapter, I could build pretty much anything I wanted, as long as it was in a small scale. I began by coming up with lots of different ideas of what would work well, and then I started building. I don't tend to plan my builds much beyond a rough idea; I just let the bricks guide me. I'm particularly happy with the way the modular city (pp.256–261) came out. Being able to make a building and then add it to a bigger city, or have your friends add to it, really appeals to me."

MICRO-MARS

Take a trip into micro-space and join the Gnome on a visit to the Red Planet! Its futuristic cityscape of shining hi-tech towers and spaceship landing platforms is out of this world. (See pp.292–293.)

ROOOOAAAR!

POCKET-SIZED GIANTS

Journey to a prehistoric world full of giant reptiles that are small enough to fit in your pocket! Just don't blame the Gnome if they escape while you're at school… (See pp.280–283.)

THE LITTLE CITY

Skyscrapers short enough for a minifigure to climb? You'll find them in a micro-metropolis, along with an office building, a construction site, a hospital and police headquarters. (See p.288.)

EVEN IN MINIATURE, THEY STILL SEEM PRETTY BIG TO ME.

I'M THE KING OF THE MICRO-WORLD!

MICRO-SCALE MODELS ARE A BIG DEAL TO ME!

255

CITY LIFE

Recreate the hustle and bustle of city life by building in micro-scale. Cities are full of structures with different shapes and colours, making them a lot of fun to design with your LEGO bricks. They're also made up of lots of smaller block sections, so you can build your city in separate parts and then combine them to make an entire micro-scaled metropolis.

Modular base is 16x16 studs

BACK TO BASICS

Try constructing your buildings on modular bases like this one. You could make each of your city's bases the same size and shape, and connect them all with LEGO Technic bricks and pins. You can assemble as many as you like – and take them apart to rearrange them whenever you want a change!

WHIZZ!

Grey LEGO Technic connector pin allows the top rotor to spin freely

HELICOPTER

This helicopter carries patients to the hospital in super-fast time. To make the tail rotor, attach a LEGO® Technic half-bush to a tap. Two 1x1 plates with clips hold the landing skids in place.

Use tiles to make a helipad for your helicopter to land on

Search your collection for printed pieces to add detail to your building

You could add a bench and some colourful scenery outside the hospital.

Tiny square windows are the backs of headlight bricks

Add pavements in a constrasting colour to the base so they can be seen clearly

HOSPITAL

A hospital is a functional building that every city should have, but that doesn't mean it has to be boring! Include little details, like some shrubbery, street lights and pavements to make your hospital a pleasant place to visit.

Thin layer of coloured stripes visually separates floors

PLASTIC FLOWERS ARE A MUST WHEN VISITING THE HOSPITAL.

AIRPORT

How about adding an airport to your city so that your micro-scale citizens can travel to other places? Prepare for take-off on this (not so) jumbo jet! You can add some mobile boarding steps to your jet by building a staircase of jumper plates with a tile on top, and wheels at the base.

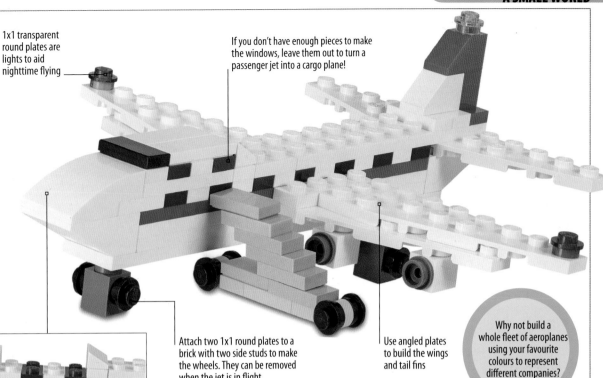

1x1 transparent round plates are lights to aid nighttime flying

If you don't have enough pieces to make the windows, leave them out to turn a passenger jet into a cargo plane!

Attach two 1x1 round plates to a brick with two side studs to make the wheels. They can be removed when the jet is in flight

Use angled plates to build the wings and tail fins

Why not build a whole fleet of aeroplanes using your favourite colours to represent different companies?

Sleek, aerodynamic nose made with slopes and curves

WINDOW SEATS

Place blue plates at intervals through the body to make windows that appear on both sides of the jumbo jet.

CONTROL TOWER

A tall air traffic control tower keeps track of the aeroplanes in the sky and on the runway. The controllers inside need to see all around, so give them windows facing in all directions using headlight bricks. A radar tower will help the controllers to track air traffic at any altitude.

Radar panels are made with grilles, but you could use tiles or plates instead

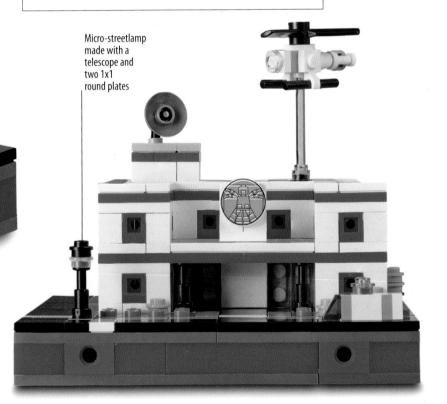

Micro-streetlamp made with a telescope and two 1x1 round plates

HOSPITAL FRONT VIEW

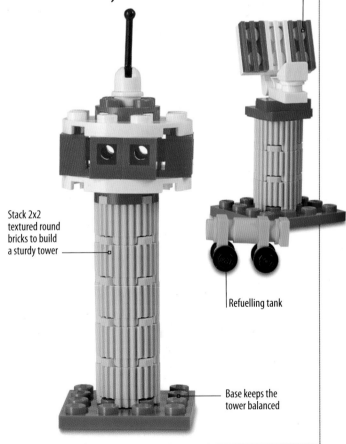

Stack 2x2 textured round bricks to build a sturdy tower

Refuelling tank

Base keeps the tower balanced

DOWNTOWN

As you build up your micro-sized city, you can add offices, stores and important civic structures such as schools, fire stations and a police headquarters. Keep the height of the storeys equal so that all of your buildings look like they are in the same scale, but use your imagination to create the rest of their details.

OFFICE BUILDING

This building is home to Octan – the imaginary fuel brand of LEGO autos everywhere – but you could become owner of your very own business by choosing your own colour scheme and decorations. If you don't want to use a printed tile as a company logo, then build any sign you like.

Air conditioning units on the roof keep the office workers cool

GOING UP!

Build each level above the ground floor in exactly the same way to make the office building look neat and professional. Use transparent pieces for big glass windows, and include vents and other details on the roof.

GREENERY

These decorative trees are constructed by stacking three 2x2 round plates for pots, and then alternating 1x1 round plates and small radar dishes to make trunks and leaves.

Window washers make the exterior look pristine

Pots are in the Octan company colours

A printed tile from a classic LEGO® Town set shows that this office belongs to Octan

An overhang above the door provides shade and shelter

Vehicles add detail to your micro-city and can be built with just a few pieces!

Don't be square. Add a doorway or a wall to the front of your building at a different angle

Make communications gear with a radar dish, a plate with a clip on top, and a tap

POLICE STATION

A micro-city's citizens may be too small to see, but they still need to be served and protected! This police station is built like the hospital (see p.256), but with more storeys and a white-and-blue colour scheme.

CALLING ALL UNITS: THERE ARE REPORTS OF A GIANT GNOME!

Include support walls between windows

Different colours and combinations of round and square 1x1 plates give vegetation a realistic look

Police vehicles can park under the elevated building

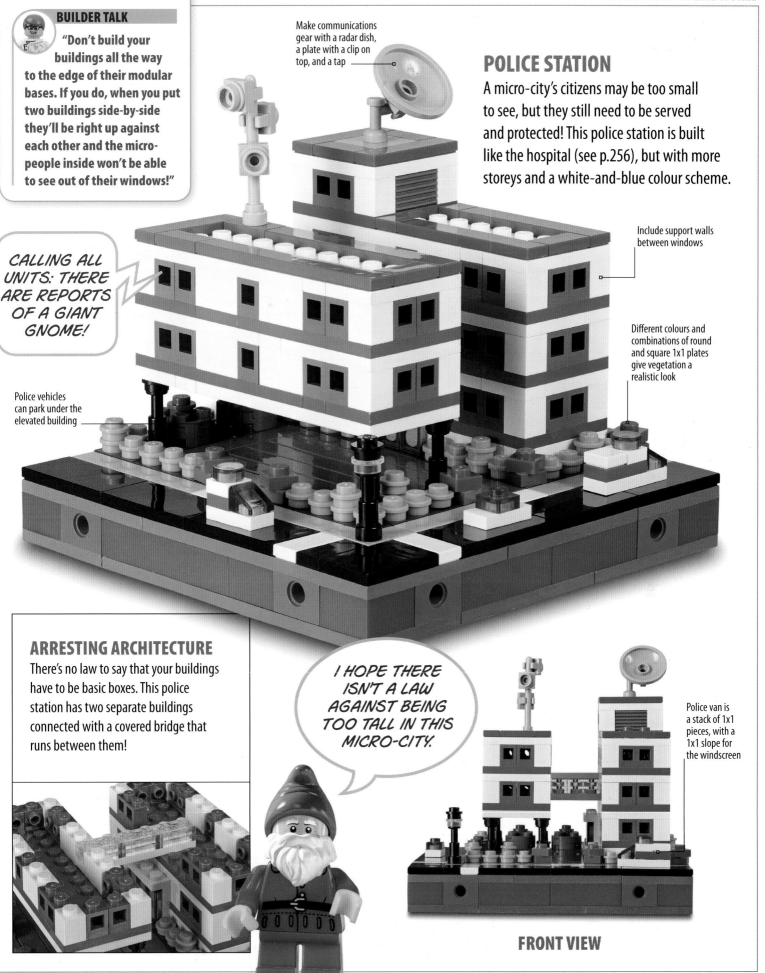

ARRESTING ARCHITECTURE

There's no law to say that your buildings have to be basic boxes. This police station has two separate buildings connected with a covered bridge that runs between them!

I HOPE THERE ISN'T A LAW AGAINST BEING TOO TALL IN THIS MICRO-CITY.

Police van is a stack of 1x1 pieces, with a 1x1 slope for the windscreen

FRONT VIEW

CITY PARK

Life in the big city can be hectic – sometimes you need to get away from it all for a bit of peace and quiet. That's why every city should have a park. But before it can be enjoyed, your park needs to be built. Here are before-and-after versions of this vital addition to your micro-city.

BUILDER TALK

"There are lots of different scales you can use when building smaller than minifigure scale. Think about what size a person would be for the building or vehicles you are making. This will help the small worlds that you build look like they fit together."

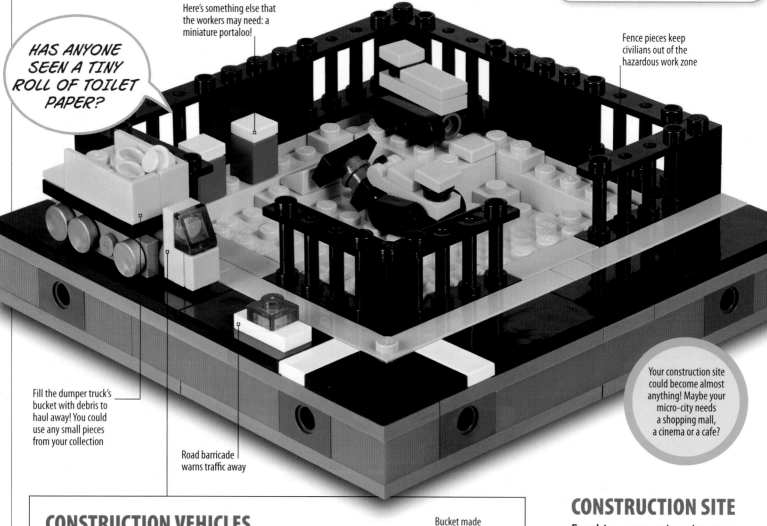

Here's something else that the workers may need: a miniature portaloo!

HAS ANYONE SEEN A TINY ROLL OF TOILET PAPER?

Fence pieces keep civilians out of the hazardous work zone

Fill the dumper truck's bucket with debris to haul away! You could use any small pieces from your collection

Road barricade warns traffic away

Your construction site could become almost anything! Maybe your micro-city needs a shopping mall, a cinema or a cafe?

CONSTRUCTION VEHICLES

Construction vehicles come in different colours, but yellow is the most classic look. Despite their size, these micro-models are very recognisable thanks to a clever choice of pieces.

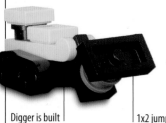

Bucket made with small corner wall elements

Digger is built around a droid torso piece

1x2 jumper plate

1x1 round tiles attached to a plate and a brick with side studs

CONSTRUCTION SITE

For this construction site, start with the modular base used for the hospital and police station. Remove the top plates so that it looks dug up and arrange bricks, plates and tiles to make mounds of freshly excavated earth.

260

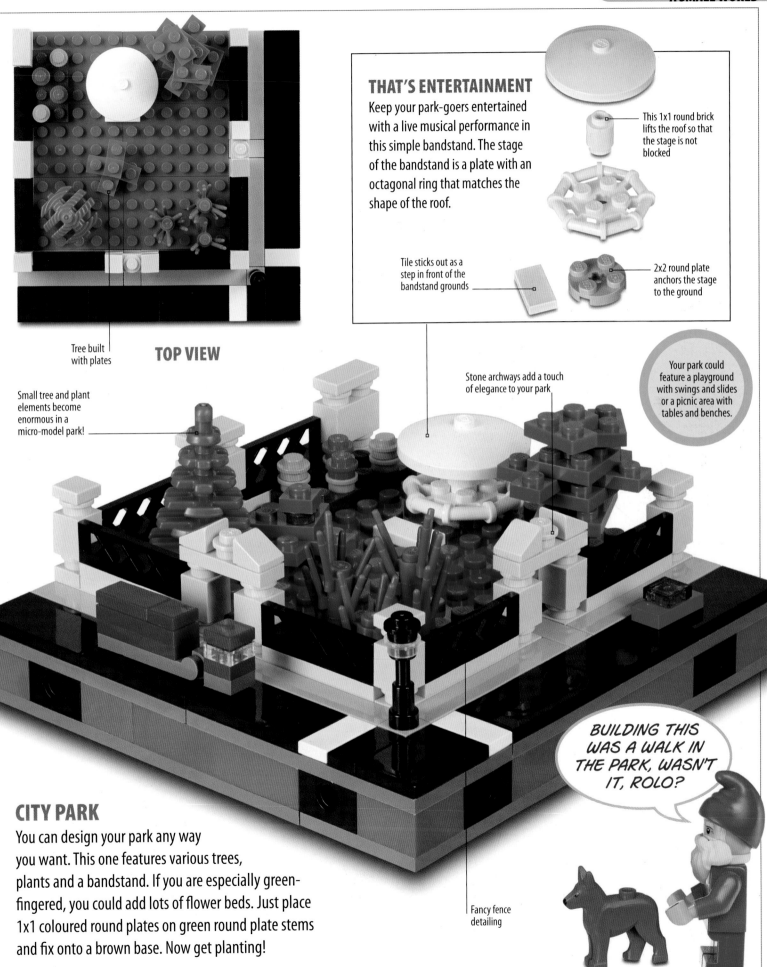

TOP VIEW

Tree built with plates

THAT'S ENTERTAINMENT

Keep your park-goers entertained with a live musical performance in this simple bandstand. The stage of the bandstand is a plate with an octagonal ring that matches the shape of the roof.

This 1x1 round brick lifts the roof so that the stage is not blocked

Tile sticks out as a step in front of the bandstand grounds

2x2 round plate anchors the stage to the ground

Small tree and plant elements become enormous in a micro-model park!

Stone archways add a touch of elegance to your park

Your park could feature a playground with swings and slides or a picnic area with tables and benches.

Fancy fence detailing

CITY PARK

You can design your park any way you want. This one features various trees, plants and a bandstand. If you are especially green-fingered, you could add lots of flower beds. Just place 1x1 coloured round plates on green round plate stems and fix onto a brown base. Now get planting!

BUILDING THIS WAS A WALK IN THE PARK, WASN'T IT, ROLO?

RACETRACK

Get out your biggest base plate and use your smallest LEGO elements to build a micro-scale racetrack! Give it all the features of the real thing: a circular course with side barriers, a starting and finish line, stands full of spectators and a set of miniature race cars. When you're done, think up rules for a racing game to play with your friends!

2...4...6...8... WHO DO WE APPRECIATE? MICRO-RACERS!

Build special obstacles like water traps, sand dunes, ramps and tunnels to change the game-play!

Use red round plates to make corner barriers that keep cars inside the track

Around the back are buildings for the pit crews who repair and maintain the cars

1x2 and 1x1 tiles make stripes that could work like the spaces on a game board

Build the road out of smooth tiles so the cars can slide along its surface

Black and white pieces mark the beginning and end of the race

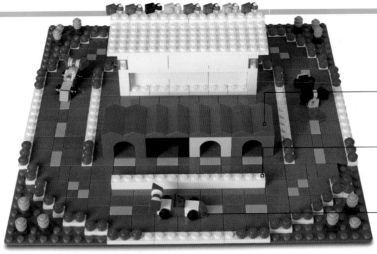

"This little 1x1 round plate can be used for all sorts of things! When I built the mini cars, I knew I'd have to use this part as the wheels and it dictated the size of the cars. You can also find it used as a nose for the mini lion on p.279."

The pit buildings are made from roof tiles and arch bricks. If you don't have these, use bricks and plates instead

A long brick or panel works for the pit wall

A race car only seats one, so you only need one window!

REAR VIEW

GRANDSTAND

What's a race without the fans? Minifigures are way too big for a micro-scale crowd, but rows of colourful stacks of two 1x1 round plates create just the right look.

Use transparent bricks for windows on the sides of the grandstands

Attach 1x1 plates with side clips to pieces with bars for tiny pennant flags

Decorate the outside with trees and bushes made from 1x1 square and round plates

TOP VIEW

I'M ASKING FOR DIRECTIONS!

WHY DO YOU KEEP STOPPING?

TINY RACERS

Build these racing cars in a similar way to the micro-cars on p.265. Removing the 2x4 plate in the middle and adding a spoiler at the back increases the car's speed.

Wheels are 1x1 round plates attached to 1x1 bricks with studs on two sides

VEHICLES

Build some micro-scale automobiles and a truck to haul them around. If it were scaled to minifigures, this car carrier would be a truly massive model, but as a micro-build, it can be made in a much more manageable size. Load up its trailer with colourful cars and take them on a road trip.

Transporter trucks come in different sizes, so try building a trailer that holds one, two or even 20 autos!

NOW THIS IS THE WAY TO TRAVEL!

Make sure your hinges are well attached as you build

Top bars are lances from minifigure knights

Wheels are from a small LEGO race car set

TRANSPORTER TRUCK

Building a fairly large micro-scale model means that you get to add in special features, such as a turning cab, spinning wheels and a trailer that works like the real thing.

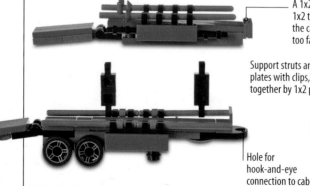

A 1x2 bracket with a 1x2 tile attached keeps the cars from moving too far forwards

Support struts are 1x1 plates with clips, held together by 1x2 plates

Hole for hook-and-eye connection to cab

DESIGNING A TRAILER

Your trailer needs to be long, wide and tall enough to hold your micro-cars. That's why it's a good idea to build the autos first and then design the trailer to fit them.

MICRO-CARS

Here are a few simple ways to use small LEGO pieces to create micro-scale automobiles. You can use the same techniques to make boxy vans, racing cars (see p.263) and stretched limousines.

Use 1x1 bricks with one side stud between the wheels and attach to the bottom of the plate

Each one of these micro-cars is built around a 2x4 plate

CAB CONSTRUCTION

The truck's cab can be long-nosed or flat-nosed, and any colour you like. This cab's window is three 1x2 transparent bricks side-by-side, with a 2x3 plate as a roof. Attach slopes to the side of the bonnet to create an angled shape.

Roof horns are minifigure binoculars

Use a cone, a telescope and a 1x1 round plate to make a smoke stack

If you don't have this ladder piece, attach grilles to bricks with side studs

*RIGHT A BIT...
LEFT A BIT...WHOA!
EASY, EASY...
LEFT A BIT...*

BUILDER TALK

"The trailer was the challenging part of this model. It was tough to make it as small as possible, while still keeping it functional. I used a hook-and-eye connection to allow the truck to make turns and the trailer to be easily removed."

Smooth tiles let autos slide into place without sticking on studs

LOAD 'EM UP!

Each level of the trailer has its own hinged ramp to let the cars drive on and off. When folded back up, the ramps lock the cars in place.

Wheels are black 1x1 round plates attached to 1x1 bricks with studs on two sides

CARGO HAULERS

With so much micro-scale construction going on, you'll need a way to transport your precious pieces from place to place. Build a freight train to move them around the country, and a cargo ship to carry them across the sea.

Logs are stacks of 1x1 round bricks, plates, and cones

Windscreen is a transparent 1x2 brick

Expand your scene with a train station, tracks, and other train styles like steam engines, bullet trains and passenger or tanker cars!

Build your freight cars like open-topped boxes, ready to fill with cargo

FREIGHT TRAIN

Freight trains transport heavy loads over long distances, so make sure your train cars are strong and sturdy. Each car carries a different cargo, but they can all be built in the same way.

If you don't have curved pieces for the roof, use a flat plate instead

Stack two 1x2 textured bricks to create the warehouse's metal door

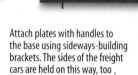

Attach plates with handles to the base using sideways-building brackets. The sides of the freight cars are held on this way, too

Trolley wheels are from airport and garage sets. You could also use skateboard wheels or small LEGO wheel hubs without tyres

Front and back windows are held on by grilles on top

THE LITTLE ENGINE

The core of the train engine is a basic stack of plates and textured bricks, beneath a roof of plates with side rails. With a window on each end, your train can travel in either direction.

Connect the carriages and engine with ball-and-socket joints

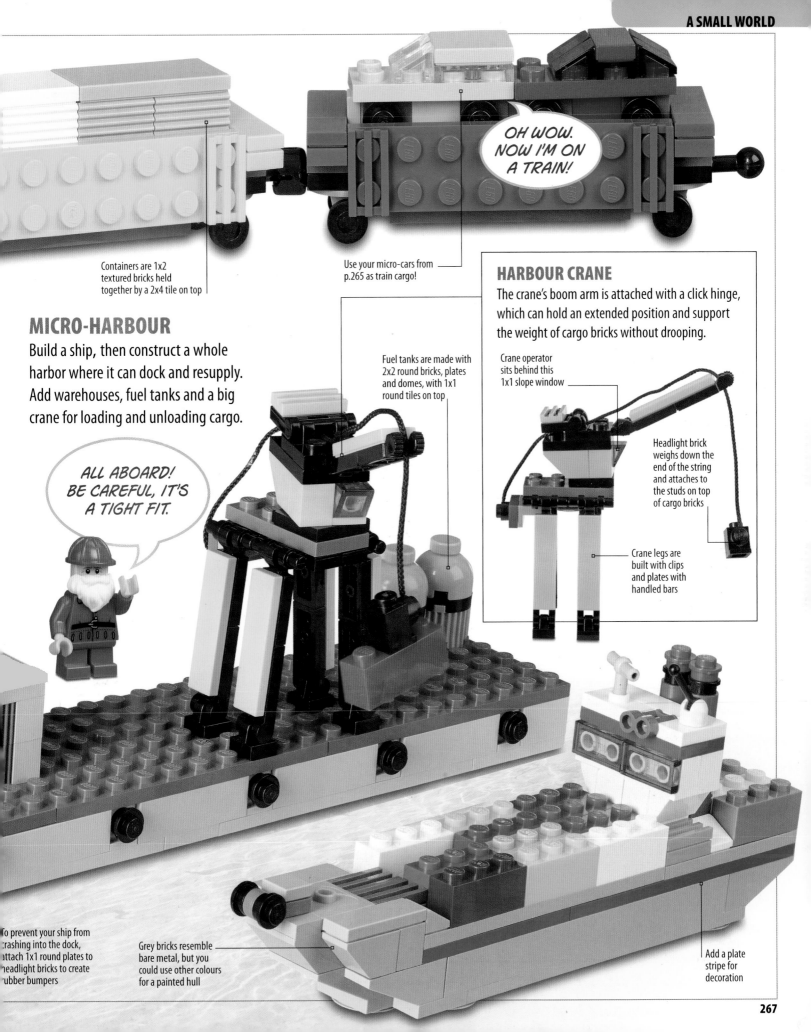

Containers are 1x2 textured bricks held together by a 2x4 tile on top

OH WOW. NOW I'M ON A TRAIN!

Use your micro-cars from p.265 as train cargo!

HARBOUR CRANE

The crane's boom arm is attached with a click hinge, which can hold an extended position and support the weight of cargo bricks without drooping.

MICRO-HARBOUR

Build a ship, then construct a whole harbor where it can dock and resupply. Add warehouses, fuel tanks and a big crane for loading and unloading cargo.

Fuel tanks are made with 2x2 round bricks, plates and domes, with 1x1 round tiles on top

Crane operator sits behind this 1x1 slope window

Headlight brick weighs down the end of the string and attaches to the studs on top of cargo bricks

ALL ABOARD! BE CAREFUL, IT'S A TIGHT FIT.

Crane legs are built with clips and plates with handled bars

To prevent your ship from crashing into the dock, attach 1x1 round plates to headlight bricks to create rubber bumpers

Grey bricks resemble bare metal, but you could use other colours for a painted hull

Add a plate stripe for decoration

OIL PLATFORM

Take your building offshore and construct a miniature oil platform to collect oil and natural gas from beneath the ocean floor – those tiny cars and trucks need to get their fuel from somewhere!

SPINNING DRILL

Think about how you can use your LEGO Technic parts to build special moving functions into your micro-models. Spin the black gear on the side of the rig, and its long drill and the flame on top rotate right along!

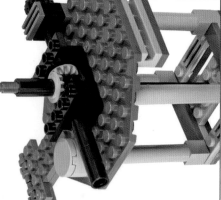

Use any flame piece from your collection, or build your own out of transparent pieces

A joystick, a tap, and a small radar dish create an array to communicate with the mainland

Crew quarters is built by stacking white and transparent pieces, with dark grey for rooftops

CAN WE ORDER A PIZZA FOR DELIVERY HERE?

MINI VEHICLES

The mini-helicopter carries workers to and from the oil platform. Its main rotor is a small tail rotor from a bigger helicopter model. The mini-sub dives under the water to check the rig and repair any problems. It is built in yellow for high visibility and uses several one-stud jumper plates.

Cockpit is built with two 1x1 slopes attached sideways

A 1x1 round plate is just the right size for a tiny propeller

Transparent element acts as a spotlight to navigate the murky seas

Pontoons are fire hose nozzles held on by clips

Helipad has a 2x2 yellow tile on top to prevent the helicopter from sliding around

FUELLED AND READY FOR TAKE-OFF!

PINT-SIZED PLATFORM

This model is based on a fixed platform oil rig, with legs that are anchored to the seabed. Most of the oil rig stays underwater, with the platform near the top sticking up above the surface. The tapering drill frame at the top of the oil platform is built like the harbour crane (see p. 267), using narrow clip-and-bar hinges.

Grey pieces look like strong steel

Try building a tanker ship or a pipeline to transport the oil back to land!

Angled supports are made with clips and plates with handles, joined together by narrow tiles

Yellow cranes move on clip hinges to lift supplies or lower the mini-sub into the water

Plates with holes lock the rig levels together, while letting the cross-axle drill pass through

REAR VIEW

Use single-piece columns for strength and stability

Meet these dolphins in their underwater habitat on p.273

★ CHALLENGE

PUZZLE PLAY

This micro-puzzle is small in size, but big on fun! Build a frame using simple bricks, then combine other pieces to make shapes to fit inside it – just like a jigsaw puzzle. Ask your friends and family to complete the puzzle. Try timing them to see who can fit the bricks inside the frame the fastest!

A puzzle shouldn't just be functional – make it decorative, too

Frame can be any shape you like!

BRICKS AND PIECES

The brick pieces you build need to fit perfectly into your frame, but create different shapes and sizes to make the puzzle a real challenge.

Join your brick shapes with 2x2 bricks, which will also make the shapes easier to move around the puzzle

Hat is a 2x2 round brick stacked on a 4x4 round plate

RAIN OR SHINE, I'M FEELING FINE.

SEAPLANE

Tim built this little plane with LEGO plate pontoons so it can land on water. Radar dishes on wheel connectors give it a pair of spinning propellers!

The umbrella's antenna handle is plugged into a headlight brick

UMBRELLA MAN

Thanks to his trusty umbrella, this top-hatted gentleman has no fear of rainy days. Tim constructed him sideways, with a head mounted on a bracket.

A transparent 1x2 brick makes a good cockpit window

Sail is a pair of opposite angled plates attached to a bracket

LIGHTHOUSE

Tan elements create a small island for this micro-scale lighthouse. The transparent yellow piece at the top is a light to warn sailing boats away from the rocky shores.

BZZZ!

HANDFUL OF BRICKS

Each of the fan builders was given a handful of common LEGO elements and asked to make as many different models as they could using only those pieces. These are the models that micro-scale building maestro Tim G. built.

SATELLITE DISH

A round plate, a radar dish and an antenna form a transmitter to help a miniature spaceport send messages into space. Will tiny aliens answer the call?

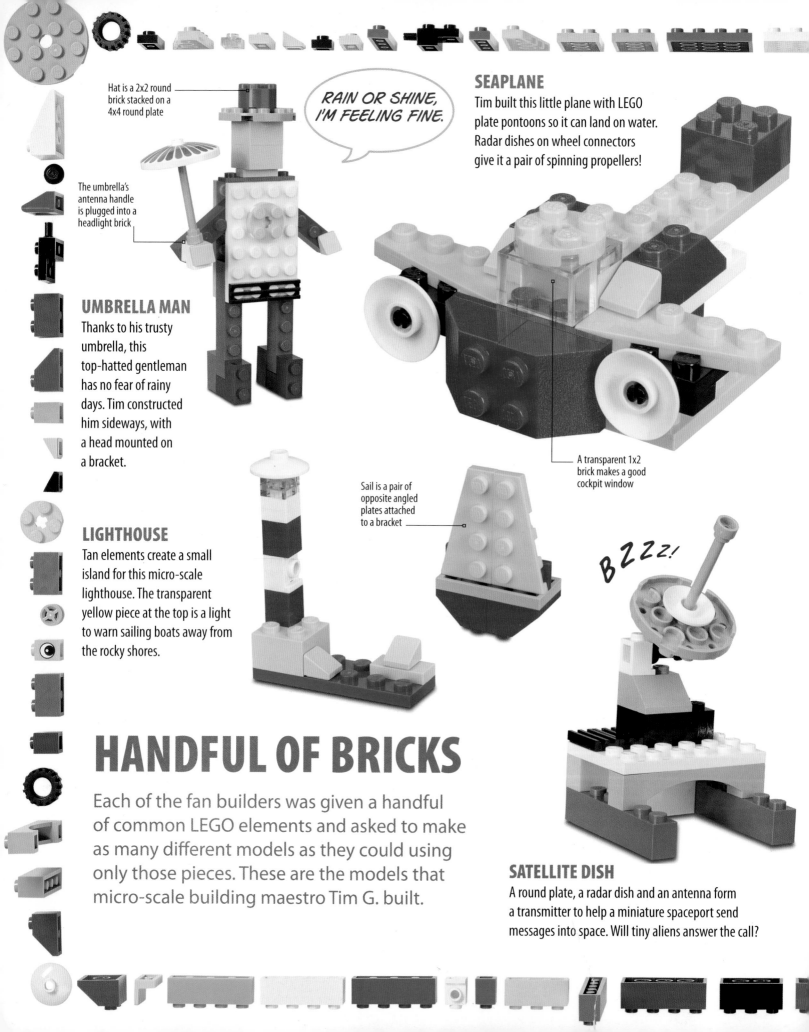

HORSE PADDOCK

Tim built his horse a set of training jumps to get it in shape for equestrian shows, as well as a water pump and a stack of hay to keep it refreshed.

Just two bricks can add a lot to a scene

A tap for a beaked head

The horse's neck and tail are centred on jumper plates

DUCK

This white duck was built out of just five pieces, including the headlight brick that gives it a turning head. Compare it to the one built by Pete and Yvonne on p.311!

ROOSTER

Cock-a-doodle-doo! This mini model captures all the familiar features of a crowing barnyard rooster, from the comb on its head to the plume of tail-feathers on its back.

SCORPION CAR

Combine a stinging arachnid with a race car, and what do you get? The fastest thing in the desert, that's what! Tim really got creative with this colourful clawed model.

There's even a hole on top where a minifigure can sit and drive!

HMMM...WHAT DOES THIS REMIND ME OF?

HANDFUL OF THOUGHTS

"I looked at the bricks I was given and thought about what they reminded me of. It was fun and challenging to build something with such a small handful!"

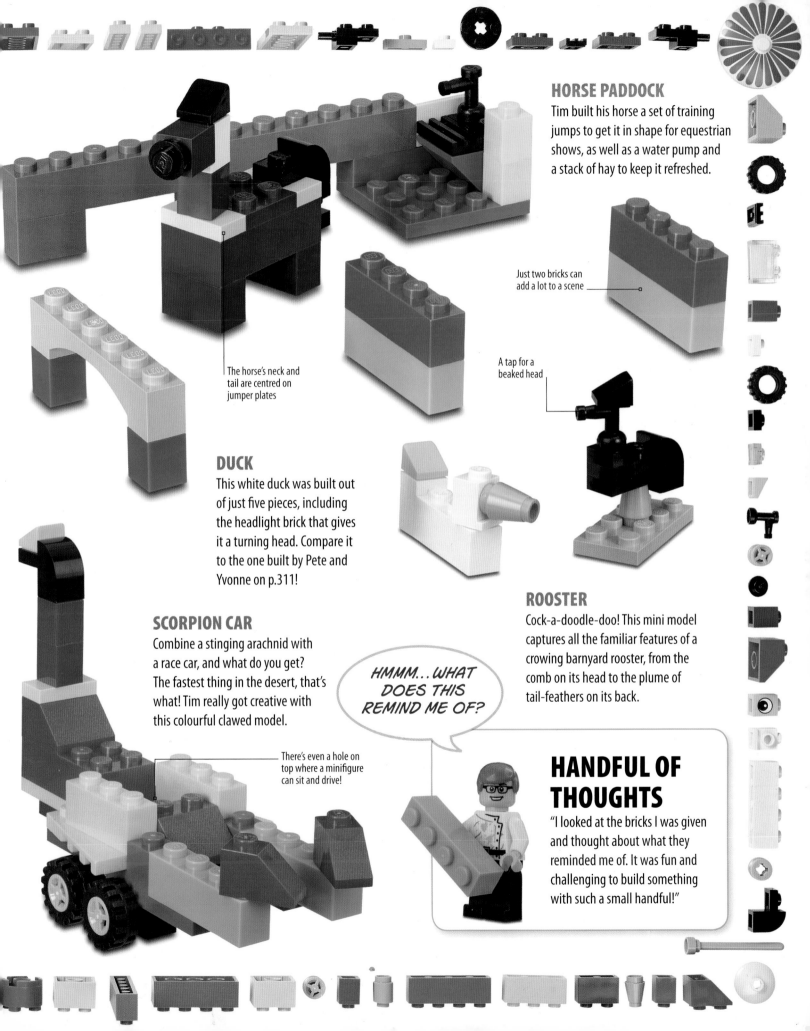

ON THE SEA FLOOR

Take a dive beneath the waves and build a scene at the bottom of the ocean! You can find lots of curious things on the sea floor, like a long-forgotten pirate's ship. You might even discover a sunken chest full of treasure with your micro-scale sub. Micro-scale building makes it easy to construct a shipwreck and all of the undersea objects that surround it.

BUILDING A WRECK

To make the ship's angled front, build a clip hinge and angle the section of the bow into position. Don't worry if there are gaps in your model — a shipwreck is called a wreck for a reason!

Only one of the ship's masts still stands

What sank this ship? Maybe you can build a hint into your own version!

Use binoculars for jet propulsion

Two curved slopes make up the sub's main body

The cockpit is 1x1 transparent tiles so aquanauts can see any underwater wrecks clearly

Robot arms for underwater exploration

UNIDENTIFIED MARINE LIFE AHEAD, CAPTAIN.

WATCH WHERE YOU'RE GOING WITH THOSE ROBOT ARMS!

Sea plants have started to grow over the wreck. You could also make barnacles with white round plates

TOP VIEW

Sunken treasure is gold 1x1 round plates, but you could use whatever colourful pieces you have in your collection

Turn to the next page to study this octopus more closely!

Use bricks with side studs to attach the sides of the hull

REAR VIEW

SHIPWRECK

To build a shipwreck, start by constructing the basic shape of a boat – just don't finish it! The parts that have been on the seabed for a long time should suggest what the ship looked like when it was complete. Use plates and tiles to create broken planks and stray pieces of hull.

Fin is a 1x1 slope

Jumper plate

DOLPHINS

It doesn't take many pieces to build a micro-scale dolphin. Use tiny slopes to give your flippered friends distinct features. Jumper plates and a plate with ring at the back will allow you to put the fins in the right positions.

Use transparent pieces to make stands for your extra objects

Pick a base plate colour that looks like a sandy ocean floor

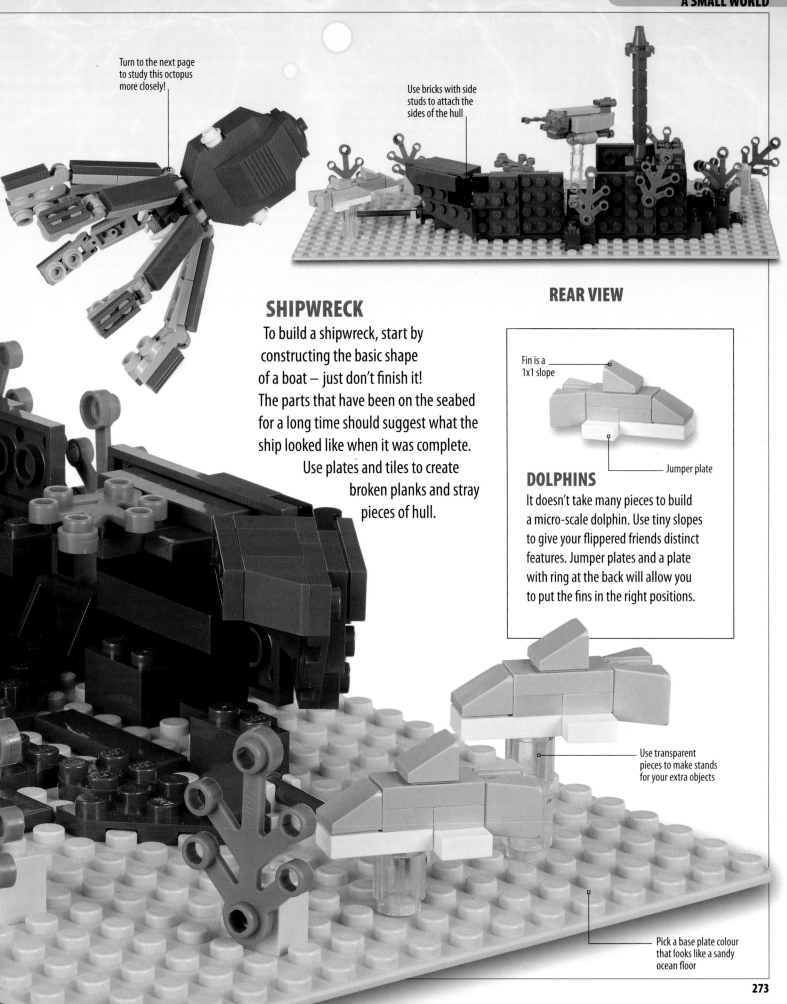

MONSTERS OF THE DEEP

The ocean is full of adventure and mystery. You never know what unusual marine life might be swimming around down there in the depths. Use your bricks to build weird and wonderful micro-scale creatures, and a fearless submarine to explore it all.

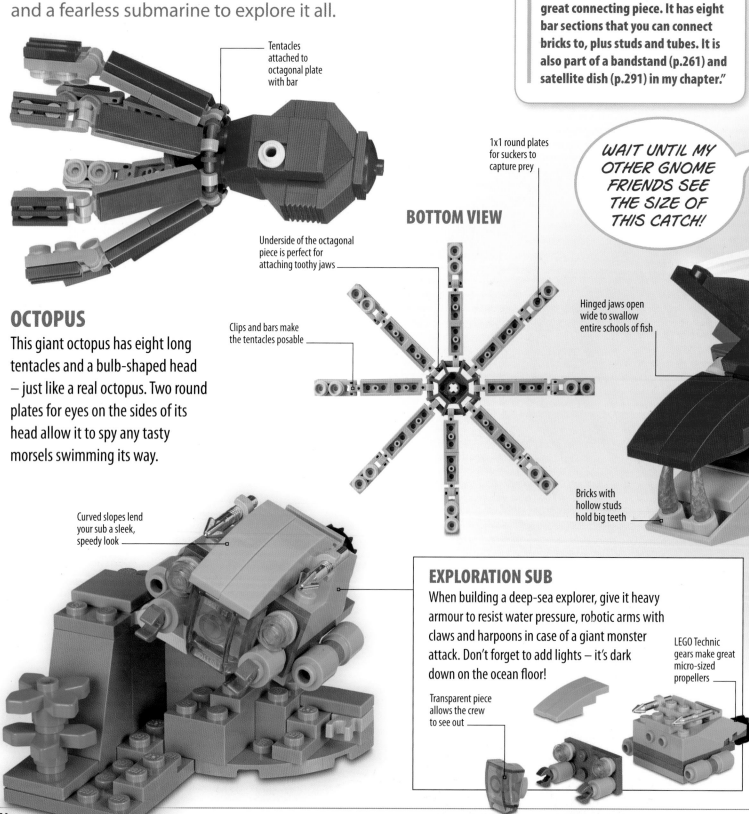

Tentacles attached to octagonal plate with bar

COOL BRICK

"This octagonal plate with bar is a great connecting piece. It has eight bar sections that you can connect bricks to, plus studs and tubes. It is also part of a bandstand (p.261) and satellite dish (p.291) in my chapter."

1x1 round plates for suckers to capture prey

BOTTOM VIEW

Underside of the octagonal piece is perfect for attaching toothy jaws

WAIT UNTIL MY OTHER GNOME FRIENDS SEE THE SIZE OF THIS CATCH!

OCTOPUS

This giant octopus has eight long tentacles and a bulb-shaped head – just like a real octopus. Two round plates for eyes on the sides of its head allow it to spy any tasty morsels swimming its way.

Clips and bars make the tentacles posable

Hinged jaws open wide to swallow entire schools of fish

Bricks with hollow studs hold big teeth

Curved slopes lend your sub a sleek, speedy look

EXPLORATION SUB

When building a deep-sea explorer, give it heavy armour to resist water pressure, robotic arms with claws and harpoons in case of a giant monster attack. Don't forget to add lights – it's dark down on the ocean floor!

LEGO Technic gears make great micro-sized propellers

Transparent piece allows the crew to see out

274

SEA SERPENT

With its snake-like body and three pairs of fins, this reptilian creature is unlike any that you'll find in the oceans of Earth. Or maybe it just hasn't been found yet! The sections of the serpent's body are held together with sturdy click hinges, providing movement for swimming, hunting and battling pesky submarines!

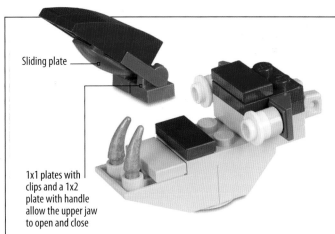

Sliding plate

1x1 plates with clips and a 1x2 plate with handle allow the upper jaw to open and close

MOUTHY MONSTER

To make a jaw strong enough to feast on plenty of fish, lock two curved bricks and a plate with handle together using a 2x2 sliding plate underneath. The lower jaw is made with inverted slope bricks held together by another sliding plate.

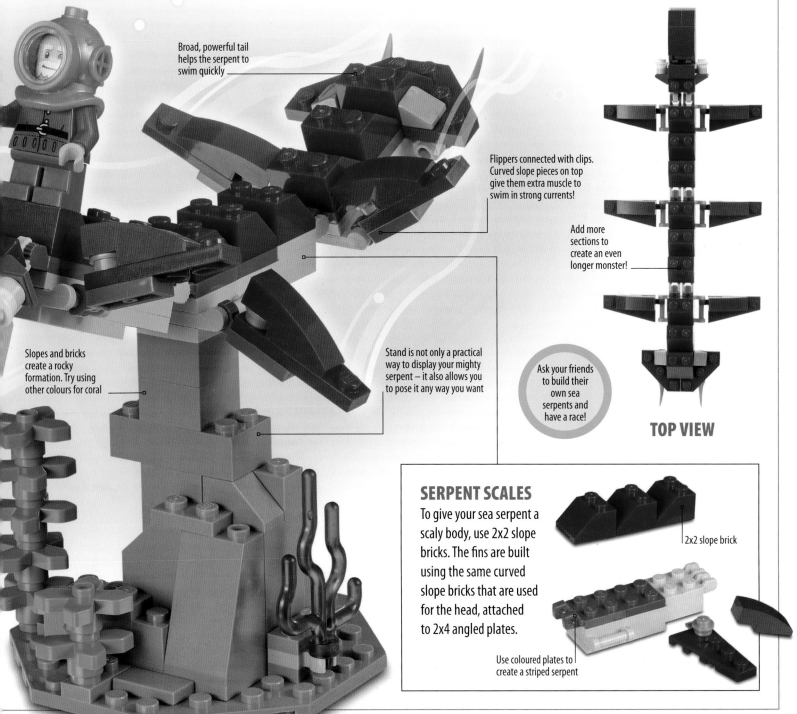

Broad, powerful tail helps the serpent to swim quickly

Flippers connected with clips. Curved slope pieces on top give them extra muscle to swim in strong currents!

Add more sections to create an even longer monster!

Slopes and bricks create a rocky formation. Try using other colours for coral

Stand is not only a practical way to display your mighty serpent – it also allows you to pose it any way you want

Ask your friends to build their own sea serpents and have a race!

TOP VIEW

SERPENT SCALES

To give your sea serpent a scaly body, use 2x2 slope bricks. The fins are built using the same curved slope bricks that are used for the head, attached to 2x4 angled plates.

2x2 slope brick

Use coloured plates to create a striped serpent

OCEAN LIFE

Not all ocean creatures are as scary as the monstrous sea serpent. These sea beasts are a bit more friendly – except perhaps for the pointy-toothed anglerfish! Look through your bricks and see what pieces would work best for animals that live in, and fly above, the sea.

1x1 brick with studs on top and two sides

Front flippers are flag pieces

Back flippers are 1x1 slopes

SEA LION

This playful sea lion gets its shape from 1x1 slopes. The front flippers are LEGO flag pieces attached to 1x2 plates with clips. You could also try buiding a different shape for a swimming pose.

FLIPPER CLIPPER

Each of the blue whale's flippers is made out of a small angled plate and a plate with handle. A piece with a clip attaches it to a sideways-facing stud on the body.

Use clips and bars for the tail too, to allow hinged movements while swimming

Plate with handle attaches underneath the angled plate

Build a waterspout out of transparent round plates and radar dish

Tiles give the top of the head a smooth surface

Tail is built sideways and attached by plates with clips on top

Small eyes are 1x1 round plates built into the model

I MAY BE MICRO-SCALE, BUT I'M STILL THE BIGGEST THING IN THE SEA!

BLUE WHALE

With micro-building, even something as big as a whale can be made portable and pocket-sized. Slope and curved pieces make for a smooth, streamlined body – search for similar shapes in your collection and use them to create your own underwater friends.

QUICK BUILD

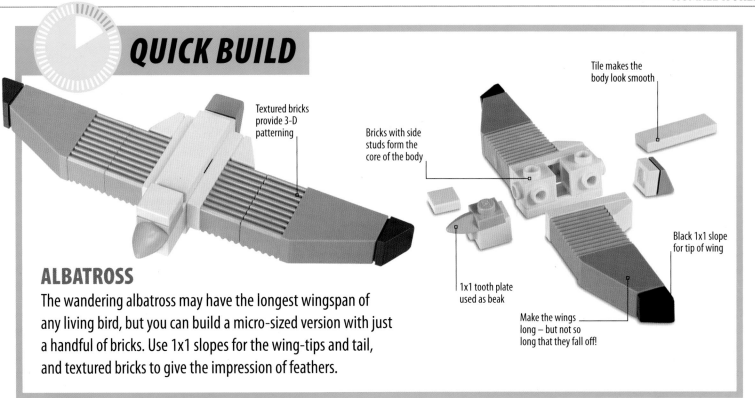

Textured bricks provide 3-D patterning

Tile makes the body look smooth

Bricks with side studs form the core of the body

Black 1x1 slope for tip of wing

1x1 tooth plate used as beak

Make the wings long – but not so long that they fall off!

ALBATROSS

The wandering albatross may have the longest wingspan of any living bird, but you can build a micro-sized version with just a handful of bricks. Use 1x1 slopes for the wing-tips and tail, and textured bricks to give the impression of feathers.

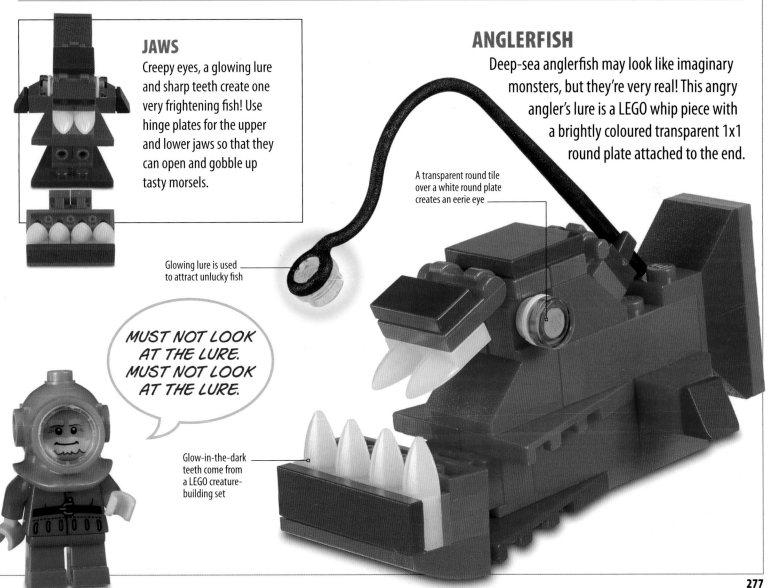

JAWS

Creepy eyes, a glowing lure and sharp teeth create one very frightening fish! Use hinge plates for the upper and lower jaws so that they can open and gobble up tasty morsels.

ANGLERFISH

Deep-sea anglerfish may look like imaginary monsters, but they're very real! This angry angler's lure is a LEGO whip piece with a brightly coloured transparent 1x1 round plate attached to the end.

A transparent round tile over a white round plate creates an eerie eye

Glowing lure is used to attract unlucky fish

MUST NOT LOOK AT THE LURE. MUST NOT LOOK AT THE LURE.

Glow-in-the-dark teeth come from a LEGO creature-building set

MICRO-AFRICA

Welcome to Micro-Africa, where miniature animals roam free. Thanks to micro-scale building, you can go wild and turn your bedroom floor into your very own wildlife park! Don't worry about fitting every tiny detail into a micro-model. The main thing is to focus on the big clues – for example, a large brown mane or a trumpeting trunk.

What other micro-animals could you build for your wildlife park? How about a snapping crocodile or a hungry hippo?

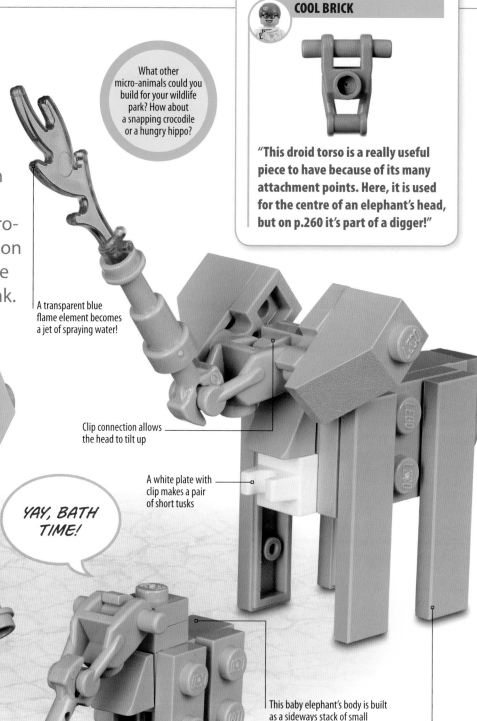

COOL BRICK

"This droid torso is a really useful piece to have because of its many attachment points. Here, it is used for the centre of an elephant's head, but on p.260 it's part of a digger!"

A transparent blue flame element becomes a jet of spraying water!

Clip connection allows the head to tilt up

A white plate with clip makes a pair of short tusks

YAY, BATH TIME!

Legs are 1x4 tiles attached to bricks with side studs

This baby elephant's body is built as a sideways stack of small bricks and plates

ELEPHANT

All you need to make a micro-model look like an elephant is a trunk and two big ears! Why not gather all of your grey bricks together and assemble an entire herd of elephants?

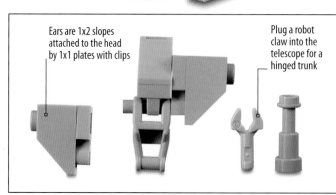

Ears are 1x2 slopes attached to the head by 1x1 plates with clips

Plug a robot claw into the telescope for a hinged trunk

HEAD AND TRUNK

When micro-building, try to find creative uses for unusual pieces. The centre of the adult elephants' heads is the torso from a minifigure-sized robot, and the end of their trunk is a telescope.

GIRAFFE

What do you think of when you picture a giraffe? Long legs, a long neck and a pattern of spots? Then those are the features that you should build into your micro-model.

HEY, THOSE ARE MY LEAVES. TAKE OFF!

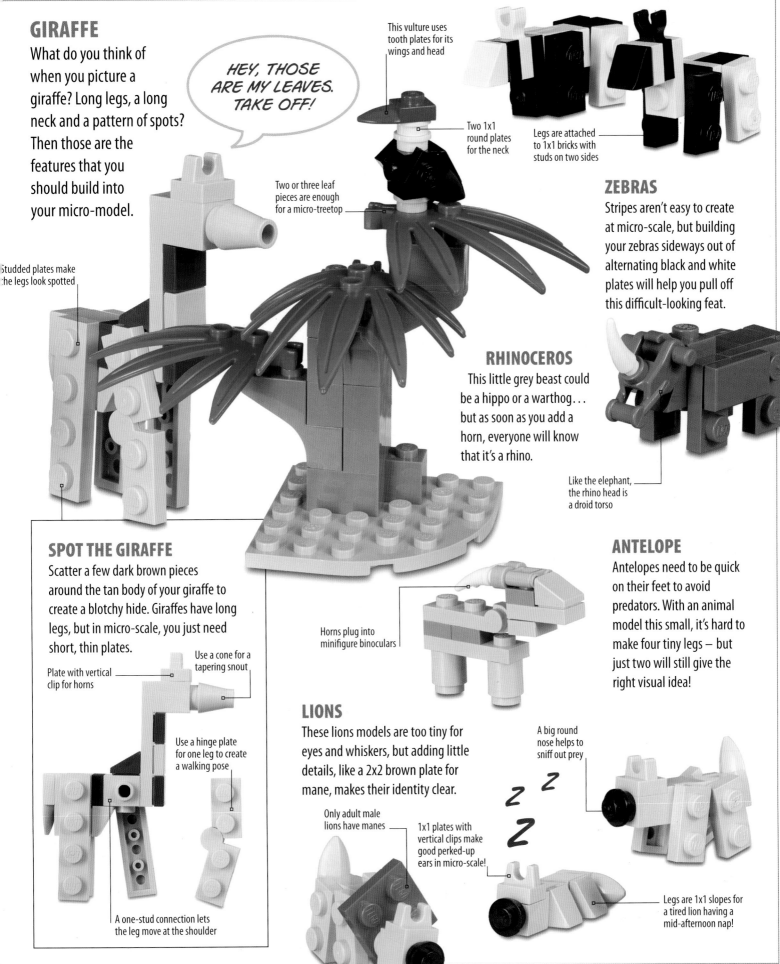

Studded plates make the legs look spotted

This vulture uses tooth plates for its wings and head

Two 1x1 round plates for the neck

Two or three leaf pieces are enough for a micro-treetop

Legs are attached to 1x1 bricks with studs on two sides

ZEBRAS

Stripes aren't easy to create at micro-scale, but building your zebras sideways out of alternating black and white plates will help you pull off this difficult-looking feat.

RHINOCEROS

This little grey beast could be a hippo or a warthog... but as soon as you add a horn, everyone will know that it's a rhino.

Like the elephant, the rhino head is a droid torso

SPOT THE GIRAFFE

Scatter a few dark brown pieces around the tan body of your giraffe to create a blotchy hide. Giraffes have long legs, but in micro-scale, you just need short, thin plates.

Plate with vertical clip for horns

Use a cone for a tapering snout

Use a hinge plate for one leg to create a walking pose

A one-stud connection lets the leg move at the shoulder

Horns plug into minifigure binoculars

LIONS

These lions models are too tiny for eyes and whiskers, but adding little details, like a 2x2 brown plate for mane, makes their identity clear.

Only adult male lions have manes

1x1 plates with vertical clips make good perked-up ears in micro-scale!

ANTELOPE

Antelopes need to be quick on their feet to avoid predators. With an animal model this small, it's hard to make four tiny legs – but just two will still give the right visual idea!

A big round nose helps to sniff out prey

Legs are 1x1 slopes for a tired lion having a mid-afternoon nap!

PREHISTORIC BEASTS

Millions of years ago, titanic dinosaurs roamed Earth. Use your LEGO bricks to create a miniature prehistoric scene populated with dinosaurs and their ancient reptilian relatives. Add forests, deserts and other environments so that it feels just like home for your Mesozoic micro-saurs!

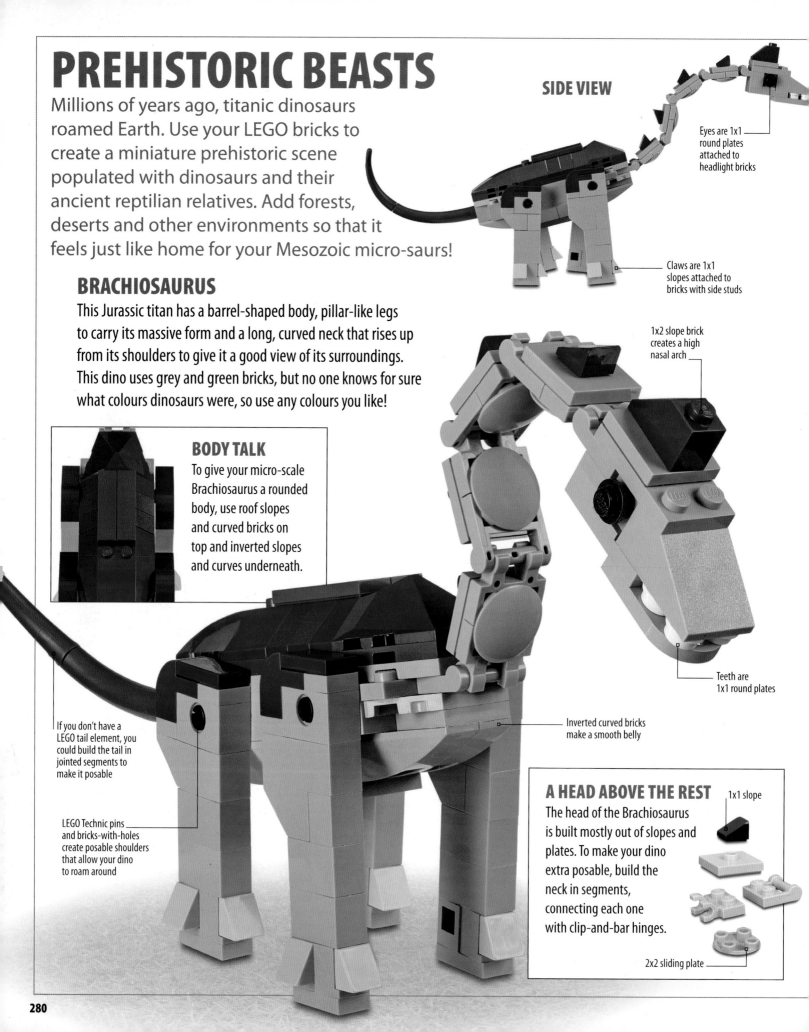

SIDE VIEW

Eyes are 1x1 round plates attached to headlight bricks

Claws are 1x1 slopes attached to bricks with side studs

BRACHIOSAURUS

This Jurassic titan has a barrel-shaped body, pillar-like legs to carry its massive form and a long, curved neck that rises up from its shoulders to give it a good view of its surroundings. This dino uses grey and green bricks, but no one knows for sure what colours dinosaurs were, so use any colours you like!

BODY TALK

To give your micro-scale Brachiosaurus a rounded body, use roof slopes and curved bricks on top and inverted slopes and curves underneath.

1x2 slope brick creates a high nasal arch

Teeth are 1x1 round plates

If you don't have a LEGO tail element, you could build the tail in jointed segments to make it posable

Inverted curved bricks make a smooth belly

LEGO Technic pins and bricks-with-holes create posable shoulders that allow your dino to roam around

A HEAD ABOVE THE REST

The head of the Brachiosaurus is built mostly out of slopes and plates. To make your dino extra posable, build the neck in segments, connecting each one with clip-and-bar hinges.

1x1 slope

2x2 sliding plate

QUICK BUILD

1x4 curved slope used for the curved back and the crested head

Clip pieces under the wings give the Pteranodon grasping claws

Bricks with side studs hold plates with handles in place

PTERANODON

Building this Pteranodon is much easier than pronouncing it! Time yourself and try to build this soaring reptile as fast as you can. Use clips and hinges for flapping wings so your creature can fly away from dangerous dinos.

VOLCANO

Build some interesting scenery for your prehistoric pals. This volcano is constructed with a mix of bricks and slopes to give it a rough, rocky shape. Add streams of orange and red slopes for a river of molten lava trickling down or build it all in brown and grey for a mountain.

Add a column of bricks or a flame piece for a mighty eruption!

HEY! IT'S NOT TIME FOR PEOPLE YET.

You can use transparent elements for lava, too, or use blue bricks to create rivers and waterfalls

A hollow interior keeps the volcano lightweight, but make sure it's well-supported so it doesn't fall apart

Start with a wide base and build up to a narrow top

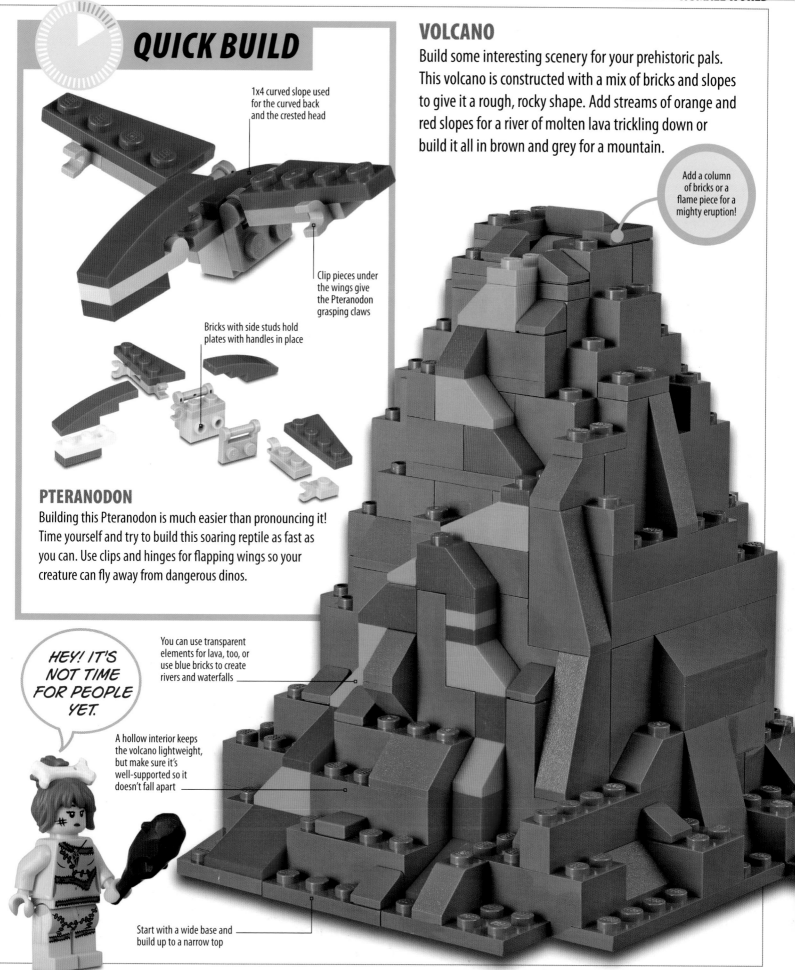

DANGEROUS DINOSAURS

Watch out! There are even more dangerous dinos about! Fortunately, as the builder, you don't have anything to fear from these micro-scaled menaces…unlike our poor tour guide, who seems to have caught more than he bargained for! What other scary, scaly dinos can you create for your micro-dino display?

GRRR!

The T-rex's sharpest teeth are made from plates with clips

Use hinges for an angled tail and head

These short (but very strong!) legs are round bricks and plates built upside down to turn the studs into toes.

TRICERATOPS

Give your Tyrannosaurus a dino to battle with! The Triceratops may be a plant-eater, but it's definitely no prehistoric pushover. Use pointy pieces to make three mighty horns for its head.

TYRANNOSAURUS REX

No micro-dino display would be complete without the most famous tyrant lizard of them all! This mini T-rex has a big toothy head, powerful legs and a pair of small arms made with robot arm pieces and claws.

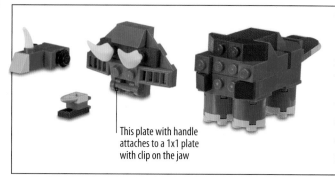

TINY 'TOPS

Use angled plates and slopes to create the Triceratops's bony neck frill. A 1x1 slope gives its head a tough beak. Below, a clip and handle connection makes a chomping jaw.

This plate with handle attaches to a 1x1 plate with clip on the jaw

AWESOME JAWS

Use bricks and slopes to give your Tyrannosaurus a strong skull with jaws that open on a clip hinge. This model uses a combination of normal and sideways building to create its shape.

BAD DINOSAUR! THAT'S MY SUPPER, NOT YOURS!

LEGO fishing rod —made for fish, not dinosaurs

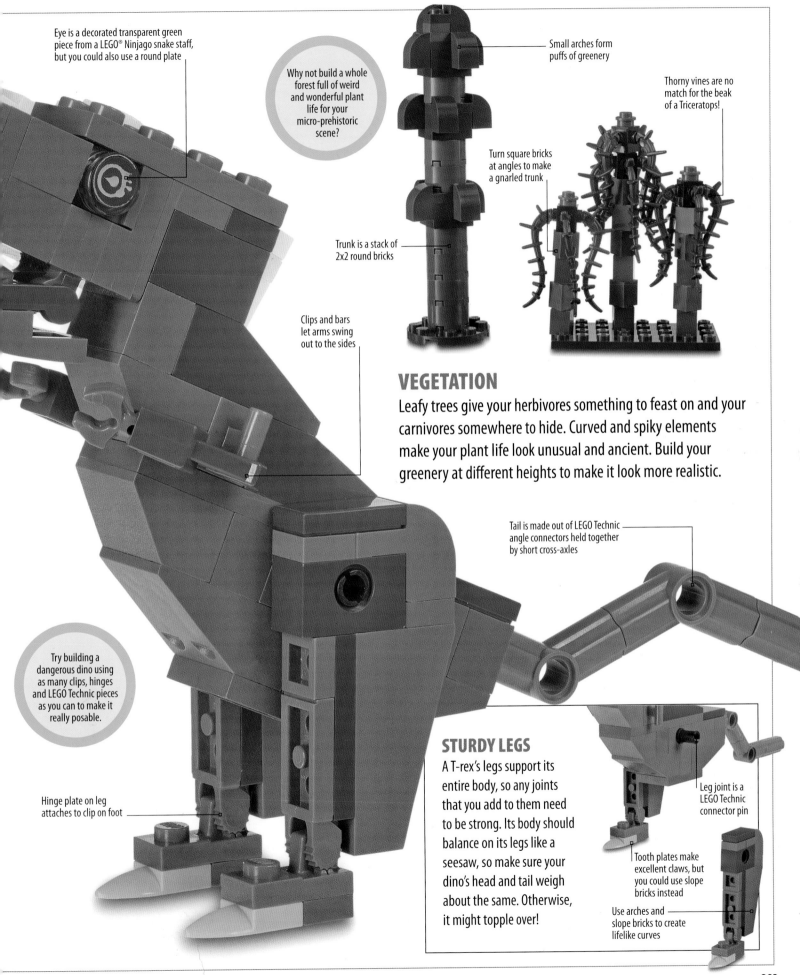

Eye is a decorated transparent green piece from a LEGO® Ninjago snake staff, but you could also use a round plate

Why not build a whole forest full of weird and wonderful plant life for your micro-prehistoric scene?

Small arches form puffs of greenery

Thorny vines are no match for the beak of a Triceratops!

Turn square bricks at angles to make a gnarled trunk

Trunk is a stack of 2x2 round bricks

Clips and bars let arms swing out to the sides

VEGETATION

Leafy trees give your herbivores something to feast on and your carnivores somewhere to hide. Curved and spiky elements make your plant life look unusual and ancient. Build your greenery at different heights to make it look more realistic.

Tail is made out of LEGO Technic angle connectors held together by short cross-axles

Try building a dangerous dino using as many clips, hinges and LEGO Technic pieces as you can to make it really posable.

STURDY LEGS

A T-rex's legs support its entire body, so any joints that you add to them need to be strong. Its body should balance on its legs like a seesaw, so make sure your dino's head and tail weigh about the same. Otherwise, it might topple over!

Leg joint is a LEGO Technic connector pin

Tooth plates make excellent claws, but you could use slope bricks instead

Use arches and slope bricks to create lifelike curves

Hinge plate on leg attaches to clip on foot

MICRO-CASTLES

Why not become king or queen of your very own micro-castle? With their mighty towers and strong stone walls, castles are a terrific subject for micro-building. As long as you include its most well-known features, even a palm-sized castle model will be instantly familiar to everybody who sees it.

Stack 1x1 round bricks and cones for small towers, and 2x2 pieces for larger ones

Add some foliage to your mountain. These pine trees are green and brown 1x1 cones and round bricks

Use grey bricks, slopes, and tiles to create micro-scale mountains

Think about what else you could add to your mountain. How about mountain goats or colourful plants?

A fortified gatehouse prevents unwelcome guests from crossing the bridge

An inverted 1x2 slope supports the base of the side tower

Transparent 1x1 plate windows are attached to headlight bricks

BUILDING THE CHATEAU

The main building is a basic stack of bricks, with grey plates to represent bare stone. The roof is built using classic LEGO roof slopes.

MOUNTAIN CHATEAU

This marvellous manor rises from a split mountain peak. Visitors must pass through a gatehouse and cross a bridge high above a flowing river. Yellow walls and a peaked blue roof make it look freshly painted and well-maintained.

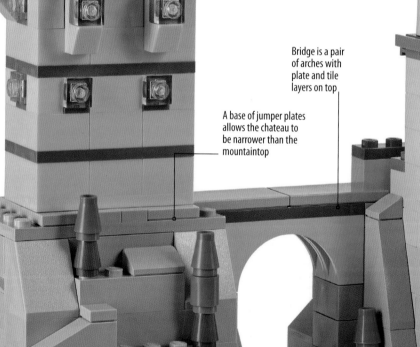

Bridge is a pair of arches with plate and tile layers on top

A base of jumper plates allows the chateau to be narrower than the mountaintop

Transparent blue tiles form a river. You could try building a waterfall on the mountainside, too!

MEDIEVAL CASTLE

This traditional medieval castle has a square stone wall for defence, with a gateway in front and sturdy round towers at the corners. Two loyal knights on horses stand guard, ready to fight off invaders!

Use 1x1 plates to create defensive crenellations on the side battlements

You could place cones on top to create a fanciful fairy tale castle

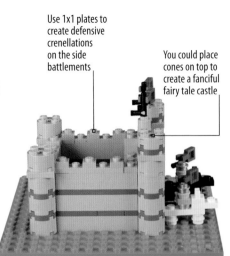

Gold 1x1 round plate adds decoration to the grey castle walls

Studs on top look like stone blocks

This 1x1 LEGO Technic brick-with-hole could be a window...or damage from a catapult attack!

SIDE VIEW

Flags are 1x1 plates with clips attached to fire hose handles

KNIGHTS

These mounted knights in shining armour are a little large for the castle's scale, but you can't build them much smaller! They are holding flags, but they could also hold lances for jousting.

I'M ON KNIGHT SHIFT.

Metallic pieces make great armour!

Horse legs are stacks of two 1x1 round plates

Narrow towers are stacked 1x1 round bricks and plates attached to jumper plates, and held in place from behind with clips and bar pieces

CONSTRUCTING THE CASTLE

The castle's corner towers are stacks of 2x2 round bricks, with dark grey round plates to give the appearance of different kinds of stone. The dark grey sides of the castle's entrance are made by attaching tiles to bricks with side studs.

Two dark brown 1x2 tiles lie in front for a wooden drawbridge

HISTORICAL BUILDINGS

Don't just stop at castles – you can build all kinds of micro-scale buildings from the past. Find pictures of a historical building and identify its most recognisable details. Then look through your bricks for pieces that are the right shape and colour to recreate those details in a tiny size.

Συνολικά, είμαι απλώς άλλο ένα τούβλο στον τοίχο.

GREEK TEMPLE

The hardest part of making a micro-scaled version of an ancient Greek temple is creating the columns. Stacks of 1x1 round bricks will work, but for even better accuracy, try barred fence pieces.

Slopes on the sides give the roof its shape

Round plates imitate sculpted details

Your temple doesn't have to be all white – classic Greek buildings and statues were often colourfully painted

Pick a country, research its historical buildings and then get building!

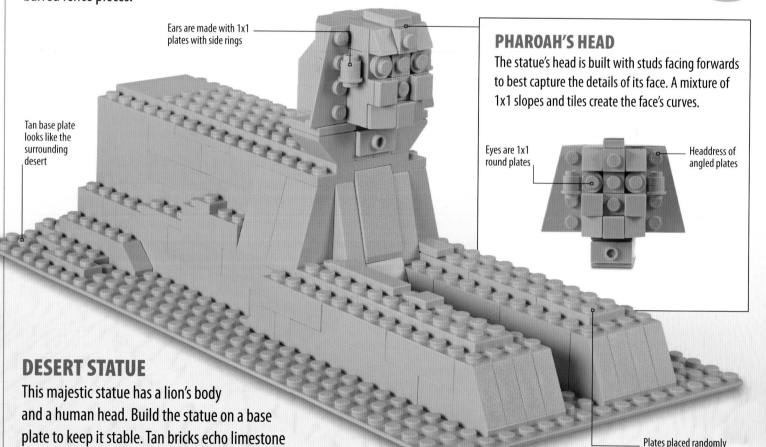

Ears are made with 1x1 plates with side rings

Tan base plate looks like the surrounding desert

PHAROAH'S HEAD

The statue's head is built with studs facing forwards to best capture the details of its face. A mixture of 1x1 slopes and tiles create the face's curves.

Eyes are 1x1 round plates

Headdress of angled plates

DESERT STATUE

This majestic statue has a lion's body and a human head. Build the statue on a base plate to keep it stable. Tan bricks echo limestone blocks, and slopes are used for angled edges.

Plates placed randomly on model create a weathered look

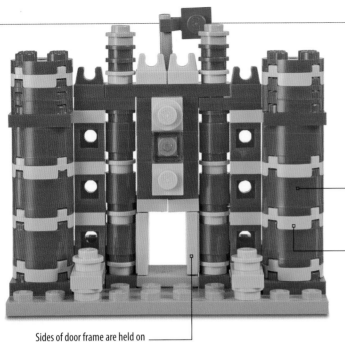

STATELY HOME

You don't always have to build the entire building. Start with an iconic part, like the front of this stately home, and then decide how much of the rest you want to make!

Side towers are made out of 2x2 round bricks and plates

Alternate bricks and plates to make colour patterns

Sides of door frame are held on by 1x1 bricks with side studs

Windmill's sails rotate on a turntable piece attached to a bracket with side studs

2x2 domed brick forms the roof of a storage silo

WINDMILL

Why not build different scenes around your micro-models? This old-fashioned windmill sits near a canal with a boat, a wooden jetty and storage silos for the grain produced by the mill.

The boat's windows are transparent 1x1 plates

Sails made from four angled plates held together with a round tile

A second plate layer raises the grass-covered land above the water

You don't have to build the entire boat, just the part that sticks up above the water

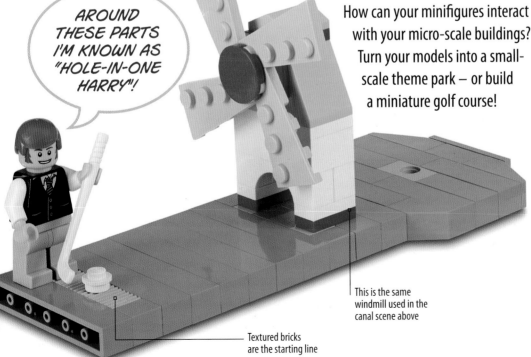

AROUND THESE PARTS I'M KNOWN AS "HOLE-IN-ONE HARRY"!

CHANGE OF SCENE

How can your minifigures interact with your micro-scale buildings? Turn your models into a small-scale theme park – or build a miniature golf course!

This is the same windmill used in the canal scene above

Textured bricks are the starting line

Aim for the brick with a hole!

Jumper plates are part of the windmill

CREATING A COURSE

This mini golf course is built like a wall on its side for a smooth surface. Bricks with side studs attach the jumper plates at the base of the windmill.

METRO SKYLINE

You've already seen how to build a modular micro-city, but you can go even smaller than that! By making individual super-micro towers, you can put together an entire metropolis, complete with monuments and skyscrapers, all small enough to display on a dinner plate. Use your pieces to create a variety of architectural wonders for a souvenir-worthy skyline.

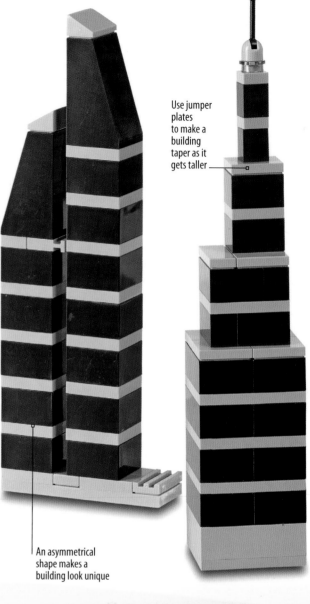

Use jumper plates to make a building taper as it gets taller

I CALL THIS CITY THE LITTLE APPLE!

CITY-SCAPE

Super-micro buildings can be as easy or complicated to build as you want them to be. Some are as simple as stacking up bricks and plates. For a more elaborate shape, incorporate slopes and jumper plates.

An asymmetrical shape makes a building look unique

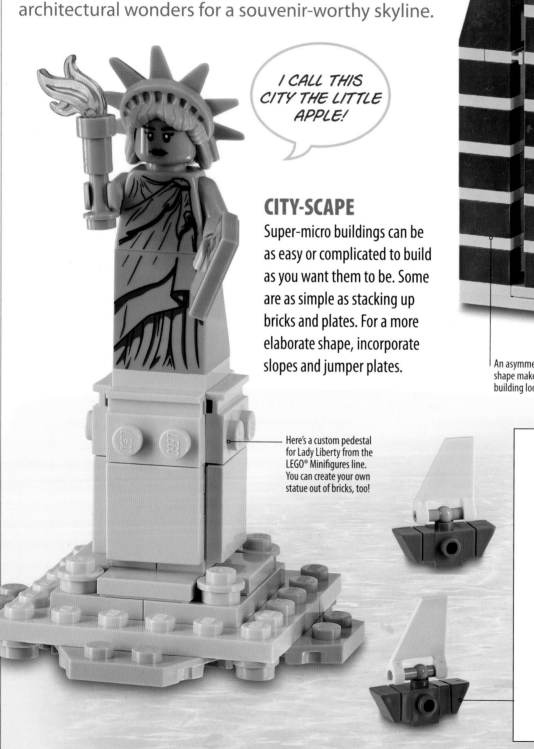

Here's a custom pedestal for Lady Liberty from the LEGO® Minifigures line. You can create your own statue out of bricks, too!

This LEGO Technic T-bar holds the sail in place

Use a flag for a triangular sail

Centre is a 1x1 brick with hollow studs on its sides

YACHT

Making a micro-scale yacht is smooth sailing if you've got the right pieces. If you don't have all of these parts, make up your own design!

Black bricks make the best shiny glass windows

Bricks with sideways studs will help you create vertical lines with plates

STRIKING SKYLINE
Think of ways to make your city buildings look interesting. Adding little details, such as antennas and exposed studs, helps create a spectacular skyline.

Antenna is a minifigure lance

The notches on the bottom of the pieces mimic little windows!

A hidden core of bricks with side studs holds this building together

Alternate stacks of bricks in one colour, and plates in another to build a basic tower

A blue tile creates a rooftop swimming pool

Smokestacks are LEGO® Alien Conquest ray guns clipped on by their handles, but you could stack round plates instead

OCEAN LINER
An ocean liner is a great way to view the city skyline from the water. With its high deck and multiple floors, it gives passengers plenty of opportunities for snapping photos of all their favourite buildings.

Cabin levels are made by alternating black and white plates

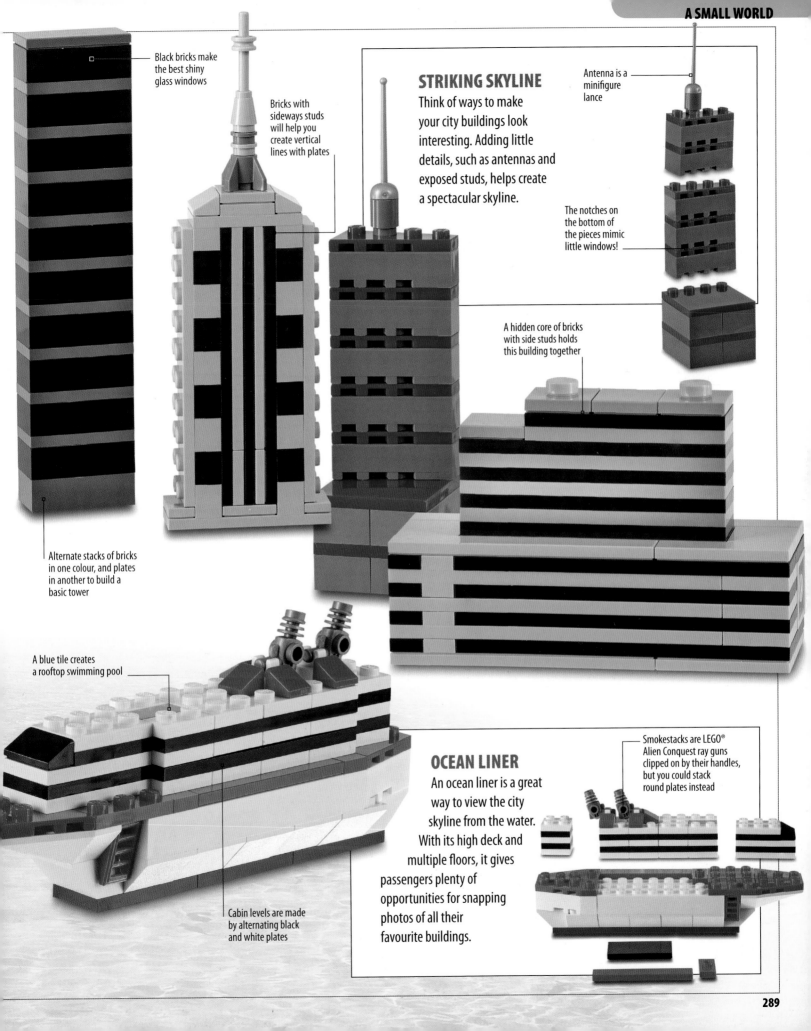

OUTER SPACE

Are you ready to boldly go where few have built before?
Then blast off for outer space and start constucting
and exploring your very own micro-scale galaxy!
To begin your cosmic journey you'll need a powerful
rocket, and a space station to be your first port of call.

Enlarged section for
carrying satellites and
other payloads

Textured bricks add
extra surface detail

3...2...1 LAUNCH

Your rocket will need removable
boosters if it's going to launch
into orbit. The boosters are
attached to the sides of the
rocket by sideways-building.

Plug in a flame
piece for a
launching effect

ROCKET

The body of this rocket is built
with 2x2 round bricks and plates,
and holds two large cones base-
to-base to create the bulge near
the top. To make the body of the
rocket more solid, and to connect
the two cones, build a long LEGO
Technic axle through its centre.

Bracket piece holds the
rocket to the gantry
during countdown

Use tiles for a
heat-resistant
platform under
the rocket

LAUNCH PAD

Before it can blast off,
your rocket needs a
launch pad. This gantry
is built with C-shaped
wall elements, but you
could also use 1x2 bricks
and 2x4 plates.

A transparent red round
plate acts as a warning
light – when it flashes,
stand clear of the launch pad!

SPACE STATION

The core of this space station is made of six half-cylinder pieces, with sturdy pylons supporting the large solar-panel "wings". The attached modules are round and domed bricks. Each one has its own function, such as astronaut quarters and labs for scientific experiments.

Tail is a 1x3 slope attached to jumper plates, topped with a 1x1 slope

SPACE SHUTTLE

A micro-scale space station needs a micro-scale spaceship! This simple ship is built in a streamlined, studs-free style, which gives it a sleek and futuristic look. Its wings include slopes attached to bricks with side studs.

A transparent grey piece provides a curved cockpit window

Blue and white colour scheme matches the rocket

Shuttle attaches to a docking tube made from 2x2 textured round bricks

Solar panels are stands from LEGO Minifigures collectible characters

Four brackets at the centre hold everything together

Create viewports with transparent 1x1 round tiles or plates

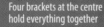

ALL IN THE DETAIL

You could make a communications dish with just a dish piece, but this detailed one is built with eight robot arm pieces, clipped to a plate with octagonal ring.

I'VE ALWAYS WANTED TO BE AN ASTROGNOME!

1x1 round plate

GREETINGS, EARTHLINGS

Build a communications dish so that our astronauts (or astrognomes) can keep in touch with Earth during their outer-space travels.

Include a computer bank and control panel, too

A 2x2 tile with one stud and a 1x1 plate with clip allow the dish to be aimed towards the sky

FUTURE WORLDS

Meet the micro-city of tomorrow! In the distant future, humanity has reached and colonized Mars. Here on the Red Planet, needle-like towers rise high into the sky and robotic machines dig for precious energy crystals. Use your smallest bricks to create your own alien landscapes and futuristic worlds – micro-scale style!

MARTIAN CITY

Build a sci-fi city with unusually shaped towers and airtight domes. These Mars Colony skyscrapers are built out of bricks and plates like any building, but with extra slopes to create interesting angles. Transparent blue pieces give the scene a unified, Space Age atmosphere.

1x2 brick with side studs and stand

1x2 slope

Place small elements inside the domes as farming crops grown by the settlers

SIDE VIEW

HOP TO THE FUTURE

A Planet Hopper with two big engines helps colonists get around Mars. You can build lots of different micro-spaceships for your landing pad.

You could expand your future-city with bridges between buildings, space elevators and extra spaceships.

Use clips to attach lightsaber blades for dust-storm sensors

A tile on an inverted slope makes a small landing pad midway up a tower

Include some small buildings to make the big ones look even taller!

Windows are transparent blue plates

Transparent domes sit on 4x4 round bricks – a perfect fit!

Landing pad is a 6x6 tile raised on legs. Add transparent 1x2 plates and wall elements for detail

SPACE CRUISER

In the future, rockets and space shuttles might be a thing of the past. Build a super-fast space cruiser that can dodge asteroids, outrace comets and fly between worlds in the blink of an interstellar eye!

Wings attach at two points for a solid connection

Each wing uses two plate-with-bar pieces to attach to the clips on the body

Cones can be boosters or blasters!

CRUISER CONSTRUCTION

The space cruiser is built around a core of bricks with side studs. Clips on the body attach a pair of sleek, flared-out wings, which are the same long, curved shape as the spaceship's top.

A LEGO Technic pin helps the saws to spin

A tall 1x1 column supports the saw arm

MINING ROVER

This Martian mining machine is out of this world! It grinds up rock with its saws, pipes the rubble through its central section for refinement, and deposits ores and crystals into the hover-truck at the other end.

Grey colour scheme looks strong and industrial

Rover wheels are mounted on 1x6 LEGO Technic bricks

Dark orange and brown plates create an uneven Martian surface. Use slopes for alien rocks

Hover-truck's jets are 1x1 plates with side rings

FUTURE TECH

The mining rover's saws are propellers from a LEGO submarine set. The pipes at the front and back are column pieces, and the heavy-treaded wheels are LEGO Technic gears.

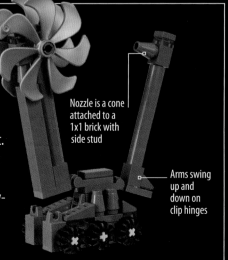

Nozzle is a cone attached to a 1x1 brick with side stud

Arms swing up and down on clip hinges

COOL BRICK

"This blade propeller makes a powerful saw for Martian mining equipment here, but it could be used as helicopter blades, a fan in a house, or as part of a set of wheels on a futuristic car!"

Go Wild!

The world is full of animals. They run, swim, fly and crawl. They can be as small as an insect or as big as a whale. They may be covered in fur, feathers or scales, with dozens of legs or none at all. But there's one thing that every animal has in common: you can build it with your LEGO® bricks. It's a wild world out there – so explore it!

HELLO, HELLO

MEET THE BUILDERS:

PETE REID AND YVONNE DOYLE

Ages: Both 38

Day Jobs: Postman (Pete); IT support (Yvonne)

LEGO Specialities: Robots, spaceships (Pete); buildings, interiors (Yvonne)

Brick Collection: A shared collection of 250,000 pieces

Favourite Bricks: 2x2 octagonal plate (Pete); 1x1 tile (Yvonne)

Did You Know? Pete and Yvonne fell in love at a LEGO event. Their eyes met over a pile of LEGO bricks.

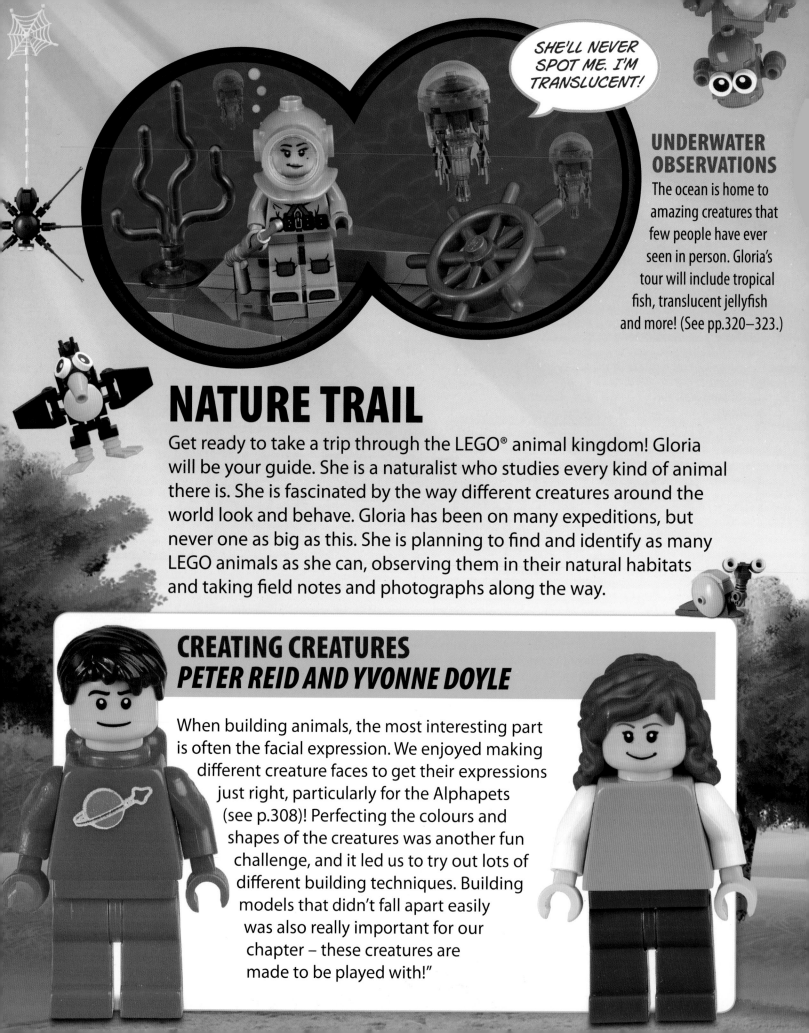

SHE'LL NEVER SPOT ME. I'M TRANSLUCENT!

UNDERWATER OBSERVATIONS

The ocean is home to amazing creatures that few people have ever seen in person. Gloria's tour will include tropical fish, translucent jellyfish and more! (See pp.320–323.)

NATURE TRAIL

Get ready to take a trip through the LEGO® animal kingdom! Gloria will be your guide. She is a naturalist who studies every kind of animal there is. She is fascinated by the way different creatures around the world look and behave. Gloria has been on many expeditions, but never one as big as this. She is planning to find and identify as many LEGO animals as she can, observing them in their natural habitats and taking field notes and photographs along the way.

CREATING CREATURES
PETER REID AND YVONNE DOYLE

When building animals, the most interesting part is often the facial expression. We enjoyed making different creature faces to get their expressions just right, particularly for the Alphapets (see p.308)! Perfecting the colours and shapes of the creatures was another fun challenge, and it led us to try out lots of different building techniques. Building models that didn't fall apart easily was also really important for our chapter – these creatures are made to be played with!"

POLAR EXPLORATION

No location is too remote and no environment too extreme for this naturalist! Gloria will travel from the frozen Antarctic to the North Pole, meeting penguins, polar bears and everything in between. (See pp.324–327.)

...AND BEYOND!

Not content to study only the animals she can find on Earth, Gloria will peer through a telescope to study strange creatures from other planets!

ON SAFARI

Kick off your animal adventure by going on an African safari! Put together a camouflaged lookout and keep watch to see what creatures wander past. Be very quiet and hold still – you don't want to scare the animals!

SAFARI... SO GOOD!

You could also build window covers to hide the lookout – or to give your minifigures some shade!

Place plants on a tan or yellow base to create a natural landscape

Use a step element or build a ladder to access the lookout

SIDE VIEW

1x2 log bricks look like side-by-side tree trunks

CAN YOU STAY ON THE STEPS, GLORIA? IT HELPS ATTRACT THE LIONS.

TREE-TOP HIDEAWAY

Palm leaves disguise the lookout's square plate roof so that the people inside won't be noticed by nearby animals. Flat and smooth shapes look artificial, so add some lumpy bits on top!

Use brown pieces so the structure blends in with the environment

LOOKOUT

On a safari you can go looking for animals, or you can wait for the animals to come to you. By building a lookout designed to blend in with the trees, your minifigures can observe the wildlife undetected.

Stilts can be 2x2 bricks or pairs of 1x2 bricks

Stilts keep the viewing platform out of reach of ground creatures

GIRAFFE

It's hard to overlook a giraffe out there on the savanna! With their long necks and legs, these towering titans really stand out in a crowd. Use 1x1 pieces to make the skinniest sections, and regular and inverted slopes for realistic angles.

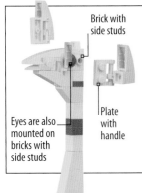

Brick with side studs

Plate with handle

Eyes are also mounted on bricks with side studs

EAR, EAR

The giraffe's ears are 1x3 curved slope pieces attached to clips. To make them move, connect the clips to plates with handles before attaching them to the bricks with side studs on the giraffe's head.

Nose is made from the same piece as the ears: a 1x3 curved slope

Use a tooth plate for a protruding lower lip

A steep slope piece adds height and strength to the base of the neck

Studs on the back are hidden by tiles

Assemble the legs and neck separately before attaching them to the body

Tail is a yellow harpoon gun with its handle plugged into a LEGO® Technic half-pin

Build even more trees and plants to add to your safari scene.

Start the body with a large plate in the middle

Feet are 1x2 slopes

Build a scene for your giraffe, with a tall, leafy tree and sand or grass for a base

This sculpted head makes an interesting lion face

THE MANE EVENT

Most of this powerful hunter's mane is built out of angled plates. A pair of brackets on each side attaches them to the head and shoulders of the lion. The central parts of the mane are built directly into the body.

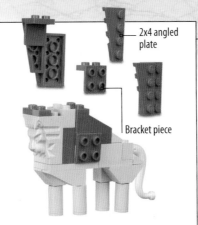

2x4 angled plate

Bracket piece

Legs are LEGO Technic pieces, but you could use 1x1 round bricks and plates instead

S-shaped tail is attached to a brick-with-hole with a LEGO Technic pin

LION

No safari would be complete without a lion sighting. Use tan pieces to build the body of this fearsome feline, and brown or black for its shaggy mane. A clever use of special pieces will give you a unique model design.

SAFARI GIANTS

What giant-sized beasts will you see on your safari? You might spot a trumpeting elephant at the watering hole, an ostrich sprinting across the plains or a herd of horned buffalo keeping an eye out for danger. Build them all for a grand wildlife adventure!

ELEPHANT

Elephants are the biggest animals you'll encounter on your expedition, so make sure you have plenty of grey bricks in your collection! Try starting your build with a six-stud-wide plate and building the body up from there.

Hinge plates attach to pieces with slopes on three sides for the flapping ears

Use slope bricks to create the shape of the elephant's angled forehead

The end of this elephant's trunk is made from a pair of 1x3 curved pieces

Attaching the legs last will make the rest of the body easier to build

SIDE VIEW

Tail piece, from a LEGO® Alien Conquest set, attaches with a hinge brick so it's posable

Build around this six-stud-wide plate

Use 2x2 round plates and bricks to make the elephant's strong, pillar-like legs

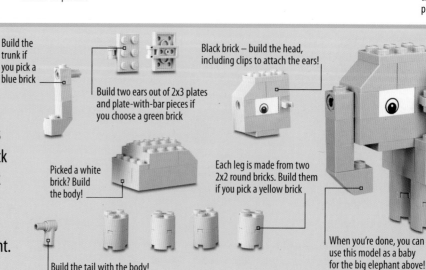

★ **CHALLENGE**

ELEPHANT STAMPEDE

Challenge your friends to an elephant race! Put five bricks of different colours into a bag and take turns picking a brick from it. The colour of the brick you pick determines which body part you can build for that turn. The winner is the first player to build a complete elephant.

Build the trunk if you pick a blue brick

Build two ears out of 2x3 plates and plate-with-bar pieces if you choose a green brick

Black brick – build the head, including clips to attach the ears!

Picked a white brick? Build the body!

Each leg is made from two 2x2 round bricks. Build them if you pick a yellow brick

Build the tail with the body!

When you're done, you can use this model as a baby for the big elephant above!

Beak is a skeleton leg from a LEGO® Ninjago set

YOU CAN'T RUFFLE MY FEATHERS – THEY'RE PLASTIC!

Centre of the head is a 1x1 brick with studs on four sides

OSTRICH

These large, flightless birds are extremely fast runners, so give your model a pair of long, straight legs. Make sure your ostrich's body is well balanced so it doesn't fall over. Female ostriches are brown or grey – why not use your pieces in those colours to build a female version?

BIG BIRD BODY

Use plates and inverted slopes to build the ostrich's lower body, with 1x1 slopes for its raised, feathery back. Attach tooth plates to brackets on both sides to create the wings. Another tooth plate is used for the tail feathers.

Tooth plate

1x1 slope piece

Stack orange, tan or pink 1x1 round plates to make the neck

Legs are telescopes, and two-toed feet are 1x1 plates with side clips

What other safari animals can you build to add to your safari scene?

2x3 angled plate

BUILD-A-BUFFALO

A pair of bricks with two side studs holds the whole model together on the inside. Angled plates attach to them sideways to create the buffalo's thick hide, and grilles make the hair of its shaggy coat.

Bricks with side studs

1x2 grille

Long curved bricks create a true-to-nature humpbacked shape

The buffalo's eyes are headlight bricks

BUFFALO

Don't be tricked by its cow-like appearance – the buffalo is as short-tempered and tough as they come! Build as many as you can and create a whole herd of these majestic, but grumpy, beasts to populate your safari scenes.

Horns from a LEGO cow plug into headlight bricks with hollow side studs

Plates with click hinges let the head hang at an angle

Use tooth plates to create short, sharp hooves peeking out from under the hair

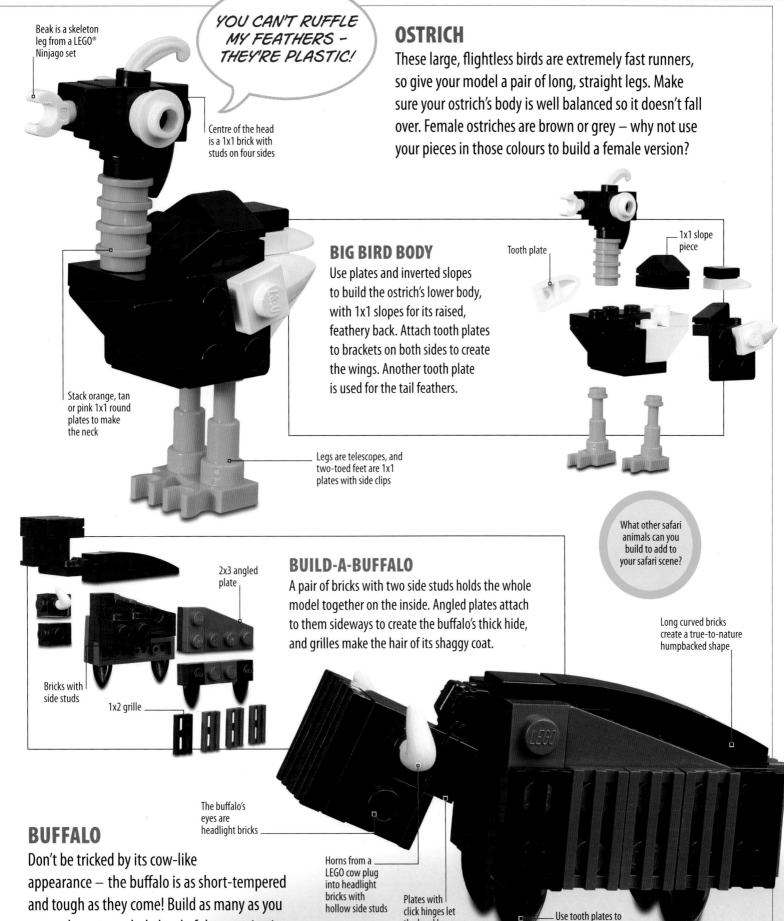

SAFARI TRUCK

Fallen trees, bumpy roads and rivers are just a few of the hazards that you will come across on your safari. You need a rugged vehicle that won't get stuck in the mud or break down in the path of a charging elephant. Build a truck that will get you everywhere you want to go – and let you make a speedy exit if you need to!

BOTTOM VIEW

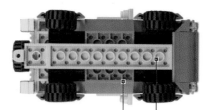

A plate with inverted slopes on its sides supports the centre of the truck

A long plate locks together the truck's underside

If your roof piece isn't long enough, extend it with plates, slopes and tiles

The roof can be removed if it's not too sunny...and there aren't any monkeys around!

THOSE LIONS SEEM TO BE GETTING CLOSE, GLORIA.

Build a trailer to attach to your truck. You could fill it with banana pieces to keep the monkeys happy!

Use multiple grilles for an impact-resistant front end. You could build up a reinforced bumper, too!

Use plates to add decorative stripes and details

Transparent slopes make bright headlights

Use tyres with big treads for traction on dust, dirt and mud

A 1x2 tile mounted on a plate with side ring makes a handy side mirror

Attach a tile to headlight bricks to create a thick door in case of an angry rhino attack!

TRUCK POWER

Your safari truck needs to be built for adventure. Include a rugged chassis to resist bumps and thumps, big tyres to drive over any obstacles, headlights to light the way in the dark and open windows so your minifigures can photograph the wildlife with ease.

GLORIA?

A blank minifigure head with a round tile on the end holds the spare tyre onto the back of the truck

A curved bar with studs keeps the photographer from falling out of the truck!

This socket piece can be used to tow other vehicles or supplies

REAR VIEW

Use grey or silver pieces to give the impression of strong metal

Small windows support the sides of the roof

UNDER THE HOOD

Most of the safari truck is built with basic LEGO bricks, but a few parts — such as the wheels, mudguards and windshield — are specific to automobile sets. If you don't have these pieces, then improvise with what you do have!

A tall roll bar holds up the back of the roof

Punctured tyres are a real problem out in the wild, so always pack a spare!

This piece can be used as a vehicle's hood or roof

A hollow space beneath the hood will keep your model lightweight and fast, but you could build an engine inside

Make sure the bottom of your truck is raised up high to clear rocks, roots and ruts

Install mudguards over the wheels

303

BARNYARD BEASTS

Expand your farm and build animals that baa, bray, moo, or neigh! They will all need their own place to live and food to eat, so do a bit of research before you build. How else will you know how to take proper care of them all?

> COUNTING THESE SHEEP MAKES ME FEEL SLEEPY... YAWN!

Sheep like to munch on low-growing plants

Make a fence out of bar or antenna pieces attached to 1x1 bricks with side studs

SHEEP PEN

When building a sheep pen, use a green base plate so your sheep have plenty of fresh grass for grazing. If you have enough pieces, build the fence all the way around and add a gate so that the farmer can get inside.

Build smaller, simpler versions of your sheep to make lambs — or skinny pink versions for shearing season!

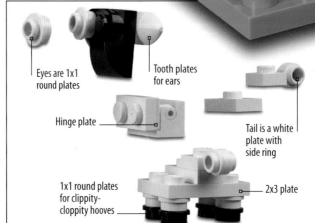

Eyes are 1x1 round plates

Tooth plates for ears

Hinge plate

Tail is a white plate with side ring

1x1 round plates for clippity-cloppity hooves

2x3 plate

SHEEP

Want to make a woolly sheep? Start with a 2x3 plate and attach a hinge for the neck. Plates with side rings sticking out create a thick and curly coat.

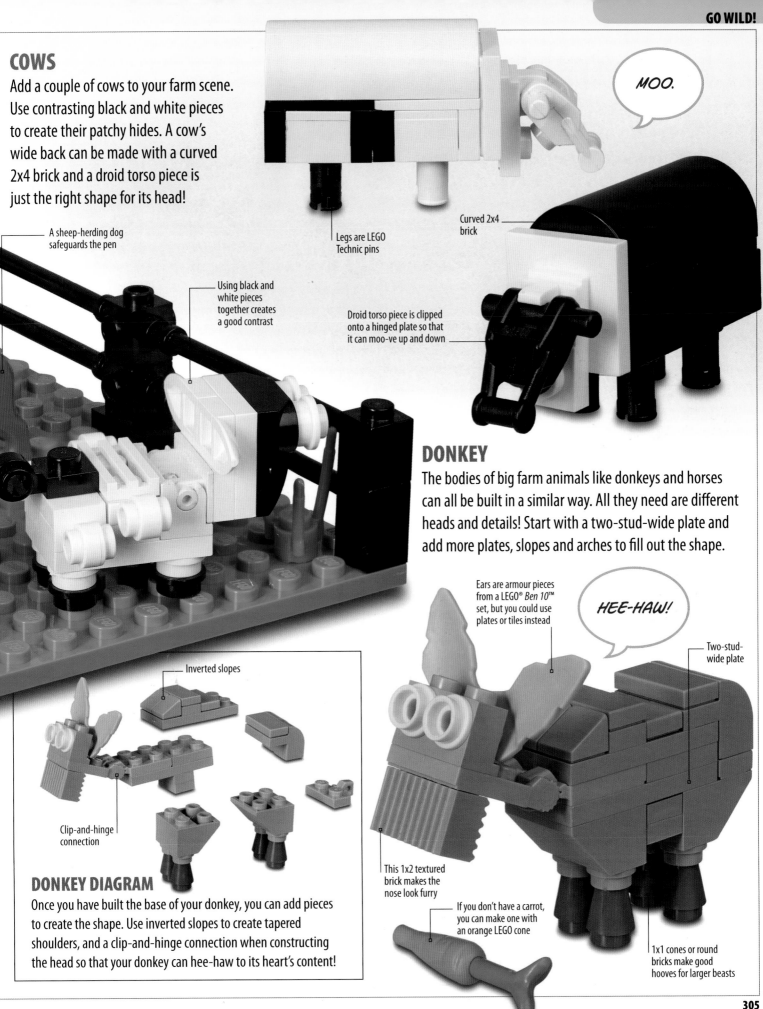

COWS

Add a couple of cows to your farm scene. Use contrasting black and white pieces to create their patchy hides. A cow's wide back can be made with a curved 2x4 brick and a droid torso piece is just the right shape for its head!

MOO.

A sheep-herding dog safeguards the pen

Using black and white pieces together creates a good contrast

Legs are LEGO Technic pins

Curved 2x4 brick

Droid torso piece is clipped onto a hinged plate so that it can moo-ve up and down

DONKEY

The bodies of big farm animals like donkeys and horses can all be built in a similar way. All they need are different heads and details! Start with a two-stud-wide plate and add more plates, slopes and arches to fill out the shape.

Ears are armour pieces from a LEGO® *Ben 10*™ set, but you could use plates or tiles instead

HEE-HAW!

Two-stud-wide plate

Inverted slopes

Clip-and-hinge connection

DONKEY DIAGRAM

Once you have built the base of your donkey, you can add pieces to create the shape. Use inverted slopes to create tapered shoulders, and a clip-and-hinge connection when constructing the head so that your donkey can hee-haw to its heart's content!

This 1x2 textured brick makes the nose look furry

If you don't have a carrot, you can make one with an orange LEGO cone

1x1 cones or round bricks make good hooves for larger beasts

FARM FOWL

You don't have to travel too far afield to discover interesting animals. Take a trip to the farm and you will find cows, pigs, horses and much more – not to mention the different kinds of birds that live there. Let's meet a few of our most familiar and favourite feathered friends.

DUCK POND

Ducks love water, so build a pond on your farm where they can quack and splash to their hearts' content. Ponds can be found anywhere, surrounded by grass or in the dirt. You could also add some frogs or fishy friends to your pond!

Use colourless transparent tiles for a frozen winter pond!

QUICK BUILD

DUCKS

These little ducks are made with just seven pieces. Start with a 1x1 brick with studs on four sides, and attach a tail, wings and a clip to hold the head.

1x1 cone for a tail

Wings are tooth plates

1x1 brick with studs on four sides

Tile for a smooth body

Head is a fire hose nozzle

DON'T MIND ME, GUYS. JUST ACT NATURAL!

Place plants at the edge of the pond or sticking out of the water

Make a still water surface with transparent blue tiles

Ducks can perch on the side or go for a swim

Build a ring of grey plates for stone, or brown for mud, around the pond

CHICKEN COOP

Your chickens will need to be protected from foxes and other predators, so build a coop to keep them (and their precious eggs) safe.

I'M FEELING COOPED UP IN HERE.

Ice cream cone tops or 1x1 round plates make egg-cellent eggs!

Grilles give the impression of a feathery back

Use small plates to make straw bedding

If you don't have these latticed fences, any fence pieces will do

You could build a fence all the way around so your chickens don't get out, and nothing else gets in!

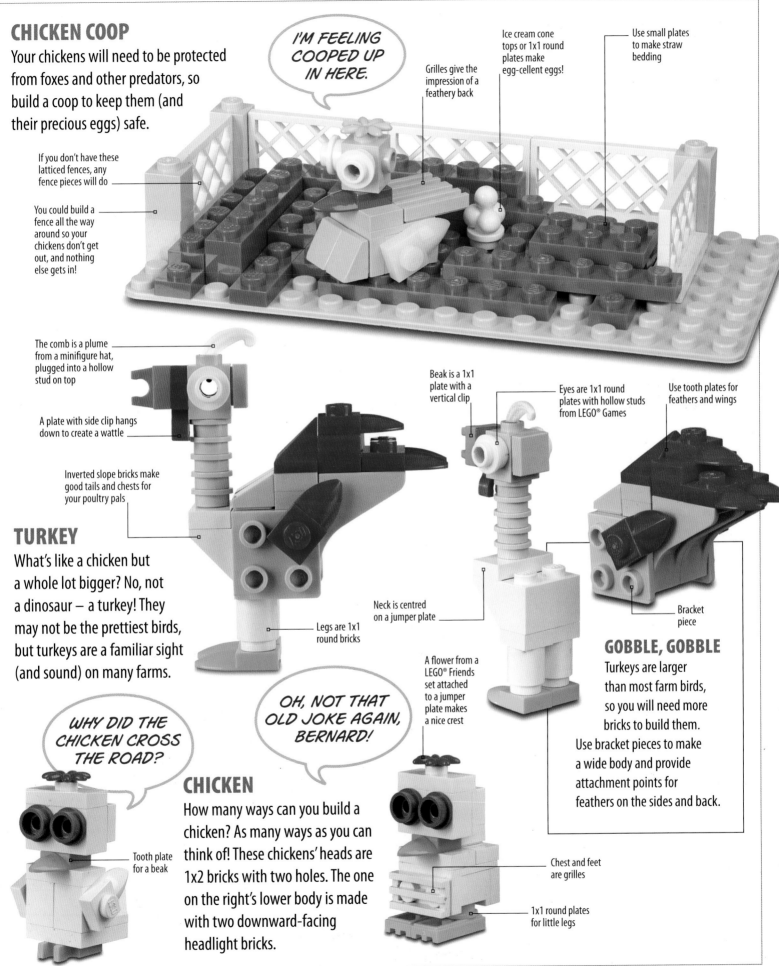

The comb is a plume from a minifigure hat, plugged into a hollow stud on top

A plate with side clip hangs down to create a wattle

Beak is a 1x1 plate with a vertical clip

Eyes are 1x1 round plates with hollow studs from LEGO® Games

Use tooth plates for feathers and wings

Inverted slope bricks make good tails and chests for your poultry pals

TURKEY

What's like a chicken but a whole lot bigger? No, not a dinosaur – a turkey! They may not be the prettiest birds, but turkeys are a familiar sight (and sound) on many farms.

Legs are 1x1 round bricks

Neck is centred on a jumper plate

Bracket piece

GOBBLE, GOBBLE

Turkeys are larger than most farm birds, so you will need more bricks to build them. Use bracket pieces to make a wide body and provide attachment points for feathers on the sides and back.

WHY DID THE CHICKEN CROSS THE ROAD?

OH, NOT THAT OLD JOKE AGAIN, BERNARD!

A flower from a LEGO® Friends set attached to a jumper plate makes a nice crest

CHICKEN

How many ways can you build a chicken? As many ways as you can think of! These chickens' heads are 1x2 bricks with two holes. The one on the right's lower body is made with two downward-facing headlight bricks.

Tooth plate for a beak

Chest and feet are grilles

1x1 round plates for little legs

307

ALPHAPETS

Building these peculiar little creatures is as easy as A-B-C! You can make all sorts of strange, silly and unusual animal faces by using LEGO tiles with printed numbers and letters. If you don't have these decorated tiles, then try other ones with interesting patterns and colours from your collection.

Back can be a slope or a curved brick

Two V tiles and a P tile create scrunched up eyes and a tongue sticking out!

With two Q tiles and an upside-down Y, this cat looks curious and hopeful

Use tooth plates for pointy, triangular ears

Red hinge plate creates a cat's collar

Four tooth plates make the front and hind feet

Base of body is a 2x3 plate

HERE, BIRDIE! TWEET, TWEET!

CATS

Use different letters to give your crouching kitty a new expression! Even without letter tiles, you can use pieces with printed grilles or dials to change your creation's face and mood.

A hinge base lets the head tilt up and down

PET PIECES

Think about how to use your pieces in different ways, like tilting a tooth plate to create a floppy ear. Experiment with your pieces and you'll discover lots of ways to fill your creations with heaps of fun.

What other animals could you add to your Alphapet collection?

Use pieces with side studs to build in different directions

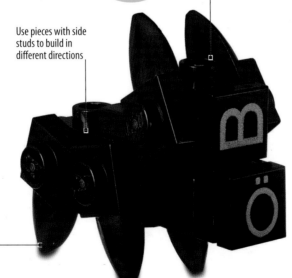

Use sideways tooth plates for stubby little legs

Angle the ears back to make the pup look like it's running

A grille creates a fuzzy white chest

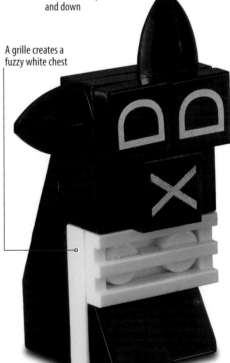

Letter Ö tiles give this bird a wide-eyed look

Fluttering wings can twist in their rings and rotate on the body's side studs

1x1 brick with side studs

Plate with side ring

BIRD BODY

Birds come in many shapes. The head and body of this bird is built around a pair of 1x1 bricks with studs on four sides.

Beak is a horn plugged into a hollow stud

BIRD

Sometimes you find the perfect piece to make an animal part. This bird's wings are a pair of LEGO minifigure fan accessories, plugged into 1x1 plates with side rings.

Neck is a 1x2 plate. Use a longer plate for a longer neck

Feet are an orange plate with clip

Turned sideways, the letter B (or the number 8) creates two eyes on a single 1x1 tile

Pick tropical colours for tropical birds!

PARROTS

Parrots come in all sorts of bright colours and vivid hues. If you build more than one, mix and match your pieces to make them really stand out.

WHO'S A PRETTY BIRD THEN?

Use different pieces to create varied plumage shapes

Make a feathered crest by attaching a minifigure neck bracket onto the top stud

TAKING WING

This parrot's wings are a pair of opposite-facing angled plates, attached to a brick with studs on its sides. What pieces from your collection would make the best bird wings?

1x1 headlight brick for the head

2x3 angled plate

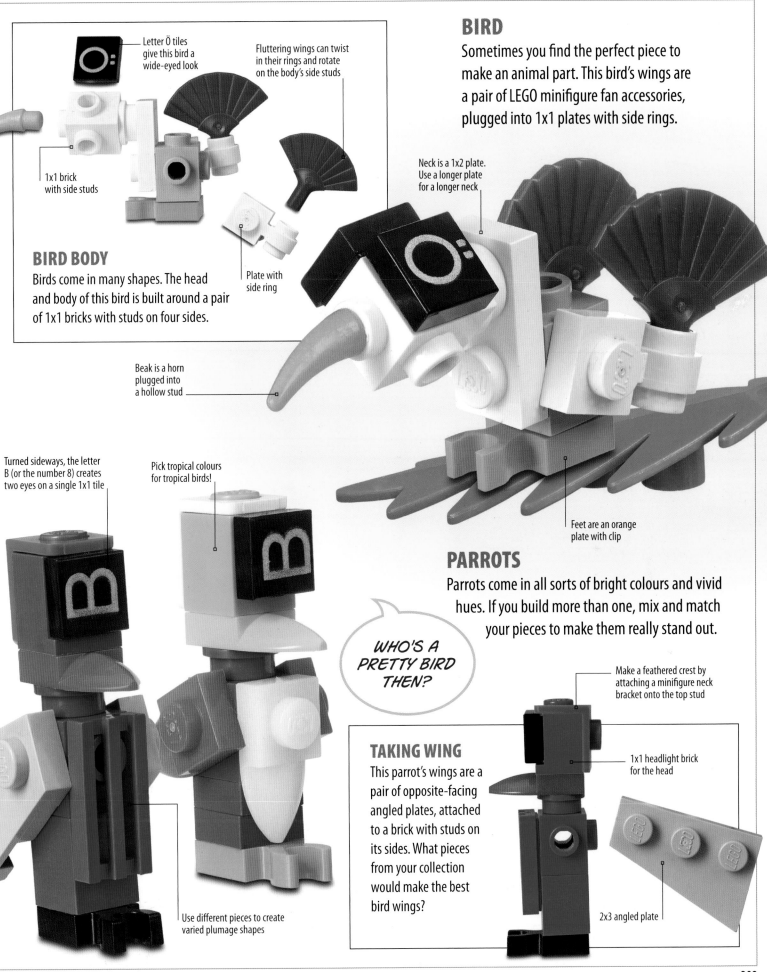

309

HANDFUL OF BRICKS

Each of our fan builders was given a handful of common LEGO elements and asked to make as many different models as they could using only those pieces. Check out the custom creations that creature-makers Pete and Yvonne built.

Eyes are radar dishes with black 1x1 round plates in the centre

PLANT

This dancing flower was born to boogie! Pete and Yvonne used one shade of green to make the stem, another for the leaves and an orange plate for a colourful blossom on top.

A sturdy base of bricks is key for a tall, thin model

CHIRP!

BIRD

Eyes, a beak, and wings are all this little bird needs to be recognisable. Placing one slope-brick foot in front of the other makes it look like it's taking a step.

Angled plate wings are attached with sideways building

It's no surprise that an antenna piece makes a great antenna!

Leave some room in the middle for your minifigure to sit in

RACE CAR

For a fast-looking auto, build a long body that's low to the ground with a raised spoiler. Turn a racer into a remote-controlled car by attaching an antenna on top.

4X4 CAR

To make a simple LEGO brick car, just include four spinning wheels and a transparent piece for a windshield. Headlights, a rear spoiler and a front grille are optional extras!

Two grilles make an extra-wide bumper

DUCK

How do you make a duck model look like it's swimming? Just build the part that's sticking out of the water, like Pete and Yvonne did here!

A 1x1 slope creates a feathery plume

Angled plates can be tail feathers, too

MOST OF OUR MODELS HAVE EYES!

HANDFUL OF THOUGHTS

"We took the bricks and sat down to build until something good happened. We had no plan — we just went with the flow! We don't normally build with such colourful and diverse LEGO elements, but we found ourselves really enjoying the challenge."

Pop a radar dish on top of an antenna for a shady umbrella

BEACH SCENE

An umbrella, a comfy reclining chair and a bottle of sunblock will help you enjoy a day at the sandy beach. Watch out for the ocean tickling your toes!

Bottle is a 1x1 round brick with a tap on top for the dispenser

With four wheels, this creation spins around and around and around!

I LOVE MY LEDERHOSEN!

WHIRLIGIG

Not every model has to be something specific. Try combining pieces in random or silly ways to make equally random or silly models!

BAVARIAN BOY

Pete and Yvonne used colorful bricks to dress this fine fellow in traditional Bavarian clothing, including a hat, shoes and a pair of leather breeches.

Innocent, wide-eyed expression

Two grilles for suspenders

Floppy ears are brown 1x2 bricks

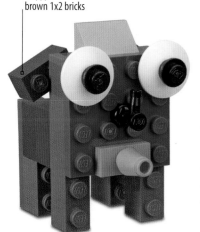

DOG

What kinds of animals can you build out of a handful of bricks? Here's a peculiar pooch with a tap for a nose and a cone for a panting tongue!

CREEPING CRITTERS

Just look at these darlings, with all of their legs and eyes and mandibles and antennae. Build some bugs and grubs, and spiders and centipedes – these little critters can be cute, too! Show how much you love them by building the creepiest crawlies you can imagine.

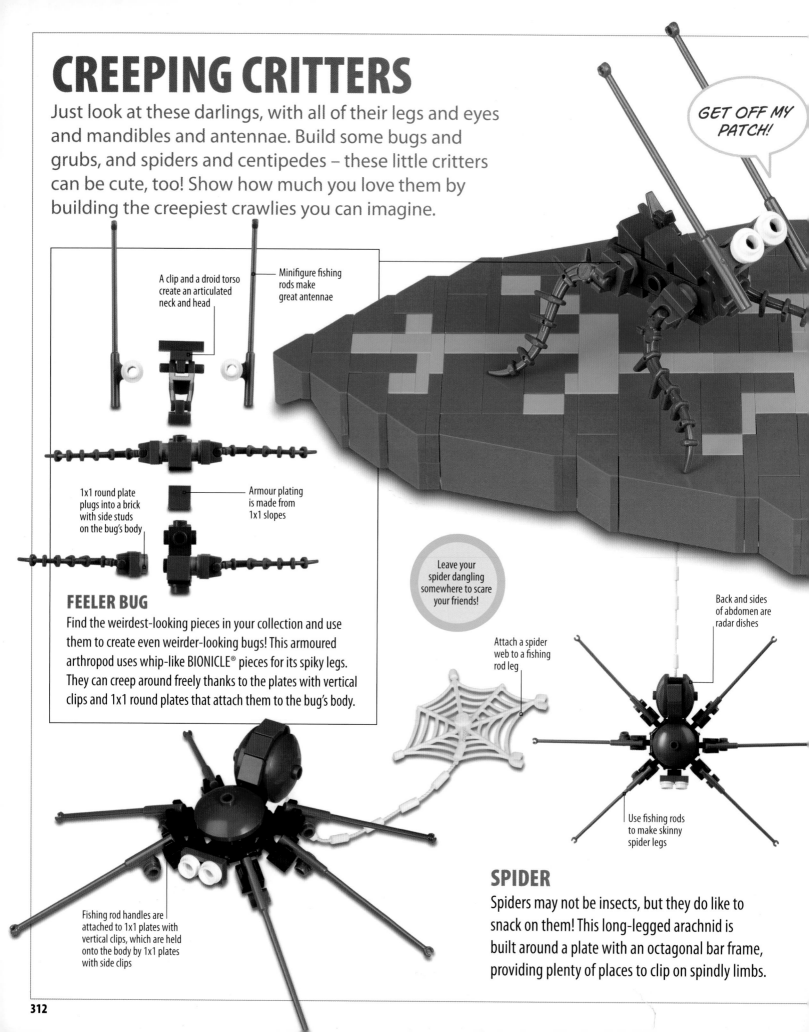

GET OFF MY PATCH!

A clip and a droid torso create an articulated neck and head

Minifigure fishing rods make great antennae

1x1 round plate plugs into a brick with side studs on the bug's body

Armour plating is made from 1x1 slopes

FEELER BUG

Find the weirdest-looking pieces in your collection and use them to create even weirder-looking bugs! This armoured arthropod uses whip-like BIONICLE® pieces for its spiky legs. They can creep around freely thanks to the plates with vertical clips and 1x1 round plates that attach them to the bug's body.

Fishing rod handles are attached to 1x1 plates with vertical clips, which are held onto the body by 1x1 plates with side clips

Leave your spider dangling somewhere to scare your friends!

Attach a spider web to a fishing rod leg

Back and sides of abdomen are radar dishes

Use fishing rods to make skinny spider legs

SPIDER

Spiders may not be insects, but they do like to snack on them! This long-legged arachnid is built around a plate with an octagonal bar frame, providing plenty of places to clip on spindly limbs.

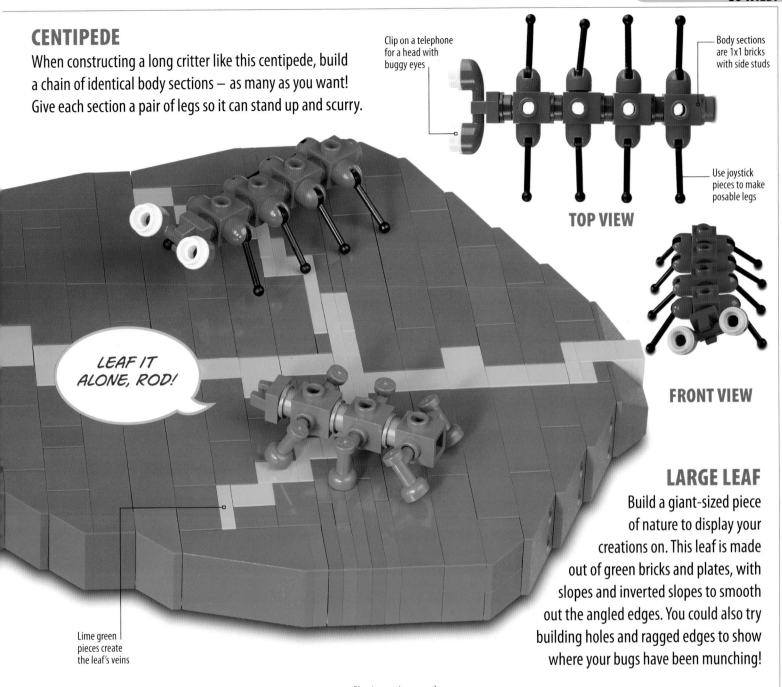

CENTIPEDE

When constructing a long critter like this centipede, build a chain of identical body sections – as many as you want! Give each section a pair of legs so it can stand up and scurry.

Clip on a telephone for a head with buggy eyes

Body sections are 1x1 bricks with side studs

Use joystick pieces to make posable legs

TOP VIEW

FRONT VIEW

LEAF IT ALONE, ROD!

Lime green pieces create the leaf's veins

LARGE LEAF

Build a giant-sized piece of nature to display your creations on. This leaf is made out of green bricks and plates, with slopes and inverted slopes to smooth out the angled edges. You could also try building holes and ragged edges to show where your bugs have been munching!

Plug in tap pieces or other small elements for legs

Head is a 1x1 plate with vertical clip

GREEN BUG

This skittering critter is built entirely out of small LEGO pieces. Its segments are made from 1x1 bricks with side studs, and 1x1 round plates in between.

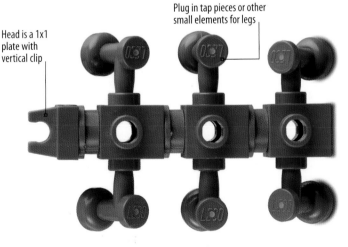

TOP VIEW

COOL BRICK

"This 1x1 brick with studs on top and four sides allows you to build outwards in lots of directions. It's a great brick for an animal head or the centre of a body."

313

MORE CREEPING CRITTERS

There are lots of other invertebrates out there that you can build! Just look under a rock, up a tree or in a garden and you're sure to find all sorts of creeping, crawling, slithering and slimy creatures to inspire your creativity.

SNAILS

Snails may not be the fastest critters around, but these ones are quick builds if you have the right parts. You could also make a slug by leaving off the shell part!

WAIT UP! YOU'RE GOING TOO FAST!

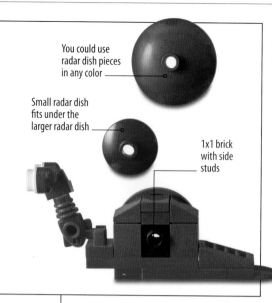

SNAIL SHELL

A snail's shell is its home, so take care when building this part! The centre of the snail's shell is a 1x1 brick with side studs. Radar dishes attach to the 1x1 brick's side studs.

You could use radar dish pieces in any color

Small radar dish fits under the larger radar dish

1x1 brick with side studs

Eyestalks are a telephone handset on a clip

A minifigure ray gun creates a detailed, angled neck

A grille slope and a tooth plate make a tapering tail

QUICK BUILD

LADYBIRDS

You can build a little ladybird out of just seven pieces. For a bigger challenge, try to change the design so that your ladybird is flying!

Body is two dome bricks held together by a small LEGO Technic axle

Use a plate with a vertical clip for mandibles

Head is a black 1x1 brick with four side studs

Gaps in shell look like a ladybird's black spots!

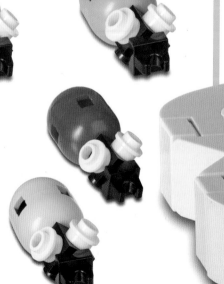

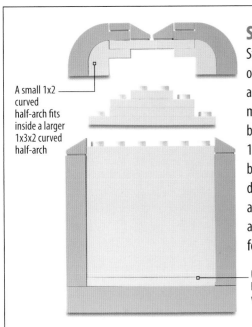

A small 1x2 curved half-arch fits inside a larger 1x3x2 curved half-arch

SLICED BREAD

Start the construction of your bread slice with a big white wall in the middle. Use tan or brown bricks for the crust. 1x1 slopes and arch bricks create the distinctive "bread" shape at the top. You could also add some green bricks for a touch of mould!

Use one big wall element or stack lots of white bricks to form the white part of the bread slice

SHOO, FLY!

To make the body of this fly, use three 1x1 bricks with studs on four sides. For the head, use another 1x1 brick with side studs, but in a different colour.

1x1 plates attach the wings to the body

Use contrasting coloured angled plates for the wings

Eyes are decorated 1x1 round tiles from a LEGO Ninjago set

Robot-claw legs plug into hollow studs

Why stop at one fly? Build a whole swarm!

A FEAST FIT FOR A FLY!

FLY AND BREAD

If you leave food out long enough, you are sure to attract some buzzing company. A slice of bread makes an inviting landing pad for a hungry fly – and it might even bring some friends!

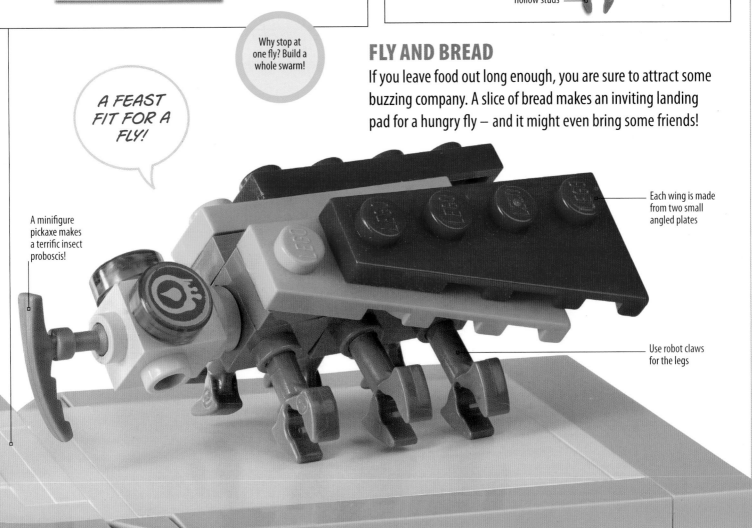

A minifigure pickaxe makes a terrific insect proboscis!

Each wing is made from two small angled plates

Use robot claws for the legs

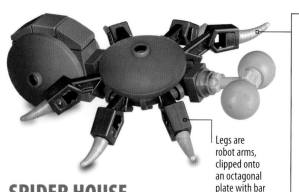

SPIDER HOUSE

Many zoos are home to different species of spiders and other invertebrates. Build some creepy-crawler creations for your zoo.

Legs are robot arms, clipped onto an octagonal plate with bar

SPIDER BELLY

To make the sides of this armoured abdomen, attach small radar dishes to bricks with side studs, then add larger radar dishes over the small ones.

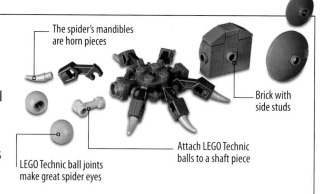

The spider's mandibles are horn pieces

Brick with side studs

Attach LEGO Technic balls to a shaft piece

LEGO Technic ball joints make great spider eyes

AT THE ZOO

A zoo is a marvellous place to see creatures from all over the world in one location. Think about what will keep your zoo animals happy, like an enclosure with climbing bars to monkey around on and trees to climb.

Use transparent 1x1 round tiles for eyes that look like they're glowing

This bug variation uses a second octagonal plate with bar for its abdomen

CHECK OUT MY "WEB" SITE!

A 1x1 round stud supports the radar dish on top

Body and head are both 1x1 bricks with studs on four sides

A minifigure pistol plugs into a cone to create a slender tail

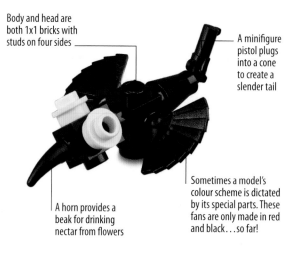

A horn provides a beak for drinking nectar from flowers

Sometimes a model's colour scheme is dictated by its special parts. These fans are only made in red and black...so far!

HUMMINGBIRD

A hummingbird is small and light, so you don't have to use a lot of bricks to build its body. LEGO minifigure fans make perfect rapidly beating wings.

SNAKE

The joints of this super-posable snake are made from droid torsos (see the Cool Brick on p.278), with segments ssembled from side-stud bricks, small plates and plates with vertical clips. If you don't have enough parts to build a snake this long, build a shorter one!

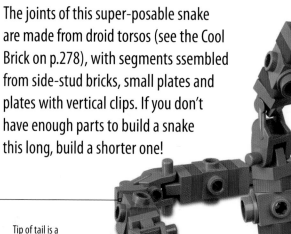

1x1 plates create brightly coloured stripes

HISSING SNAKE

The snake's head is a 1x1 brick with four side studs. A round brick is used for a nose and its hissing tongue is a unicorn's horn!

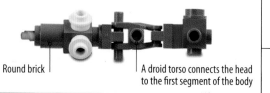

Round brick

A droid torso connects the head to the first segment of the body

Tip of tail is a robot claw

MONKEY

Monkeys are always up to something, so let them play by giving them different head and limb positions. This one is designed to sit on the ground. Its head is built upside down to give it a cheeky and whimsical expression!

Hinge plates allow its legs to swing out to the sides

One 2x2 dome gives the monkey's snout a little round mouth, and another gives it a bellybutton!

Climbing bars built out of LEGO Technic bricks and long bar elements

Arms are ray guns from the LEGO® Minifigures range

Top of head is a 2x2 slide plate from underneath a boat

Use plates with side rings to make the monkey's ears

Eyes are attached to headlight bricks

MONKEY BUSINESS

To make this cheeky monkey's head, use a 2x2 dome connected to bricks with side studs. If you don't have plates with printed eyes, any 1x1 round pieces will do!

This small tree is built with bricks, small plant leaves and regular and inverted slopes

This monkey's legs are 1x2 curved half-arches, and its feet are tooth plates

MONKEY PEN

You can build an animal enclosure out of bricks, fence pieces, or even a ring of clipped-together ladders. Fill your zoo displays with objects that will keep the animals inside exercised and entertained.

A rubber auto tyre can provide hours of interaction for a curious primate

WHAT'S THAT, GLORIA? WHY OF COURSE YOU CAN HAVE A BANANA!

Plates with vertical clips make hands that can hold onto objects

OOO! OO!

MADE-UP CREATURES

Imagine discovering a creature that no one has ever seen before. What would it look like? Maybe it's something totally alien that could never possibly exist on our planet. What kinds of made-up creatures can you build with your bricks?

"The ray gun is a space weapon, but it's used here as part of the dancing alien's leg! You will also see it used as part of a snail's head (p.314) and a monkey's elbow (p.317)."

Head is one giant eyeball made from two radar dishes, held together by a pulley wheel

I'VE GOT MY EYE ON YOU!

Lower arms are 2x2 domes connected with a short LEGO Technic cross-axle

Fire hose nozzles attached to clips give the shoulders and hips plenty of movement

Build the arms and legs first before attaching them to the main body

A droid torso and a clip create a posable neck to attach the head to the body

ALIEN OBSERVER

Play with shapes and proportions. This creature may have two arms, two legs and a head, just like humans do, but the way those body parts are built makes it very different indeed.

REAR VIEW

Top and bottom body sections are built around 1x1 bricks with studs on four sides, with a droid torso in between

A small transparent radar dish over a larger white one creates a wide, staring eye

DANCING GOOFBALL

Here's another creature with a big eye, but that's where the similarities end. With its strong legs and suction-cup feet, it must come from a world with really low gravity!

Brown radar dishes make alien shoes that are built for dancing!

Multi-jointed neck is built out of plates with clips and handles

Body is an octagonal plate with bar, covered by a radar dish

LASER LEGS

Two ray guns with a tap element in the middle make up each leg. The ray guns' handles plug into hollow studs on the body and feet.

Tap piece

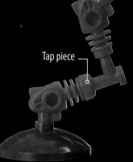

BLUE BOUNCER

This alien creature loves to hop around on its frog-like feet. Everything it meets is a delightful surprise – that's why its eyes and mouth are so round!

Eyes are made with transparent round tiles, white radar dishes and paddles

Legs are made with 1x1 plates and tap elements

How do you make the eyes stick up in a V-formation? Just rotate the 1x1 brick with four side studs at the back!

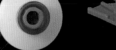

Eyestalks are paddles plugged into 1x1 cones

REAR VIEW

Flippers make great imaginary creature feet

Mouth is a 1x1 round plate

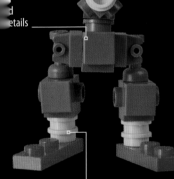

details

GARDEN GREEB

Nobody knows where this creature came from, but it sure hates it when you forget to water the garden. Make sure it gets plenty of sunlight to help it grow!

1x3 plates make feet that are perfectly camouflaged for standing near carrots!

Yellow socks made from pairs of 1x1 round plates

UNDERCOVER ALIENS

Even if you only have a few pieces, you can still make a wild and wacky alien creature. Build a whole crew and give them different hats to help them blend in on Earth. Use a minifigure hat, or simply a small cone or round brick.

CREATURE-CREATION

The head of this strange alien is a 1x1 brick with four side studs, with bulging eyes made from hollow-stud LEGO Games round plates. The body is a 2x2 dome on top of a 2x2 round plate. Its snow shoe feet connect to the body with 1x1 round plates.

A 1x1 round plate also attaches the alien's hat to its head

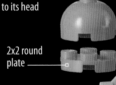

2x2 round plate

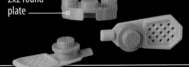

Cap from a lumberjack in the LEGO Minifigures series

A small cone makes a great fez!

Clown bowler hat from the LEGO Minifigures series

inifigure
or
hoes for
g feet

I HAVE A UNIQUE STYLE.

TROPICAL FISH

Strap on a snorkel and check out these eye-catching underwater fish! Some sea creatures are patterned to blend in with their environments, but not these flashy fellows. Their vivid colourations stand out from the crowd. Use your most colourful bricks to make some tropical fish friends of your own.

A 1x1 plate with a vertical clip makes a pair of fishy lips

Use different slope shapes and colours to build different types of fish

AXLE-EYED FISH

Here's a novel way to make fish eyes! Build a 1x2 LEGO Technic brick with a cross-shaped hole into the head, then slide a short cross-axle through and add a half-bush on each side.

Put slopes together with their matching inverted slopes to give your fish a diamond-shaped body

Attach a 1x1 round plate or tile to a big radar dish for a fish eye

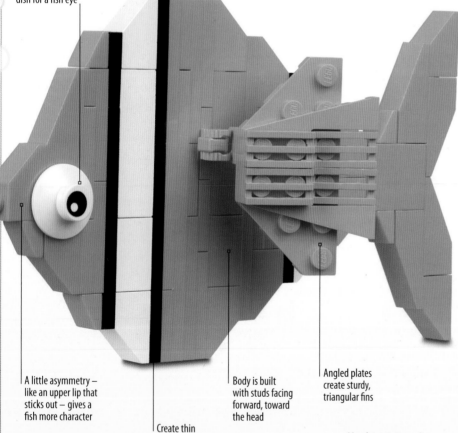

CLOWNFISH

Do you have a lot of orange bricks and slopes? Then build a cheerful clownfish! Except for the eyes and fins, its brightly hued body is built like a wall and entirely flat. Its body is very narrow, so attach its left fin higher than the one on its right. By putting the left fin's own click hinge plate lower than the right fin's, you will even both sides out.

Eyes are upside down radar dishes attached to a brick-with-hole

You could add a hinge here to make the tail swing from side to side

A little asymmetry – like an upper lip that sticks out – gives a fish more character

Create thin black stripes with plates and thick white stripes with bricks

Body is built with studs facing forward, toward the head

Angled plates create sturdy, triangular fins

Mouth is a 1x1 round plate plugged into the bottom of an inverted slope

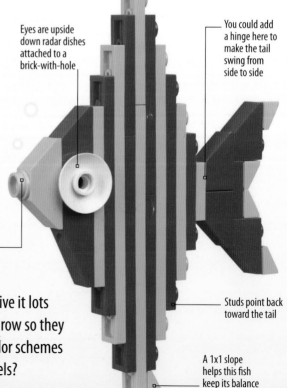

STRIPY FISH

Build a fish's body entirely out of plates to give it lots of skinny stripes. Stagger the plates in each row so they all stay locked together. What other wild color schemes can you come up with for your marine models?

Studs point back toward the tail

A 1x1 slope helps this fish keep its balance

Build top fins out of slopes, plates and tiles

Radar-dish eye also attaches to a brick with side studs

Telephone handset

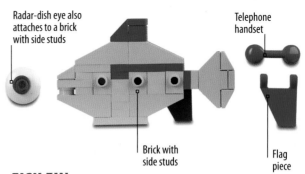

Brick with side studs

Flag piece

FISH FIN

To make this fish's fin, attach a telephone handset to bricks with side studs that are built into the fish's body. Clip a flag onto the telephone's handle to make a fin that can move up and down as the fish swims.

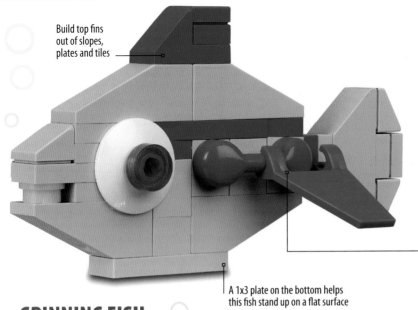

A 1x3 plate on the bottom helps this fish stand up on a flat surface

GRINNING FISH

A 1x1 plate inside its mouth gives this odd fish a round-toothed smile. A transparent red tile attached to a radar dish for an eye adds to its strange appearance!

SMALL FISH

Use little slopes to build a little fish. Small slopes give your model all kinds of interesting angled shapes and patterns.

Eye is a 1x1 round plate plugged into a 1x1 brick-with-hole

WHY ARE FISH SO SMART?

Side fins are held on by brackets

Use two 1x3 slopes to make the tail

BECAUSE WE ARE ALWAYS IN A SCHOOL!

Radar dish eyes are held in place by a 1x1 brick with studs on two sides

BIG-HEADED FISH

Not every fish has to be made out of straight lines and angles. Use curved bricks to add smooth, rounded features to your aquatic creations. Curved pieces also make a fish look graceful and streamlined.

The body is built from the bottom up, starting with a 1x6 plate

Create a layered effect by nesting clear pieces inside each other

MARINE LIFE

Fish aren't the only creatures that you'll find beneath the waves. The oceans are teeming with life, from the tiniest shrimp to the largest whale. Some of them swim, some of them float and some scuttle along the bottom. Look through your pieces for something that reminds you of an animal that lives underwater – then start building!

Top is a stack of clear and transparent blue radar dishes in different sizes

UMBRELLA JELLYFISH

Do you have a lot of transparent elements in your collection? Then build a jellyfish! Start with an umbrella-shaped dome on top, and add trailing tentacles below.

If you use a dome for the top, add a round plate or brick underneath it

DOME JELLYFISH

Some jellyfish can grow quite large. Mix white or light-coloured pieces with your transparent elements to make the biggest jellyfish you can assemble!

Fill out the centre with a stack of transparent blue round pieces

I HAVE THE STRANGEST CRAVING FOR PEANUT BUTTER.

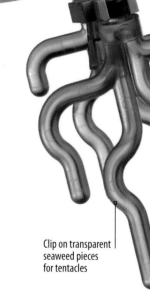

A sliding plate makes the top rounded and smooth

Clip on transparent seaweed pieces for tentacles

JELLY BELLY

The innermost part of this jellyfish's floating body is a white 1x1 brick with side studs. Transparent purple flames are plugged into 1x1 plates with side rings on the four sides.

1x1 round plates link the plates with side rings to the centre brick

A transparent blue grille looks like three short tentacles

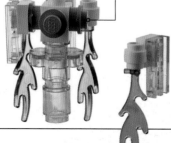

Dome is the bottom half of a crater-pocked rock sphere

Central body is a 2x2 round brick, with four 1x1 round bricks attached underneath

CRATER JELLYFISH

This jellyfish is constructed entirely out of transparent blue pieces. Build a stand to make it "float" and place it near a light source for an otherworldly glow.

Tentacles are transparent flame pieces

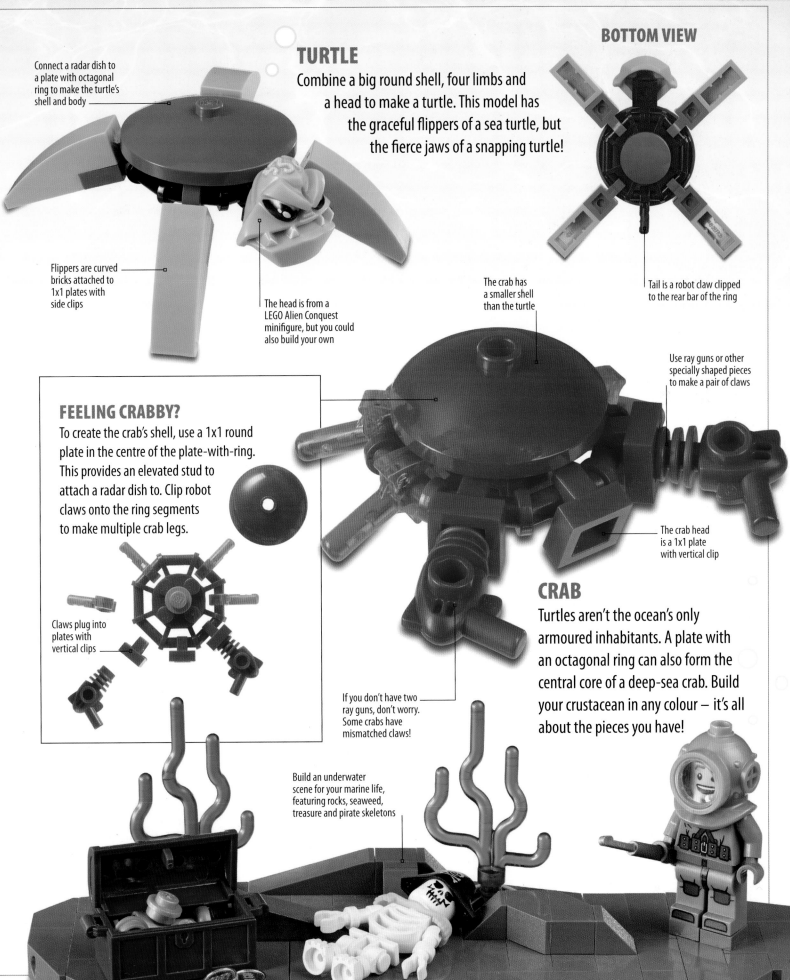

BOTTOM VIEW

Connect a radar dish to a plate with octagonal ring to make the turtle's shell and body

TURTLE

Combine a big round shell, four limbs and a head to make a turtle. This model has the graceful flippers of a sea turtle, but the fierce jaws of a snapping turtle!

Flippers are curved bricks attached to 1x1 plates with side clips

The head is from a LEGO Alien Conquest minifigure, but you could also build your own

The crab has a smaller shell than the turtle

Tail is a robot claw clipped to the rear bar of the ring

Use ray guns or other specially shaped pieces to make a pair of claws

FEELING CRABBY?

To create the crab's shell, use a 1x1 round plate in the centre of the plate-with-ring. This provides an elevated stud to attach a radar dish to. Clip robot claws onto the ring segments to make multiple crab legs.

Claws plug into plates with vertical clips

The crab head is a 1x1 plate with vertical clip

CRAB

Turtles aren't the ocean's only armoured inhabitants. A plate with an octagonal ring can also form the central core of a deep-sea crab. Build your crustacean in any colour – it's all about the pieces you have!

If you don't have two ray guns, don't worry. Some crabs have mismatched claws!

Build an underwater scene for your marine life, featuring rocks, seaweed, treasure and pirate skeletons

AT THE POLES

If you think winter is tough where you live, try living in the Arctic or the Antarctic! The animals there have to be tough, hardy and well-insulated against the cold. Build an icy polar scene and some creatures to fill it, but be warned – you may need to use all of your white bricks!

When building a background, add higher ridges to create far-off hills and snow banks

POLAR PEAKS

Use your micro-scale building skills to make a miniature background for your icy scene. A mixture of white and grey pieces creates a stark and atmospheric snow-capped mountain vista.

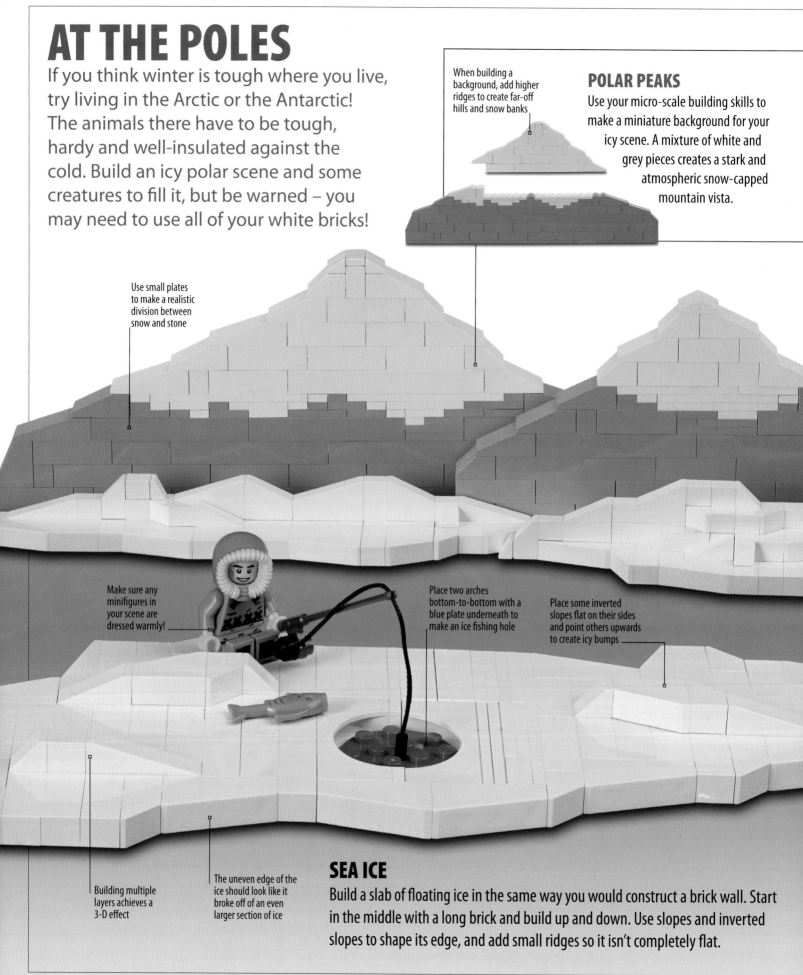

Use small plates to make a realistic division between snow and stone

Make sure any minifigures in your scene are dressed warmly!

Place two arches bottom-to-bottom with a blue plate underneath to make an ice fishing hole

Place some inverted slopes flat on their sides and point others upwards to create icy bumps

Building multiple layers achieves a 3-D effect

The uneven edge of the ice should look like it broke off of an even larger section of ice

SEA ICE

Build a slab of floating ice in the same way you would construct a brick wall. Start in the middle with a long brick and build up and down. Use slopes and inverted slopes to shape its edge, and add small ridges so it isn't completely flat.

COOL BRICK

"This 1x1 tooth plate makes great feet, beaks and teeth! It can also be used to create feathers, as seen on the ducks and chickens on pp.306–307."

PENGUINS

Start your penguin with a 1x1 brick with studs on all four sides. Add a round plate for a neck, black tooth plates for wings and 1x2 tiles in front and back.

1x1 brick with studs on four sides

Tooth plate for wings

A black back against deep, dark water hides the penguin from predators hunting above

Why not add an igloo to keep your minifigures warm on cold polar nights?

By including bricks with side studs in your ice slab wall, you can attach the mountains as vertical walls

Binoculars make keen eyes for spotting fish

Baby penguins are covered in fuzzy down to keep them warm until they are grown-up

One-stud connections let you swivel and pose the head and wings

Use a tooth plate for a pointy beak

Feet are a single 1x1 plate with side clip

Use a 1x1 round tile for a penguin chick's belly

MUSH, DOGGIES! WE'VE GOT TO GET HOME BEFORE RUSH HOUR!

DOG SLED

Move over, snowmobile – out here on the polar ice, canine power is the way to travel! Start your dog sled with a 2x4 plate and attach a pair of runners for smooth movement over snow.

If you don't have hockey sticks for runners, use poles or bars instead

You could add a longer section at the back for carrying important supplies

An angled front cuts down on wind resistance for faster speed

Round plates on the end of string elements attach to studs on the backs of LEGO dogs

ARCTIC ANIMALS

To see the wildest animals on the planet, you've got to travel to the ends of the Earth. Here at the North Pole, it's eat or be eaten…and few creatures are as good at eating as these ones! Build some ferocious predators to fill your polar scene. What other cold-weather animals could you build?

KILLER WHALE

To build this mighty killer whale's streamlined body, start in the middle with a long, two-stud-wide black brick or plate. Use white pieces for its stomach and a patch on its body.

Use arches to build the rounded snout

Add 1x1 round plates for the top teeth, too

Hinge plate

CHILLY CHOMPERS

The killer whale's mouth is full of 1x1 round plate teeth, surrounding a pink tile tongue. Its upper jaw is attached with a hinge so it can open and close for a great big chomp.

If you build a bigger killer whale model, you could use cones as pointy teeth!

Attach the white section under the jaws with jumper plates

Use jumper plates to center a dorsal fin, built from slope and curved bricks

The whale's eyes are transparent 1x1 round plates attached to headlight bricks

WHY CAN'T THERE BE PENGUINS ON MY PAGE?

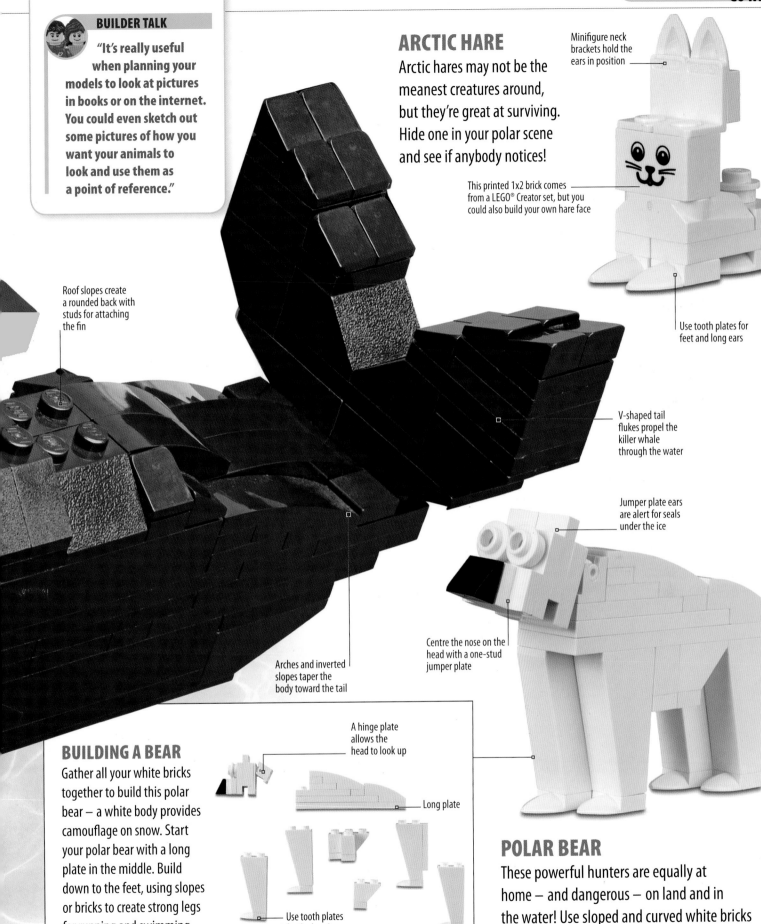

ARCTIC HARE

Arctic hares may not be the meanest creatures around, but they're great at surviving. Hide one in your polar scene and see if anybody notices!

Minifigure neck brackets hold the ears in position

This printed 1x2 brick comes from a LEGO® Creator set, but you could also build your own hare face

Use tooth plates for feet and long ears

Roof slopes create a rounded back with studs for attaching the fin

V-shaped tail flukes propel the killer whale through the water

Jumper plate ears are alert for seals under the ice

Centre the nose on the head with a one-stud jumper plate

Arches and inverted slopes taper the body toward the tail

BUILDING A BEAR

Gather all your white bricks together to build this polar bear – a white body provides camouflage on snow. Start your polar bear with a long plate in the middle. Build down to the feet, using slopes or bricks to create strong legs for running and swimming.

A hinge plate allows the head to look up

Long plate

Use tooth plates for the bear's clawed feet

POLAR BEAR

These powerful hunters are equally at home – and dangerous – on land and in the water! Use sloped and curved white bricks to build the body of a mighty polar bear.

THINGS THAT GO BUMP
IN THE NIGHT

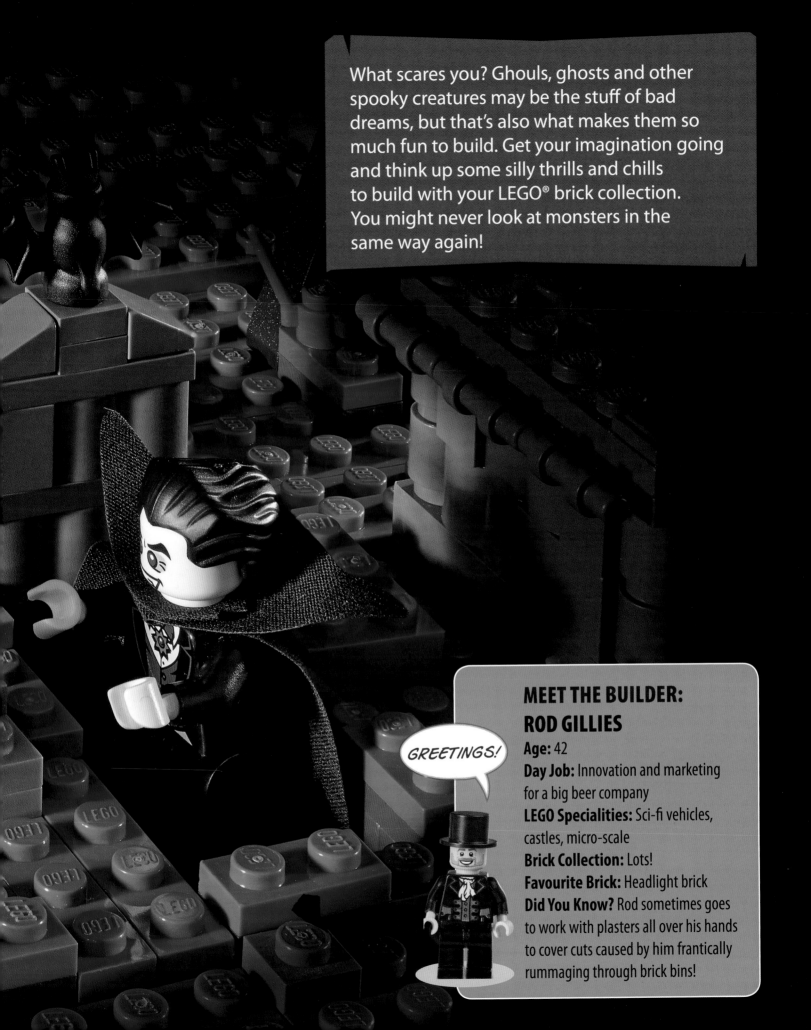

What scares you? Ghouls, ghosts and other spooky creatures may be the stuff of bad dreams, but that's also what makes them so much fun to build. Get your imagination going and think up some silly thrills and chills to build with your LEGO® brick collection. You might never look at monsters in the same way again!

GREETINGS!

**MEET THE BUILDER:
ROD GILLIES**
Age: 42
Day Job: Innovation and marketing for a big beer company
LEGO Specialities: Sci-fi vehicles, castles, micro-scale
Brick Collection: Lots!
Favourite Brick: Headlight brick
Did You Know? Rod sometimes goes to work with plasters all over his hands to cover cuts caused by him frantically rummaging through brick bins!

I'M TIMMY AND I'M NOT FRIGHTENED OF ANYTHING.

...BUT I AM!

FRIGHT NIGHT

Meet Timmy. He's an ordinary boy who adores scary things. He thinks that bad dreams are the best! Timmy has spent all day reading scary books, watching scary movies and thinking up scary stories. He even ate a big piece of cheese right before bedtime! Now Timmy is about to go on a wild ride through the realm of nightmares. Time to see if Timmy is as brave as he thinks he is.

I've got a BONE to pick with you, Timmy!

SKELETON CHASE

Yikes – pursued by a giant skeleton! But that's the least of Timmy's worries... because he is about to meet a whole graveyard full of them! (See p.362.)

To ensure a nightmare night, Timmy eats small "cheese" slopes just before he goes to bed

BUILDING BAD DREAMS
ROD GILLIES

"For my theme, I wanted to tackle some of the classic scares we're all familiar with from movies and books – but with a comic twist, since they're all LEGO creations! I also wanted to make my own creations different in style to the official LEGO® Monster Fighter sets. For most of the bigger models, I sketched out rough drawings in advance, but for the details or for smaller creations I tended to get inspired by just picking up bricks and seeing what happened!"

BZZZ! WHRRR! Sweet dreams do not compute!

Find out how to make Timmy's bed on p.344

ROBOT ATTACK

Look out! An army of rampaging robots is just one of the frights that Timmy will be encountering tonight. (See p.352.)

HOW NICE, A VISITOR!

WE HAVEN'T HAD ONE OF THOSE IN CENTURIES!

HOUSE OF VAMPIRES

Have you ever wanted to tour a vampire's haunted castle? It looks like Timmy's nightmare is taking him there, whether he likes it or not! (See p.336.)

SPOOKY CIRCUS TRAIN

"Whoooooo wants to see the greatest show in Nightmare Land?" Timmy's nightmare starts with a circus train – but it isn't for any ordinary circus. The engine is decorated with bones, and the clowns and ringmaster are all skeletons! The circus is usually a place for laughs and cheers, but in the realm of bad dreams, it can be very spooky indeed.

COOL BRICK

"LEGO® Technic half-pin connectors let you link regular bricks to LEGO Technic pieces through sideways building. They can also make great details on their own when they are a contrasting colour to the piece they are plugged into."

ALL ABOARD!

If you have some LEGO train wheel bases, use them to build a circus train for a nightmare carnival. Make an engine in front and a car for it to pull. Inside could be snakes, spiders, or something even scarier!

COME ONE, COME ALL, TO THE NIGHTMARE CARNIVAL!

Build a hollow box for the freight car

Turn plates sideways to build letters. Pick a colour that will stand out against the background

If you don't have this "cow catcher" piece, build one out of slope bricks

WE ONLY RUN A SKELETON SERVICE.

White robot arms create ribcage-like decorations on the engine's sides

Smokestack connects to 2x2 plate

Bone elements are held on by clips

A set of wheels at each end means you can make the freight car as long or as short as you want

Train connector to link cars together

EERIE ENGINE

The locomotive is based on an old-style steam engine. Use roof slopes to build the tube-like shape of the front boiler, and include a small cabin in back for the ectoplasmic engineer.

Even the jolliest jester looks creepy with a skeleton head

Blue LEGO Technic half-pins provide detail

The skull has LEGO Technic bricks-with-holes for eye sockets and a brick with a cross-axle hole for its nose

FRONT VIEW

FORTUNE TELLER

In the land of nightmares, fortune tellers never warn you about tomorrow's surprise math test. Mix and match minifigure parts and accessories to populate your carnival with colourful performers and other odd characters.

I SEE NICE THINGS IN YOUR FUTURE.

NO! I LIKE HORRIBLE THINGS!

Crystal ball is a transparent minifigure head piece under a transparent 2x2 hollow dome

Bell is a 1x1 round plate and a 2x2 round brick attached to a radar dish with a printed swirl

GAME OF STRENGTH

You don't have to add bone details to this test-your-strength game to make it spooky. Just build it out of clashing colours and give it a scary attendant – it will fit right in with your nightmare carnival!

Use a tooth plate to mark the strongest swing

Build the game as a long, thin base with a short wall at one end, and then flip it up

Hammer is a long bar, a brick with a hollow side stud, two 1x1 plates and a 1x1 tile

NIGHTMARE CARNIVAL

"Last stop! Everybody off!" The carnival is a maze of games, rides and snack booths, each with its own scary twist. Timmy likes cotton candy, but he is pretty sure he doesn't want to try the rotten candy that they're selling here! Build fiendishly fun rides and attractions to give visitors to your nightmare carnival a good scare.

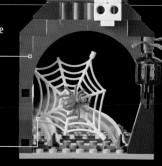

Make sure the tunnel arches are high enough for the car and passengers to roll through

A spider in a web makes any scene look extra-spooky!

ENTRANCE VIEW

GHOSTLY RIDE

You don't have to build the entire carnival ride — just a stretch of track and a haunted interior. Build spooky details into the wall that will make the riders jump in their seats!

Old-fashioned lamps are four-forked palm tree tops with transparent 1x1 round plates inside and a small radar dish as a lid

Lock pieces together well so the arches don't fall apart

Use textured bricks in the back wall to make it look old and decrepit

Sign is a sideways wall of stacked green and black bricks and plates

Add plants, cats, bats and frogs to bring your scary ride to life

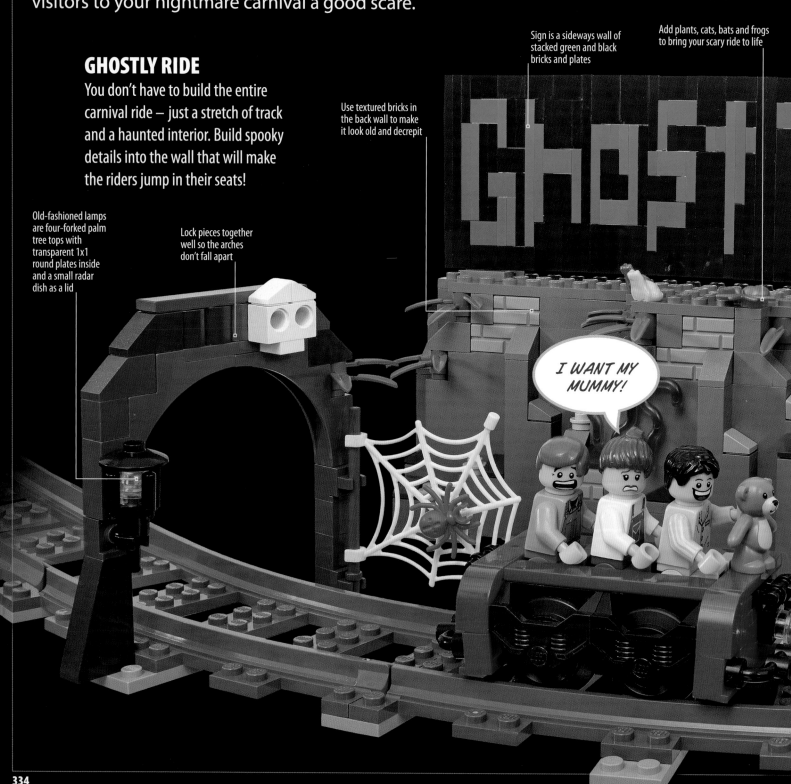

I WANT MY MUMMY!

ON TARGET

Use printed tiles and microfigures from LEGO® Games as targets for a carnival shooting game. Hit one and you will get a prize… but are you sure you want whatever it is that you'll win?

IF YOU MISS, YOU HAVE TO SIT ON THE SHELF.

Crossbow handles are plugged into jumper plates

Make a striped awning with arch pieces in alternating colours

Use stacked-up log bricks or 1x2 brown bricks to make the stall's wooden sides

Where will your ghost train go next? Will there be more track, or a sheer drop?

CRAZY CAR

Use a pair of train wheel bases to make a small ride car. A 2x6 hollow space on top is just the right size for three frightened minifigures to sit inside. Build your car in a colour that stands out against the wall's dark background.

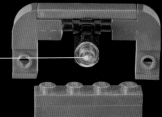

Car is symmetrical front-to-back so it can roll either way

Headlight is a 1x1 transparent yellow round plate

Bumpers are sideways-built curved bars with studs attached to headlight bricks

HAUNTED HOUSE

Next, Timmy dreams about a house where monsters live. It has all kinds of creepy rooms and an attic full of specters! A haunted house is more than just a brick building with creatures placed inside. Think about what kinds of rooms your monsters would like, and don't forget the most important part of the model: the ghosts!

Black fence pieces look like a foreboding iron railing

Mix round and square plates in different colours to make a low stone wall

Spider web attaches to a bar mounted on clips in the wall

A LEGO Technic brick creates a hole for bats to fly in and out!

Blood-red rooftops add to the haunted ambience

FRONT VIEW

Sprinkle in some dark grey bricks for an old stone building

Build bricks with side studs into the walls to attach vines and ivy to the outside

Get your teeth into this Vampire Car build on p.342!

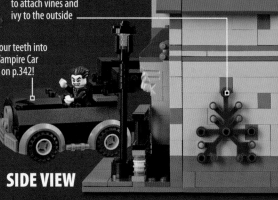

SIDE VIEW

UP-SCARES, DOWN-SCARES

This model is half house and half castle, full of musty old history. Inside are cavernous chambers with arches and alcoves that could hide all manner of scary things. It is built in two halves — each half is connected by 1x2 hinge bricks so it can swing open, revealing the shadowy, haunted interior.

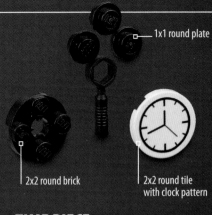

1x1 round plate

2x2 round brick

2x2 round tile with clock pattern

TIME PIECE

It won't take a long time to build this clock! A printed round tile is used for the clock face and a minifigure wrench for the pendulum.

A pair of plates with handles becomes a gothic carved windowsill

BOO!

Use an arch or build a column in the middle of the open side to support the roof bricks overhead

Why not extend your haunted house? Fill it with more rooms full of spooky stuff to scare visitors!

Upper storey lifts off, making it easier to access the study

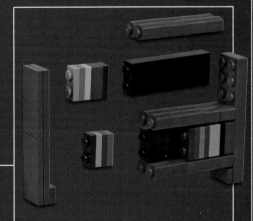

HELLO! IT MUST BE TIME FOR SUPPER!

THE MASTER'S LAIR

The cultured Count has his own library and study in the main downstairs chamber. His prized bookcase is built sideways, with stacks of coloured 1x2 plates as books on the shelves.

Jumper plates in the tile floorboards connect animals and objects

WITCH'S HOVEL

The witch seemed nice enough until she asked Timmy to sweep the floor. No matter how hard he tries to hold on, the broom just keeps flying around and making an even bigger mess! The witch who lives in this small shack could be good or bad. Fill it with potions, knick-knacks, and other components for casting magic spells!

THIS JOB REALLY SWEEPS YOU OFF YOUR FEET!

Stack up varied grey bricks to build a stone chimney

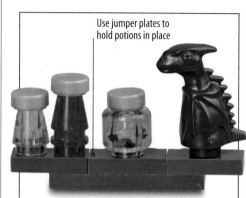

Use jumper plates to hold potions in place

SHELF OF SPELLS

Shelves help the witch keep her magical potions and lotions well-organised. For bottles and jars, use different coloured transparent round pieces and put 1x1 round plates or tiles on top as lids.

WHILE YOU'RE UP THERE, CAN YOU DUST THE CHIMNEY?

Stone doorway is built on jumper plates so it sticks a little way out of the wall

The interior door frame is built with inverted slopes

MAGIC SHACK

The witch's hovel has hinge bricks built into the chimney so it can open up to show off the interior. Inside are shelves full of everything a witch could need for brewing up hexes, curses and strange elixirs.

Use jumper plates in the floor to keep furniture and accessories from sliding around when the model is moved

The table legs are telescopes

If your shack is too small for a bubbling cauldron, use a barrel instead!

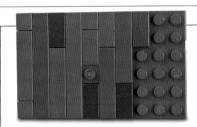

Attach a tile at an angle to the stud on a 1x1 plate to patch a hole in the worn-out roof

RAMSHACKLE ROOF

Build a layer of tiles onto a large plate for a roof made of wooden planks. Different shades of brown will make it look like some of the boards have been repaired and replaced.

Table legs are 1x1 round bricks on top of 1x1 round tiles

TOP TABLE

Assemble a table to lay out all the ingredients for your next spell. This one uses brown plates, tiles, clips and jumper plates.

Use slope bricks at the top of the frame to support the angle of the roof

White walls with black outlines resemble old, timber-framed construction

Place wild plants around the outside of the hovel

REAR SIDE VIEW

Window is attached to jumper plates

Door is attached with clip-hinges

Cobblestone path is made with 1x1 tiles

FRONT VIEW

Every witch should have a broom

Rat is safe from the witch's cauldron...for now!

Talking goblin head keeps the witch company

MONSTER MOTORS

What is that terrifying growling sound? Is it a werewolf? A dinosaur? No – it's a crazy custom car with a monster at the wheel! Build a pint-sized auto to fit your favourite LEGO monster minifigure. Give it a design and colour scheme that reflects what kind of creature drives it, and roll it around to wreak some havoc!

This engine piece can be found in many LEGO vehicle sets

Bricks with side studs and half-arch bricks at the front of the car allow you to attach a sideways-built bumper

FRONT VIEW

IF I GET A FLAT TYRE, I USE A PUMPKIN PATCH!

Curved elements mimic a pumpkin's shape

PUMPKIN CAR

What could be a better ride for a pumpkin-headed monster than a pumpkin-themed car? With its bright orange colour scheme and rounded curves, this model definitely shows its jack-o'-lantern influence.

Big exposed wheels and engine capture the look of a classic hot rod racer

CAR NO WORK. FRANKIE USE HIS BOLTS.

FRONT VIEW

MONSTER CAR

Use pieces that resemble wood, aluminum and brass to build a chugging, puffing steampunk roadster fit for a makeshift monster assembled by mad science! Try combining your more unusual pieces to create even more unusual shapes.

Stack two plates with handles for a double bumper

Ray guns attach to silver telescopes held on by clips

STEAM POWER

The engine is built with a mix of metallic-coloured elements. Gold robot arms and cones plugged onto silver ray gun handles give it six smokestacks for venting heat and steam.

Gold robot arms

Wagon wheels look rickety and old-fashioned

"The headlight brick is a really useful brick! It lets you do loads of cool things, like attaching bricks sideways or putting bricks 'studs in' on the back of them."

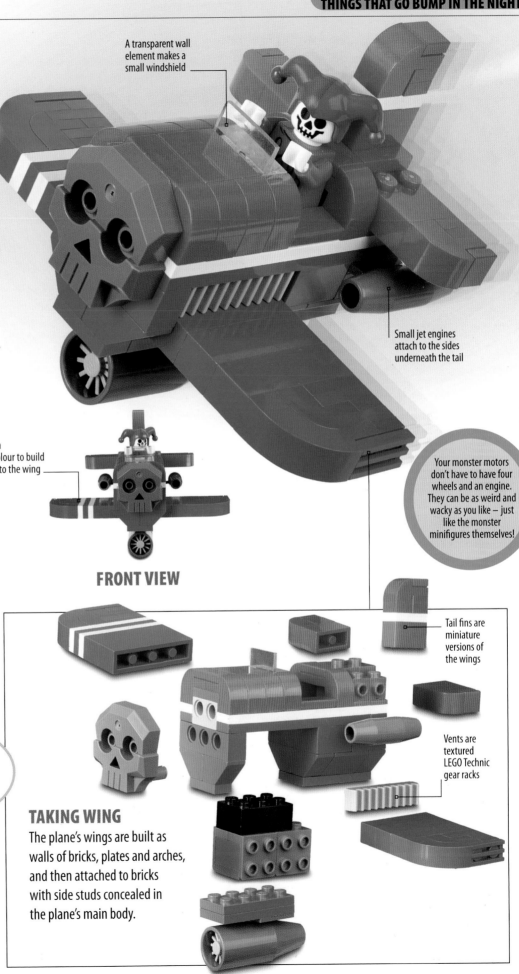

A transparent wall element makes a small windshield

Small jet engines attach to the sides underneath the tail

JESTER JET

You can use the same building techniques that you would use to make a mini monster car to build a haunted plane! Use arches, tiles and sideways building to make its surface smooth and aerodynamic.

Use plates in a contrasting colour to build thin stripes into the wing

Your monster motors don't have to have four wheels and an engine. They can be as weird and wacky as you like – just like the monster minifigures themselves!

FRONT VIEW

Inverted slopes make the underside look more rounded

SIDE VIEW

IS THAT WHAT THEY CALL A SCAREPLANE?

Tail fins are miniature versions of the wings

Vents are textured LEGO Technic gear racks

TAKING WING

The plane's wings are built as walls of bricks, plates and arches, and then attached to bricks with side studs concealed in the plane's main body.

MONSTER RACE

Scary racers, start your engines! Timmy has no idea how he has ended up as a referee for this race – as the racers career down the track, he realises that he has no idea what the rules are, either! Build more monster cars to add to your monster collection – which one do you think would win in a monster race?

Headlights are unnecessary when the driver can see in the dark!

A 2x3 curved plate with hole creates a tombstone-like decoration

FRONT VIEW

GETTING STUCK IN TRAFFIC DRIVES ME BATTY!

Use a grille and two grille slopes to make a ribbed bumper

VAMPIRE CAR

Vampires are associated with the colour black, bats and coffins. That's why this model reflects all three! Roof slopes give the car the long, angular shape of a coffin and the curved fins on the back are reminiscent of a bat's sweeping wings.

Close-fitting mudguards around the wheels provide a sleek silhouette

Plates with handles add side details

Neon green bulbs make the engine look like it's powered by swamp water!

Use slope bricks to make angled surfaces

A textured brick makes a good small car grille

FRONT VIEW

SWAMP MONSTER CAR

Create a complementary colour scheme by matching your car to the look of its driver. Can you tell that the swamp monster's favourite colour is green? Transparent and bubble-like elements add to the auto's aquatic appearance.

Big tyres for traction on marshy terrain

Match the details to the monster – build a skull-faced car for a skull-faced clown!

CREEPY CLOWN CAR

What kind of colour scheme should you give your custom car model? Clashing colours will really jump out and say "Boo!" to onlookers. If your driver has green hair, try a fiery red race car and add a yellow stripe to represent blazing speed!

FRONT VIEW

An auto hood or roof piece also works well as a rear spoiler

Nothing says "fast" like a giant plume of flame blasting out of the back of your vehicle!

⭐ **CHALLENGE**

Stack bricks in alternating colours to create checkered race markers

SCARY RACING

Challenge your friends to build their own monster mini-cars and race to become King or Queen of the Monsters. Build obstacles and ramps to make it super challenging – and super scary! Take turns giving your car a quick one-handed push and see who can reach the finish line first.

Build lots of ramps in different sizes

ROCKET RACER

Use round pieces to build a jet engine, with a hole in the centre for the flame element's peg. The front piece of the car is built with four curved macaroni bricks and matches the look of the red 4x4 round plate at the back.

Plug ray gun handles into bricks with hollow side studs to make angled engine exhaust pipes

A blue driver's seat makes this car's colour scheme even more clashing!

DO YOU KNOW THE WAY TO THE BLOOD BANK?

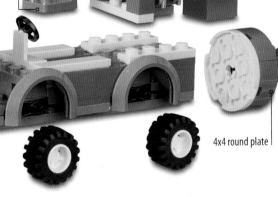

Curved macaroni brick

Snap 1x1 round plates into the skull's eye sockets for eerie, staring headlights

4x4 round plate

SWEET DREAMS

"Phew, thank goodness that's over," Timmy says as he opens his eyes. But a sudden rattling tells him that he is still stuck in the nightmare! A bedroom is a place of safety and comfort. . .so where better to hide a spooky scare? Whether you build a skeleton in the closet or a monster under the bed, there won't be any sweet dreams here tonight!

Use printed or stickered tiles for wall decorations

A treasure chest can double as a trunk for storing clothes and toys

YIKES!

Attach decorations to brackets or bricks with side studs in the walls

Inverted slopes form braces for the bookshelf

A black section of wall behind the wardrobe makes it look dark and shadowy when the door is opened

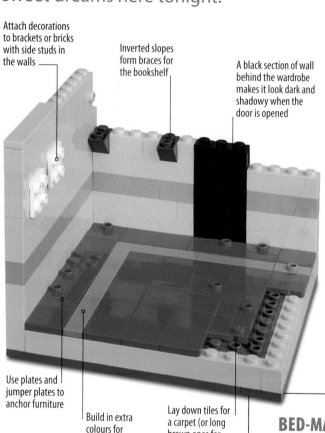

Use plates and jumper plates to anchor furniture

Build in extra colours for wallpaper and rug designs

Lay down tiles for a carpet (or long brown ones for a wooden floor)

ROOM DESIGN

You can use this basic design to make lots of different kinds of rooms. It's just a floor and two walls, built up the normal way. The details and contents are up to you!

BED-MAKING

Use plates to build the bed's frame and legs. Place small arches over the edges and fill in the centre with tiles to make a patterned blanket or bed cover.

There's some space under the bed, so why not add a creature there?

Lay a white tile across some jumper plates for the pillow

Include a plate to attach a sleeping minifigure or give a frightened one somewhere to stand

Colourful plates and tiles create some bedtime books

Hide the top studs under tiles and slopes

Since the wardrobe rests against the side of the main model, you don't need to build a back wall!

The tall bricks on the sides are specially designed with connections for the door pieces

Use 1x1 round plates for short legs

WICKED WARDROBE

Build a frame with doors to make an opening wardrobe. What's lurking inside your wardrobe? Use hinge pieces to attach a skeleton at an angle so it looks like it's lunging out to grab someone!

BUILDING A BEDROOM

Why not base your model on your own bedroom? Try to match your bed, floor, furniture and even the pictures and posters on your walls. Or you could build the bedroom that you would love to have...in your dreams!

QUICK BUILD

Scatter toys on your bedroom floor. This toy car is a jumper plate with a 1x1 square tile on top

LEGO Technic ball-joint pieces attach to studs on the floor

SCARY FACES

Build some scary faces to display on your shelves or desk to give your friends a fright. Gather all your small pieces together and get prepared to scare!

Brown plates create a tuft of monster hair

Use black plates for a crooked smile

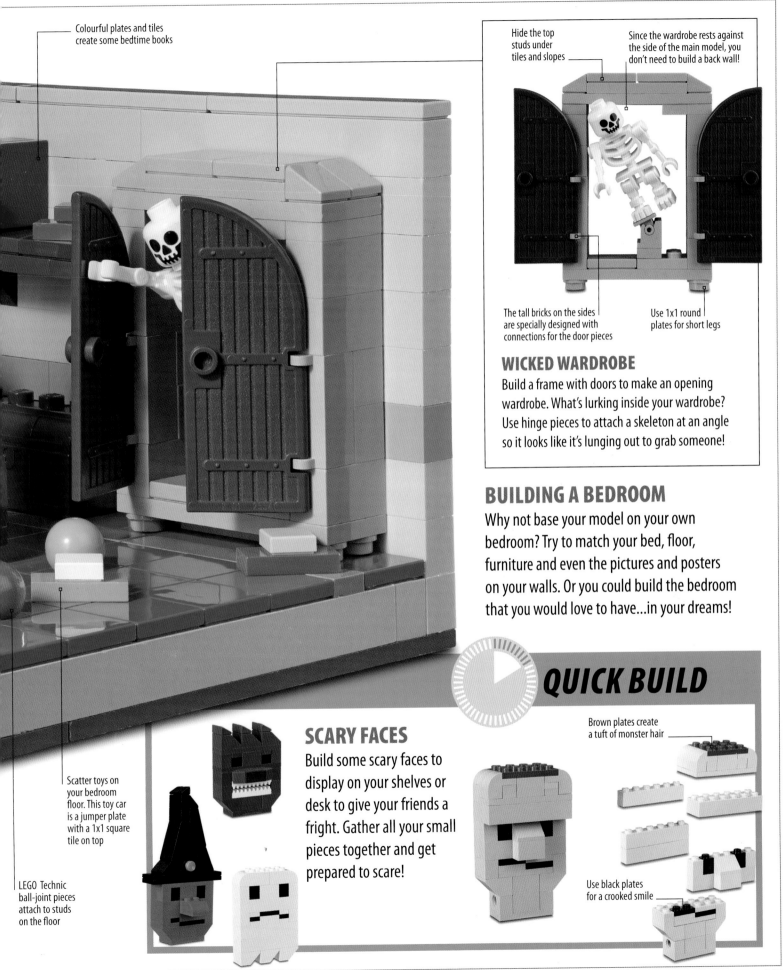

SOMETHING IN THE BATH

Fleeing into the bathroom doesn't help
Timmy. There are all kinds of strange noises
in the plumbing…and what just made that
splash?! An ordinary home can become
an extraordinary one in the world of bad
dreams. Bathrooms are just the start – think
about what you can do to transform a kitchen
or living room scene into some silly, scary fun!

Red and blue round
plates on top of faucets
show which is for hot
water and which is for cold

Sink and
bathtub are
attached to the
wall using bricks
with side studs

A black nighttime
background
establishes the
time and makes
the monster stand
out even more

LEGO® Alien
Conquest head

BATHROOM NIGHTMARE

This bathroom is built in much the
same way as the bedroom on p.344,
but with different fixtures and
furnishings. The familiar tub, sink
and toilet make it clear where in
the house this particular scare is
taking place!

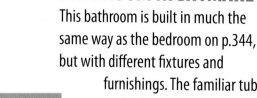

BOO!

BOO
HOO!

TENTACLES IN THE TUB

Use bricks with holes and side studs to build the bathtub.
The creature under the water is built with tail elements
plugged into the bricks. Attach the tub to the bathroom
floor using plates and
bricks with
side studs.

Exposed studs make
the red floor look like
a deep-pile carpet

KNOCK KNOCK!

Mum, there's a monster outside! A spooky face
in the window turns a simple home-life scene
into the start of an alien invasion. Building it
in a slightly larger scale makes the minifigure
look like a small (and very scared) child.

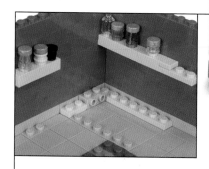

Place arches
on their sides to
make rounded
corners like a
real bathtub

White bricks for
bubbles created
by the bath beast!

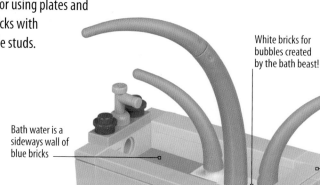

Bath water is a
sideways wall of
blue bricks

346

Attach two-stud-wide plates into the wall to create shelves

EEK! WHAT WAS IN THAT BOTTLE OF BUBBLE BATH?

BUILDER TALK

"Sometimes it's worth starting with the hardest bit of a model and then working your way back. I built the curved ends of the tub and sink first and finished with the bits against the wall, and then attached them to the rest of the bathroom."

Instead of using tentacle pieces, you could create your own creature underneath the water!

It's no surprise that LEGO tiles make ideal bathroom floor tiles!

A brick-with-hole acts as a drain to keep the tub from over-filling

SIDE VIEW

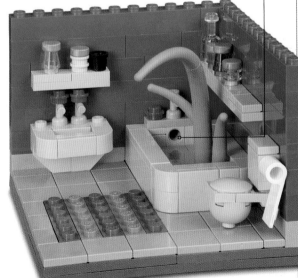

For a bath mat, use tiles with exposed studs to create the impression of deep, fuzzy material – and to attach a fleeing minifigure

PERILOUS POTTY
This looks like a perfectly normal toilet, but who knows what could be lurking in there? The bowl is an upside-down 2x2 dome, clipped to the wall by the plate with handle above it.

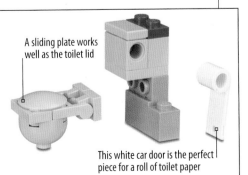

A sliding plate works well as the toilet lid

This white car door is the perfect piece for a roll of toilet paper

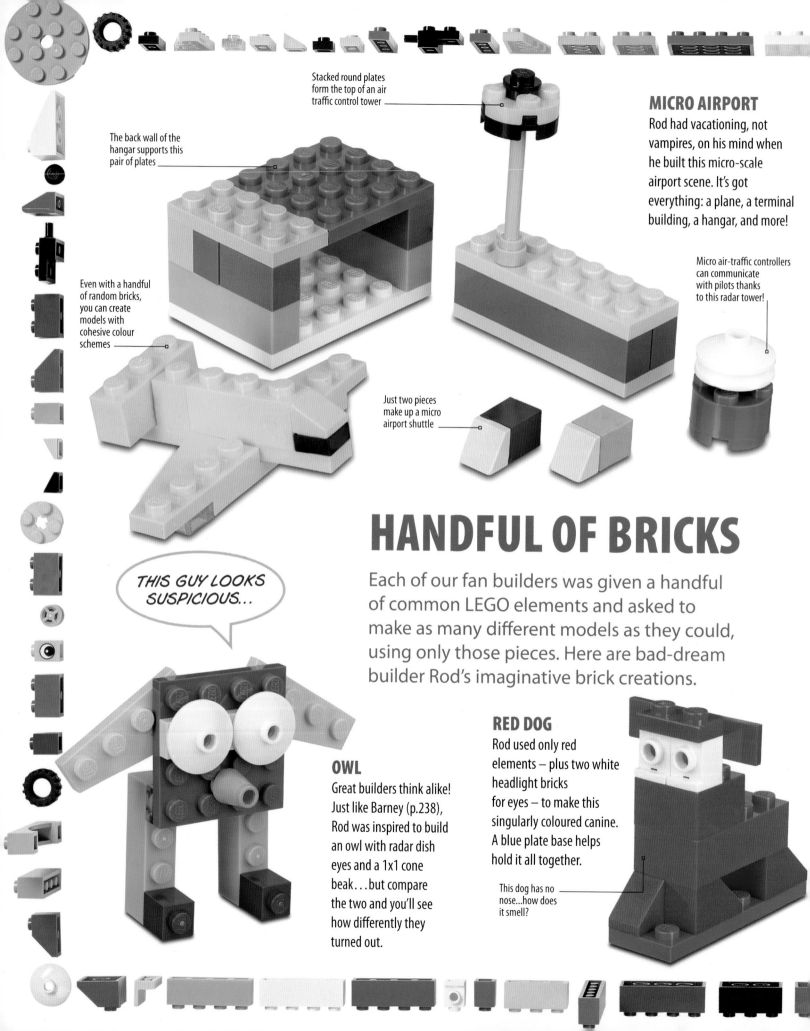

Stacked round plates form the top of an air traffic control tower

The back wall of the hangar supports this pair of plates

Even with a handful of random bricks, you can create models with cohesive colour schemes

MICRO AIRPORT

Rod had vacationing, not vampires, on his mind when he built this micro-scale airport scene. It's got everything: a plane, a terminal building, a hangar, and more!

Micro air-traffic controllers can communicate with pilots thanks to this radar tower!

Just two pieces make up a micro airport shuttle

HANDFUL OF BRICKS

Each of our fan builders was given a handful of common LEGO elements and asked to make as many different models as they could, using only those pieces. Here are bad-dream builder Rod's imaginative brick creations.

THIS GUY LOOKS SUSPICIOUS...

OWL

Great builders think alike! Just like Barney (p.238), Rod was inspired to build an owl with radar dish eyes and a 1x1 cone beak...but compare the two and you'll see how differently they turned out.

RED DOG

Rod used only red elements – plus two white headlight bricks for eyes – to make this singularly coloured canine. A blue plate base helps hold it all together.

This dog has no nose...how does it smell?

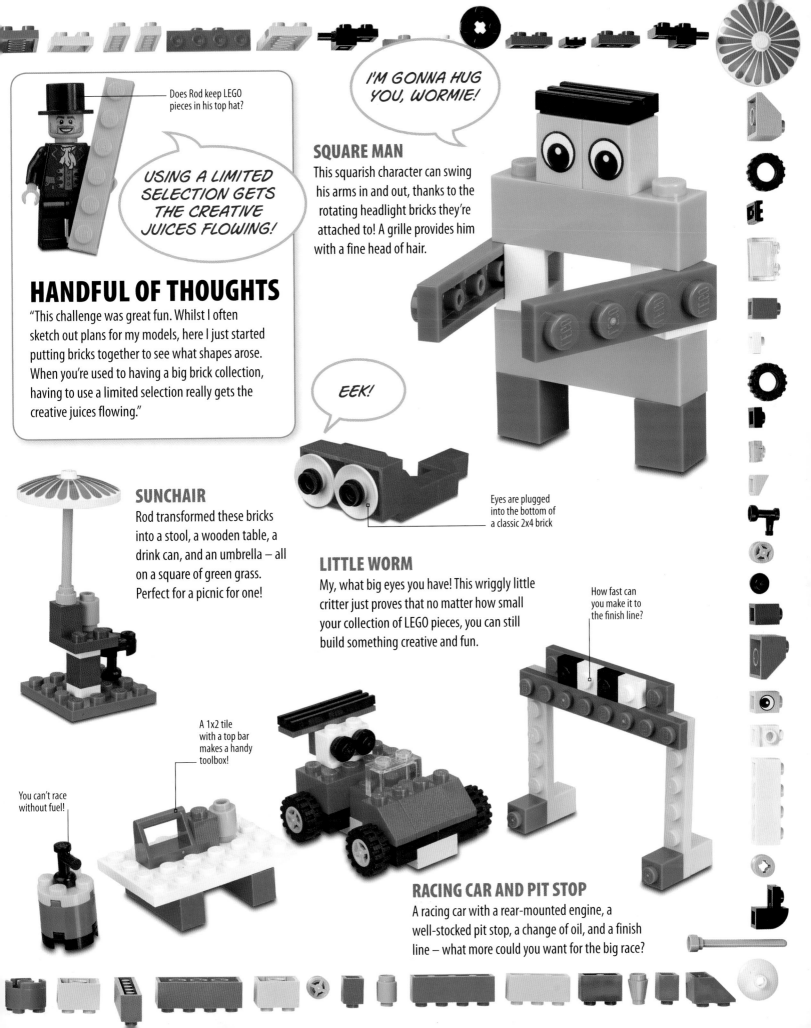

Does Rod keep LEGO pieces in his top hat?

USING A LIMITED SELECTION GETS THE CREATIVE JUICES FLOWING!

HANDFUL OF THOUGHTS

"This challenge was great fun. Whilst I often sketch out plans for my models, here I just started putting bricks together to see what shapes arose. When you're used to having a big brick collection, having to use a limited selection really gets the creative juices flowing."

I'M GONNA HUG YOU, WORMIE!

SQUARE MAN

This squarish character can swing his arms in and out, thanks to the rotating headlight bricks they're attached to! A grille provides him with a fine head of hair.

EEK!

Eyes are plugged into the bottom of a classic 2x4 brick

LITTLE WORM

My, what big eyes you have! This wriggly little critter just proves that no matter how small your collection of LEGO pieces, you can still build something creative and fun.

How fast can you make it to the finish line?

SUNCHAIR

Rod transformed these bricks into a stool, a wooden table, a drink can, and an umbrella – all on a square of green grass. Perfect for a picnic for one!

A 1x2 tile with a top bar makes a handy toolbox!

You can't race without fuel!

RACING CAR AND PIT STOP

A racing car with a rear-mounted engine, a well-stocked pit stop, a change of oil, and a finish line – what more could you want for the big race?

MAD SCIENTIST'S LAB

Timmy should have heeded the warning on the sign outside, but when he sees the flashing lights and hears the weird noises from inside the lab, he can't resist taking a peek! Build a mad scientist's laboratory to conduct strange experiments in and fill it with machines, devices and mysterious chemicals.

ON THE SLAB
Use a 2x6 plate as the base for a monster-building operating table. A hinge placed underneath allows it to lie flat or be raised up at an angle.

Two 1x1 slopes make a cradle for the monster's head

The studs of a 1x2 plate attach to the holes in the minifigure's legs to hold it in place

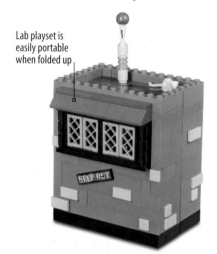

Lab playset is easily portable when folded up

FRONT SIDE VIEW

Windows let in light so the details on your model can be seen clearly

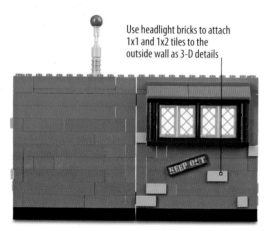

Use headlight bricks to attach 1x1 and 1x2 tiles to the outside wall as 3-D details

OPEN FRONT VIEW

MAKING SCIENCE

The mad scientist's laboratory is built as a small box that opens up to reveal a larger space for playing and storytelling. Inside are the scientist's latest projects: a pair of mechanical robots and a monster that he's bringing to life!

To find out how to build your own robots, turn to p.352

A red LEGO Technic ball at the top of a spire collects electricity from lightning storms to power the mad scientist's work

To prevent the halves from wobbling, place one hinge near the bottom and one near the top

LAB EQUIPMENT

Your lab will need equipment to concoct all sorts of weird and wonderful distillations. Build pipes and tubes out of faucets, lightsaber handles, round bricks, LEGO Technic T-bars and other interestingly shaped elements.

Only using grey pieces makes this look like a very complicated piece of machinery!

FRESHLY BREWED!

What else could you add to your lab? Fill the empty space with even more wacky equipment!

NEXT SUBJECT!

The scientist's assistant rolls in his next experimental subject. The trolley is a simpler version of the operating table, with a pair of wheels at the bottom so it can be pushed around.

THESE TEST SUBJECTS SURE ARE BONE IDLE.

A plate with handle lets a minifigure hold on at the top

Tiles with printed gauges and dials are very helpful for building machinery

Grille locks the headlight bricks together

Skeleton's feet plug into headlight bricks

'BOTS ON THE LOOSE

Oh no! When Timmy opened the door to the lab, something got out. In fact, a whole lot of somethings did! Now his dream is full of clanking, stomping, beeping robots. When you build your own LEGO brick robots, you can make them big, small, round, square, or anything in between. Give them lots of metallic pieces and mechanical detail.

MEGA 'BOT

Do you have a favourite minifigure? Then blow it up – in scale, that is! This one is based on the Clockwork Robot. Use your bricks to construct a giant-sized version with as many of the same colours and details as possible.

Stack a 2x2 round tile on a 2x2 round plate to make the classic stud on top of the head

Eyes are 1x1 square plates mounted on radar dishes

The head is built just like the body, only smaller

Use a large turntable for your mega 'bot's neck

Posable robotic claws are built from clips, plates with handles, sliding plates and 1x1 slopes

SIDE VIEW

Tiles, grilles, radar dishes and round plates recreate the original printed details on the minifigure in 3-D

Attach tiles to side studs for smooth surfaces

TITANIUM TORSO

The giant robot's torso has a core of bricks with side studs. Plates and tiles are attached to create the look of a smooth body with bolts around the chest, just like on the minifigure!

It doesn't matter what colour bricks you use on the inside – they'll be hidden from view!

Feet are tipped with grille slopes

IT REALLY CAPTURES MY WINNING SMILE!

Clockwork Robot

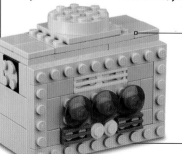

Why not extend your 'bot family? Baby Bot might like an older brother and sister!

'BOT HEAD

To allow Mrs. Bot to turn her head, use a jumper plate with a tile on each side. Her wide jaw is made from a 2x3 curved plate with hole. Give Mrs. Bot a cute bow by attaching two 1x1 slopes.

1x1 slope

2x3 curved plate with hole

Jumper plate

A free-rotating LEGO Technic pin allows the arm to swing back and forth

Elbow is a 1x1 round tile attached to a half-pin

MRS. BOT

Dark red pieces, silver accents and lots of round elements give this robot a stylish art deco design. Her skirt is a Technic wheel element from a LEGO® Star Wars™ set.

Eyes are silver 1x1 round plates attached to headlight bricks

Shoulders are ray guns with their handles plugged into headlight bricks

Each foot is made from a 1x2 plate and a 1x2 tile flipped upside down

Use 1x1 round bricks for the legs, lower arms and parts of the torso

SIDE VIEW

FAMILY PHOTO TIME, EVERYBODY!

Grille-slope mouth creates a quirky expression

A plate with handle built into the body adds a projecting decoration

Arm built out of LEGO Technic cross-axle connectors

Upper legs are barrel-shaped droid body elements linked by a LEGO Technic pin

Feet are inverted slopes attached to corrugated tubes by a LEGO Technic axle-with-stud

Grilles become treads on the bottom of the feet

MR. BOT

This retro, industrial-looking robot is built mostly out of grey pieces to imitate metal. His arms swivel at the shoulders, and an unusual upside-down construction gives his feet treads.

BABY BOT

What's the smallest robot you can build? This miniature marvel is made out of just eight pieces, starting with a brick with two side studs for its body!

Wide eyes are a binocular piece attached to a 1x1 round plate

1x1 plates with side clips make tiny arms

Legs are 1x1 cones plugged into a 1x2 jumper plate

ROBOT RAMPAGE

"You dare to unleash robots in MY city?" says the Inventor. "Let's see how they do against my own mechanical minions!" Suddenly there are two armies of robots battling it out in Timmy's dream. Build some 'bots that are designed for demolition and destruction! Give them claws, spikes and any other tools they'll need to mash, smash, crunch and munch their rivals.

Golden eyes plug into the bases of headlight bricks that are turned on their backs

A plate with a handle creates a bar to protect the robot's head

Tiles printed with dials make great robotic features

Big feet keep this 'bot from toppling over

Antenna picks up commands from its inventor

One-stud connections let the head and shoulders be posed

SIDE VIEW

TORNADO-TRON

This riotous red robot can spin its body around to send enemies toppling to the ground. Its boxy construction shows that it's tough and ready to rumble.

2x2 turntable

SPIN CYCLE

A 2x2 turntable in the middle of the model lets its upper body rotate freely with a flick of your finger. Or hold it by the shoulders and make its legs spin around!

A plate with side bars creates an antenna on each side of the head

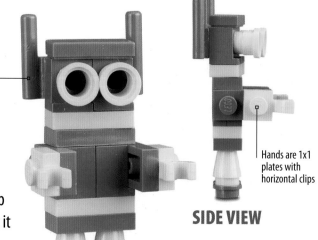

Hands are 1x1 plates with horizontal clips

SIDE VIEW

Legs are 1x1 cones with round plates at the base

ROBOTS: ATTACK! OOPS, DID I FORGET TO BUILD AN OFF BUTTON?

ZOOM-BOT

What this robot lacks in size, it makes up for with speed. Its legs are jets to rocket it around and its claws pack an electric zap that sends bigger 'bots packing!

CHOMP CHOMP

BIT-OR

It can be fun to build a robot model around one particular feature – such as a giant set of teeth! This fellow's chompers can reduce its rivals to scrap in seconds.

Teeth are 1x4 LEGO Technic gear racks

Round plates for eyes are attached to headlight bricks

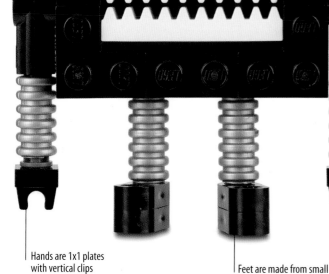

HEAVY METAL

The toothy robot's limbs are sheathed in silver corrugated tubes. Thread LEGO Technic cross-axles with studs on the ends through the tubes to connect LEGO Technic pieces to regular bricks.

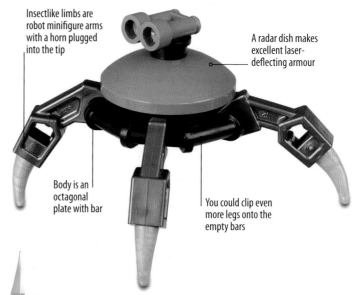

Use LEGO Technic pins to connect the arms to the body

Insectlike limbs are robot minifigure arms with a horn plugged into the tip

A radar dish makes excellent laser-deflecting armour

Body is an octagonal plate with bar

You could clip even more legs onto the empty bars

Hands are 1x1 plates with vertical clips

Feet are made from small LEGO Technic liftarms

SPI-DRONE

Not all robots have to be humanoid – let their missions determine their form. With its stealthy shape and dark colour scheme, this automated arachnoid is designed to scramble across walls and ceilings as it snoops on its unwitting foes.

⭐ **CHALLENGE**

MINIFIGURE MEMORY

Gather a heap of your scariest minifigures and challenge your friends to a minifigure memory test! Give your friends some time to look over the minifigures, then hide them all behind a blanket and remove one. The winner is the first friend to correctly guess which minifigure is missing.

THE MUMMY'S TOMB

When Timmy calls for his mummy, this isn't what he meant. Archaeological sites are a great place to discover the past, but in the world of nightmares, they are also home to venomous snakes, moving statues, hidden traps and pharaohs' curses!

ANCIENT RUINS

When constructing a building that is thousands of years old, don't just make clean, smooth walls. Include pieces that are rounded or textured to show its age. Off-colour bricks will make it look like bits of the original stone have fallen away.

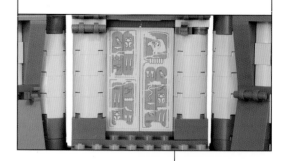

Hinges make the side walls angle in, or you could build one straight long wall

Plates with handles resemble decorative carvings

The addition of some leaves shows how nature has crept into the ruin

WHO DARES TO ENTER MY TOMB?

Scattered tan tiles on the ground give the impression of an old temple taken over by the desert

MUMMY ATTACK!

When the hidden stand behind the door bricks is pushed, the door bricks topple forward, making the lurking mummy smash through the wall!

The mummy stand is connected to the base by a hinge

Mummy's feet are attached to studs

What other nightmarish creatures could be hiding in your ancient ruins?

STONE PROTECTOR

Use a rotating turntable base to create a special action function: a wall that spins around to reveal one of the tomb's guardian statues. . .or a secret treasure!

Place another turntable on top of the moving wall so that the roof stays still while it rotates

Brick-built statue of the jackal-headed god Anubis

Slope bricks help make the ruins look old and weathered

N-N-N-NOT ME, OLD CHAP!

M-M-ME NEITHER!

OPEN

Make a strong support column from a stack of 2x2 round bricks and a long LEGO Technic cross-axle through the middle

Door bricks sit on smooth tiles so they fall easily when the mummy is pushed forward

CLOSED

SKELETON

Well, that was some gratitude! As soon as Timmy finished putting the skeleton together, it started chasing him and threatening to gobble him up. It is certainly a good thing that it is all bones and no tummy. Look through your collection for long bars, curved elements and oddly shaped pieces, and use them to build a big, scary skeleton!

BOO!

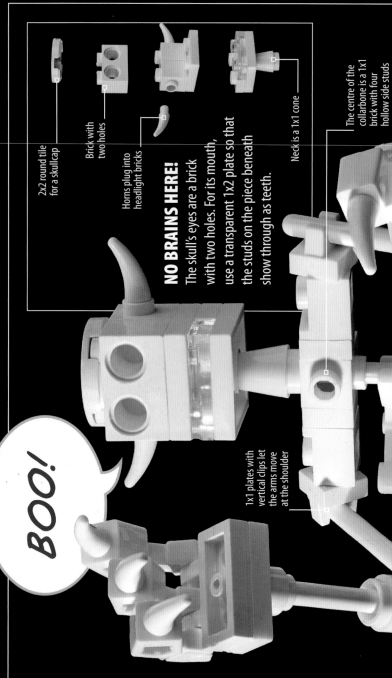

NO BRAINS HERE!

The skull's eyes are a brick with two holes. For its mouth, use a transparent 1x2 plate so that the studs on the piece beneath show through as teeth.

2x2 round tile for a skullcap

Brick with two holes

Horns plug into headlight bricks

Neck is a 1x1 cone

The centre of the collarbone is a 1x1 brick with four hollow side studs

The hands are built just like the feet, but tipped with claws

A 1x2 plate with handle creates the back of the pelvis

Top of the legs are round bricks

1x1 plates with vertical clips let the arms move at the shoulder

Skeleton's ribs are minifigure skeleton arms!

The spine is a long rod piece

Hips are headlight bricks attached sideways to a brick with four side studs

Shoulder blades are 1x1 plates with side rings

SKELETAL SPECIES

Who says this has to be a human skeleton? Make it a monster by adding horns, claws and oversized hands and feet. Now it looks both grim and a little bit goofy – just right for a LEGO brick nightmare!

Position big feet at an angle to help the skeleton keep its balance

REAR VIEW

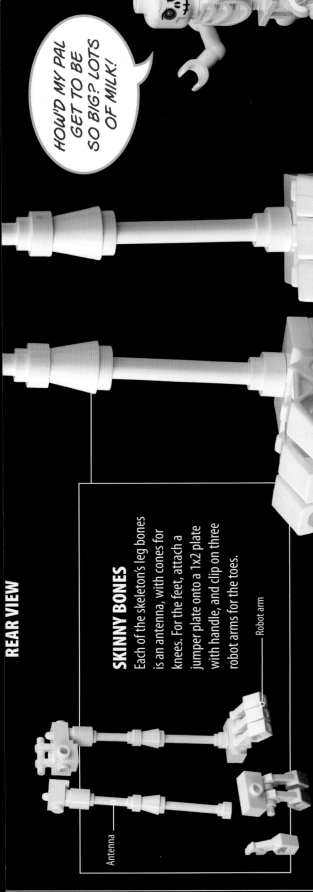

HOW'D MY PAL GET TO BE SO BIG? LOTS OF MILK!

SKINNY BONES

Each of the skeleton's leg bones is an antenna, with cones for knees. For the feet, attach a jumper plate onto a 1x2 plate with handle, and clip on three robot arms for the toes.

Robot arm

Antenna

MONSTER BOX

Here's a monstrous box that you could use to hide your secret treasures. A sinister skeleton guardian will scare off anyone who tries to sneak a peek! What will you store inside?

SCARE IN THE BOX

This scary skeleton is designed to sit in the box, with its bony fingers draped over the edge. The posable fingers are robot claws clipped onto a plate with handles.

LEGO Technic angle connectors form the skeleton's elbows

Use a grille to make a mini ribcage

Skull attaches to jumper plate

Arms are cross-axles

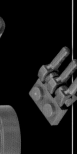

Skull is a sculpted piece, but you could build your own

Top edge is lined with tiles

The box's sides are square wall elements

If you don't have these tall bricks for the corners, then stack up regular 1x1 bricks

VAMPIRE'S CASTLE

Timmy runs away from the skeleton as fast as his little legs will carry him, until he reaches the steps of a big stone castle. "Velcome, child," he hears as the door slowly creaks open. "Von't you come in for a bite?" Vampires like to hide in castles during the day, and the older the better. Give your castle lots of classic furnishings and décor!

CRYPT SWEET CRYPT

Look at pictures of old castles and mansions to get ideas for your vampire's lair. For colours, use grey to resemble stone, with black and red accents. Avoid open windows – vampires aren't too fond of sunlight!

Moon (a printed glow-in-the-dark radar dish) is attached to the black rear wall using a brick with side stud

A couple of slopes can make an entire peaked rooftop

Use the backs of headlight bricks for dark, square windows

PLEASED TO EAT–I MEAN MEET YOU!

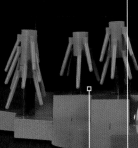

Trees are brown telescopes with upside-down flower stems on top

Pillars are plates with handles built sideways

Alternate 2x2 tiles to make a checkerboard floor pattern

MICRO-TRANSYLVANIA

If you don't have enough pieces to make an entire vampire castle, create a micro-scale façade with your smallest LEGO pieces! Give it classic monster story details, such as a rocky mountain peak, a spooky forest and a big full moon outside.

COSY COFFIN

What makes a castle feel like a vampire's home? Spooky colours and details like chains and trap doors help, but a coffin for a bed really makes the model complete. If you don't have a LEGO coffin, build your own. You could look at the graves on p.362 for inspiration!

WINDOWS

For windows that look like they belong to a room that was built centuries ago, combine window frame pieces with latticed window elements. Surround them with grey arches and bricks to resemble stone blocks.

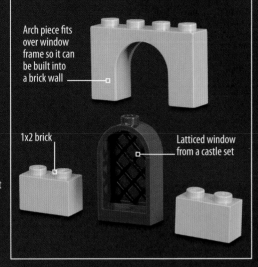

Arch piece fits over window frame so it can be built into a brick wall

1x2 brick

Latticed window from a castle set

Make a bigger window out of sideways fence pieces and plug transparent 1x1 round plates into the gaps for a stained glass effect

A large arch creates the shape of a large window

OLD STONES

This part of the castle has been around for a long, long time. Slopes and unfinished edges make a stone wall look like it is falling apart and textured bricks add to the appearance of decay and disrepair.

Candlestick is made from a telescope, a LEGO Technic half-pin, and a minifigure screwdriver for the wick

EEEK! EVEN I'M SCARED HERE.

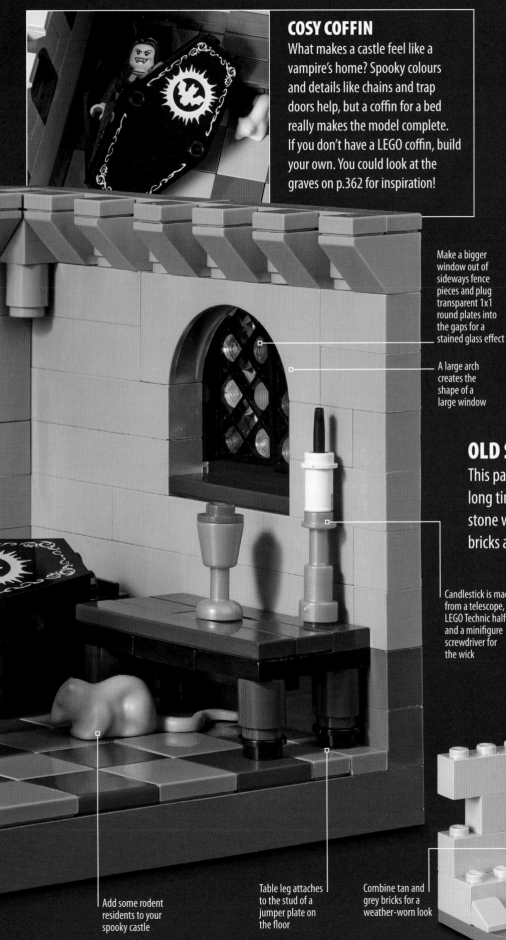

Add some rodent residents to your spooky castle

Table leg attaches to the stud of a jumper plate on the floor

Combine tan and grey bricks for a weather-worn look

GRAVEYARD

"Join us, Timmy," says the voice from under the ground. "Take a rest with us." There's nothing spookier than an old cemetery at midnight. Anything could pop out from under those headstones! When creating a creepy graveyard scene, make it look decrepit and crumbling by making the stones uneven and falling apart. Don't forget to add a forbidding crypt or tomb.

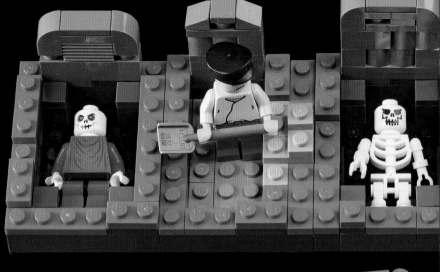

THE PERFECT FIT

To make a grave the right size for a minifigure, build it around the figure so it's guaranteed to fit! When building the headstone, combine grey log bricks with smooth bricks to create a weathered stone surface.

1x2 log brick

Bricks topped with smooth tiles in the corners of the grave let the cover rest in place without sticking

Build bricks-with-holes into the sides of the plots and click the sections together with LEGO Technic connector pins

Build on top of a 4x6 plate to make a removable cover for a grave

Use small round plates and tiles to build a decorative stone slab

GRAVE MATTERS

Each plot in the cemetery should have enough room for a grave with a headstone at the top. Make the stones as simple or as elaborate as you like. A mix of both will make your model look varied and interesting!

THAT JOKE ALWAYS TICKLES MY FUNNY BONE!

HEY, GET BACK IN THERE!

Flowers show that someone has been tending this particular grave

Use brown plates for piles of dug-up earth

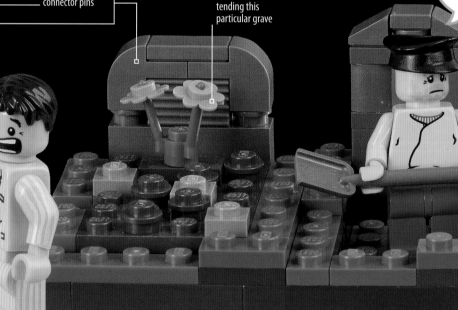

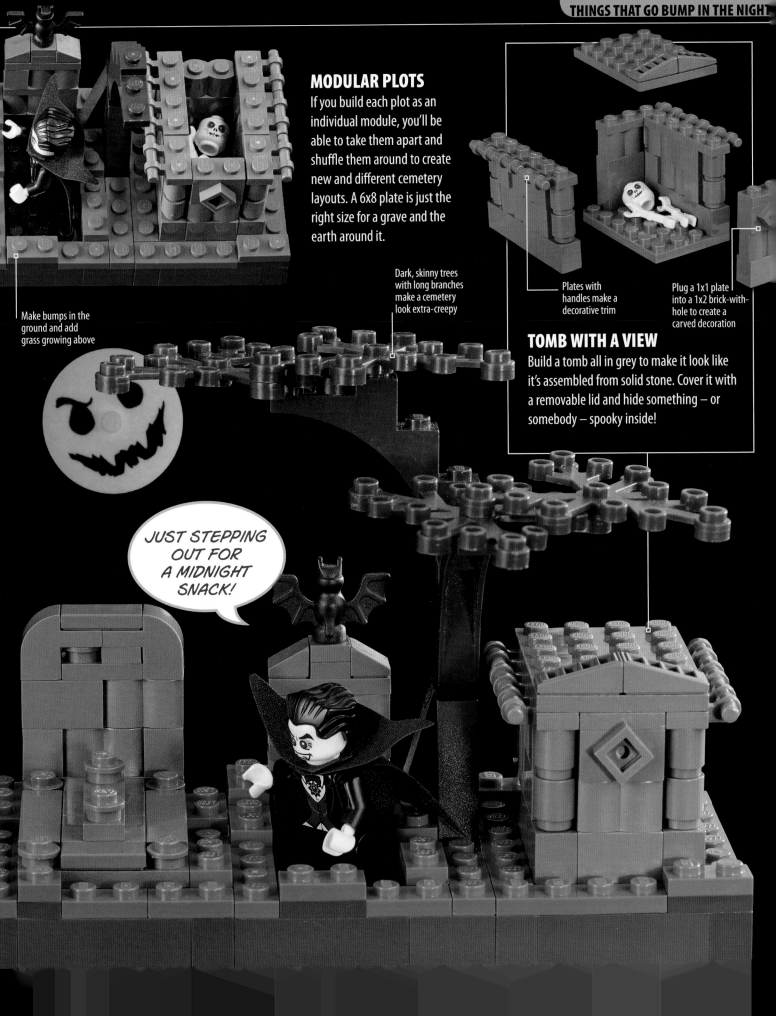

MODULAR PLOTS

If you build each plot as an individual module, you'll be able to take them apart and shuffle them around to create new and different cemetery layouts. A 6x8 plate is just the right size for a grave and the earth around it.

Make bumps in the ground and add grass growing above

Dark, skinny trees with long branches make a cemetery look extra-creepy

Plates with handles make a decorative trim

Plug a 1x1 plate into a 1x2 brick-with-hole to create a carved decoration

TOMB WITH A VIEW

Build a tomb all in grey to make it look like it's assembled from solid stone. Cover it with a removable lid and hide something – or somebody – spooky inside!

JUST STEPPING OUT FOR A MIDNIGHT SNACK!

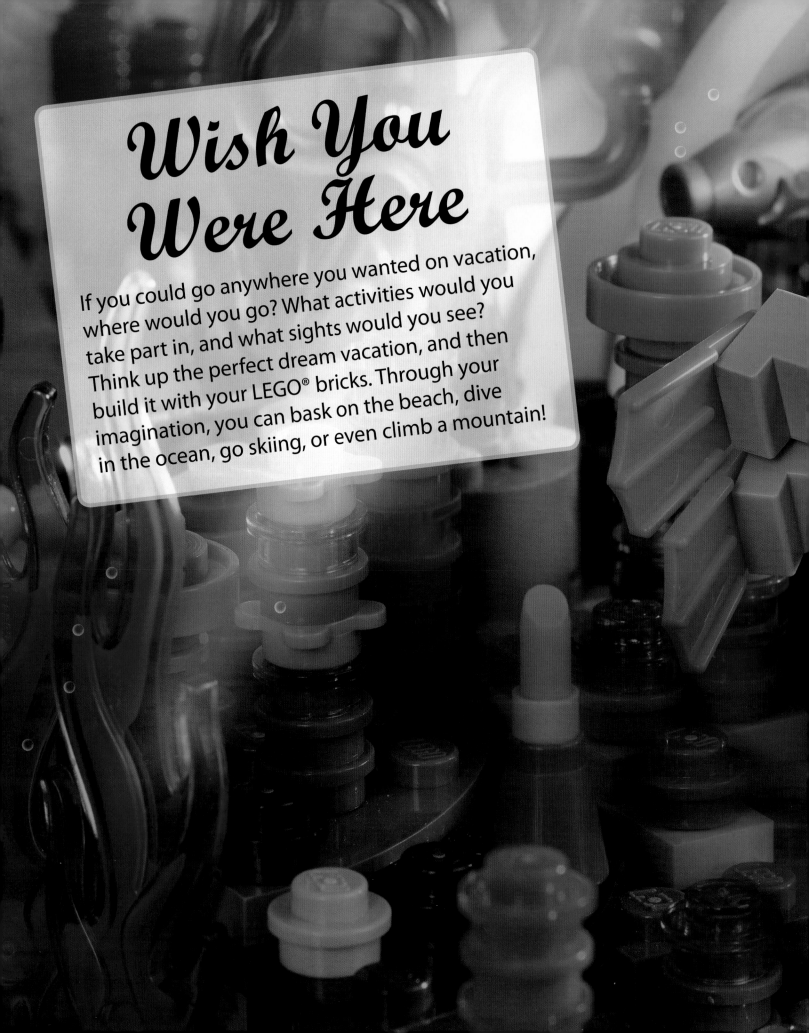

Wish You Were Here

If you could go anywhere you wanted on vacation, where would you go? What activities would you take part in, and what sights would you see? Think up the perfect dream vacation, and then build it with your LEGO® bricks. Through your imagination, you can bask on the beach, dive in the ocean, go skiing, or even climb a mountain!

G'DAY!

MEET THE BUILDER:
TIM JOHNSON
Age: 42
Day Job: Digital producer
LEGO Speciality: Microscale architecture
Brick Collection: 120,000 pieces
Favourite Brick: 1x2 tile with grille
Did You Know? Tim used to keep
all his empty LEGO boxes as a child,
and still has them 30 years later.

DID YOU PACK YOUR TICKETS? INTERGALACTIC PASSPORT? RAY GUN?

EARTH MISSION

Glax is a space-travel journalist who has just received a very exciting interstellar mission from his boss, Zorg. Glax is to travel to a remote planet called "Earth" and experience all of its best vacation spots and leisure pursuits, then write about it all for the Space Network. The entire galactic quadrant will be reading his daily reports! Glax's job has taken him all over the known universe, but this will be his first time on Earth. He hopes the locals are nice and he doesn't lose his luggage!

ZORG

YEP, YEP, AND DOUBLE-YEP!

GLAX

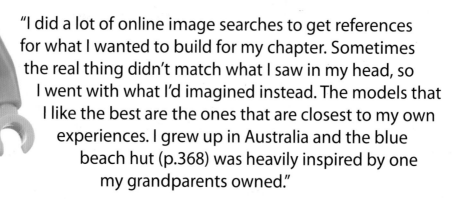

Glax quickly discovers the sweet, cool concoction known as "ice cream"

HAVE A GREAT TIME!

MAKING VACATIONS
TIM JOHNSON

"I did a lot of online image searches to get references for what I wanted to build for my chapter. Sometimes the real thing didn't match what I saw in my head, so I went with what I'd imagined instead. The models that I like the best are the ones that are closest to my own experiences. I grew up in Australia and the blue beach hut (p.368) was heavily inspired by one my grandparents owned."

Space Network

6,846

Home   Aliens   Inbox

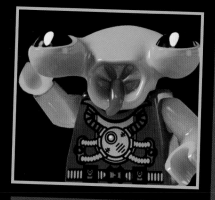

Wall   **Photos**   **Info**

GLAX

... is somewhere special. Here's a hint: it's round and blue-green. Give up? It's Earth!

Profile

Name: Glaxxico8791
Location: Pluuvonic Nebula
Occupation: Freelance tourist
Likes: Solar sailing
Dislikes: Wormholes

Friends   7,946,462

HANNO   **ROX**

DOLO   **ZORG**

YOXY   **PX200-E**

ZX81   **COLIN**

GLAX commented on his own picture

Here I am going up a mountain in a cable-mounted travel pod. When I get to the top, I will strap boards onto my feet and slide back down!

GLAX commented on his own picture

I have enjoyed resting in the rays of Earth's sun, next to an artificial body of water with an elevated launch platform. Note: human waiters do not enjoy being splashed.

ZORG commented on your picture
That strange Earth food looks a little like you, Glax.

GLAX commented on his own picture

Today I explored the Earth ocean aboard a floating vehicle shaped like a giant piece of fruit. Later, I lay down on some sand until I turned from green to red. Humans have very strange hobbies!

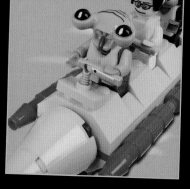

GLAX commented on his own picture

BEACH HUTS

Greetings from Earth! Glax's holiday has begun with a trip to something called "The Beach," a sandy desert next to a large expanse of water. Humans must be partly solar-powered, because they sure enjoy lying out in the sun! Build a stretch of beach for your vacationing minifigures to enjoy. Include beach huts so they can relax in carefree comfort.

Brown bush pieces look like dry beach plants

REAR VIEW

HOME ON THE SAND

At a beach hut, vacationers can change into bathing suits, grab a snack, or snooze in the shade. To make one, build a small one-room house with lots of seaside details. Include a sandy beach around it!

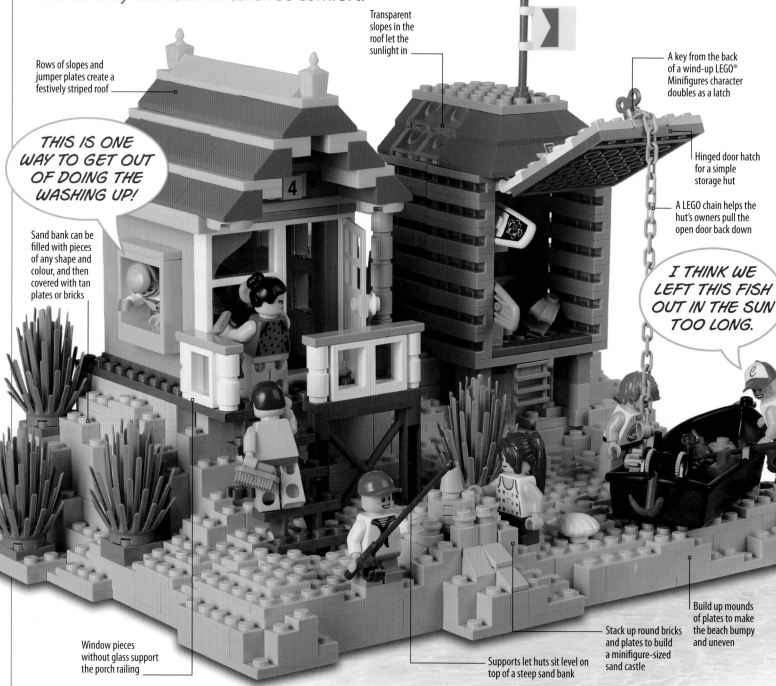

Rows of slopes and jumper plates create a festively striped roof

Transparent slopes in the roof let the sunlight in

A key from the back of a wind-up LEGO® Minifigures character doubles as a latch

Hinged door hatch for a simple storage hut

A LEGO chain helps the hut's owners pull the open door back down

THIS IS ONE WAY TO GET OUT OF DOING THE WASHING UP!

Sand bank can be filled with pieces of any shape and colour, and then covered with tan plates or bricks

I THINK WE LEFT THIS FISH OUT IN THE SUN TOO LONG.

Window pieces without glass support the porch railing

Supports let huts sit level on top of a steep sand bank

Stack up round bricks and plates to build a minifigure-sized sand castle

Build up mounds of plates to make the beach bumpy and uneven

COOL BRICK

"I love the 1x4 bricks with grooves for creating textures. A wall of them resembles corrugated metal. If you leave the short end exposed in a wall, it looks a little like a window."

FRONT VIEW

A tile with a number identifies the vacation hut

SURF HUT

The surfers who own this hut have cheered it up by painting a mural on the back wall. Inside are shelves for their surfboards and clips to hold their favourite beach gear.

Mural is built on a small plate and attached to the interior wall using bricks with side studs

HUT CONSTRUCTION

Try building each hut as a separate mini-scene and then connecting their sections of beach together. They can be identical buildings in different colours, or totally individual designs.

Include beach accessories like shells, fishing poles and swimming equipment

A small ladder provides quick and easy access

Tell a story with your scene. These surfers have just returned from a fishing trip in their rowboat. Time for a beach cook-out!

▶ QUICK BUILD

MICRO BEACH HUT

A big beach hut may take a while to assemble, but you can put together a micro-scale version in no time at all. When you've finished, build even more to make a whole ocean-view scene!

A bracket allows the doors to be attached sideways

Use jumper plates to centre the roof slopes

Build matching shapes with different doors and decorations

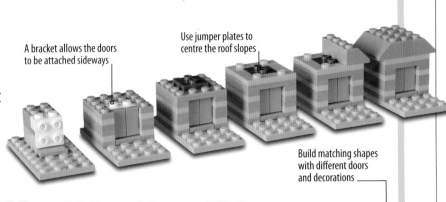

ICE-CREAM STALLS

While at the beach, Glax samples a unique human delicacy: a wafer rolled into a cone and filled with a frozen substance that has something to do with Earth cows. Believe it or not, it tastes much better than it sounds! Who doesn't love sweet, cold ice cream on a sunny day? Build a stall so your beach-goers can enjoy some of their own!

ACK! BRAIN FREEZE!

Hinge cylinder underneath the ice-cream sign snaps onto the back of the kiosk

Arch is supported by columns built from 1x1 round bricks and plates

This ice-cream scoop started out as a LEGO® Ninjago nunchuk handle!

SMALL KIOSK

This stall is just big enough for a vendor and a freezer full of frozen treats. Give it a bright colour scheme and an eye-catching sign overhead, as well as a shade to block the sun on hot summer days.

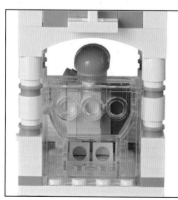

FREEZER
Inside the stall is a freezer full of ice-cream flavours. If you don't have this single transparent piece, you can build your own out of LEGO windows, tiles, and hinge pieces.

SIGNAGE
No sunbather will miss this sign! Its scoops are built around two brackets and two inverted brackets. An upside-down 2x2 cone is held on by a long rod piece.

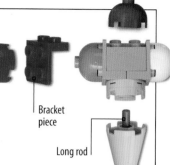

Bracket piece

Long rod

Big scoops are 2x2 domes in different colours

Alternate curved bricks of the same shape to make a striped awning for the stall's roof

Transparent elements look like glowing lights

1x1 round plates underneath give the awning a fringe

1x1 round plates make good single-serving scoops

Build in textured bricks for detail

Hat comes from a LEGO
butcher minifigure

Refrigerated display
under the counter is made
with two transparent
windshield pieces

REAR SIDE VIEW

Transparent goblet
for a dessert glass

A sink for cleaning
up melted ice cream

The hut is built
on a raised cement
platform of grey plates,
but sand has piled up
around its base

AWNING CONSTRUCTION

The front awning is attached to
the roof by click hinges, letting it
fold down when the hut is
closed at night!

Plate with
click hinge

LARGE HUT

For a more crowded beach or resort, you'll need a bigger
ice-cream stall. This one looks cool and classy with its extended
awning, transparent counter and lots of dessert-making
equipment. Its kitchen has something for every hot beach-goer!

I LEARNED
TO DO THIS
AT SUNDAE
SCHOOL!

Beach umbrella pole
plugs into the centre
of a 2x2 round brick

A 1x1 round plate attaches
this LEGO® Technic ball-joint
piece to its goblet cone

BEACH ACCESSORIES

Before visiting an Earth beach, Glax recommends that you obtain a personal seating device to avoid getting sand in your spacesuit. Here are some items that will make a trip to the beach even more fun.

A radar dish mounted on a group of 1x1 round plates provides a freshly scooped curve

If you don't have enough pieces in the same color, pick something similar for a ripple of colour

Scoops don't all have to be this size and shape – they can look any way you like!

Use a red 2x2 dome for a cherry on top, or smaller pieces for nuts and sprinkles

Make some of these pieces brown or black for chocolate chips

WHAT'S THE SCOOP?

How do you build a big scoop of ice cream? Make a round, bumpy shape out of 2x2 round bricks and place a circular plate or brick on top to hold them together.

KING-SIZED CONE

This giant cone is made by building ringed layers of 2x2 round bricks and log bricks that get smaller as they get closer to the bottom.

Use tan, brown, or white bricks for the cone

A plate layer every few rows makes the cone strong and sturdy

The upside-down cone at the tip is held on by a LEGO Technic cross-axle

ICE CREAM CONE

Why should minifigures have all the fun? Put your bricks together and build a life-sized ice cream cone for yourself. Just don't try to eat it – this colourful plastic treat is for play and display purposes only!

I'LL BET I'VE GOT THE BIGGEST ICE CREAM CONE IN THE WORLD!

DECK CHAIR

A portable deck chair is perfect for sitting
out in the sun near the ocean or by the side of a pool.
Just fold it up and take it along with you wherever
you want to go!

Try building an
even smaller deck
chair so it's
minifigure size.

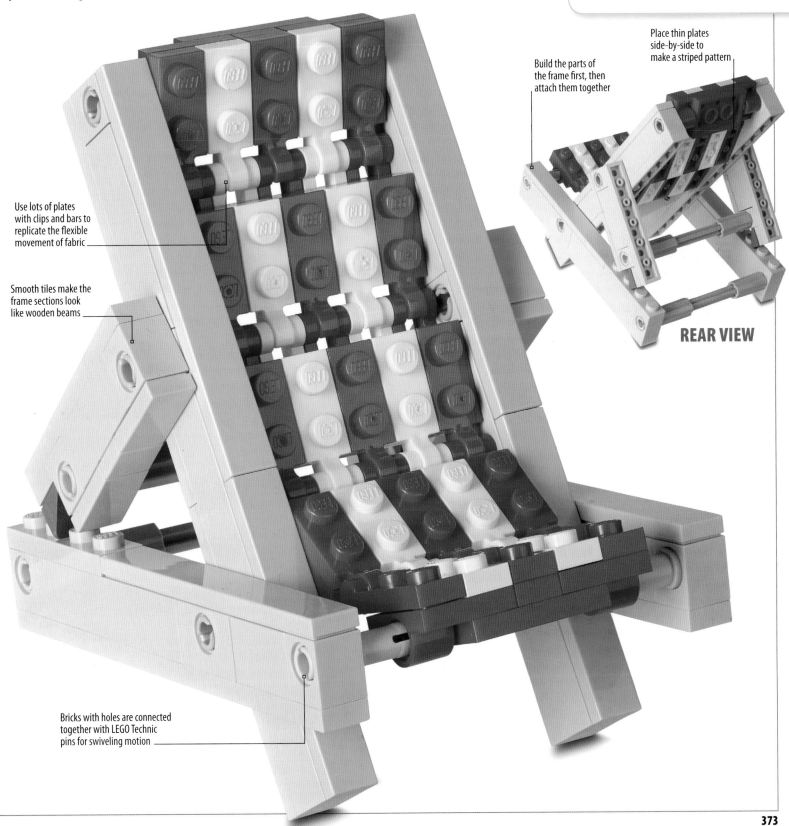

Place thin plates
side-by-side to
make a striped pattern

Build the parts of
the frame first, then
attach them together

Use lots of plates
with clips and bars to
replicate the flexible
movement of fabric

Smooth tiles make the
frame sections look
like wooden beams

REAR VIEW

Bricks with holes are connected
together with LEGO Technic
pins for swiveling motion

BEACH BOATS

Glax observes some humans going out on the water inside small floating crafts that lack even basic antigravity propulsion. Perhaps this is an activity that he should attempt as well? Going out in a boat turns a trip to the beach into an adventure on the water, whether you're going fast or taking your time. Build one and try it out!

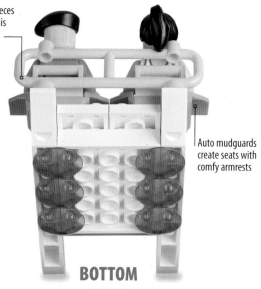

There are lots of other pieces that can substitute for this rectangular bar element

Auto mudguards create seats with comfy armrests

BOTTOM VIEW

I LIKE THE VIEW.

AND I LIKE THE EXERCISE!

PADDLE BOAT

A paddle boat moves when you turn its foot pedals. The more you pedal, the faster it goes! Build a paddle boat to be flat and stable for a comfortable ride. With two seats, friends can team up for twice the boating fun.

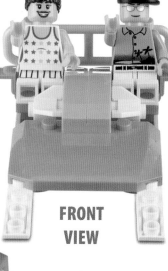

FRONT VIEW

A car roof is a simple way to make the front of the boat, but you could build it out of plates instead

Use long inverted curve bricks to make floatation pontoons

PEDAL POWER

The pedals are round bricks with fins from a rocket. They are connected together by a LEGO Technic cross-axle that passes through a pair of bricks-with-holes so the pedals can spin.

Curved bricks cover and hide the rotating pedal function

Use plates to lock the bricks-with-holes together on the top and bottom

Cross-axle

Pedal

Try building a spinning paddle-wheel under the boat, or one on each side!

Fire fighter hose nozzles plugged into jumper plates give the passengers something to hold onto

Not enough yellow pieces? Add spots, or make a green, red or over-ripe brown banana instead!

Black tooth-shaped piece resembles a banana's stem – or use a 1x1 cone or round brick

1x1 slopes fill in the gaps on the sides

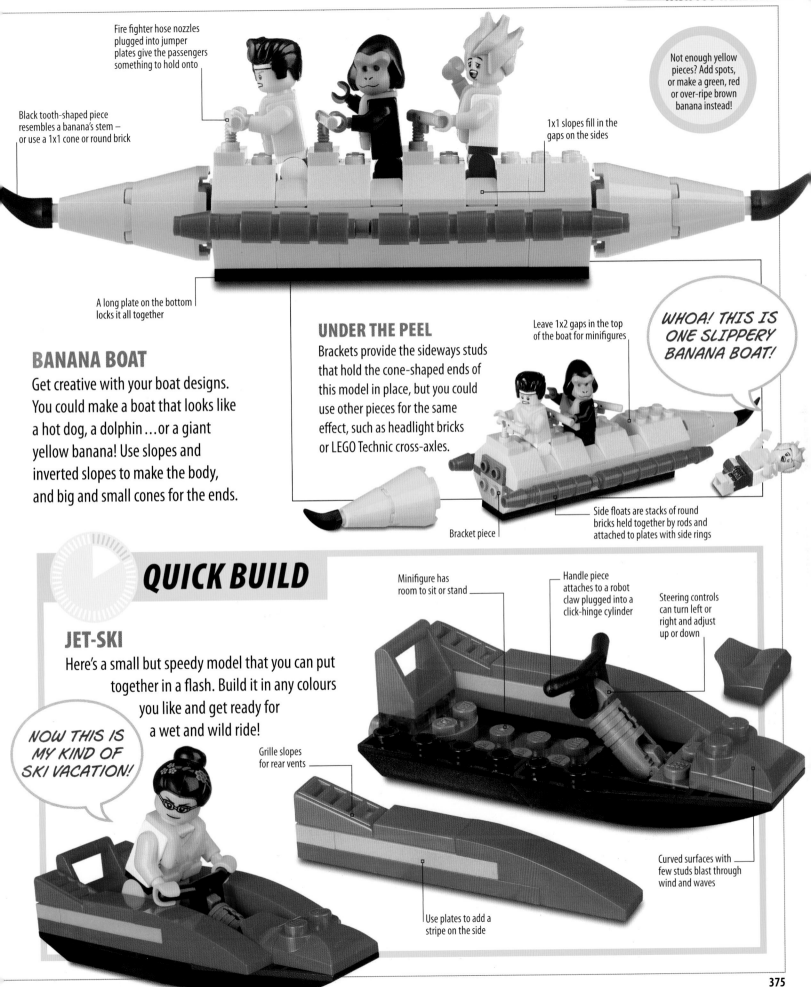

A long plate on the bottom locks it all together

BANANA BOAT

Get creative with your boat designs. You could make a boat that looks like a hot dog, a dolphin…or a giant yellow banana! Use slopes and inverted slopes to make the body, and big and small cones for the ends.

UNDER THE PEEL

Brackets provide the sideways studs that hold the cone-shaped ends of this model in place, but you could use other pieces for the same effect, such as headlight bricks or LEGO Technic cross-axles.

Leave 1x2 gaps in the top of the boat for minifigures

WHOA! THIS IS ONE SLIPPERY BANANA BOAT!

Side floats are stacks of round bricks held together by rods and attached to plates with side rings

Bracket piece

QUICK BUILD

Minifigure has room to sit or stand

Handle piece attaches to a robot claw plugged into a click-hinge cylinder

Steering controls can turn left or right and adjust up or down

JET-SKI

Here's a small but speedy model that you can put together in a flash. Build it in any colours you like and get ready for a wet and wild ride!

NOW THIS IS MY KIND OF SKI VACATION!

Grille slopes for rear vents

Curved surfaces with few studs blast through wind and waves

Use plates to add a stripe on the side

HOTEL POOL

After Glax's beach adventure, he discovers a building where individual hibernation pods can be rented for the night. Amazingly, it includes its own miniature ocean! A hotel swimming pool provides even more opportunities for vacation fun. Your minifigures can swim, splash, play water-tag, and even take a leap from the high diving board!

SWIMMING POOL

Build a big swimming pool for a vacation hotel! You can make rippling water by adding layers of transparent blue pieces over a base of blue plates. Include other familiar pool features, such as a diving board and a lifeguard. If you don't have enough pieces to build an entire pool, just make part of one!

Binoculars and a floatie ring are a lifeguard's most important gear

Place the lifeguard's seat on a raised platform so he can spot any trouble

Use 1x2 wall elements to make ladder steps

Use small tiles and round plates to create waves

Attach the top half of a minifigure to the water surface to make it look like he is submerged in water!

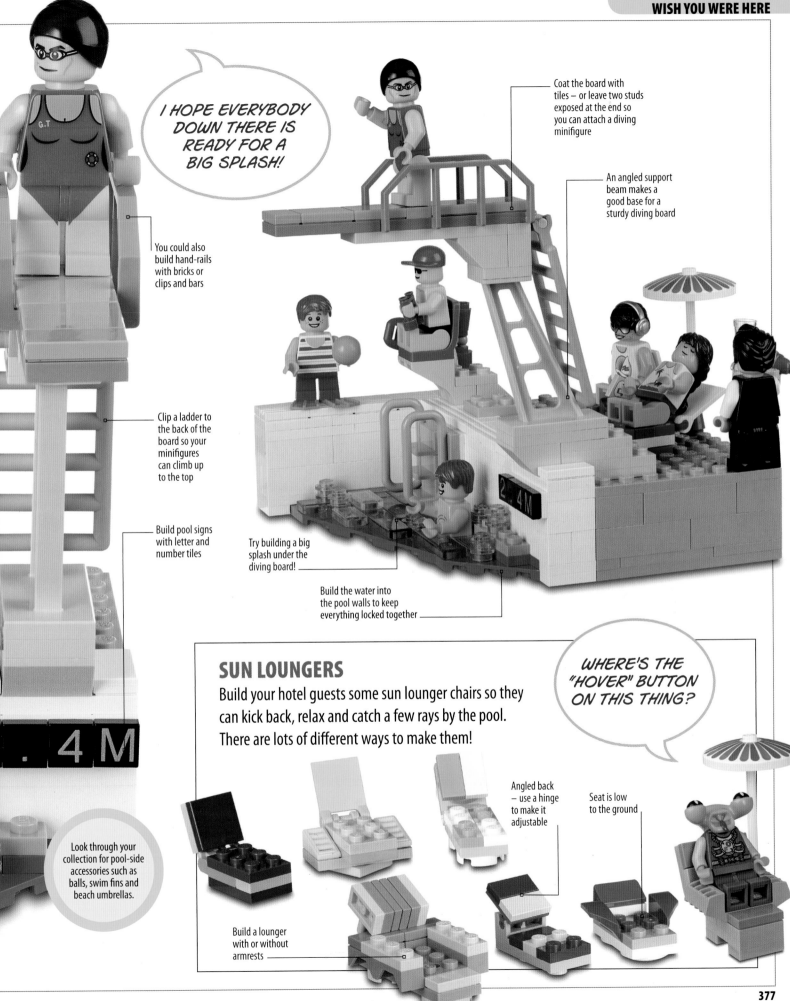

I HOPE EVERYBODY DOWN THERE IS READY FOR A BIG SPLASH!

Coat the board with tiles — or leave two studs exposed at the end so you can attach a diving minifigure

An angled support beam makes a good base for a sturdy diving board

You could also build hand-rails with bricks or clips and bars

Clip a ladder to the back of the board so your minifigures can climb up to the top

Build pool signs with letter and number tiles

Try building a big splash under the diving board!

Build the water into the pool walls to keep everything locked together

SUN LOUNGERS

Build your hotel guests some sun lounger chairs so they can kick back, relax and catch a few rays by the pool. There are lots of different ways to make them!

WHERE'S THE "HOVER" BUTTON ON THIS THING?

Angled back — use a hinge to make it adjustable

Seat is low to the ground

Look through your collection for pool-side accessories such as balls, swim fins and beach umbrellas.

Build a lounger with or without armrests

MAKING A SPLASH

Glax's afternoon at the pool has left him soaked. He tries to dry himself by using a rapid-velocity acceleration ramp, but that only results in him becoming wetter! Make a towering waterslide and send your minifigures screaming with laughter into the water below.

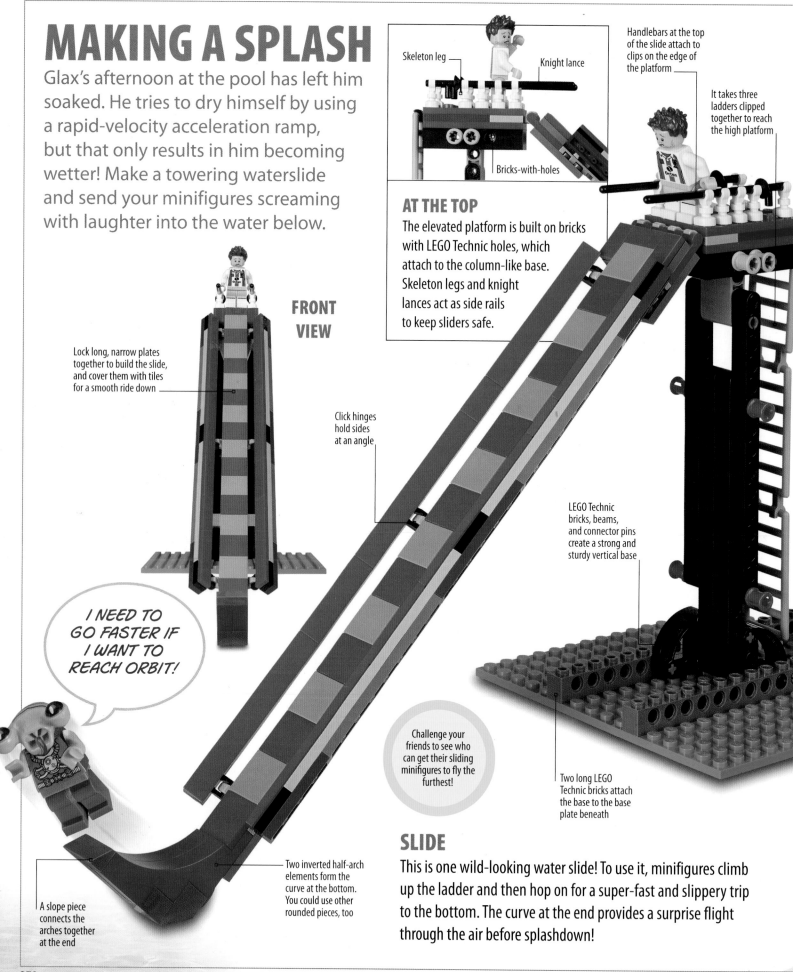

Skeleton leg

Knight lance

Handlebars at the top of the slide attach to clips on the edge of the platform

It takes three ladders clipped together to reach the high platform

Bricks-with-holes

AT THE TOP
The elevated platform is built on bricks with LEGO Technic holes, which attach to the column-like base. Skeleton legs and knight lances act as side rails to keep sliders safe.

FRONT VIEW

Lock long, narrow plates together to build the slide, and cover them with tiles for a smooth ride down

Click hinges hold sides at an angle

LEGO Technic bricks, beams, and connector pins create a strong and sturdy vertical base

I NEED TO GO FASTER IF I WANT TO REACH ORBIT!

Challenge your friends to see who can get their sliding minifigures to fly the furthest!

Two long LEGO Technic bricks attach the base to the base plate beneath

Two inverted half-arch elements form the curve at the bottom. You could use other rounded pieces, too

A slope piece connects the arches together at the end

SLIDE
This is one wild-looking water slide! To use it, minifigures climb up the ladder and then hop on for a super-fast and slippery trip to the bottom. The curve at the end provides a surprise flight through the air before splashdown!

SURFBOARDS

Surfboards come in lots of different sizes – though you probably haven't seen too many like this! There are official minifigure-scaled LEGO surfboard elements, but you can also build your own out of plates, boat parts and other long, flat and curved pieces.

WHOA. THESE ARE SOME RIGHTEOUS BOARDS, DUDE!

The long, curved pieces at the front and back come from airplane, boat, helicopter and spaceship sets

The bigger you make your surfboard, the more colours and patterns you can build into it

TOP VIEW

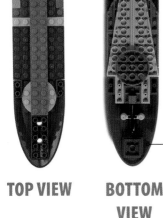

TOP VIEW

BOTTOM VIEW

TOP VIEW

Use tiles for smooth, flat surfaces on top

A LEGO Technic connector pin connects this fin piece to a plate-with-hole on the board's underside

The bottom of this board uses rectangular, angled and even circular plates

The size of these surfboards is determined by the size of the special parts on the ends

TOP VIEW   **BOTTOM VIEW**

BOTTOM VIEW

Construct ramps and obstacles for an even bigger challenge!

★ *CHALLENGE*

BAGGAGE CART STACKER

Have you ever tried to cross a busy airport with a cart full of luggage? Build a simple base with wheels, add a brick to it, and roll it over to a friend, who adds another brick and rolls it back with a single push. Who will be the first to topple the truck?

Can you place your bricks in a way that makes your opponent's bricks off-balance?

Try building rolling bases of different shapes, or using different-sized wheels

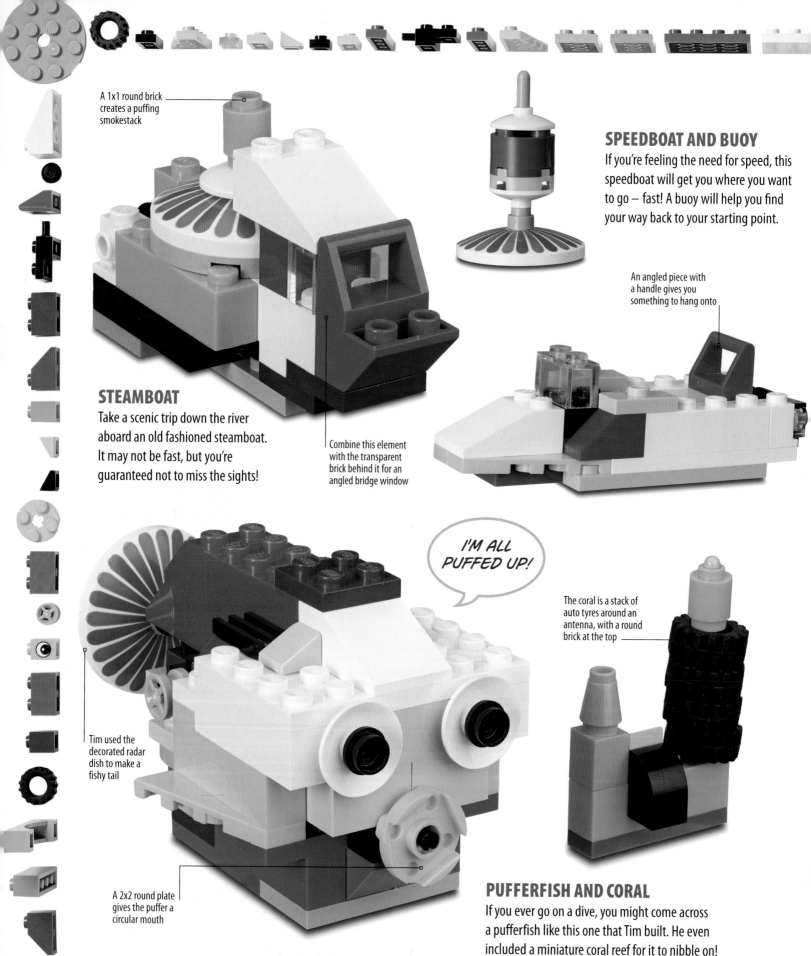

A 1x1 round brick creates a puffing smokestack

SPEEDBOAT AND BUOY

If you're feeling the need for speed, this speedboat will get you where you want to go – fast! A buoy will help you find your way back to your starting point.

An angled piece with a handle gives you something to hang onto

STEAMBOAT

Take a scenic trip down the river aboard an old fashioned steamboat. It may not be fast, but you're guaranteed not to miss the sights!

Combine this element with the transparent brick behind it for an angled bridge window

I'M ALL PUFFED UP!

The coral is a stack of auto tyres around an antenna, with a round brick at the top

Tim used the decorated radar dish to make a fishy tail

A 2x2 round plate gives the puffer a circular mouth

PUFFERFISH AND CORAL

If you ever go on a dive, you might come across a pufferfish like this one that Tim built. He even included a miniature coral reef for it to nibble on!

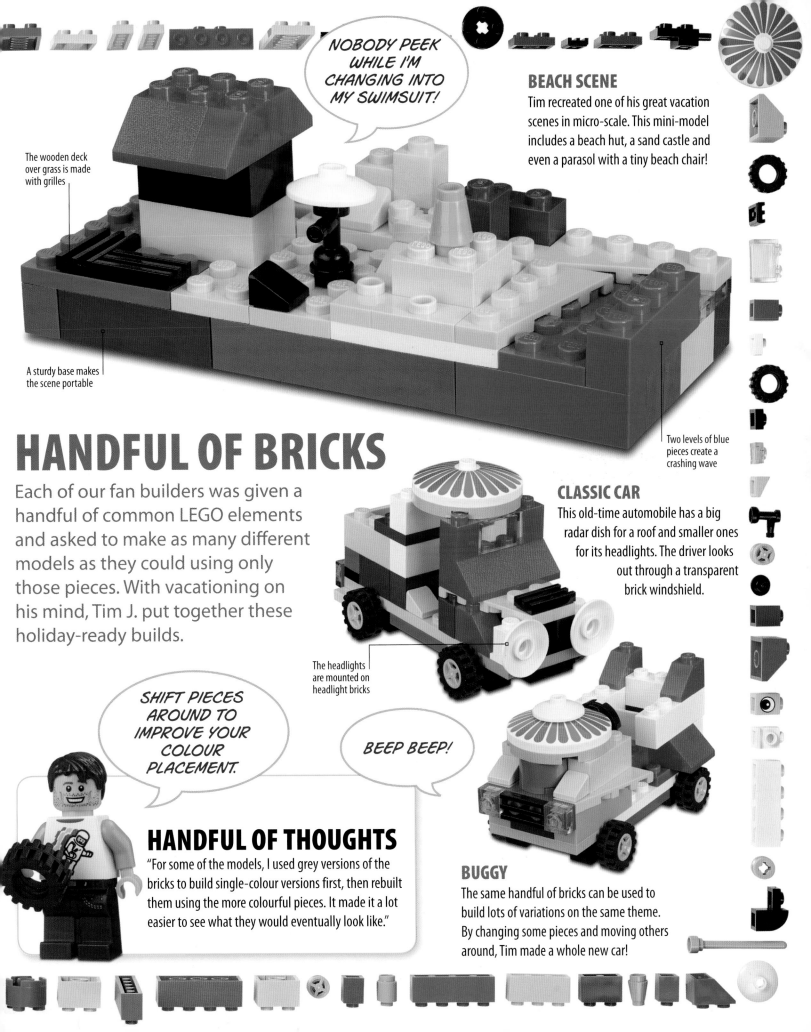

NOBODY PEEK WHILE I'M CHANGING INTO MY SWIMSUIT!

BEACH SCENE

Tim recreated one of his great vacation scenes in micro-scale. This mini-model includes a beach hut, a sand castle and even a parasol with a tiny beach chair!

The wooden deck over grass is made with grilles

A sturdy base makes the scene portable

Two levels of blue pieces create a crashing wave

HANDFUL OF BRICKS

Each of our fan builders was given a handful of common LEGO elements and asked to make as many different models as they could using only those pieces. With vacationing on his mind, Tim J. put together these holiday-ready builds.

CLASSIC CAR

This old-time automobile has a big radar dish for a roof and smaller ones for its headlights. The driver looks out through a transparent brick windshield.

The headlights are mounted on headlight bricks

SHIFT PIECES AROUND TO IMPROVE YOUR COLOUR PLACEMENT.

BEEP BEEP!

HANDFUL OF THOUGHTS

"For some of the models, I used grey versions of the bricks to build single-colour versions first, then rebuilt them using the more colourful pieces. It made it a lot easier to see what they would eventually look like."

BUGGY

The same handful of bricks can be used to build lots of variations on the same theme. By changing some pieces and moving others around, Tim made a whole new car!

BENEATH THE SEA

Diving under the sea is like exploring a whole different world. The fish remind Glax of some of his friends back home! Whether you're diving from a speedboat on the surface or swimming down near the sea floor, you're sure to see scenery and animals that you've never encountered before when you venture beneath the waves.

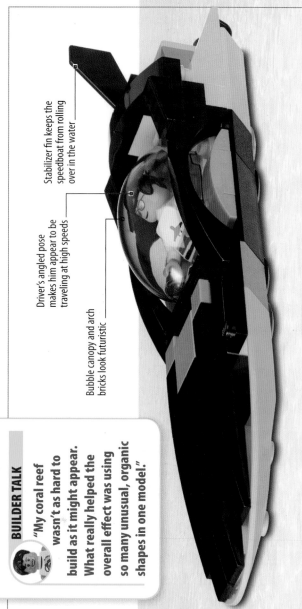

Stabilizer fin keeps the speedboat from rolling over in the water

Driver's angled pose makes him appear to be traveling at high speeds

Bubble canopy and arch bricks look futuristic

LUXURY SPEEDBOAT

For the ultimate in sea thrills, build a super-fast speedboat and hang on tight! Long curved and inverted-curve bricks make this boat's nose look smooth and streamlined. Give your speedboat a big engine and a windshield to protect the driver from water spray.

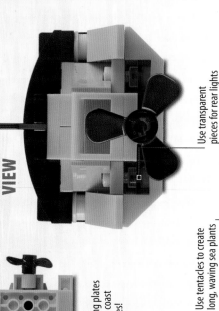

REAR VIEW

Use transparent pieces for rear lights

BOTTOM VIEW

Place round sliding plates on the bottom to coast across flat surfaces!

REAR VIEW

LEGO Technic balls attached to the ends of transparent flexible pipes

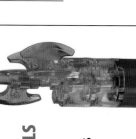

CLEVER CORALS

Coral structures should look unique. This one is built by clipping transparent blue axe heads onto a rod sticking out of a stack of 2x2 round bricks.

Use tentacles to create long, waving sea plants

SCHOOL DAYS

Build a floating school of fish by clipping them above a bar piece using robot or skeleton arms. Create even stranger ocean life with brushes from a LEGO® Friends set!

Blue brush head

Brown bar piece

CORAL REEF

Start your coral reef by adding bricks to a base plate to make an uneven sandy, rocky surface. Use some of your most unusual and colourful pieces to build different types of plant or coral. Ice cream scoops, barbell weights, and even lipstick create a colourful reef that any diver would want to explore!

For branching coral, plug flame pieces into hollow studs and central holes of round bricks and plates

LEGO Friends flower ornaments create a sea anemone's mouth

A LEGO banana becomes a yellow sea slug!

Brown brooms inserted into hollow cones

An overlapping mound of red flowers (some raised on plates beneath) forms a single coral colony

HOW MANY FISH CAN YOU SEE?

Plug in green flames for leafy kelp

Pile up plates as sand banks

Transparent antenna elements

Glow-in-the-dark elements bring the reef to life at night. You could place light-up bricks under transparent pieces, too!

EXTREME SPORTS

Glax thinks he has finally discovered how humans get into orbit. They climb up mountains! For a real rugged outdoor adventure, try a day of rock-climbing – or let your minifigures do it for you! You can give them an extra thrill by building a bungee jump up at the top!

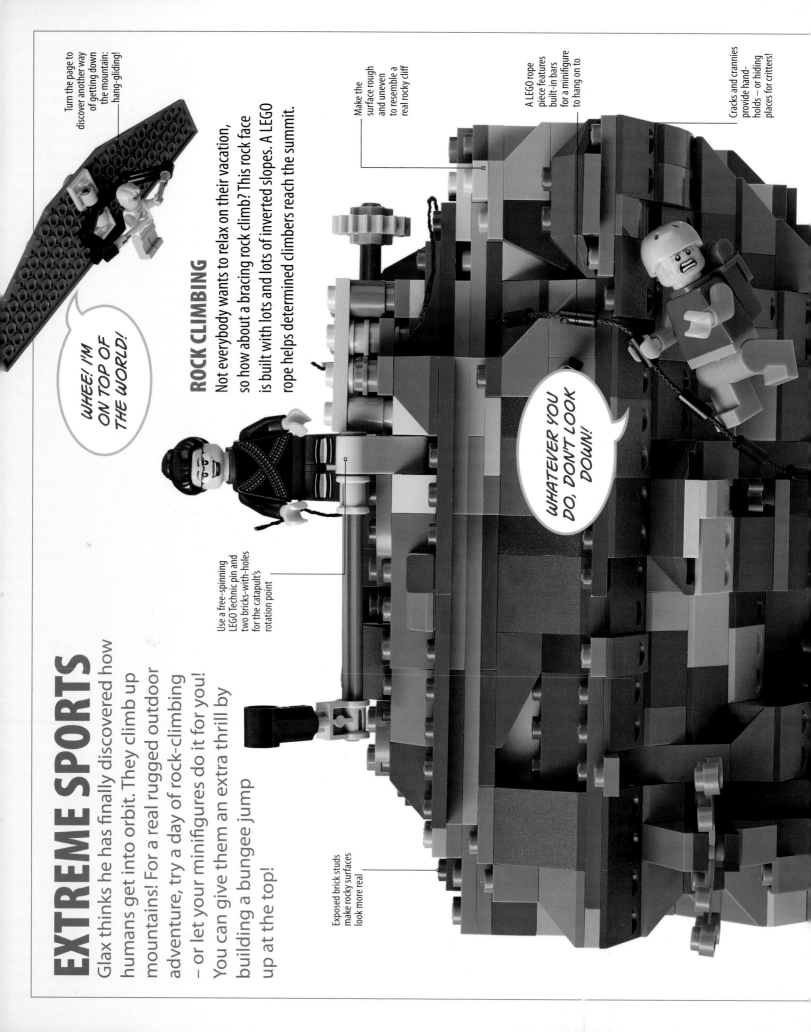

Turn the page to discover another way of getting down the mountain: hang-gliding!

WHEE! I'M ON TOP OF THE WORLD!

ROCK CLIMBING

Not everybody wants to relax on their vacation, so how about a bracing rock climb? This rock face is built with lots and lots of inverted slopes. A LEGO rope helps determined climbers reach the summit.

Make the surface rough and uneven to resemble a real rocky cliff

A LEGO rope piece features built-in bars for a minifigure to hang on to

Cracks and crannies provide hand-holds – or hiding places for critters!

WHATEVER YOU DO, DON'T LOOK DOWN!

Use a free-spinning LEGO Technic pin and two bricks-with-holes for the catapult's rotation point

Exposed brick studs make rocky surfaces look more real

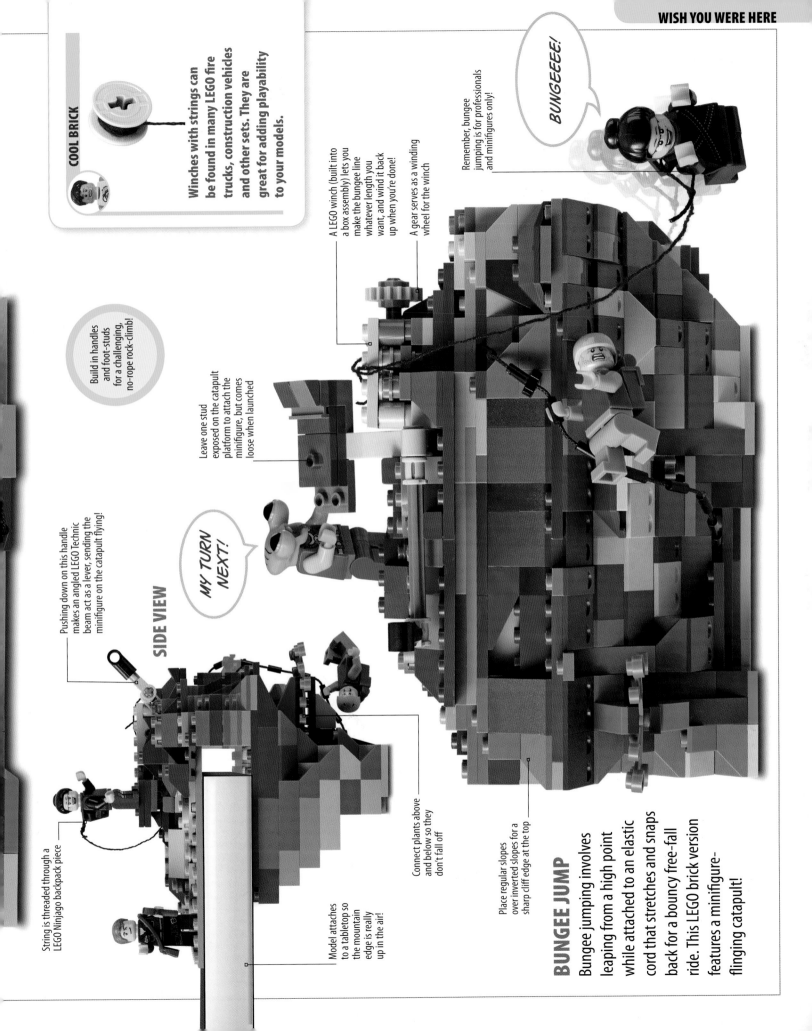

COOL BRICK

Winches with strings can be found in many LEGO fire trucks, construction vehicles and other sets. They are great for adding playability to your models.

A LEGO winch (built into a box assembly) lets you make the bungee line whatever length you want, and wind it back up when you're done!

A gear serves as a winding wheel for the winch

Remember, bungee jumping is for professionals and minifigures only!

BUNGEEEE!

Build in handles and foot-studs for a challenging, no-rope rock-climb!

Leave one stud exposed on the catapult platform to attach the minifigure, but comes loose when launched

MY TURN NEXT!

SIDE VIEW

Pushing down on this handle makes an angled LEGO Technic beam act as a lever, sending the minifigure on the catapult flying!

String is threaded through a LEGO Ninjago backpack piece

Model attaches to a tabletop so the mountain edge is really up in the air!

Connect plants above and below so they don't fall off

Place regular slopes over inverted slopes for a sharp cliff edge at the top

BUNGEE JUMP

Bungee jumping involves leaping from a high point while attached to an elastic cord that stretches and snaps back for a bouncy free-fall ride. This LEGO brick version features a minifigure-flinging catapult!

ADVENTURES UP HIGH

These humans cannot seem to decide whether they want to go up or down. Not only do they climb and bounce, but they even strap on giant wings and fly! Send your minifigures to even greater heights by building entire mountains for them to scale and colourful hang gliders to help them sail safely back down to the ground below.

THIS IS SO MUCH FUN, I MIGHT NEVER COME BACK DOWN...

A long LEGO Technic pin at the top centre attaches the frame to two plates-with-holes, one in front and one behind

Main glider wing is made with two large, mirror-image angled plates

Thanks to the LEGO Technic pin connection, the harness frame can swing left and right as the minifigure pilot shifts weight to steer

HANG GLIDER

Help your vacationing minifigures see the sights from a bird's-eye view with a hang glider! Gliders are much smaller and easier to build than full aeroplanes. All you need is a flat wing surface and a way for a pilot to hang on beneath.

MINIFIGURE MOUNTAIN

Let's hope your minifigures aren't afraid of heights, because they're going on an exciting mountaineering vacation! Use basic bricks to build a tall mountain – then take turns against your friends to race your minifigures to the top. To make your minifigures' mountain climb even more of a challenge, you could use small coloured pieces as distance markers, stopping your minifigures only at points of the same colour.

Where in the world is your mountain located? Use different colours to create brown desert cliffs, green jungle slopes, or black and red volcanoes.

Use white bricks for a snow-capped peak

Small, coloured pieces make distance markers

Build your mountain as tall as you want it to be!

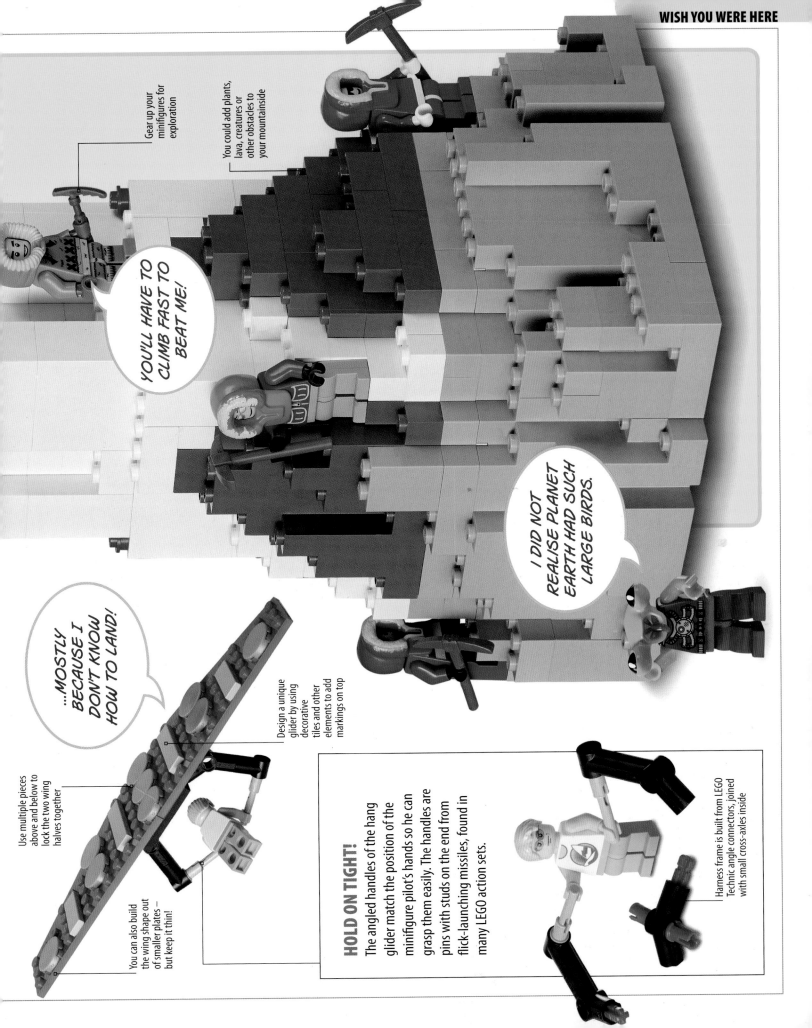

Gear up your minifigures for exploration

You could add plants, lava, creatures or other obstacles to your mountainside

YOU'LL HAVE TO CLIMB FAST TO BEAT ME!

I DID NOT REALISE PLANET EARTH HAD SUCH LARGE BIRDS.

...MOSTLY BECAUSE I DON'T KNOW HOW TO LAND!

Design a unique glider by using decorative tiles and other elements to add markings on top

Use multiple pieces above and below to lock the two wing halves together

You can also build the wing shape out of smaller plates — but keep it thin!

HOLD ON TIGHT!

The angled handles of the hang glider match the position of the minifigure pilot's hands so he can grasp them easily. The handles are pins with studs on the end from flick-launching missiles, found in many LEGO action sets.

Harness frame is built from LEGO Technic angle connectors, joined with small cross-axles inside

MOUNTAIN BIKING

How can Glax get back down from the mountain? He looks for a jetpack vendor, but instead finds a friendly Earthling who trades a foot-powered, two-wheeled contraption for Glax's favourite disintegrator blaster. Do you have a few LEGO bicycles? Then build a bumpy, rocky dirt path down the mountain for them to ride and race along!

Include small round and square pieces for pebbles and other outdoor details

DO YOU GUYS EVER FEEL LIKE WE'RE JUST GOING AROUND IN CIRCLES?

BUNGEEEE!

I'M WINNING! I'M WINNING!

WAIT FOR ME! I WANT TO RACE TOO.

BIKE TRACK

Turn LEGO bicycles into mountain bikes by building an outdoor track for them to race on. Make the track as big or small as you like, and add stunt features such as ramps, pits and obstacles to steer around.

No need to build supports – LEGO bicycles stand up by themselves

If you don't have a LEGO bicycle, try building your own!

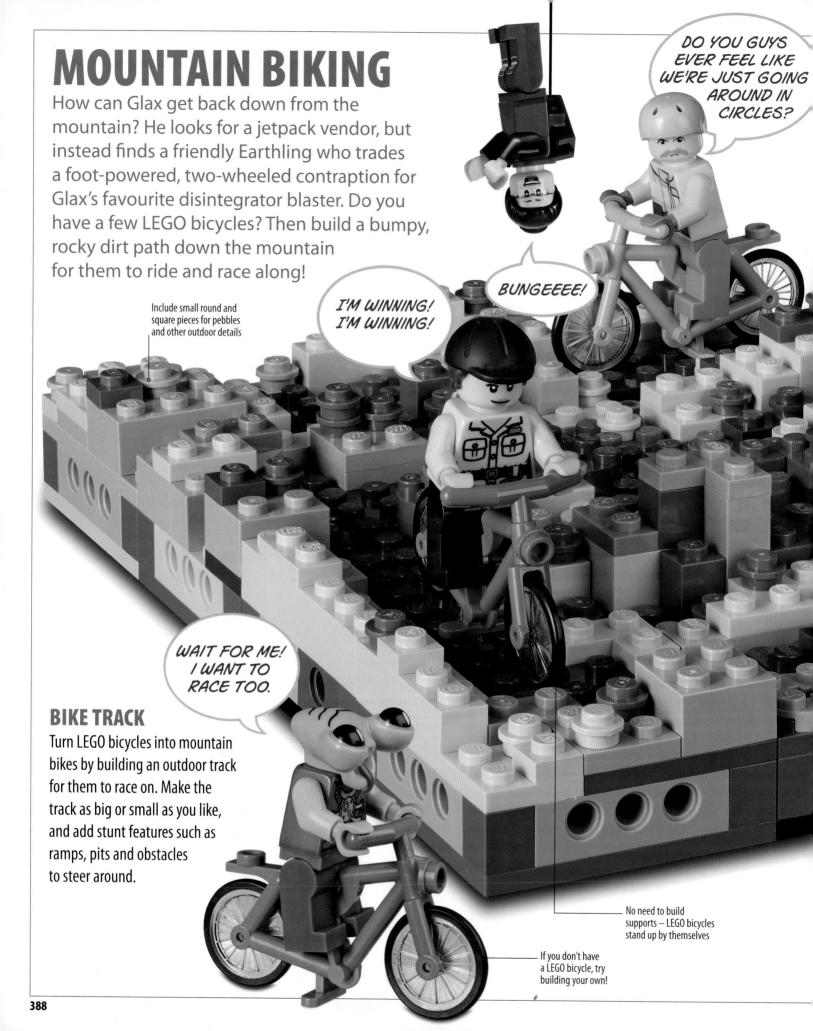

Sturdy headgear is important when biking, especially on uneven terrain

WHEE!

TRACK LAYOUT

To make your track interesting, vary your paths – make straight lines, tight corners, T-junctions, crossroads, zig-zags and dead ends. You could also include growing plants, fallen tree trunks, and narrow streams or even rivers for the bikes to jump over!

Raised plates in the same colour as the trail create a realistic surface

Rearrange the sections to build a new course!

Use brown plates to make dirt trails

Consider building part of your trail out of slope bricks and racing your bikes to the bottom!

CONNECTING YOUR COURSE

To make a modular bike course, construct each section on a 6x6 plate with 1x4 LEGO Technic bricks on their sides. Connect the sections with LEGO Technic pins so that their paths line up to create a complete track.

If you don't have enough 1x4 LEGO Technic bricks, use two 1x2 ones instead

Since the middle will be covered, you can use any colours you want!

Fill in the corners with 1x1 bricks

WATER ADVENTURES

When the humans talked about "white water rafting," Glax did not expect to be floating down a rushing river at high speeds, narrowly avoiding many large rocks. This is even better than asteroid-surfing! Build a big raft or a kayak and send your most daring minifigures on a thrilling ride through the rapids.

Take a camping trip by storing backpacks and outdoor supplies in the kayak!

NO ONE BEATS ME TO THE FINISH LINE!

BLUE KAYAK

This simple kayak is built around a pair of inverted curved wedge elements – a common piece that can be found in many LEGO sets. Plates arranged around the top give it a traditional kayak's partially covered deck.

Place your paddler in the centre of the kayak for balance

A covered top keeps water from getting in

CAN'T YOU JUST ENJOY THE RIDE?

This double-ended paddle is made from a long bar and two sets of hinged pieces

KAYAK CONSTRUCTION

The space between the two curved wedges is filled by an inverted 2x4 double slope piece. Add more to make a longer kayak with room for extra paddlers!

Double angled plates match the shape of the wedges underneath

A two-stud-wide gap in the centre leaves room for a minifigure paddler

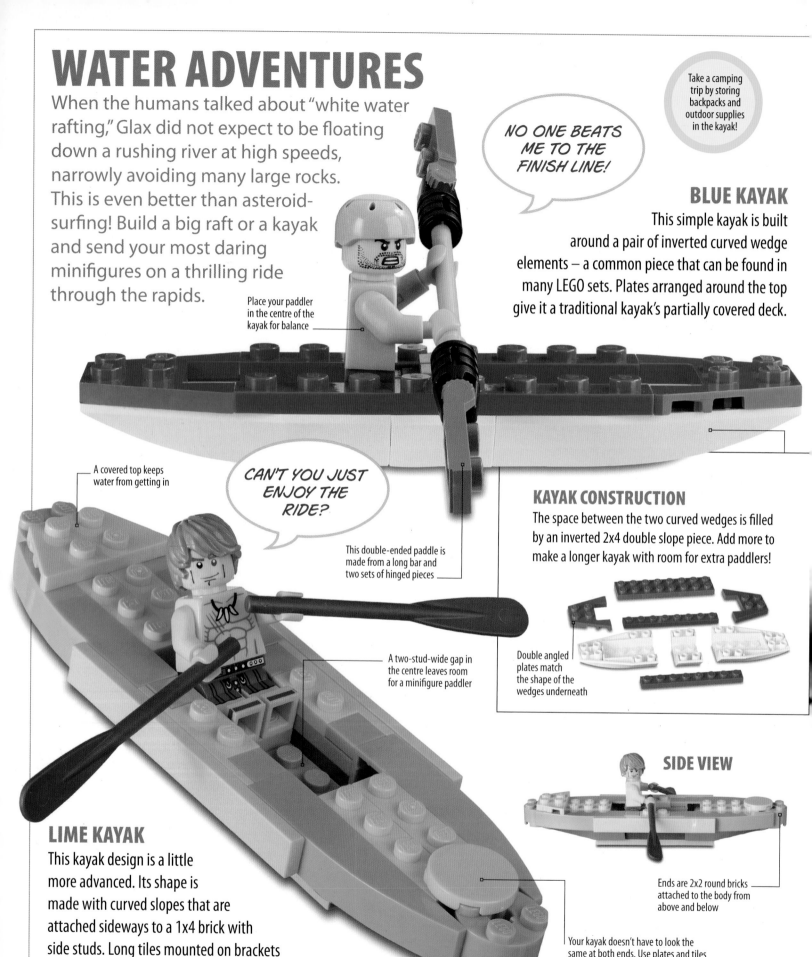

LIME KAYAK

This kayak design is a little more advanced. Its shape is made with curved slopes that are attached sideways to a 1x4 brick with side studs. Long tiles mounted on brackets in the centre lock the slopes in place.

SIDE VIEW

Ends are 2x2 round bricks attached to the body from above and below

Your kayak doesn't have to look the same at both ends. Use plates and tiles to make the front and back different

Curved arch brick

FULL OF AIR

A row of curved arch bricks almost all the way around gives the raft its rounded, air-filled appearance. You can also use angled slopes, or even make a ring of regular bricks.

A staggered front end helps the raft look angular, but not too pointy

BOTTOM VIEW

Sliding plates allow the raft to glide along easily

If you don't have this headgear, you could use construction helmets or astronaut helmets

You could add a motor here at the back!

REAR VIEW

I THINK I MIGHT HAVE GOTTEN ON THE WRONG BOAT!

Make sure there's enough space for a team of minifigures with oars or paddles

If you don't have enough oar elements, try building your own!

Use bright colours so your raft can be easily spotted in the water

WHITE WATER RAFT

This type of raft is usually inflatable and made of tough rubber, so your model should have rounded curves instead of square edges. Build it wide and low so it won't tip over in rough water!

The front is a little higher than the rest of the raft

SKIING

It may look like ice cream, but Glax finds Earth snow much less tasty, especially without chocolate syrup on top. On the other hand, it's great for skiing! Equip your minifigures with skis or snowboards and build them a snowy slope to slide down. Carry your skiers up to the top in an electric cable car and let the cold-climate adventures begin!

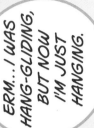

ERM... I WAS HANG-GLIDING, BUT NOW I'M JUST HANGING.

Cable is a flexible LEGO tube, but you can use a long bar or even a string!

Bricks and plates with click hinges create a bent armature between the roof and the cable

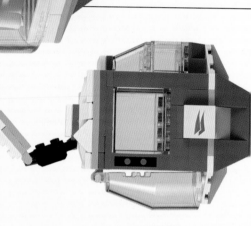

Big windows will let your passengers see the snowy landscape

Use a printed tile for the ski resort's logo

If you don't have this piece you could use a window or a windscreen instead

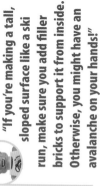
STAY CONNECTED

A plate with side ring provides a secure connection and lets the cable car slide up and down the tube – or use a clip instead!

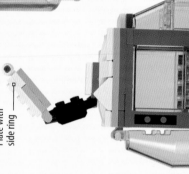

Plate with side ring

CABLE CAR

Build an enclosed cable car to carry multiple minifigures up the slopes. It should be lightweight and sturdy enough to hang from the cable without coming apart. Add bricks inside so your skiers have benches to sit on, and leave plenty of space for skiing gear.

Hinged spaceship canopy door opens to let skiers get on and off

A tile with caution stripes says "Watch your step!"

Add white pieces to the roof for a coating of snow

SKI SLOPE

You can build a ski slope of any size and shape – from an easy nursery slope for beginners to a steep mountainside for fearless experts. Find all of the white slope bricks in your collection and start building!

You could attach curved bricks to make gentler, more rounded snowdrifts.

If you don't have minifigure skis and ski poles, improvise! Use long, thin plates to make skis and rods or anything skinny with a handle for the poles

Sharp peaks look like mountains far off in the distance

LEFT-SIDE VIEW

You could cover the ground with white tiles for the appearance of freshly fallen snow

Use multiple layers to connect white plates together to make a wide base

Add transparent blue pieces for icy details

RIGHT-SIDE VIEW

It looks like some of these skiers need a little more practice

IT DIDN'T SHOW THIS IN THE HOLIDAY BROCHURE!

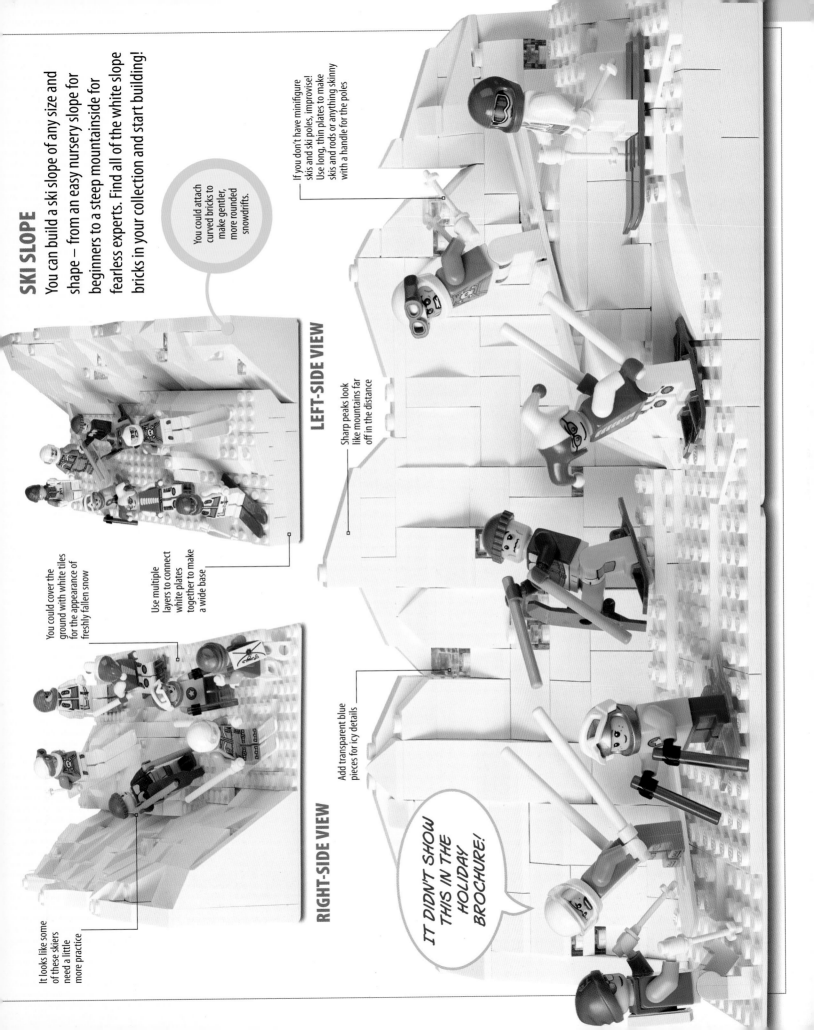

SNOW TRANSPORTS

What's the best way for an alien tourist to trek around on a snow-covered mountain? Earth technology has provided visitors with several useful options. Whether they choose to drive through the drifts on a snowmobile or surf down the slopes on a snowboard, it's a whole lot easier than using snow shoes to get where you need to go!

SNOWMOBILE

Who needs roads? When you have a snowmobile, you can go anywhere...as long as it's covered in snow! Give your snowmobile skis in front for steering, and a treaded tire in back for traction and power.

SIDE VIEW

Attach a four-stud-wide front end to a three-stud-wide back with jumper plates

A bracket lets you attach these curved bricks using sideways building

A clipped-on flap keeps snow from spraying on anyone behind the snowmobile!

Short minifigure skis are held by tap elements, which plug into 1x1 plates with side rings on the snowmobile

A hinge plate holds the controls at a comfortable angle

A long, free-spinning LEGO Technic pin holds the tyre in place

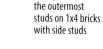

Use latticed elements to form a railing to keep the riders in place – or use regular 1x4 bricks

2x12 plate attaches to 1x4 bricks with side studs on the base

Strings attach to the outermost studs on 1x4 bricks with side studs

Curve made from four arch pieces attached to a 1x4 plate

TOBOGGANS

A toboggan is the perfect snow transport. It's fun, fast and you can fit a few minifigure friends aboard it if you make yours long enough. You need a wide, flat base, an upwards-curving front, spots for riders to sit or stand and strings for steering.

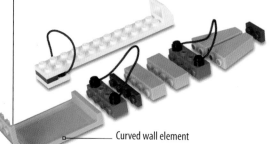

Curved wall element

SIDEWAYS SLIDER

The J-shaped nose of this toboggan is made from a tall, curved wall element. Most of the rest is built sideways, from a combination of bricks, plates and slopes.

SNOWBOARD JUMP

It's like surfing on a frozen wave! Give your snowboarding minifigures something to really jump about by building a snowy-looking stunt ramp. Assembling the slope is relatively easy, but the curve at the bottom may take a bit of clever construction.

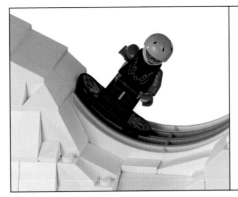

HALF-PIPE

This stunt, the half-pipe, was built by connecting four large arches side-by-side with tiles and plates with clips. They attach to the rest of the snowboarding model upside-down!

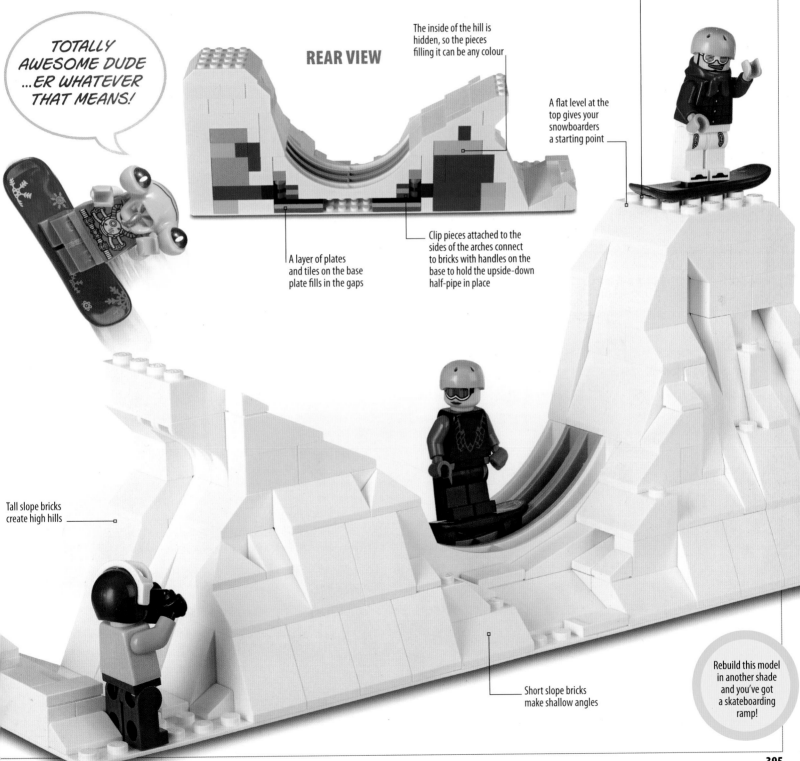

TOTALLY AWESOME DUDE ...ER WHATEVER THAT MEANS!

REAR VIEW

The inside of the hill is hidden, so the pieces filling it can be any colour

A flat level at the top gives your snowboarders a starting point

Clip pieces attached to the sides of the arches connect to bricks with handles on the base to hold the upside-down half-pipe in place

A layer of plates and tiles on the base plate fills in the gaps

Tall slope bricks create high hills

Short slope bricks make shallow angles

Rebuild this model in another shade and you've got a skateboarding ramp!

SKI HOTEL

Skiing may not be as cold as wading through the nitrogen streams of Pluton IV, but it's still nice to have somewhere to warm up at the end of a long day on the slopes. Build a lodge where your winter vacationers can relax and thaw out by the fire. If you're lucky, Glax won't have finished off all of the hot chocolate!

ALPINE HOTEL

Before you start building, do some planning. Pick out doors and windows you would like to use (or you could construct your own), and choose colours that look good together. Don't forget to think about the little details that will bring your hotel to life!

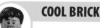

The undersides of bricks add their own interesting effects

Use white slopes to make a snow-covered rooftop

Windows with shutters help keep out the cold

Clips in the wall hold ornamental bars

Fence elements can also be a terrace's railing

Auto mudguards make good arches over windows

Plates between brick layers add decoration and support

ALL THIS SHOVELLING SURE KEEPS YOU TOASTY!

A lamppost with a telescope base helps late arrivals find their way to the front door

Stack extra white plates for deeper snow on the ground

Shovel the entrance so your door has enough clearance to swing open!

396

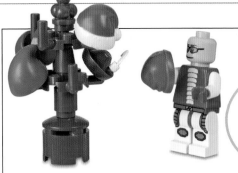

LOOKS LIKE SANTA HAS ARRIVED ALREADY!

HOTEL-BUILDING

If you only assemble the front of the hotel, you can keep the back open to move your minifigures around the different rooms and floors. Make sure the bottom floor is strong so that it doesn't fall apart as you add the higher levels.

Build in a peaked roof for a traditional Alpine-style building

HOME COMFORTS

Your hotel will need some amenities to keep the vacationers happy. Include things like chairs, telephones, cabinets, a fireplace and a hatstand for storing hats and ski equipment.

You can store all kinds of odd objects up in the attic!

The split flue carries smoke from the fireplace on the middle floor to the chimneys on the roof

Looks like this bat has found somewhere warm to stay for the winter!

Pillars and inverted slopes help bear the weight of the structures above them

Transparent yellow 1x1 round plates create soft interior lights

Stack log bricks to make traditional log columns and walls

Include a magazine rack in reception!

397

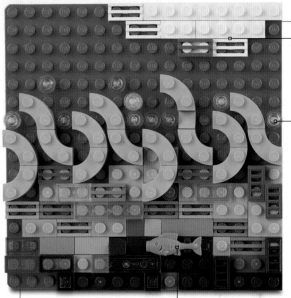

White pieces for a hint of cloud

Stacks of 1x1 round plates form bubbles and ocean froth

Use clips to attach fish and other objects or accessories

HOLIDAY POSTCARDS

Although Glax's holo-camera ran out of power (who knew the sockets were incompatible?), he has learned about the human custom of sending each other images of places where they have been. Build a one-of-a-kind vacation postcard using your LEGO pieces! You can design a flat mosaic, or add layers and accessories to make your postcard really pop.

OCEAN SURF

Start your postcard by picking a base plate (or putting several together) in the colour that you want for a background. You can make ocean waves with curved macaroni bricks and other water effects with transparent tiles and grilles!

You can use tiles to make a school of fish

Make waving lines of tiles for long strands of seaweed

Mix dark green pieces in for deeper water

Use round pieces to make organic, living shapes and forms

SHARK SCENE

Frame an animal in the postcard just like you would in a photograph. To make a shark's distinctive shape, try building an outline first and then carefully removing it to add the body colour underneath. When you put the outline back again, you'll have a coloured-in creature!

EVEN ALIENS LEAVE IT UNTIL THE LAST DAY TO WRITE POSTCARDS!

Your postcard doesn't have to be flat – use grille slopes to add some depth to the surf

Teeth are 1x1 slopes attached to the side studs of headlight bricks

Step-shaped angled bricks can be used to make undersea plants

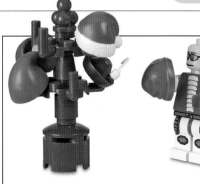

LOOKS LIKE SANTA HAS ARRIVED ALREADY!

HOTEL-BUILDING

If you only assemble the front of the hotel, you can keep the back open to move your minifigures around the different rooms and floors. Make sure the bottom floor is strong so that it doesn't fall apart as you add the higher levels.

Build in a peaked roof for a traditional Alpine-style building

HOME COMFORTS

Your hotel will need some amenities to keep the vacationers happy. Include things like chairs, telephones, cabinets, a fireplace and a hatstand for storing hats and ski equipment.

You can store all kinds of odd objects up in the attic!

The split flue carries smoke from the fireplace on the middle floor to the chimneys on the roof

Looks like this bat has found somewhere warm to stay for the winter!

Pillars and inverted slopes help bear the weight of the structures above them

Transparent yellow 1x1 round plates create soft interior lights

Stack log bricks to make traditional log columns and walls

Include a magazine rack in reception!

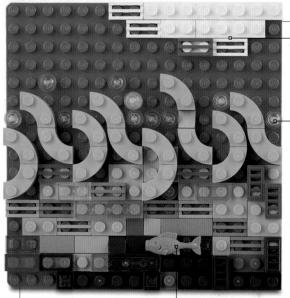

White pieces for a hint of cloud

Stacks of 1x1 round plates form bubbles and ocean froth

Use clips to attach fish and other objects or accessories

HOLIDAY POSTCARDS

Although Glax's holo-camera ran out of power (who knew the sockets were incompatible?), he has learned about the human custom of sending each other images of places where they have been. Build a one-of-a-kind vacation postcard using your LEGO pieces! You can design a flat mosaic, or add layers and accessories to make your postcard really pop.

OCEAN SURF

Start your postcard by picking a base plate (or putting several together) in the colour that you want for a background. You can make ocean waves with curved macaroni bricks and other water effects with transparent tiles and grilles!

You can use tiles to make a school of fish

Make waving lines of tiles for long strands of seaweed

Mix dark green pieces in for deeper water

Use round pieces to make organic, living shapes and forms

SHARK SCENE

Frame an animal in the postcard just like you would in a photograph. To make a shark's distinctive shape, try building an outline first and then carefully removing it to add the body colour underneath. When you put the outline back again, you'll have a coloured-in creature!

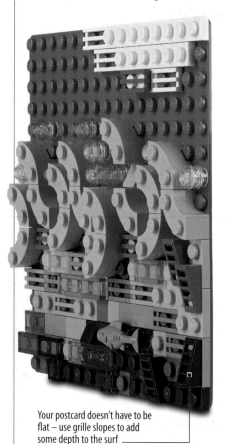

Your postcard doesn't have to be flat – use grille slopes to add some depth to the surf

Teeth are 1x1 slopes attached to the side studs of headlight bricks

Step-shaped angled bricks can be used to make undersea plants

EVEN ALIENS LEAVE IT UNTIL THE LAST DAY TO WRITE POSTCARDS!

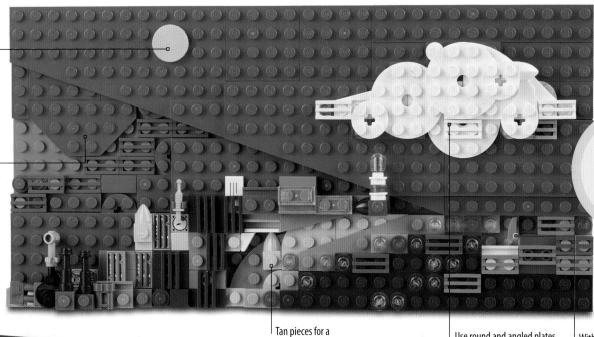

Sometimes simple works – like a bright yellow 2x2 round tile for the sun

Blue sky plates are layered on top of green hills in the background

Search for old postcards around your house and use them for inspiration!

Tan pieces for a sandy shoreline

Use round and angled plates to make clouds, with grilles for the wispy bits

With multiple layers, you can hide parts of elements to change them into something else – like letting the point of a gold pickaxe stick up as a sailboat's tiny sail!

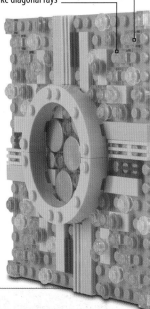

SEASIDE TOWN

When you've got the hang of building postcards, try making one in a style that's a little more advanced. This scene of a small town by the sea uses layers of plates along with grilles, a letter, binoculars, a nunchuk handle, telescopes and even a doctor's needle to create three-dimensional details.

Striped lighthouse is a red headlight brick, three 1x1 round plates and a transparent bulb piece on top

Symmetrical geometric designs are a good way to practise building LEGO brick mosaics

Use one stud jumper plates to get your piece placement just right

Different shades of yellow make the sun look like it is blazing with light

Use 1x1 plates to make diagonal rays

BUILDER TALK

"These mosaic models look best at a distance because the shapes blend together better. While building, move away from your model to see if your additions look good."

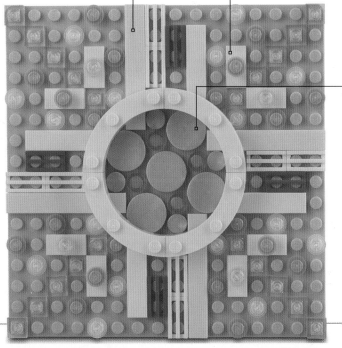

Gold-coloured elements make the centre even more radiant

THE SUN

Be creative with your postcards! While you should never look directly at the sun, you can still build your own version to enjoy. Use warm brick colours to make a circle and then add rays pointing in all directions.

HANDFUL OF BRICKS LIST

4x4 plate x 1

2x2 inverted slope x 1

2x2 brick x 3

2 x 4 brick x 2

2x2 plate x 2

1x2/1x4 angle plate x1

1x6 plate x 2

2x2 slope x 3

Antenna x1

1x2 slope x 2

2x3 slope x 1

1x1 slope x 4

1x1 brick eyes x 2

1x2 tile with top bar x 1

1x2 plate x 1

1x1 round brick x 1

2x4 angled plate x 2

1x2 curved half-arch x 1

1x3 brick x 2

4x4 round plate x 1

2x2 round brick x 1

DK | Penguin Random House

For DK Publishing
Senior Editor Laura Gilbert
Project Editor Hannah Dolan
Editors Jo Casey, Emma Grange, Shari Last, Catherine Saunders, Lisa Stock, Victoria Taylor, Tina Jindal, Matt Jones
Senior Designer Natan Martin
Art Editors Dimple Vohra, Pallavi Kapur, Karan Chaudhary
Assistant Art Editor Ishita Chawla
Designers Owen Bennett, Jill Bunyan, Lynne Moulding, Robert Perry, Sam Richiardi, Lauren Rosier, Lisa Sodeau, Ron Stobbart, Rhys Thomas, Toby Truphet
Senior Jacket Designer Mark Penfound
Senior DTP Designer Kavita Varma
Senior Producer Charlotte Oliver
Managing Editor Simon Hugo
Design Manager Guy Harvey
Creative Manager Sarah Harland
Art Director Lisa Lanzarini
Publisher Julie Ferris
Publishing Director Simon Beecroft

For the LEGO Group
Project Manager Mikkel Joachim Petersen
Assistant Licensing Manager Randi Kirsten Sørensen
Senior Licensing Manager Corinna van Delden
Designer Melody Louise Caddick
Building Instruction Developer Alexandra Martin
Model makers Sebastiaan Arts, Stephen Berry, Yvonne Doyle, Rod Gillies, Tim Goddard, Deborah Higdon, Tim Johnson, Barney Main, Pete Reid, Duncan Titmarsh, Andrew Walker

Photography by Gary Ombler, Brian Poulsen and Tim Trøjborg

First published in the United Kingdom in 2015
by Dorling Kindersley Limited
80 Strand, London WC2R 0RL

Contains content previously published in LEGO® *Play Book* (2013)
and *The LEGO® Ideas Book* (2011)

001-288806-Oct/15

Page design copyright © 2015 Dorling Kindersley Limited.
A Penguin Random House Company

Acknowledgements

Dorling Kindersley would like to thank: Stephanie Lawrence, Randi Kirsten Sørensen, Mikkel Petersen, Melody Caddick, Corinna van Delden and Alexandra Martin at the LEGO Group; Sebastiaan Arts, Stephen Berry, Yvonne Doyle, Rod Gillies, Tim Goddard, Deborah Higdon, Tim Johnson, Barney Main, Pete Reid, Duncan Titmarsh (www.bright-bricks.com) and Andrew Walker for their amazing models; Jeff van Winden for additional building, Daniel Lipkowitz for his inspiring text; Gary Ombler, Brian Poulsen and Tim Trøjborg for their brilliant photography; Rachel Peng and Bo Wei at IM Studios; Emma Grange, Lauren Nesworthy, Lisa Stock, Sarah Harland and Matt Wilson for editorial and design assistance.

1x1 brick x 7

4x6 plate x 1

1x1 headlight brick x 2

1x4 brick x 6

1x2 brick x 5 (including 1 transparent)

1x6 brick x 2

1x2 jumper plate x 3

2x3 brick x 1

1x1 round plate x 2

1x2x1 panel x1

2x2 radar dish x 2

1x4 plate x 2

Wide rim, wide tire, and 2x2 axle plate with 1 pin x 4

1x1 cone x 1

2x6 plate x 3

1x1 plate x 4

2x4 plate x 2

1x2 grille plate x 2

Tap x 1

1x6 arch brick x 1

2x2 round plate x 2

4x4 radar dish x 1